THREE CONTRIBUTIONS
TO THE DEVELOPMENT OF
ACCOUNTING THOUGHT

THE DEVELOPMENT OF CONTEMPORARY ACCOUNTING THOUGHT

Advisory Editor
Richard P. Brief

Editorial Board
Gary John Previts
Basil S. Yamey
Stephen A. Zeff

*See last pages of this volume
for a complete list of titles.*

THREE CONTRIBUTIONS TO THE DEVELOPMENT OF ACCOUNTING THOUGHT

Edited by
Maurice Moonitz

ARNO PRESS

A New York Times Company
New York • 1978

Editorial Supervision: LUCILLE MAIORCA

———◆———

Reprint Edition 1978 by Arno Press Inc.

THE DEVELOPMENT OF CONTEMPORARY ACCOUNTING THOUGHT
ISBN for complete set: 0-405-10891-5
See last pages of this volume for titles.

Manufactured in the United States of America

———◆———

Library of Congress Cataloging in Publication Data
Main entry under title:

Three contributions to the development of accounting
     thought.

     (The Development of contemporary accounting thought)
     Reprint of articles published between 1917 and 1970
in various journals.
     CONTENTS: Moonitz, M.   Three contributions to the
development of accounting principles prior to 1930.--
Federal Reserve Board. Uniform accounts.--Esquerré,
P-J. Correspondence. [etc.]
     1. Accounting--United States--History--Addresses,
essays, lectures. I. Moonitz, Maurice. II. Series.
HF5615.U5T45   657'.0973   77-87315
ISBN 0-405-10928-8

CONTENTS

THREE CONTRIBUTIONS TO THE DEVELOPMENT OF ACCOUNTING PRINCIPLES PRIOR TO 1930

Maurice Moonitz

Three Contributions to the Development of Accounting Principles Prior to 1930

MAURICE MOONITZ*

"Confound these thieving ancients for stealing all our modern ideas."

The part played by various agencies in the development of accounting principles in this country since 1930 is well documented.[1] The period before 1930 is not so well known, except for a project undertaken in 1917. The purpose of this note is to offer a review of that project and two other developments which help explain how we got where we are with respect to accounting principles.

Uniform Accounts (1917)

At the request of Edwin N. Hurley, then Vice-Chairman and later Chairman of the Federal Trade Commission, the President of the American Association of Public Accountants (predecessor of the American Institute of Accountants), J. Porter Joplin, appointed a special committee to confer with the trade commission on all questions of accounting. Robert H. Montgomery was Chairman of the eight-member committee.

The most important accomplishment of the committee was the "promulgation of a programme for audit procedure which was prepared at the request of the Federal Trade Commission, approved by the commission and transmitted to the Federal Reserve Board. . . ." The audit program in its final form was unanimously approved by the members of the council.[2]

The Federal Reserve Board published the text in the *Federal Reserve Bulletin* (April 1, 1917) and reprinted it in pamphlet form in 1917 and again in 1918 for general distribution. The text also appeared in the *Journal*

---

* Professor of Accounting, University of California, Berkeley.

[1] See, for example, *Audits of Corporate Accounts* (New York: AICPA, 1934; reprinted 1963) and Reed K. Storey, *The Search for Accounting Principles* (New York: AICPA, 1964).

[2] Report of the Committee on Federal Legislation, *American Institute of Accountants Year Book, 1917*, p. 217.

of Accountancy, June 1917, and the *Canadian Chartered Accountant*, July 1917.

Several titles were used:

(i) The original text was titled "Uniform Accounts."

(ii) The 1917 Reprint carries the expanded title: "Uniform Accounting— A Tentative Proposal Submitted by the Federal Reserve Board. . . ."

(iii) The 1918 Reprint is titled: "Approved Methods for the Preparation of Balance Sheet Statements—A Tentative Proposal. . . ."

In 1929, a revision was prepared by the Institute and published by the Federal Reserve Board under the title: "Verification of Financial Statements (Revised)—A Method of Procedure Submitted by the Federal Reserve Board. . . ." The text appeared also in the *Journal of Accountancy*, May 1929. This 1929 publication marked the end of the role of the AICPA as expert adviser to other organizations in this field. The 1936 revision, entitled "Examination of Financial Statements by Independent Public Accountants," was prepared and published by the Institute.

ACCOUNTING PRINCIPLES

Although "Uniform Accounts" and its successors dealt mainly with auditing procedures and form of financial statements, certain accounting principles are set forth. Examples:

(i) "The auditor should satisfy himself that inventories are stated at cost or market prices, whichever are the lower at the date of the balance sheet.

"No inventory must be passed which has been marked up to market prices and a profit assumed that is not and may never be realized. If the market is higher than cost, it is permissible to state that fact in a footnote on the balance sheet."

(ii) Factory overhead: "(The auditor should satisfy himself) that no selling expenses, interest charges, or administrative expenses are included in the factor overhead cost."

(iii) Discounts: "Trade discounts should be deducted from inventory prices, but it is not customary to deduct cash discounts. However, this may be done when it is the trade practice so to do."

(iv) Overhead in self-constructed equipment: "While it may be considered permissible to make a charge for factory overhead cost to additions to property such as, e.g., time of superintendent and his clerical force employed on construction work, etc., it cannot be deemed conservative business practice, inasmuch as the probabilities are that the overhead charges of a plant will not be decreased to any extent even though additions are not under way; and, therefore, the absorption of part of these charges when additions are in progress has the effect of reducing the operating costs, as compared with months in which no construction work is under way."

(v) Net sales: "Allowances to customers for trade discounts, outward freights, reductions in prices, etc., should be deducted from the sales in the profit and loss account, as the amount of net sales is the only figure of interest to the bankers."

(vi) Surplus additions and deductions: "Items of unusual or extraordinary profit which do not belong strictly to the period under audit, or cannot be said to be the legitimate result of the ordinary transactions of the concern, should be entered here and verified with the surplus account."

(vii) Materiality: "Where the market values of securities are less than the book value, *save where the variation is so small as to be trifling*, a reserve for loss in value on the balance sheet date must be set up." *Verification of Financial Statements* (1929) alters the sense somewhat: "Where the *total* market value of marketable securities is less than the *total* book value, *save where the difference is small*, a reserve for loss in value must be set up on the balance sheet." *Examination of Financial Statements* (1936) completes the transition to the present usage: "If the total market value of securities included under current assets is less than the total book value *by any material amount*, a reserve . . . should be provided . . . (emphasis added).

SIGNIFICANCE

The 1917 and 1929 publications were prepared by the Institute but disseminated by the commercial bankers of the country. The principles, rules, and procedures contained in these publications were accordingly taken seriously by businessmen and their outside accountants since the success or failure of a loan application to a commercial bank turned in part on the financial statements submitted to the banker. The effective enforcer of these principles, rules, and procedures was the banker, not the accountant or his professional organization. The origin of many of our present-day accounting customs and habits will be found in the decades during which the special interests of the short-term credit granter shaped the "principles" of accounting.

"Students Department" of the Journal of Accountancy

Almost from its first issue, the *Journal of Accountancy* published unofficial solutions to questions and problems in the examination for admission set by the Institute or in the CPA examinations set by states such as New York and Pennsylvania. These undoubtedly had some influence in shaping the background and attitudes of entrants to the profession. Of much more positive influence, however, was the "Students Department" started in January 1914 and edited by Seymour Walton, a practicing accountant and the proprietor and driving force behind the Walton School of Commerce (primarily a correspondence school). In the "Foreward" to the Students Department in that first issue, Walton stated that "It is not intended to lay out a connected course of business instruction such as is already given by many excellent schools of commerce and accounting in our larger cities. The intention is rather to supplement the work of these institutions by the discussion of subjects and the exposition of principles, as brought out in the solution of problems given in CPA examinations. . . ." As illustrated below, Walton was true to his word. The Students Department is a gold mine of information on the accounting principles of the time, and the reasons for their existence.

Walton carried the burden alone from January 1914 until October 1917. That issue tells us that Walton was "assisted by H. A. Finney." Walton died on June 26, 1920, at the age of 74 (he was born February 15, 1846). Apparently he had prepared enough copy in advance so that it is not until the September 1920 issue that the by-line read "Edited by H. A. Finney." In November 1925, the by-line indicated that Finney was "assisted by H. P. Baumann." Later, Baumann became an associate editor and then took over as editor in November 1928. He served in that capacity until March 1947, when Thomas W. Leland of Texas A and M succeeded him.

While Walton and Finney were editors, the Students Department discussed various topics at considerable length and undoubtedly exerted considerably influence on students and practitioners alike. For example, they both stressed the mathematics of finance (compound interest calculations). This emphasis, and with it the facility of the practicing arm of the profession to make constructive use of compound interest calculations, is lost somewhere in the 1930's, to be restored in the 1960's as "capital budgeting" became important. Furthermore, as Walton's protégé, and later his successor, Finney's views and attitudes were being crystallized into the form they took in his textbooks, the first of which appeared in 1924. These textbooks in the earlier editions were characterized by close attention to practice and procedure, extensive illustrations, excellent problem material, and no documentation whatsoever for the relatively sparse discussion of "theory." [3]

Finney was well aware of what he was doing. At an informal meeting in the late 1940's, he stated that his mission in writing his texts was to convey what was done in practice, whether that practice was good, bad, or indifferent. He did not conceive of his mission as consisting of a reexamination of accounting at either the practical or the theoretical level.

Here is just a random sampling of what did appear in the Students Department. The August 1917 issue contained a long essay (12 pages) on partnerships. It also contained a three-page critique of an article that had appeared in an earlier issue of the Journal. We find in the same issue a three-page analysis of "mystical and symbolic arithmetic" that was apparently popular at the time. According to Walton, many persons were mystified by a magical identity. In the case of all the "heads of state" of the countries

---

[3] It is not until the middle or late 1940's that we find even a single footnote reference in the Finney series.

involved in World War I, identical results were obtained if you added four amounts together: (1) the year of birth; (2) the year they assumed their present position (king, emperor, prime minister, president); (3) their age in the current year; and (4) the number of years in their present office. As Walton comments: "Ask John Smith when he was born, when married, how old he is, and what anniversary of his marriage occurs this year. . . . The age . . . must be calculated as at the birthday that occurs this year." The sum of the four numbers will always be precisely twice the current year, e.g., two times 1969, or 3938.

The October 1917 issue included a problem from a June 1917 CPA examination that required the candidate to calculate depreciation by three different methods—(1) straight-line; (2) constant percentage of diminishing value; and (3) annuity. The May 1925 issue contained a seven-page letter from Paul-Joseph Esquerré regarding a "statement of *resources* and their application" (emphasis added) that had been called for in the May 1921 Institute examination. Finney replied (14 pages) in the June 1925 issue, under the title "The Statement of Application of *Funds*—A Reply to Mr. Esquerré" (emphasis added). This exchange of views by these two leading textbook authors highlighted a difference of opinion regarding the "funds statement" that still exists—Esquerré advocated the "all-resources" type of statement, after the manner of Perry Mason in *Accounting Research Study No. 2*, "Cash Flow Analysis and the Funds Statement," [4] while Finney held out for a statement accounting for variations in net working capital.

Special Bulletins

When the library of the American Institute of Accountants opened in April 1918, it included a bureau of information to answer inquiries from members. The Special Committee on Administration of Endowment reported to the annual meeting in 1920 that it had authorized the librarian to issue special bulletins concerning questions and answers that passed through the bureau of information. Thirty-three bulletins were published under this authorization from January 1920 to December 1929. A detailed list of these bulletins and their contents is appended.

In the foreword to Special Bulletin No. 1 (January 1920), L. S. Miltimore, Librarian, stated: "In sending out answers, the Bureau of Information does not claim to be presenting the last word in any subject. The opinions expressed are those of one, two, or three accountants of good standing who have set forth their views in response to request from the Bureau of Information. The opinions are transmitted under the distinct understanding that they are purely advisory and in no sense intended to be dictatorial." These bulletins were printed and distributed to the members of the Institute. The extent of attention given to any one question varied from a

---

[4] AICPA, 1961.

line or two to several pages. The entire set of 33 bulletins covered not more than 185 printed pages. Nevertheless, these bulletins constitute an additional source of information on the practice of the day.[5]

Appendix

American Institute of Accountants
List of Special Bulletins Distributed to Membership 1920–1929, Inclusive

No.	Date	Topics Covered
1	January 1920	Tobacco manufacture—pricing of graded leaf tobacco Taxes—excess profits tax Automobile tire factor—unit for cost purposes Profits—allocation Depreciation rates Bonus and income tax Reserve for relining furnaces
2	March 1920	"Suggestions for professional conduct." Reprinted from the *Bulletin* of Haskins and Sells, January 15, 1919 Breweries—depreciation rates Mining company—valuation of land
3	May 1920	Moving pictures—depreciation rates Cattle industry—depreciation practices Tobacco manufacture; bonus and income tax—continuation of discussion in Bulletin No. 1.
4	July 1920	Moving pictures; mining company—continuation of previous discussion Merchandise in transit Cotton mills—land, buildings, machinery and equipment Automobile insurance—unearned premium calculation
5	September 1920	Film exchanges—accounting principles Merchandise in transit—comment on previous reply Motor buses—accounting system Depreciation—ice industry Motor trucks—burden distribution in manufacture Breweries—depreciation rates
6	November 1920	Fire loss—operating expense or capital loss Breweries—continuation of previous discussion Turpentine leases—depreciation Seed beans—inventory pricing Bolts and nuts—financial statements Negligence—auditor's liability Drafts—contingent liability Depreciation—contract interpretation

[5] These Special Bulletins and other documents are reproduced in *Accounting Principles and Auditing Standards—Source Documents. Two Parts.* (Supply now exhausted, according to AICPA.) Photocopied in 1963 and distributed in 1964 to the following universities: California, Berkeley; California, Los Angeles; Chicago; City of New York; Columbia; Cornell; Harvard; Illinois; Indiana; Iowa; Michigan; Michigan State; Minnesota; New York; North Carolina; Northwestern; Ohio State; Pennsylvania; Stanford; Texas; Washington; Wisconsin.

Appendix—*Continued*

No.	Date	Topics Covered
		Steel vessels—percentage of scrap
		Time-keeping and payroll distribution—system
7	December 1920	Inventories, commitments, and foreign exchange
8	February 1921	Piano manufacturing costs—system
		Shipbuilding—expense ratios
9	September 1921	Depreciation for brick manufacture
		Wholesale bakeries—labor cost distribution
		Taxicabs—depreciation rate
		Steamship companies—extraordinary repairs
		Funded debt—definition
		By-products—valuation
		Non-par value shares—how to handle in the accounts
		Dividends—relation to appraisals
		Mortgages—second mortgage acquired at a discount
10	October 1921	Cash commissions on capital stock
		Consolidations—surpluses carried through merger
		Fire losses—profit on insurance settlement
		Royalty on sand
		Non-par-value shares—comment on previous answer
		Mortgages—comment on previous answer
		Bonds—held in replacement fund
		Discounts—revenue or reduction in cost?
		Depreciation—relation to profits or losses
		Amounts due from officers and employees—classification
		Overhead expenses—allocation to departments
11	December 1921	Balance sheets—subsequent events
		Accounting for special industries and trades—sources of information
		Non-par-value shares—continuation of previous discussion
		Automobile insurance companies—systems
12	June 1922	Dividends—relation to depletion reserve
		Chain drug stores—perpetual inventories
		Agent's commissions—accounting treatment
		Automobile sales—systems
		Stock without par value—treatment
		Bond premium—life tenant or remainderman?
		Certificates—form of audit report
13	July 1922	Newspaper subscriptions—realization of revenue
		Depreciation on insulation in cold storage warehouses
		Balance sheets—extent of disclosure
		Capital stock—opening entries
		Jewelry—operating expenses
		Coconut oil industry—depreciation rates
		Depreciation on school buildings
14	August 1922	Tannery equipment—repairs
		Dividends—criticism of previous discussion
		Imprest fund—definition
		Bonds—installment payments
		Estate accounts—income in tax regulations

Appendix—*Continued*

No.	Date	Topics Covered
15	October 1922	Capital stock—fraudulent issue Public stenographer—operating expenses Bonus—calculation Bonus contract—cash or accrual Newsprint paper mill—spoiled material as cost element Land company—assets at "ridiculously low valuation" Newspapers—startup costs Brokers—valuation of open positions Moving expenses—deferred charge
16	November 1922	Bonus—continuation of previous discussion Bank balances—form of confirmation reply Balance-sheet—treatment of sold receivables Cafeteria chain restaurants—operating ratios Depreciation of wood working machinery Customer's accounts—internal control Unrealized gross profit from leases—when realized Executorship accounts—authority for principles adopted Schools—system Financial acceptance companies—system Department stores—turnover by departments
17	February 1923	Capital stock—comment on previous answer Newsprint paper mill—ditto Stock dividends—no-par shares Commissions—method of calculation Dividends from depletion reserve Ice cream costs Mortgage investment company—amortization of dis-discount
18	March 1923	Lumber brokers—cost ratios Dual-teller settlement system—bank operation Federal income tax—deductibility of dividends "Normal"—meaning in tax law of 1919 Reserves for contingencies—used to equalize profits Surplus—capitalization Bonds—held in treasury
19	May 1923	Dividends—comments on previous answer Students' accounts—system for schools Interest during construction—public utility Municipal departments of finance—internal control Subsidiary companies—tax aspects Depreciation—bill boards Cost of construction—cost-plus contract
20	September 1923	Bonds—continuation of previous discussion Expenses—startup costs Beet sugar companies—cost of inventory Automobile body plants—burden rates Estate accounting—principal versus income Bakeries—cost analysis

Appendix—*Continued*

No.	Date	Topics Covered
21	December 1923	Preferred stock—valuation
		Insurance premiums—classification
		Customers' accounts—verification
		Expenses—continuation of previous discussion
		Salt—chart of accounts for salt mining company
		Paper industry—classes of accounts
		Mining companies—various operating problems
		Silk hosiery company—depreciation rates
		Newspaper costs—comparative data
		Treasury Department's adjustment of depreciation
		Capital gain—two-year holding period
		Valuation of copyrights
22	February 1924	Customers' accounts—continuation of previous discussion
		Bakeries—ditto
		Depreciation—hotels
		Retirement of preferred stock
		Partner's loss
		Candy store serving light luncheons—operating ratios
		Automobile agencies—operating ratios
		Florists' shops—operating ratios
		Selling expense—capitalization
23	April 1924	Equity in purchased property
		Fire loss adjustment
		Collections—internal control
		Acquisition of real estate—elements of cost
		A corporation problem—withdrawals by principal owner
		Depreciation—marble company
		Depreciation—flour milling industry
		Consolidation of accounts—real estate subsidiary
		Chocolate and chocolate products—turnover
		Export accounts receivable—verification
		Cost of salt
		Hardware—manufacturing expenses
24	January 1925	Consolidation of statements—real estate subsidiary
		Equity in purchased property—continuation of previous discussion
		Bonds—ditto
		Mining companies—ditto
		Serially maturing funded debt—balance sheet treatment
		Valuation of raw silk inventories
25	February 1925	Depreciation—ball parks
		Charges of public accountants
		Building material trade—costs of operation
		Distribution of cost on the basis of sales in a patent litigation case
		Lumber inventory
		A merger—accounting entries
		Salt-cost

Appendix—*Continued*

No.	Date	Topics Covered
		Depreciation on sheds—retail lumber yards
		Accountant's liability
		Converters of cotton goods—bad debts experience
26	March 1926	Distribution of overhead
		Bond discount
		Real estate improvements
		Certified balance sheets
		Installment furniture business—bad debt experience
27	May 1926	Irrigation project—expenditure for joint facility (canal)
		Sick leaves—practice in large accounting firms
		Rate base—position of franchise and of operating loss
		Report notes—restrictions on use of accountant's opinion
		Change of entries—retroactive salary increase
		Interest charged to construction—implicit interest
		Steel plants—miscellaneous operating items
		Musical records—depreciation rate on matrices
		Fertilizer industry—repairs as percentage of net sales
28	December 1926	Cheque dated back—cash book kept open
		Interest charged to construction—continuation of previous discussion
		Rate base—ditto
		Corporation accounts—paid-in surplus; current liability
		Athletic clubs—depreciation; organization costs
		Valuation of sugar property—components of cost
		Capital stock without par value—classification
		Merchandise shipments—loss on purchase commitment
		Rate of interest—calculation of effective rate
29	January 1928	Appraisal of fixed assets—recording as unrealized profit
		Canning costs—overhead allocation
		Contingent reserves—relation to profit-and-loss
		Corporation accounting—appraisal surplus and dividends
		Corporation finance—equity method, investment in subsidiaries
		Depreciation of greenhouses
		Laundries cost accounting
		Participation mortgage bonds—restrictive covenants
		New York franchise tax bill—year applicable
30	March 1928	Gas and water works companies—auditing
		Joint fees—public accountants
		Valuation of licensed abstractor's business
		Participation mortgage bonds—continuation of previous discussion
		Partnership withdrawals—partner's withdrawals as an asset
		Promotion expenses—capitalization
		Restaurants—cost of sales

Appendix—*Continued*

No.	Date	Topics Covered
		State franchise tax on business corporations—year applicable
		Repurchase agreements—disclosure of contingent liability
		Taxation of corporation shares received as management fee
31	June 1928	Accrual of contractor's profits
		Manufacturing confectioners' costs
		Newspaper publishing accounting—operating data
		Pricing inventories of scrap metals
		Underwriting expenses for mortgage-bond issues
		Valuation of goodwill—publisher of a city directory
		Valuation of licensed abstractors' business—continuation
		Verification of customers' securities—audit procedure
32	March 1929	Amusement park accounting—cost allocation
		Calculation of interest—accounts payable for merchandise
		Consolidated balance sheet—extent of control
		Cost of engravings to lithographers—amortization of cost of stones
		Depreciation of office building and equpiment
		Payroll book as evidence
		Sugar refinery problem—accounting for "boneblack"
		Taxes on coal mines—undeveloped land
		Use of term "working capital"
33	December 1929	Stock dividends—accounting by recipient

UNIFORM ACCOUNTS

Federal Reserve Board

UNIFORM ACCOUNTS

At the request of Edwin N. Hurley, then vice-chairman, and
later chairman of the Federal Trade Commission, the president of the
American Association of Public Accountants, J. Porter Joplin, appointed a special committee to confer with the trade commission on
all questions of accounting. Robert H. Montgomery was chairman of
the eight member committee.

The most important accomplishment of the committee was the
"promulgation of a programme for audit procedure which was prepared
at the request of the Federal Trade Commission, approved by that
commission and transmitted to the Federal Reserve Board...." The
audit program in its final form was unanimously approved by the
members of the council.[1]

---

[1] Report of the Committee on Federal Legislation, American
    Institute of Accountants Year Book, 1917. p. 217.

The Federal Reserve Board published the text in the Federal
Reserve Bulletin and reprinted it in phamplet form in 1917 and again
in 1918 for general distribution. There was neither title page nor
preface in the original publication which is reproduced on pages 1-
15. The title page and preface of both of the reprints follow the
article on pages 16-19.

All differences in text between the original and the reprints are noted beneath the reproductions. The only other differences are in layout, punctuation, and capitalization.

Uniform Accounts.

The following tentative proposal has been submitted by the Federal Reserve Board for the consideration of banks, bankers, and banking associations; of merchants, manufacturers, and associations of manufacturers; and of auditors, accountants, and associations of accountants:

Through the courtesy of the Federal Trade Commission the Federal Reserve Board has been enabled to take advantage of a large amount of information and data which the Trade Commission acquired in connection with the study of the statements made by merchants, manufacturers, etc., as showing the condition of their business. Because this matter was clearly of importance to banks and bankers, and especially to the Federal Reserve Banks which might be asked to rediscount commercial paper based on borrowers' statements, the Federal Reserve Board has taken an active interest in the consideration of the suggestions which have developed as a result of the Trade Commission's investigation, and now submits in the form of a tentative statement certain proposals in regard to suggested standard forms of statements for merchants and manufacturers.

The problem naturally subdivides itself into two parts. (1) The improvement in standardization of the forms of statements; (2) the adoption of methods which will insure greater care in compiling the statements and the proper verification thereof.

In recent years bankers through their associations and otherwise have made rapid progress in the direction of more uniform and complete forms of statements. Much has also been accomplished in the improvement of the quality of the statements rendered and in securing statements which do not depend [for their accuracy on the borrowers' statement alone but are verified to a greater or less extent by independent scrutiny and audit. The advantage of a statement certified by trustworthy public accountants over an unverified statement is evident. At the present time, however, there is no uniformity as to the extent of verification in the case of statements put forward as having been verified.

The Federal Trade Commission in the course of its investigation of business conditions has been strongly impressed with the lack of uniformity and has enlisted the aid of the American Institute of Accountants with a view to remedying the condition. It has found that verified statements may be divided broadly into—(a) Those in which the certificate is based on an examination of the books without personal superivsion of inventories and independent appraisal of all assets with the aid of technical appraisers, and (b) statements verified with the personal supervision of inventories and independent appraisal of all assets.

The value of the two classes of audits and their relation to each other depends to a great extent upon the character and magnitude of the business involved.

In some cases method (b) has advantages over method (a). In other cases, notably those of large companies in which personal supervision of inventories is arduous and perhaps impracticable and the value of an independent appraisal of assets is liable to be considerably exaggerated, the reverse may be true. That is to say, a verification based upon the books themselves without an appraisal may be and often is the safer method of procedure. It is highly desirable gradually to educate the business world to the great importance of a complete form of audit statement, although any plan for immediate adoption intended to produce practical results must recognize that under present practice probably more than 90 per cent of the statements certified by public accountants are what are called balance-sheet audits, such as are described in paragraph (a) above referred to.

As a first step toward the standardization of balance-sheet audits and to insure greater care in compiling and verifying statements the Federal Trade Commission requested the American Institute of Accountants to prepare a memorandum on balance-sheet audits. This memorandum was duly prepared and approved by the council of the institute representing accountants in all sections of the country.

After approval by the Federal Trade Commission the memorandum was placed before the Federal Reserve Board for consideration. The Federal Reserve Board, after conferences with representatives of the Federal Trade Commission and the American Institute of Accountants, and a careful consideration of the memorandum in question, has accepted the memorandum, given it a provisional or tentative indorsement, and submitted it to the banks, bankers, and banking associations throughout the country for their consideration and criticism.

---

*Appeared in June 1917 issue of Journal of Accountancy, pp. 401-23, titled "Uniform Accounting." Also appeared in Canadian Chartered Accountant, July 1917, pp. 5-33.

1/ This paragraph deleted in reprints and the information included on the cover and title pages. (See pp. 16-17 and 18-19.)

2/ "borrowers'" changed to "borrower's" in the reprints.

The recommendations in the memorandum apply primarily to what are known as balance-sheet audits. This is an initial step which may easily be succeeded by future developments tending still further to establish uniformity and covering more fully the field of financial statements.

GENERAL INSTRUCTIONS FOR A BALANCE SHEET AUDIT OF A MANUFACTURING OR A MERCHANDISING CONCERN.

The scope of a balance sheet audit for a fiscal year or other operating period of an industrial or mercantile corporation or firm comprises a verification of the assets and liabilities, a general examination of the profit and loss account, and, incidental thereto, an examination of the essential features of the accounting.

Trial balances of the general ledger, both at the beginning and end of the period under review, should be prepared in comparative form and checked with the ledger. The items in the trial balances should be traced into the balance sheets before the assets and liabilities are verified, to prove, among other things, that no "contra" asset or liability has been omitted from the accounts, that the assets and liabilities have been grouped in the same manner at the beginning and end of the period, and also that the balance sheets are in accordance with the books. The disposition of any general ledger assets and liabilities that may have been scrapped, sold, written off, or liquidated during the period under review should be traced and noted in the working papers. Furthermore, a general scrutiny of the general ledger should be made to see that the accounts, if any, that have been opened and closed during the year have no bearing on the company's financial position at the close of the fiscal period.

The auditor should obtain a copy each of the balance sheet at the beginning and the end of the period to be audited, and should make a comparison between them, so that a comprehensive view may be had by him of the changes in the figures during the period under review. A statement of the disposition of the profits should then be prepared from this comparative balance sheet as a further aid in impressing the meaning of the figures upon the mind of the auditor.

The verification of assets and liabilities for convenience will be considered in the order in which the items appear in the form of balance sheet attached hereto. This form of statement has been determined by the desire to meet as

87199—17——6

nearly as possible the requirements and practice of Federal Reserve Banks.

SPECIFIC INSTRUCTIONS AND SUGGESTIONS RELATING TO THE SEPARATE HEADINGS.

CASH.

The cash on hand preferably should be counted after banking hours on the last day of the fiscal period to be covered by the audit, and the amount thereof, together with the cash stated to be in the bank, reconciled with that shown by the cashbook. The cash, bills receivable, and investments must be examined on the same day, so as to make it impossible for a treasurer to make up a shortage in one asset by withdrawing negotiable funds temporarily from another.

In counting the cash on hand the auditor must see that all customers' checks produced to him as part of the cash balance have been duly entered in the cashbook prior to the close of the period and should note the dates and descriptions of such checks, and also the dates and descriptions of all advances made from cash and not recorded on the books. Advances to employees should be strictly investigated, and if any are secured by personal checks the auditor should see that the checks are certified by the bank on which they are drawn before the close of the audit.

Certificates must be obtained, as of the evening of the closing date, from the banks in which cash is deposited, by or mailed directly to, the auditor himself. The balances as shown by the certificates must be reconciled with those shown on either the cashbook, the checkbook stubs, or bank registers, taking into consideration outstanding checks.

In verifying the outstanding checks there is only one safe and satisfactory method of proving their accuracy, and that is to compare the credit side of the cashbook from the last day of the fiscal period backward, item by item, with the checks returned from the bank for such period as may be necessary to account for all current outstandings. Any old checks not yet cashed by banks should be made the subject of special inquiry. When this work is completed, a list of the outstanding checks so ascertained should be prepared, showing the dates of the checks and compared with the actual checks returned from the bank at a later date, and any not so returned should be specially investigated. Special care is necessary to see that no checks for cash purposes are drawn

3/ Reprints read "the beginning and at the end..."

4/ Reprints read "balance sheets..."

at the close of the period and entered in the next period.

Where the currency and bank transactions are kept together in the cashbook and the auditor does not count the cash until a date subsequent to the close of the fiscal year, he must, in addition to verifying the bank balances as of the close of the year, verify them as of the date of the count of cash. This is absolutely essential when it is considered that, although the cash on hand, which forms only part of the balance, at the date of the count is correct, it does not follow that the total cash is correct.

When receipts are shown in the cash books as being deposited in the bank on the last day of the fiscal period, but are included in the reconciliation statement on account of their not being paid into the bank until the next day, the auditor must obtain letters from the banks acknowledging such deposits.

The deposits shown in the pass books should be checked in detail for the last two or three days of the fiscal period from the books to prove that they were composed of bona fide checks, and that no check drawn by the company was deposited in a bank without being credited to the bank on which it was drawn prior to the close of the fiscal period.

So that the auditor may satisfy himself that deposits are promptly made in bank each day, and that the same checks are paid into bank as are received, it is advisable to call for a number of deposit slips and compare them with the receipts as shown by the cashbook for the days in which the deposits are made. To make such verification absolute the deposit slips should be obtained from the banks.

When the practice of a company is to pay all of its cash receipts into bank, they should be compared and reconciled with the total deposits, as shown by the bank books, and similarly the disbursements should be reconciled with the total checks drawn.

Outstanding checks not examined at a previous audit on account of not having been returned by the banks must be called for and traced into the cashbook at the beginning of the current audit.

NOTES RECEIVABLE.

A list of notes receivable outstanding at the end of the fiscal period should be prepared showing the dates the notes are made, the customers' names, the date due, the amounts of the notes and the interest, if any, contained in the notes. If discounted the name of the discounting bank should be noted and verification obtained from the bank.

The outstanding notes must be carefully examined with the notes-receivable book, and with the list prepared by or produced to the auditor, the due dates and the dates of making the notes being carefully checked, and when notes have been renewed the original dates should be recorded. When notes have been paid since the close of the fiscal year, the cash should be traced into the books of the company, and when they are in the hands of attorneys or bankers for collection certificates should be obtained from the depositaries.

When notes receivable are discounted by banks the company has a liability therefor which should appear on the balance sheet. Lists of discounted notes not matured at the date of the audit should be obtained from the banks as verification and their totals entered under 20a if the cash therefor is shown as an asset.

The value of collateral, if any, held for notes should be ascertained, as it frequently happens that the notes are worth no more than the collateral.

Notes due by officials and employees must always be stated separately from customers' notes, as must also notes received for other than trade transactions.

Notes due from affiliated concerns must not be included as customers' notes, even though received as a result of trading transactions. Affiliated companies' notes should be shown as a separate item of current assets or as other assets as the circumstances warrant. They may be fairly included in current assets if the debtor company has ample margin of quick assets over its liabilities, including such notes. The term "Quick assets" is used here in the sense in which it is used by Federal reserve practice. "Current assets" is used to comprise these assets and other assets which though current are excluded in determining the eligibility of the paper for Federal Reserve purposes.

Optional.—The best verification of notes receivable is an acknowledgment by the party named in each note as the payor on the due date that the note is a bona fide obligation. Therefore if time permits, and the client does not object, it is advisable to obtain such written confirmation for each note. The auditor should personally mail the letters, inclosing stamped envelope for reply addressed direct to himself.

ACCOUNTS RECEIVABLE.

The bookkeepers of the accounts-receivable ledgers should be asked to draw off lists of the open balances at the end of the fiscal period, and distributions of the total columns should be shown on the lists according to the age of the accounts, e. g., not yet due, less than 30 days past due, more than 30 days past due. The accounts paid since the close of the fiscal period should be noted in the lists before taking up the matter of past due accounts with the credit department, as payment is the best proof that an account was good at the date of the audit.

The totals of the lists of outstanding accounts should agree with the controlling account in the general ledger if separate ledgers are kept. When credit balances appear on customers' accounts they should be shown on the balance sheet as a separate item and not deducted from the total of debit balances; and debit balances on the accounts-payable ledgers should be treated in the same manner.

The lists must be footed and compared in detail with the customers' accounts in the ledgers.

The composition of outstanding balances should always be examined, as it frequently happens that while a customer may be making regular payments on his account, old items are being carried forward which have been in dispute for a considerable period of time. Such items and accounts which are past due should be taken up with the credit department or some responsible officer, and the correspondence with the customers examined, so that the auditor may form an opinion of the worth of the accounts and satisfy himself that the reserve for bad and doubtful accounts set up by the company is sufficient.

Trade discounts (and also so-called cash discounts, if exceeding 1 per cent) and freights allowed by the company should be inquired into, and if they have been included in the accounts receivable a reserve therefor should be set up in the balance sheet. Also inquiries should be made regarding customers' claims for reductions in prices and for rebates and allowances on account of defective materials, so that it may be seen that a sufficient reserve has been established therefor.

Inquiry must be made as to whether any of the accounts receivable have been hypothecated or assigned, and the sum total of accounts so listed entered under 20b.

The auditor should satisfy himself that the bad debts written off have been duly authorized by responsible officials.

Accounts due from directors, officers, and employees must be stated in the balance sheet separately and not included as trade accounts. This applies also to deposits as security, guaranties, and other extraordinary items not connected with sales.

Accounts due from affiliated concerns must not be included as customers' accounts, even though arising as a result of trading transactions. Affiliated companies' accounts should be shown as a separate item of "current assets" or as "other assets," as the circumstances warrant. They may be fairly included as "current assets" if the debtor company has ample margin of quick assets over its liabilities, including such accounts.

Optional.—The best verification of an open balance is a confirmation by the customer; therefore, if time permits and the client does not object, it is advisable to circularize the customers. The auditor should personally see the circulars mailed after comparing them with the lists of outstanding accounts. The envelopes for replies sent with the circulars should be addressed direct to the auditor.

In large concerns the system of accounting is generally so arranged that it would be almost impossible for accounts to be paid and not correctly credited on the accounts-receivable ledgers, but in small concerns, with imperfect systems, such occurrences are quite possible, so much so, in fact, that it is generally admitted that the risk of errors and omissions decreases in direct proportion to an increase in bookkeeping.

SECURITIES.

Under this caption must be listed securities in which surplus funds of the company or firm have been temporarily invested and which are considered as available as "quick assets," i. e., can be turned into money in time of need. Where stocks or bonds represent control or a material interest in other enterprises the ownership of which carries more or less value to the holder outside of the return thereon they should be considered as fixed assets.

A list of investments should be prepared showing—

The dates of purchases.
Descriptions of the investments.
Par value of the investments.
The denomination of the shares.

The number of shares or bonds owned.

The total capital stock of the various companies.

The amounts paid for the investments.

The interest and dividends received.

The market values of the investments.

The surplus or deficit shown by the balance sheets of the companies where no market quotations are available.

If hypothecated, with whom and for what purpose.

This list must be compared with the ledger accounts concerned and the total of amounts paid according to the list must agree with the balance of the investment account or accounts.

The securities must be examined by the auditor in person or he must secure confirmation of their existence from those who hold them as collateral. Those in possession of the company must be counted and examined as soon as possible after the audit starts, and all of them must be submitted to him at one time. It is much more satisfactory to see the actual securities than to verify cash receipts and other evidences therefor after the audit has progressed some time.

Certificates out for transfer must be verified by correspondence.

Where the market values of securities are less than the book values, save where the variation is so small as to be trifling, a reserve for loss in value on the balance sheet date must be set up.

Care must be taken to see that the certificates are made out in favor of the company, or that they are indorsed or accompanied by powers of attorney when they are in the names of individuals.

Coupons on bonds must be examined to see that they are intact subsequent to the latest interest payment date.

The investment schedule must show that the total interest and dividends receivable by the company have been duly accounted for; the income from the investments shown in the profit and loss account must be in accord with this schedule.

When market quotations can not be obtained for investments, the balance sheets of the companies in which investments are held must be examined so that the auditor may form an idea of their value.

In verifying purchases of stock exchange securities the brokers' advices must in all cases be examined in connection with the verification of the purchase price.

Investments in deeds and mortgages must be supported by both the mortgages and insurance policies, and, furthermore, it must be shown that all assessed taxes on the property have been duly paid, that the mortgages have been properly recorded, and that the insurance policies are correctly made out to the company.

If any of the securities have been hypothecated the fact and amount (book value) must be stated under 20d of the balance sheet.

INVENTORIES.

Under this caption must be included only stocks of goods owned and under control of the owner. Stocks are often hypothecated and if this is the case the fact should be stated on the balance sheet.

Inasmuch as the accuracy of the profit and loss account is absolutely dependent upon the accuracy of the inventories of merchandise at the beginning and end of the period under review, this part of the verification should receive special attention. When a balance-sheet audit is being made for the first time, the inventory at the beginning of the period should receive as much attention as that at the end, and the auditor should take every precaution to satisfy himself that both inventories were taken on the same basis.

An acceptable program of audit for inventories is as follows:

(1) Secure the original stock sheets if they are in existence and carefully test the typewritten copies with them and with tickets, cards, or other memoranda that show the original count.

(2) See that the sheets are certified to or initialed by the persons who took the stock, made the calculations and footings, and fixed the prices, and satisfy yourself that they are dependable and responsible persons. Obtain a clear and detailed statement in writing as to the method followed in taking stock and pricing it; also a certificate from a responsible head as to the accuracy of the inventory as a whole.

(3) A thorough test of the accuracy of the footings and extensions should be made, especially of all large items.

(4) The inventories should be compared with the stores ledger, work in progress ledgers and finished product records and stock records as to quantities, prices, and values, and any material discrepancy should be thoroughly traced.

(5) Where stock records are kept and no physical inventory is taken at the time of the audit, ascertain when the last physical inventory was taken [and compare it with the book records. If no recent comparison is possible, select a few book items of importance and personally compare with the actual stock on hand.

(6) Where no stock records are kept, a physical inventory should be taken preferably under the general direction of the auditor. After the inventory is completed, he should apply the same tests to verify its accuracy as if the inventory had been taken before his arrival upon the scene.

(7) When the cost system of a company does not form a part of the financial accounting scheme there is always a chance that orders might be completed and billed, but not taken out of the work in progress records. Especially is this the case when reliance is placed on such records to the extent that a physical inventory is not taken at the end of the period to verify the information shown therein. In these cases the sales for the month preceding the close of the fiscal period should be carefully compared with the orders in progress as shown by the inventory, to see that nothing that has been shipped is included in the inventory in error. Cost systems which are not coordinated with the financial accounts are unreliable and frequently misleading. Special attention should be called to every case in which the cost system is not adequately checked by the results of the financial accounting.

(8) Ascertain that purchase invoices for all stock included in the inventory have been entered on the books. Look for postdated invoices and give special attention to goods in transit.

(9) See that nothing is included in the inventory which is not owned but is on consignment from others. If goods consigned to others are included, see that cost prices are placed thereon, less a proper allowance for loss, damage, or expenses of possible subsequent return. This does not include goods at branches, as the valuing of such stocks will be governed by the same principles as apply at the head office.

(10) Ascertain that nothing is included which has been sold and billed, and is simply awaiting shipment.

(11) If duties, freight, insurance, and other direct charges have been added, test them to ascertain that no error has been made. Duties and freight are legitimate additions to the cost price of goods, but no other items should be added except under unusual circumstances.

(12) As a check against obsolete or damaged stock being carried in the inventory at an excessive valuation, the detailed records for stores, supplies, work in progress, finished products, and purchased stock in trade, should be examined and a list prepared of inactive stock accounts, which should be discussed with the company's officials and satisfactory explanations obtained.

(13) The auditor should satisfy himself that inventories are stated at cost or market prices, whichever are the lower at the date of the balance sheet. No inventory must be passed which has beem marked up to market prices and a profit assumed that is not and may never be realized. If the market is higher than cost it is permissible to state that fact in a footnote on the balance sheet.

(14) It may be found that inventories are valued at the average prices of raw materials and supplies on hand at the end of the period. In such cases the averages should be compared with the latest invoices in order to verify the fact that they are not in excess of the latest prices, and also with the trade papers, when market prices are used, to see that they are not in excess of market values.

(15) Make an independent inspection of the inventory sheets to determine whether or not the quantities are reasonable, and whether they accord in particular instances with the average consumption and average purchases over a fixed period. Abnormally large quantities of stock on hand may be the legitimate result of shrewd foresight in buying in a low market, but may, on the other hand, arise from serious errors in stock taking.

(16) Always attempt to check the totals by the "gross profit test" and compare the percentage of gross profit shown with that of previous years. In a business where the average gross profit remains fairly constant this test is a dependable one, because, if the rate of gross profit is apparently not maintained and the discrepancy can not be satisfactorily accounted for by a rise or fall in the cost of production or of the selling price, the difference will usually be due to errors in stock taking.

(17) In verifying the prices at which the work in progress is included in the inventory, a general examination and test of the cost system in force is the best means of doing this work satisfactorily. In a good cost system little difficulty will be found with the distribution of

the raw materials, stores, and pay roll, but the distribution of factory overhead cost is one that should receive careful consideration, the main points to be kept in view being:

(a) That no selling expenses, interest charges, or administrative expenses are included in the factory overhead cost.

(b) That the factory overhead cost is distributed over the various departments, shops, and commodities on a fair and equitable basis.

(18) No profit should be included in the price of finished products or stock in trade. The price list should be examined to see that the cost prices of stock are below the selling prices after allowing for trade discounts, and if they are not a reserve should be set up on the balance sheet for this loss. If the company takes immediate steps to increase the selling price, however, the amount of this reserve may be limited to the loss on goods which may have been sold since the close of the period to the date of the discovery.

(19) In the case of companies manufacturing large contracts it is frequently found necessary to make partial shipments thereof. The question then arises as to whether it is permissible to include the profits on these partial shipments in the profit and loss account. As a matter of fact, it is evident that the actual cost can not be known until the order is completed. It may be estimated that a profit will ultimately be made, yet unforeseen conditions, such as strikes, delays in receiving material, etc., may arise to increase the estimated cost. It is better not to include the profits on partial shipments, but information of this character which may have its influence in the decision of the banker upon a proposed loan may properly be laid before him. Of course, an exception should be made in cases where the profit on the partial shipments largely exceeds the selling price of the balance of the order.

(20) The selling prices for contract work in progress should be ascertained from the contracts, and where it is apparent that there will be a loss on the completed contract a due proportion of the estimated loss should be charged to the period under audit by setting up a reserve for losses on contracts in progress.

(21) If a company has discontinued the manufacture of any of its products during the year, the inventory of such products should be carefully scrutinized and, if unsalable, the amount should be written off.

(22) The inventory should be scrutinized to see that no machinery or other material that has been charged to plant or property account is included therein.

(23) Partial deliveries received on account of purchase contracts for material, etc., should be verified by certificates from the contractors, both as to quantities and prices.

(24) Advance payments on account of purchase contracts for future deliveries should never appear in an inventory, but be shown on the balance sheet under a separate heading.

(25) Trade discounts should be deducted from inventory prices, but it is not customary to deduct cash discounts. However, this may be done when it is the trade practice so to do.

(26) While the inventory is being verified, the auditor should ascertain the aggregate sales for the last year. If the turnover has not been rapid, it may be due to a poor stock of goods. Some business men dislike to sell below cost and would rather accumulate a big stock of old goods than dispose of the old and unseasonable stock at a sacrifice. The usual outcome is that the stock becomes unwieldy and funds are lacking to purchase new goods. The inventory and the gross sales may, therefore, have a direct connection.

(27) It may be well to reiterate that interest, selling expenses, and administrative expenses form no part of the cost of production, and therefore should not be included in the inventory in any shape.

COST OF FIXED PROPERTY.

In preparing the leading schedules for the accounts grouped under this heading, such as real estate, buildings, plant, machinery, etc., the balances at the beginning of the period, the additions to or deductions from the accounts during the year, and the balances at the end of the period must be shown.

The total of the balances at the beginning of the period must agree with the cost of property figures given in the balance sheet at that date, and the balances at the end of the period with the amount shown in the balance sheet that is being audited. The charges entering into the additions must be verified in detail, and in this connection the following notes are of value:

(1) Authorizations for the expenditure made during the year should be examined, and where the costs of the additions have overrun the sums authorized, inquiries should be made in regard thereto. The authorizations should show the accounts to which the expenditures are chargeable, the amounts thereof, the ap-

provals of the comptroller and manager, and descriptions of the jobs. When the authorizations are not specific as to the work done, the actual additions should, if possible, be inspected.

(2) The auditor should satisfy himself before approving additions that they were made with the object of increasing the earning capacity of the plant, and that they are not of the nature of either renewals or improvements, and in this connection changes in the production and capacity of the plant should receive consideration.

(3) To verify the pay roll and store and supply charges to jobs, one or two pay roll distribution reports should be examined in detail, and also one or two storehouse reports. In cases where large purchases have been made from outside parties for capital construction work, the vouchers therefor should be examined and the usual precautions taken to see that they are properly approved for the receipt of materials, prices, etc.

(4) For purchases of real estate the title deeds should be examined, together with the vouchers, and it should be seen that the deeds have been properly recorded.

(5) While it may be considered permissible to make a charge for factory overhead cost to additions to property such as, e. g., time of superintendent and his clerical force employed on construction work, etc., it can not be deemed conservative business practice, inasmuch as the probabilities are that the overhead charges of a plant will not be decreased to any extent even though additions are not under way, and, therefore, the absorption of part of these charges when additions are in progress, has the effect of reducing the operating costs, as compared with months in which no construction work is under way.

(6) Construction work in progress at the end of the fiscal period should be shown in the balance sheet under the heading of fixed assets and not as part of the inventories. This is important to bear in mind because construction work is not an asset that can be quickly turned into money, while everything in the inventory is supposed to be realizable in cash within a reasonably short time.

(7) The auditor should inquire as to whether any installments are due on account of construction work in progress which is being carried on by outside parties; and if so, the liabilities for these installments should be included in the balance sheet, as they may have a direct bearing on the amount of available cash on hand.

(8) When a company uses leasehold properties the leases should be examined and notes made of the periods covered, so that it may be seen that improvements, etc., on such properties are written off over the periods covered by the leases.

(9) The auditor should satisfy himself that the reserves for depreciation of buildings, machinery, equipment, etc., are adequate to reflect the deterioration in the value of the fixed properties. If in his opinion the reserves shown on the balance sheet are insufficient, he should call attention to the matter in his certificate.

(10) Care should be taken to insure that property destroyed by fire or otherwise prematurely put out of service is correctly treated in the books. Any portion of the original charge for such property which is not recoverable through insurance, as salvage or otherwise, and has not been provided for by the depreciation scheme should be written off.

It is to be observed that the foregoing notes are to be applied only to cost of properties incurred during the period under audit. In addition, information may usefully be obtained on broader lines in regard to the composition of the real estate, building, and machinery accounts, and showing what principal property is represented thereby and how the accounts have been built up from year to year for a reasonable time past if not from the inception of the business. The information derived therefrom is valuable only in indicating the progressive policy of the concern, the extent to which it reinvests undivided surplus in its plant, etc. Beyond these facts the banker who is asked for ordinary discounts or short-term loans is not interested; he looks more to the quick assets for his security.

Optional.—When the loan is greater than the quick assets seem to justify the auditor should suggest a reliable verification of the cost of property prior to the period under audit. Such action may become necessary even to the extent of calling for an appraisement by disinterested outside experts.

DEFERRED CHARGES TO OPERATIONS.

Under this heading in the balance sheet are grouped such items as unexpired insurance, bond discounts applicable to a future period, prepaid royalties, experimental charges, etc. After the clerical accuracy of the deferred charges has been verified the auditor should satisfy himself that they are properly carried forward to future operations.

Wherever possible, documentary proof must be produced in support of the items carried forward, as, for example, with unexpired insurance the policies must be examined to verify the dates of expiration, the amounts covered, and the proportion of the premiums carried forward; with royalties the agreements must be examined; with experimental charges the vouchers and particulars of the work done must be looked into, etc.

The examination of the deferred charges will usually furnish the auditor with valuable information in regard to the accounts of the company, as, e. g.:

(1) The verification of experimental charges carried forward will generally furnish information as to the production and future policy of the company.

(2) Royalty vouchers will generally furnish a check on the production of mines.

(3) An examination of the insurance policies will show if the properties are mortgaged or covered by lien, and thus be an additional verification of the liability for mortgages on real estate, buildings, etc., shown in the balance sheet.

(4) The assets covered by insurance will be ascertained and if any omissions are discovered they should be mentioned.

NOTES AND BILLS PAYABLE.

Under this caption appear notes payable and drafts accepted. Schedules should be prepared under the subcaptions, and in columns headed:

Date of making the notes or drafts.
Due dates.
Names of creditors.
Collateral hypothecated.
Additional indorsers.
Interest accrued to date of audit.
Notations of renewals (as information of this nature furnishes a guide to the state of the concern's credit).

The schedule must be compared with the notes-payable book and the total of the aggregate must agree with the balance of the ledger account of notes payable.

Statements must be obtained from all banks and brokers with whom the concern does business, showing all notes and drafts discounted or sold by them for the benefit of the concern. These statements when received must be checked against the loans shown on the con-

cern's books and approved in the minutes of a company.

Inasmuch as a note is a negotiable instrument, care must be taken to see that all of those recorded as paid during the year under audit have been properly discharged, and the canceled notes are the best evidence of this fact.

Careful attention should be given to the collateral deposited for loans and statements as to the existence of such collateral should be obtained from the holders thereof. Such hypothecation of any of the concern's assets should be accounted for on the balance sheet.

When practicable the auditor might suggest to the client the advisability of drawing notes payable on blanks bound in a book, like a check book, with a stub for each blank, the blank and the stub to bear identical numbers. The officer, or officers, signing the notes could, in such case, initial the stub as a certificate to the amounts, payees, and terms of the notes issued. If this were done, the auditing of bills payable would be greatly facilitated.

ACCOUNTS PAYABLE.

A list of balances due on open accounts must be prepared and carefully checked with the ledger accounts, care being taken to see that no open account on the ledger has been omitted from the list. It should be ascertained that the balances represent specific and recent items only. When any account does not appear regular a statement from the creditor should be obtained. If there are many such accounts in dispute, and they amount to so large a sum as to affect appreciably the total of current liabilities, the general causes for the disputes should be inquired into and note made of the matter for the consideration of the banker.

In concerns with modern voucher systems accounts payable are easily verified, as all liabilities are then included in the books when incurred. Care should be taken, however, to see that all goods received on the last day of the fiscal period, as shown by the receiving records, and also all goods that were in transit and belonged to the concern on that date, are included as liabilities, and the corresponding assets included in the inventories. This test is necessary, as an increase in the accounts payable may have a very important bearing on the financial position of the concern if the cash on hand is small.

Monthly expenses outstanding can usually be ascertained by a comparison of the expenses of the last month of the fiscal period with previous months, and those of the year with the previous year. The voucher record should, however, be examined for the months subsequent to the close of the fiscal year, in case any expenses included therein are applicable to the fiscal period under audit.

When a first-class voucher system is not in operation the auditor must take additional precautions to satisfy himself that all liabilities are included in the accounts, among which may be mentioned:

(1) Payments made in the months subsequent to the date of the fiscal period as shown by the cashbook, which should be carefully scrutinized to see that none of them is applicable to the period under review.

(2) The file of bills not vouchered or entered on the books should be examined to see that none of them belongs to the period under audit.

(3) A careful perusal of the minutes of a company may further assist the auditor in determining liabilities.

When a company has large purchase contracts in force for future deliveries they should be examined, for if the contract prices are greater than market prices, it might be necessary to set up a reserve for this loss. Any debit balance due to advance payments on such contracts or to any other cause should be shown on the balance sheet under a separate heading.

If the business under audit is one where there is any possibility of goods having been received on consignments, and part or all of such goods having been sold without a liability therefor having been shown in the books, the auditor must use all due diligence to cover the point fully. This may readily happen, as consignment accounts are usually treated as memoranda only.

If inquiry develops the fact that goods have been received on consignment, all records in connection therewith should be called for. If the goods have all been sold, the consignor's account should show the full amount due, and if the debt is a current one, the amount will appear among accounts payable due to trade creditors. Where only part of the goods have been sold, the net proceeds due to the consignors should be shown on the balance sheet under the caption of "Accounts payable consignors."

As an additional precaution against the omission of liabilities a certificate should be obtained from the proper officer or member of the concern stating that all outstanding liabilities for purchases and expenses have been included in the accounts of the period under review or of

87199—17——7

former periods. In many cases it is also advisable to obtain a certificate from the president stating that all liabilities for legal claims, infringements of patents, claims for damages, bank loans, etc., have been included, as he may be the only executive officer of the company to know the extent of such obligations.

CONTINGENT LIABILITIES.

It is not enough that a balance sheet shows what must be paid; it should set forth with as much particularity as possible what may have to be paid. It is the duty of an auditor who makes a balance sheet audit to discover and report upon liabilities of every description, not only liquidated debts but possible debts. The following are the usual forms under which contingent liabilities will be found:

Indorsements.—Inquiry of the officers or partners of the concern should be made as to whether any indorsement of outside paper has been made and as to any security received to protect the concern. Such inquiry should be particularly strict if it is known that any of the officers or partners are interested in other enterprises. Similar action should be taken in the matter of—

GUARANTIES.

Unfulfilled contracts.—Contracts to accept the delivery of goods contracted for before the date of the balance sheet, may call for the payment of large sums of money within a short time. In the case of raw materials for a manufacturer, this might be a perfectly legitimate reason for seeking a temporary loan pending production and sale, but for a merchant whose balance sheet shows a large stock of goods on hand, it might indicate a real liability impending with assets of a doubtful character to offset it. In every audit, therefore, the auditor should call for copies of all orders for future delivery, and if such orders call for stock in excess of the current and reasonable prospective demand, mention should be made on the balance sheet and a report submitted, the details depending on the circumstances of each particular case.

Items other than those arising from the specific hypothecation of current assets to be listed under item 20 should appear as a footnote on the liability side of the balance sheet, the total amounts being stated for each subheading and such additional report made as will convey clear information to the banker.

6/ In reprints paragraph ends with the word "enterprises."
  Then follows:
    "Guaranties.—Similar action should be taken in the
  matter of guaranties."
  Note: The center heading "Guaranties" is omitted in reprints.

ACCRUED LIABILITIES.

Under this caption are grouped such items as interest, taxes, wages, etc., which have accrued to the end of the period under audit, but are not due and payable till a later date. The verification of such items can be accurately made from the books and records. Special attention may be directed to the following:

Interest payable.—Many of the liabilities which appear on a balance sheet carry interest. Such items as bonds and notes payable are obvious, but the auditor should also consider the possibility of accounts also bearing interest, as enough book accounts, when past due, do bear interest to warrant inquiry being made. Loan accounts of partners and officers of corporations almost invariably bear interest; also judgments, overdue taxes, and other liens.

Taxes.—The amount of accrued State and local taxes can be ascertained from an examination of the latest tax receipts; though in some cases, as the period for which the taxes are paid is not shown on the face of the receipt, it may be necessary to make inquiries of the proper taxing authorities as to the period covered.

Under the Federal income tax law a tax of 2 per cent is imposed upon the net profits of a corporation, which must be paid even if the corporation is dissolved before the end of the year during which the tax is imposed. As the tax is specifically based upon the net profits of a particular period, although payable some months thereafter, the tax accrues throughout the specified period, and if a net profit is disclosed upon the closing of the books at any date during the year, a reserve of 2 per cent must be shown on the balance sheet as an accrued tax.

Wages.—Where the date of the balance sheet does not coincide with the date to which the last pay roll of the period under audit has been calculated, the amount accrued to the date of the balance sheet must be ascertained and entered as a liability, unless such amount is trifling. It will suffice to take the proportion of a full week's pay roll (six days) without reference to possible daily variations.

Water rates, etc.—Where bills for such expenses as water, gas, etc., are not rendered monthly, the auditor must enter the accrual of the proper proportion since the last bill as a liability.

Traveling expenses and commissions.—It is important to note whether the accounts of all traveling salesmen have been received and entered before the books are closed. The auditor should secure a list, and if any report was not so entered, provision should be made for it unless the amount is likely to be trifling.

Ample provision should be made for all commissions eventually payable on sales which have been billed to customers. As commissions are frequently not payable to salesmen until the sales have been collected from the customers, accrued commissions are often omitted from the books. As they must, however, be paid out of the proceeds of the sales on which the full profit has already been taken into the accounts, they should be set up as an accrued liability.

Legal expense.—All concerns have more or less litigation. Before the books are closed the lawyers should be requested to send in a bill to date. If one is not found, the auditor should ascertain the amount, if any, probably due and set it up as an accrued liability.

Damages.—If the concern is insured against liability for damages to employees or the public a proportion of the premiums paid in advance for the unexpired time covered by the insurance will appear in "Deferred charges." But there may be claims or suits for other damages not covered by insurance and where the auditor finds any evidence which leads him to suspect there may be liability of this nature he should insist upon being informed of all the facts. He can then form an opinion as to the amount that should be set up as an accrued liability, or if the outcome is uncertain as a reserve against possible loss.

BONDED AND MORTGAGE DEBT.

A copy of the mortgages must be examined and the terms thereof noted. The amount of bonds registered, issued, and in treasury, rate of interest, and duration of the bonds, should be shown on the face of the balance sheet. A certificate should be obtained from the trust company certifying the amount of bonds outstanding, etc., as verification of the liability stated in the balance sheet. The interest on the bonds outstanding, shown in the balance sheet, should be calculated and reconciled with the interest on bonds, as shown in the profit and loss account.

Sinking-fund provisions in mortgages should be carefully noted and care should be taken to see that they are provided for in the accounts of the company, and any default noted in the balance sheet.

Bonds redeemed during the period or previously should be examined to see that they have been properly canceled, or, if they have been destroyed, a cremation certificate should be obtained from the trustees.

Mortgages sometimes stipulate that the current assets must be maintained at a certain amount in excess of the current liabilities, and the auditor must give due consideration to such matters and any other stipulation in regard to the accounts, or any audit thereof, that may be referred to in the trust deed, and see that they have been complied with.

Mortgages.—As a mortgage derives its chief value from the fact that upon registry it becomes a lien, the auditor should verify the existence of such an obligation by inspecting the public records, not only with reference to such as may be found on the company's books but also any that may still appear on the public records as unsatisfied. If the auditor lacks the necessary facilities for making a search it will be worth his while to arrange with a local lawyer or title company whereby, for a small fee, any mortgages or judgments entered against the concern under audit will be reported to him.

In any event the auditor must verify the amount as recorded in the account, the rate, the due date, and the property covered thereby.

It should be borne in mind that a payment on account of a mortgage must be recorded or the entire amount will remain as an encumbrance on the property. Therefore, if payments on account appear, the auditor should ascertain if they have been so recorded; if not the fact should be noted on the balance sheet.

Judgments.—The same procedure should be followed in verifying judgments as in verifying mortgages. As many business men consider that the entry of an invoice is an admission of liability, and will not permit the entry of a claim which they propose to fight, it is sometimes difficult for an auditor to find any evidence of such liens. Even admitting the fact they may still refuse to allow the judgment to be entered on the books as a liability in which case it is proper for the auditor to include it as a footnote on the balance sheet as a contingent liability.

Unpaid interest.—When considering the matter of liens it should be noted that interest unpaid is a lien as well as unpaid principal, so where the auditor finds evidence of interest on liens being in default, he should add it to the principal in each case.

CAPITAL STOCK.

As a rule trust companies are the transfer agents for the capital stock of large corporations and for verification purposes it is sufficient to obtain letters from them certifying to the capital stock outstanding.

Where companies issue their own stock, the stock registers and stock certificate books should be examined and compared with the lists of outstanding stockholders.

On the balance sheet each class, if more than one, of stock must be stated, giving amount authorized, issued, and in treasury, if any. In the case of companies with cumulative preferred stocks outstanding a note must be made in the balance sheet of the dividends accrued but not yet declared.

If stock has been sold on the instalment plan, the auditor should ascertain that the calls have been promptly met and whether any are in arrears. If special terms have been extended to any stockholder, approval of the board of directors is necessary and the minutes should be examined accordingly.

If any stock has been sold during the period under audit, the auditor should verify the proceeds of the sales.

SURPLUS.

The auditor should give consideration to the surplus at the beginning of the period. This item represents the accumulated profits prior to the beginning of the fiscal period under review, and should be compared with the surplus shown on the balance sheet of the previous year, and with the ledger account, to see that it corresponds, and if it does not, a reconciliation statement should be prepared giving full details of the differences.

PROFIT AND LOSS.

The auditor should obtain the profit and loss statement for three years, at least, including the period under audit, and after verifying them by comparison with the ledger account, prepare a statement in comparative form. This comparison will furnish valuable information to the banker as to the past progress of the concern under audit.

A satisfactory form of profit and loss account is annexed hereto, but any other form giving substantially similar information is acceptable.

While it would be impracticable in an ordinary balance sheet audit, and, at the same time, somewhat useless to make a detailed check of all the transactions entering into the composition of the profit and loss account, there are certain main principles to be kept in view which are briefly outlined below:

SALES.

Whenever it is possible, the quantities sold should be reconciled with the inventory on hand at the beginning of the period, plus the production, or purchases, during the period, less the inventory on hand at end of the period.

Where a good cost and accounting system is in force, the sales records will very probably be in good shape, but nevertheless, the auditor should satisfy himself from the shipping records that the sales books were closed on the last day of the fiscal year, and that no goods shipped after that date are included in the transactions.

When an audit is being made for the first time, the auditor should satisfy himself that the sales at the beginning of the period were recorded in accordance with the dates of shipments. Such verifications can be made conveniently by a direct comparison of the shipping memoranda with the invoices billed.

Allowances to customers for trade discounts, outward freights, reductions in prices, etc., should be deducted from the sales in the profit and loss account, as the amount of net sales is the only figure of interest to the bankers.

The future bookings at the close of the fiscal year should be looked into, as a comparison of orders on hand with corresponding periods of other years furnishes the bankers with an idea of the concern's business outlook.

COST OF SALES.

The inventory at the beginning of the period, plus purchases during the period, less inventory at the end of period, gives the cost of sales. In a manufacturing concern the factory cost of production takes the place of purchases. These items will have already been verified in auditing the balance sheet, but nevertheless care should be taken to see that this heading has not been made a dumping ground for charges which would be more properly embraced under the heading of special charges. The composition of the items entering into the cost of sales should be traced in totals into the cost ledgers or accounts.

GROSS PROFIT ON SALES.

This is obtained by deducting the cost of sales from the net sales. The ratio of gross profits to net sales should be calculated and compared.

SELLING, GENERAL AND ADMINISTRATIVE EXPENSES.

Under these general headings should be set down the expenses itemized to correspond with the titles of the ledger accounts kept in each division. In checking the totals of each account with the statement for the period under audit, special attention should be given to credits in these accounts should be given to see that none have been made for the sale of capital assets and for other items which should not appear in expense accounts. The percentages of the totals of each division and of the aggregate total to net sales should be calculated for each year for comparison.

NET PROFIT ON SALES.

This is obtained by deducting the aggregate total of the selling, general, and administrative expenses from the gross profit on sales, and shows the net earnings of the concern on its real business. Ratio to sales should be calculated for each year for comparison.

OTHER INCOME.

Under this heading is embraced any income that may be derived from sources outside of sales, such as income from investments, interest, discounts, etc. Schedules should be prepared of each item, and the auditor should satisfy himself of their accuracy and of the propriety of including them as income.

DEDUCTIONS FROM INCOME.

Under this heading are grouped such items as interest on bonded debt, interest on notes payable, etc. The same procedure of verification as in the case of other income should be followed.

NET INCOME—PROFIT AND LOSS.

Adding other income to gross income and deducting deductions from income gives the net income or profit and loss for the period, which is the amount that should be carried to the surplus account.

SURPLUS ADDITIONS AND DEDUCTIONS.

Items of unusual or extraordinary profit which do not belong strictly to the period under audit, or can not be said to be the legitimate result of the ordinary transactions of the concern, should be entered here and verified with the surplus account. Similarly, deductions should be treated. Also dividends declared should be entered in the surplus account and as an item under this caption, inasmuch as it is the usual custom to declare dividends "from net earnings and surplus." After adding special credits to and deducting special charges from the net income we have the total profit and loss for the whole period from all sources which, added to the surplus balance at the beginning of the period, gives us the surplus at the end of the period, which should agree with the surplus as stated on the balance sheet.

GENERAL.

These instructions cover audits of small or medium-sized concerns. In large concerns having, for instance, tens of thousands of accounts or notes receivable, the detail procedure suggested would be impracticable, and internal check should make it unnecessary. In such cases only tests can be made, but the auditor must always be prepared to justify his departure from a complete program by showing that the purposes sought to be accomplished thereby have been adequately effected by his work.

Any extensive clerical work, such as preparations of lists of notes receivable, etc., should be performed by the client's staff, so as to avoid unnecessary employment of professional staff in merely clerical work and consequent undue expense.

FORM OF CERTIFICATE.

The balance sheet and certificate should be connected with the accounts in such a way as to ensure that they shall be used only conjointly. This rule applies also to any report or memorandum containing any reservations as to the auditor's responsibility; any qualification as to the accounts, or any reference to facts materially affecting the financial position of the concern.

The certificate should be as short and concise as possible, consistent with a correct statement of the facts, and if qualifications are necessary the auditor must state them in a clear and concise manner.

If the auditor is satisfied that his audit has been complete and conforms to the general instructions of the Federal Reserve Board, and that the balance sheet and profit and loss statement are correct, or that any minor qualifications are fully covered by the footnotes on the balance sheet, the following form is proper:

I have audited the accounts of Blank & Co. for the period from.. to ....and
     I certify that the above balance sheet and statement of profit and loss have been made in accordance with the plan suggested and advised by the Federal Reserve Board and in my opinion set forth the financial condition of the firm at .... and the results of its operations for the period.

                (Signed)   A. B. C.

[Form for profit and loss account.]

Comparative statement of profit and loss for three years ending 19

	Year ending—		
	19—	19—	19—
Gross sales........................	$........	$........	$........
Less outward freight, allowances, and returns....................			
Net sales................			
Inventory beginning of year...........			
Purchases, net........................			
Less inventory end of year...........			
Cost of sales.....................			
Gross profit on sales.............			
Selling expenses (itemized to correspond with ledger accounts kept)...........			
Total selling expense...........			
General expenses (itemized to correspond with ledger accounts kept)....			
Total general expense			
Administrative expenses (itemized to correspond with ledger accounts kept)			
Total administrative expense.....			
Total expenses...................			
Net profit on sales..............			
Other income:			
Income from investments..........			
Interest on notes receivable, etc....			
Gross income....................			
Deductions from income:			
Interest on bonded debt...........			
Interest on notes payable..........			
Total deductions			
Net income—profit and loss.........			
Add special credits to profit and loss....			
Deduct special charges to profit and loss			
Profit and loss for period........			
Surplus beginning of period............			
Dividends paid.......................			
Surplus ending of period...........			

7/ In reprints, report is all in one paragraph.

-14-

[Form of balance sheet.]

ASSETS.

Cash:
1a. Cash on hand—currency and coin........ ....
1b. Cash in bank............................. ....

Notes and accounts receivable:
3. Notes receivable of customers on hand (not past due)......................... ....
5. Notes receivable discounted or sold with indorsement or guaranty.............. ....
7. Accounts receivable, customers (not past due)............................. ....
9. Notes receivable, customers, past due (cash value, $......)................... ....
11. Accounts receivable, customers, past due (cash value, $......).............. ....
Less:
13. Provisions for bad debts.. ....
15. Provisions for discounts, freights, allowances, etc. ....
....

Inventories:
17. Raw material on hand.................... ....
19. Goods in process........................ ....
21. Uncompleted contracts........ ....
Less payments on account thereof.................... ....
23. Finished goods on hand................. ....
....

Other quick assets (describe fully):
....
....

Total quick assets (excluding all investments).. ....

Securities:
25. Securities readily marketable and salable without impairing the business....... ....
27. Notes given by officers, stockholders, or employees......................... ....
29. Accounts due from officers, stockholders, or employees.......................... ....

Total current assets................. ....

Fixed assets:
31. Land used for plant..................... ....
33. Buildings used for plant................. ....
35. Machinery.............................. ....
37. Tools and plant equipment.............. ....
39. Patterns and drawings.................. ....
41. Office furniture and fixtures............. ....
43. Other fixed assets, if any (describe fully). ....
....
....

Less:
45. Reserves for depreciation............ ....
Total fixed assets.............. ....

Deferred charges:
47. Prepaid expenses, interest, insurance, taxes, etc......................... ....
Other assets (49)........................... ....

Total assets................. ....

LIABILITIES.

Bills, notes, and accounts payable:
Unsecured bills and notes—
2. Acceptances made for merchandise or raw material purchased........ ....
4. Notes given for merchandise or raw material purchased............... ....
6. Notes given to banks for money borrowed................... ....
8. Notes sold through brokers.......... ....
10. Notes given for machinery, additions to plant, etc.................... ....
12. Notes due to stockholders, officers, or employees...................... ....

Unsecured accounts—
14. Accounts payable for purchases (not yet due)....................... ....
16. Accounts payable for purchases (past due)........................ ....
18. Accounts payable to stockholders, officers, or employees.............. ....

Secured liabilities—
20a. Notes receivable discounted or sold with indorsement or guaranty (contra).................... ....
20b. Customers' accounts discounted or assigned (contra)........... ....
20c. Obligations secured by liens on inventories...................... ....
20d. Obligations secured by securities deposited as collateral............... ....

22. Accrued liabilities (interest, taxes, wages, etc....................... ....
Other current liabilities (describe fully):
....
....

Total current liabilities................. ....

Fixed liabilities:
24. Mortgage on plant (due date ....).. ....
26. Mortgage on other real estate (due date ....).................. ....
28. Chattel mortgage on machinery or equipment (due date ....)............. ....
30. Bonded debt (due date ....)........ ....

32. Other fixed liabilities (describe fully):
....
....

Total liabilities................. ....

Net worth:
34. If a corporation—
(a) Preferred stock (less stock in treasury)................. ....
(b) Common stock (less stock in treasury)................. ....
(c) Surplus and undivided profits.. ....
Less—
(d) Book value of good will.......... ....
(e) Deficit................. ....
....

36. If an individual or partnership—
(a) Capital....................... ....
(b) Undistributed profits or deficit.. ....

Total........................... ....

UNIFORM ACCOUNTING

A TENTATIVE PROPOSAL SUBMITTED BY THE FEDERAL RESERVE BOARD
WASHINGTON

FOR THE CONSIDERATION OF

BANKS, BANKERS, AND BANKING ASSOCIATIONS; MERCHANTS, MANUFACTURERS, AND ASSOCIATIONS OF MANUFACTURERS; AUDITORS, ACCOUNTANTS, AND ASSOCIATIONS OF ACCOUNTANTS

REPRINTED FROM FEDERAL RESERVE BULLETIN
APRIL, 1917

WASHINGTON
GOVERNMENT PRINTING OFFICE
1917

PREFACE.

The following tentative proposal for a uniform system of accounting to be adopted by manufacturing and merchandising concerns appeared in the April (1917) number of the Federal Reserve Bulletin, and is now reprinted for more general distribution.

It is recognized that banks and bankers have a very real interest in the subject, because they are constantly passing upon credits based upon statements made by manufacturers or merchants.

It is quite as much of vital interest to merchants and manufacturers, because they realize that their credit sometimes suffers by reason of losses incurred by bankers through credits given to merchants and manufacturers whose statements do not correctly reflect true conditions.

Lastly, it is of immense importance to auditors and accountants, because they have a professional as well as a practical interest in having the character of their professional work thoroughly formulated and standardized. Losses incurred by bankers by reason of credits given to merchants or manufacturers, if such credits were given because the statements were either actually false or misleading in their nature, tend to discredit accountancy as a profession and to shake the confidence of bankers in the real value of any statements.

Hence it is that the Federal Reserve Board puts out this tentative proposal with the hope of encouraging the fullest criticism and discussion.

90910°—17

3

APPROVED METHODS FOR THE PREPARATION OF BALANCE SHEET STATEMENTS

A TENTATIVE PROPOSAL SUBMITTED BY THE FEDERAL RESERVE BOARD

WASHINGTON

FOR THE CONSIDERATION OF

BANKS, BANKERS, AND BANKING ASSOCIATIONS; MERCHANTS, MANUFACTURERS, AND ASSOCIATIONS OF MANUFACTURERS; AUDITORS, ACCOUNTANTS, AND ASSOCIATIONS OF ACCOUNTANTS

REPRINTED FROM FEDERAL RESERVE BULLETIN
APRIL, 1917

WASHINGTON
GOVERNMENT PRINTING OFFICE
1918

PREFACE.

The following tentative proposal for uniform methods for the preparation of balance sheet statements to be adopted by manufacturing and merchandising concerns appeared in the April (1917) number of the Federal Reserve Bulletin under the caption "Uniform Accounting," and is reprinted for more general distribution.

It is recognized that banks and bankers have a very real interest in the subject, because they are constantly passing upon credits based upon statements made by manufacturers or merchants.

It is quite as much of vital interest to merchants and manufacturers, because they realize that their credit sometimes suffers by reason of losses incurred by bankers through credits given to merchants and manufacturers whose statements do not correctly reflect true conditions.

Lastly, it is of immense importance to auditors and accountants, because they have a professional as well as a practical interest in having the character of their professional work thoroughly formulated and standardized. Losses incurred by bankers by reason of credits given to merchants or manufacturers, if such credits were given because the statements were either actually false or misleading in their nature, tend to discredit accountancy as a profession and to shake the confidence of bankers in the real value of any statements.

Hence it is that the Federal Reserve Board puts out this tentative proposal with the hope of encouraging the fullest criticism and discussion.

3

RESOURCES AND THEIR APPLICATION

Paul-Joseph Esquerré

Correspondence

RESOURCES AND THEIR APPLICATION

Editor, The Journal of Accountancy:

Sir: At the examination of May, 1921, the following problem was submitted to the American Institute candidates:

Prepare a statement of resources and their application for the twelve months ended December 31, 1920, using the following data:

THE HALL MANUFACTURING CO.

BALANCE-SHEETS

Assets

	Dec. 31, 1919	Dec. 31, 1920
Cash	$5,000	$1,800
Accounts receivable	30,000	32,000
Raw material	12,000	14,500
Goods in process	16,000	17,500
Finished goods	21,000	19,000
Land	70,000	100,000
Buildings	115,000	170,000
Machinery	90,000	100,000
Tools	26,000	23,000
Patents	30,000	28,000
Discount on bonds	....	2,000
Investment in stocks	25,000	....
Advances to salesmen	500	1,000
Unexpired insurance	300	250
	$440,800	$509,050

Liabilities

	Dec. 31, 1919	Dec. 31, 1920
Accounts payable	$35,000	$10,000
Notes payable	25,000	5,000
Bank loans	20,000	....
Bonds payable	200,000	300,000
Reserve for depreciation, buildings and machinery	20,000	29,000
Reserve for bad debts	1,200	1,500
Reserve for construction	16,000	20,000
Capital stock	100,000	100,000
Surplus	23,600	43,550
	$440,800	$509,050

Following is an abstract of the surplus account:

	Dec. 31, 1919	Dec. 31, 1920
Balance, January 1, 1920		$23,600
Add net profits for 1920		8,950
" appraisal increase in land		30,000
Total		$62,550
Deduct credit to reserve for construction	$4,000	
Dividends paid December 31, 1920	15,000	19,000
Balance, December, 1920		$43,550

Depreciation was provided during the year as follows:

Credited to reserve for depreciation, buildings and machinery $10,000
Written off from tools 5,000
Written off from patents 2,000

During the year machinery which cost $7,000 was sold for $6,000. The loss was absorbed in the reserve for depreciation.

A solution of this problem appears in volume XXXII, pages 66 and 67, of THE JOURNAL OF ACCOUNTANCY.

I know that THE JOURNAL OF ACCOUNTANCY does not claim that the solutions which it publishes are official, but there is no doubt that all the students of accounting who read THE JOURNAL believe that they are. The students enrolled in my correspondence course are asked to solve the problem referred to in the foregoing, and the unanimity with which they copy the solution published by THE JOURNAL is an evidence of their belief in its orthodoxy and official character.

My personal belief is that the solution at issue is not a good one; that it is not true to accounting principles, and that, in order to balance, it violates accounting. It is because I hope to stir the interest of accountants in general, and bring about a salutary discussion of the points at issue, that I ask you to publish this letter in your JOURNAL. I have no desire to advertise myself or my course; I am actuated only by my firm belief in the truth and sacredness of accounting principles.

After having presented a comparative balance-sheet at the beginning and at the end of the calendar year 1920, showing increases and decreases of assets, liabilities, reserves and surplus, the editor of the *Students' Department* offers the following statement:

STATEMENT OF APPLICATION OF FUNDS, YEAR ENDED DEC. 31, 1920

Funds provided:

By net profits before providing for depreciation and bad debts		$8,950.00
Add depreciation		
Building and machinery	$10,000	
Tools	5,000	
Patents	2,000	
		17,000.00
Add provision for bad debts		300.00
		$26,250.00
By issue of bonds		
Par	$100,000	
Less discount	2,000	
		98,000.00
By sale of investments in stocks		25,000.00
By sale of machinery		
Cost	$7,000	
Less loss charged to reserve	1,000	
		6,000.00
Total funds provided		$155,250.00

which were applied as follows:

To purchase of fixed assets:

Buildings............................	$55,000	
Machinery...........................	17,000	
Tools...............................	2,000	
		$74,000.00
To payment of dividends....................		15,000.00
To increase in working capital and deferred charges (exhibit "C").................		66,250.00
		$155,250.00

Exhibit "C", to which the above refers, is made up of the following increases and decreases:

Increase of accounts receivable...................	$2,000	
" " raw materials.......................	2,500	
" " goods in process....................	1,500	
		$6,000.00
Decrease " accounts payable....................	$25,000	
" " notes payable......................	20,000	
" " bank loans........................	20,000	
		65,000.00
		$71,000.00
" " cash...............................	$3,200	
" " finished goods.....................	2,000	
		5,200.00
Increase of working capital.....................		$65,800.00

The editor of the *Students' Department* uses the term "funds" but does not say whether these funds are cash or asset funds. His terminology indicates that cash is at issue, since he says that the funds provided were applied to purchase assets and pay dividends; but it also indicates that assets are at issue, since he says that funds were applied to "increase in working capital." I assume, of course, that the editor did not mean to say that cash had been applied to reduce the asset cash, and above all to reduce the asset finished goods.

Passing now to the source of the very funds which were applied, I find that "tools" which must have been consumed by, and charged to, operations, since the decrease suffered by the asset has not been set aside out of profits, have produced $5,000 of cash or asset funds; that the amortization of patent value (which the editor refers to as "depreciation") has been written off the asset, charged to operations as a profit-and-loss charge, but, nevertheless, has produced $2,000 of cash or asset funds. Whether it is cash or asset funds which the editor has in mind makes no difference whatever; in either case, he advances the theory that one of the means of providing funds is to consume assets or to write off intangibles.

The solution of your editor gives the impression that the profits of the year were $26,250 before providing for depreciation and bad debts. That is true only provided the profit-and-loss account reads as follows:

PROFIT-AND-LOSS ACCOUNT

Provisions for reserves:		Operating profits..	$26,250.00
For depreciation of B. & M.	$10,000.00		
" accounts receivable	300.00		
" depreciation of tools	5,000.00		
" " " patents	2,000.00		
	$17,300.00		
Balance transferred to surplus	8,950.00		
	$26,250.00		$26,250.00

But the profit-and-loss account does not read that way, because the writing off of the asset "tools" in the amount of $5,000 is not "depreciation" and, therefore, has not been set aside out of profits. The writing-off of tools is the result of an inventory which, when opposed to the prior inventory and to subsequent purchases, shows that the operations have actually consumed a value of $5,000 which must be considered as cost of goods manufactured, or, at any rate, as a profit-and-loss charge operating against inaccurate operating profits. The same thing is true of patents: in this case, as well as in the case of tools, a reserve was not created; the patents lost a value proportionate to the amortization of their active life, and, therefore, the loss was charged to operating profits which were too high. Thus the profit-and-loss account must read:

PROFIT-AND-LOSS ACCOUNT

Provisions for reserves:		Operating profits..	$19,250.00
For depreciation of B. & M.	$10,000.00		
" accounts receivable	300.00		
	$10,300.00		
Balance transferred to surplus	8,950.00		
	$19,250.00		$19,250.00

In reality, the actual profits of the company are, not $19,250, but $18,250, since the surplus reserved for depreciation of buildings and machinery has suffered a loss of $1,000. This loss the company's accountant did not fail to take into consideration when rendering the income-tax report. This report, when it was rendered in 1920, must have been as follows:

Operating profits............................		$19,250.00
Deduct:		
Loss on machinery sold.....................	$1,000.00	
Depreciation of machinery and buildings......	10,000.00	11,000.00
Taxable income.......................		$8,250.00

The reserve for bad debts is excluded because, in 1920, it was not an allowed deduction, and, further, because, as there had been no loss of the previous reserve, an increase of that old reserve was purely sentimental and, therefore, useless.

There is not, to my knowledge, a principle of accounting which links the new resources obtained during a period with the cash receipts, and the resources of a prior period, consumed in the present one, with the cash disbursements. It appears to me that your editor's solution is brought to a balance by forcing the funds, i. e., by making them come from sources which are impossible.

Of course, you expect me to submit to your readers what I believe to be the true solution of the problem at issue. Here it is:

STATEMENT OF RESOURCES AND APPLICATIONS

(a) Increase of corporate wealth:

(1) Through appraisal of land up to the market value thereof at 12/31/20— (Credited to surplus)...............			$30,000.00
(2) Through acquisition of fixed assets:			
Tools............................		$2,000.00	
Buildings........................		55,000.00	
Machinery:			
New machinery acquired $17,000			
Less old machinery sold.. 6,000		11,000.00	68,000.00
(3) Through increase of operating assets:			
Raw materials....................		$2,500.00	
Goods in process.................		1,500.00	
Accounts receivable (including advances to salesmen $500.00).......:		2,500.00	6,500
Total 1, 2 and 3...............			$104,500.00
(4) Through the retention, as an asset, of the discount lost on bond issue...........			2,000.00
(5) Through the release of liens encumbering assets:			
Cancellation of bank loans..........		$20,000.00	
Reduction of acc'ts payable.........		25,000.00	
" " notes payable.........		20,000.00	65,000.00
			$171,500.00

(b) Decrease of corporate wealth:

(1) Through decrease of assets:			
Investment in bonds..............		$25,000.00	
Finished goods...................		2,000.00	
Unexpired insurance..............		50.00	
Cash...........................		3,200.00	
			$30,250.00

(2) Through consumption of assets by operation:	
Tools consumèd by process..........	$ 5,000.00
(3) Through amortization of intangible values—patents.....................	2,000.00
(4) Through loss on machinery, resulting from sale	1,000.00
(5) Through distribution of surplus earned in past periods	15,000.00
Total 1, 2, 3, 4 and 5................	$53,250.00
(6) Through use of credit:	
Increase of liability for corporate bonds through issue thereof............	100,000.00
Total decrease of corporate wealth	$153,250.00

(c) Net increase of wealth through reinvestment of profits of the calendar year as follows:

(1) Net profits after appropriations, i. e., net profit transferred to surplus.........		$8,950.00
(2) Appropriated out of current earnings:		
For depreciation of buildings & machinery........................	$10,000.00	
For increase of reserve for acc'ts rec....	300.00	
		10,300.00
		$19,250.00
(3) Deduct loss of surplus previously appropriated.		
Loss of reserve for depreciation of machinery and equipment.........		1,000.00
Net profits reinvested, to secure net increase of wealth........		$18,250.00

I beg to point out to your readers that this solution expresses a perfectly well known and eminently sound principle of business philosophy. It says that a concern obtains new wealth by:

(1) increasing its assets,
(2) relieving its assets of the liens which encumber them.

It says, further, that a concern diminishes its wealth by

(1) decreasing its assets,
(2) using its credit,

and it ends by saying that the net increase of wealth obtained in a period results from the net increase of assets, made possible by the reinvestment of profits, as measured by the net increase of surplus.

It is my contention that both the layman and the accountant can understand the statement which I have submitted; whereas neither the accountant

429

nor the layman can understand the statement submitted by the editor of your *Students' Department*.

In support of this contention, permit me to say that, very recently, I had in my office, seeking advice, one of the partners in a firm of accountants. This accountant had been asked by a new client to check up "a statement of resources obtained and applied" produced by his predecessor on the lines of the statement which I have criticized in the foregoing.

The client professed inability to understand the said statement, and the accountant proclaimed loudly that he could not "make head or tail" out of it. He was convinced that a figure had been used to balance the statement, which was merely a "forced figure." My opinion was in every way corroborative of his.

Trusting that you will see your way clear to publish this letter, in the interest of our beloved theory of accounting.

Very truly yours,

PAUL-JOSEPH ESQUERRÉ.

New York, March 26, 1925.

THE STATEMENT OF
APPLICATION OF FUNDS

H. A. Finney

Students' Department

EDITED BY H. A. FINNEY

THE STATEMENT OF APPLICATION OF FUNDS

A REPLY TO MR. ESQUERRÉ

There appeared in the correspondence department of THE JOURNAL OF ACCOUNTANCY for May, 1925, a communication from Mr. Paul-Joseph Esquerré in which he expresses disapproval of the form of the statement of application of funds used in a solution which was published in the *Students' Department* for July, 1921. While Mr. Esquerré's letter is, specifically, a criticism of a particular solution, it is, in its broader implications, an expression of disapproval of the general form of the statement of application of funds which is in more or less general use, and of which the solution in question was merely an illustration.

I am in agreement with Mr. Esquerré that the statement of application of funds has not yet been perfected. No doubt certain elements of the statement as usually prepared are difficult for the layman to comprehend, particularly the theory underlying the adding back of depreciation to the profits to determine the total funds provided by the profits. This procedure and the theory on which it is based should not be especially difficult for the trained accountant to comprehend, but if the statement were perfected so that the layman would understand it as readily as he understands the profit-and-loss statement and the balance-sheet its usefulness would be greatly enhanced.

The statement of application of funds has considerable value. Undoubtedly its potential value is greater than its present realized value for the very reason that it does tax the understanding of some laymen and even some accountants. It is therefore to be hoped that Mr. Esquerré's letter will "stir the interest of accountants in general, and bring about a salutary discussion of the points at issue." The columns of the *Students' Department* are open for, and the editor will welcome, solutions of the problem in question which readers may care to submit as contributions to the discussion. If, out of such contributions, a form should be found which would be a real improvement of the old form, Mr. Esquerré's letter would prove to have been a service to the profession.

It is, of course, a matter of personal concern to the editor of this department that Mr. Esquerré saw fit to make use of such expressions as "forcing the funds" and "forced figure." The first reading of the letter left the editor with the impression that he had been accused of a mathematical forcing of a balance, and it is not unlikely that many readers obtained the same impression. Such an accusation would of course have been unwarranted and untrue, as can be determined by an inspection of the problem and the solution, which are reprinted hereinafter for purposes presently to be mentioned.

Upon second reading, it appeared more likely that Mr. Esquerré meant to convey the thought that figures were grouped in a manner which was not in accordance with his interpretation of the requirements of accounting principles. If this is the correct interpretation of his remarks, it is to be regretted that, in stating what merely amounts to a difference of opinion as to correct principle and procedure, use was made of words charged with so aspersive a connotation.

497

If, as it is hoped, this discussion is to result in constructive suggestions for the improvement of the form of the statement of application of funds, it is perhaps desirable to reprint, so that they will appear in one issue, the problem, the solution as it originally appeared in the *Students' Department*, and Mr. Esquerré's suggested statement. It may also be helpful to explain how the original statement was prepared, to comment to some extent on Mr. Esquerré's criticisms, and to analyze his statement in order to determine whether it is an improvement or not. There follows, then, the problem:

Problem

Prepare a statement of resources and their application for the 12 months ended December 31, 1920, using the following data:

THE HALL MANUFACTURING COMPANY—BALANCE-SHEET

Assets

	Dec. 31, 1919	Dec. 31, 1920
Cash	$5,000	$1,800
Accounts receivable	30,000	32,000
Raw material	12,000	14,500
Goods in process	16,000	17,500
Finished goods	21,000	19,000
Land	70,000	100,000
Buildings	115,000	170,000
Machinery	90,000	100,000
Tools	26,000	23,000
Patents	30,000	28,000
Discount on bonds		2,000
Investment in stocks	25,000	
Advances to salesmen	500	1,000
Unexpired insurance	300	250
	$440,800	$509,050

Liabilities

Accounts payable	$35,000	$10,000
Notes payable	25,000	5,000
Bank loans	20,000	
Bonds payable	200,000	300,000
Reserve for depreciation, buildings and machinery	20,000	29,000
Reserve for bad debts	1,200	1,500
Reserve for construction	16,000	20,000
Capital stock	100,000	100,000
Surplus	23,600	43,550
	$440,800	$509,050

Following is an abstract of the surplus account:

Balance January 1, 1920		$23,600
Add net profit for 1920		8,950
Add appraisal increase in land		30,000
Total		62,550
Deduct credit to reserve for construction	$4,000	
Deduct dividend paid December 31, 1920	15,000	19,000
Balance, December 31, 1920		$43,550

Depreciation was provided during the year as follows:

Credited to reserve for depreciation, buildings and
machinery.................................. $10,000
Written off from tools....................... 5,000
Written off from patents..................... 2,000

During the year machinery which cost $7,000 was sold for $6,000. The loss was absorbed in the reserve for depreciation.

The statement of application of funds is based on the increases and decreases of assets and liabilities shown by a comparative balance-sheet; but it is impossible to use these items of increase and decrease in the statement of application of funds without first giving serious consideration to the question whether any funds (or if the word "resources" is preferred, the reader is privileged to substitute that word wherever the editor uses the word "funds," it being the thought that each of these words conveys a broader meaning than mere cash) have been provided or any funds applied in ways which are significant but which are not brought to light by the comparative balance-sheet.

For instance, the increase in the surplus during the year is clearly not the amount which the profits have contributed in the way of funds during the year—if for no other reason, because dividends have been paid. Such payments constitute an application of funds which should be shown on the statement, and the charge of the dividends to the surplus has had the effect of reducing the increase in surplus for the year to an amount less than the profits. Hence, after determining the increase or decrease in each item which appears in the balance-sheets, it is necessary to give consideration to any adjustments which must be made in order to obtain more correct figures to include in the statement of application of funds.

The accompanying working papers show the increases and decreases in the various balance-sheet items, and the adjustments:

The first column of the working papers contains the balance-sheet as of December 31, 1919; the second column that of December 31, 1920. The third and fourth columns show the net debits in excess of the net credits, or vice versa, in each account during the year and the amounts of such net debits or net credits. The changes during the year are classified as debits and credits rather than increases and decreases in order that the items in the adjustment columns (5) and (6) may be uniformly applied to them as debits and credits.

Since it is known that the increase in surplus does not represent the amount of funds provided by profits, this increase, $19,950, is transferred by adjustment (A) to a lower space, where room will be available for the application of all necessary adjustments.

If the fact of the appraisal had not been stated, the increase of $30,000 in the land account would appear to have resulted from the application of funds of an equivalent amount in the purchase of land. But the problem states that the land was merely written up by a credit to surplus. The increase in the land account can not properly be shown as resulting from an application of funds, because the increase resulted from a mere book entry which did not require funds. This item must therefore be eliminated, and the elimination is accomplished by the credit adjustment entry (B) on the land line. But, on the other hand, the increase of $19,950 in surplus has been partly caused by this book

499

WORKING PAPERS

	(1) Balance-sheets Dec. 31, 1919	(2) Dec. 31, 1920	(3) Net change Debit	(4) Net change Credit	(5) Adjustments Debit	(6) Adjustments Credit	(7) Working capital and deferred charges Increase	(8) Working capital and deferred charges Decrease	(9) Funds Applied	(10) Funds Provided
ASSETS										
Cash	$5,000	$1,800		$3,200				$3,200		
Accounts receivable	30,000	32,000	$2,000				$2,000			
Raw material	12,000	14,500	2,500				2,500			
Goods in process	16,000	17,500	1,500				1,500			
Finished goods	21,000	19,000		2,000				2,000		
Land	70,000	100,000	30,000			$30,000 B				
Buildings	115,000	170,000	55,000						$55,000	
Machinery	90,000	100,000	10,000		{ $1,000 H / 6,000 I }				17,000	
Tools	26,000	23,000		3,000	5,000 F				2,000	
Patents	30,000	28,000		2,000	2,000 G					
Discount on bonds		2,000	2,000			2,000 K				
Investment in stocks	25,000			25,000						$25,000
Advances to salesmen	500	1,000	500				500			
Unexpired insurance	300	250		50				50		
	$440,800	$509,050								
LIABILITIES										
Accounts payable	$35,000	$10,000	$25,000				$25,000			
Notes payable	25,000	5,000	20,000				20,000			
Bank loans	20,000		20,000				20,000			
Bonds payable	200,000	300,000		$100,000	$2,000 K					$98,000
Reserve for depreciation	20,000	29,000		9,000	10,000 E	$1,000 H				
Reserve for bad debts	1,200	1,500		300	300 J					
Reserve for construction	16,000	20,000		4,000	4,000 C					
Capital stock	100,000	100,000								
Surplus	23,600	43,550		19,950	19,950 A					
	$440,800	$509,050	$168,500	$168,500						

Funds provided by profits:					
Increase in surplus		19,950 A			
Appraisal increase in value of land		4,000 C			
Credit to reserve for construction		15,000 D			26,250
Dividends paid	30,000 B				
Provisions for depreciation:					
Buildings and machinery		10,000 E			
Tools		5,000 F			
Patents		2,000 G			
		300 J			
Increase in reserve for bad debts		6,000 I			
Funds applied to payment of dividends	15,000 D			$15,000	
Funds provided by sale of machinery					6,000
			66,250	66,250	
	$95,250	$95,250	$71,500	$155,250	
Increase in working capital and deferred charges			$71,500	$155,250	

entry; certainly this credit to surplus did not provide funds, and if we are to adjust our surplus account increase figure to the true amount of the funds provided by profits the $30,000 must be adjusted out of the surplus. This is accomplished by the debit adjustment entry (B).

There has been transferred out of surplus during the year an item of $4,000 which was credited to a reserve for construction. This reserve is merely an appropriated surplus account, and the $4,000 transferred out of surplus during the year must be returned to it in our working papers in order to adjust the surplus increase for the year to the true amount of funds provided by profits. This transfer is accomplished by adjustment entry (C).

During the year dividends were paid in the amount of $15,000. This payment constituted an application of funds; moreover, it reduced the balance of the surplus account and consequently caused the increase in the surplus to be less than the funds provided by the profits. Adjustment is therefore made by entry (D) to add this item back to the surplus increase, to determine the funds provided by the profits and to set up on a separate line the amount of funds applied in the payment of dividends.

Entry (E) transfers out of the reserve for depreciation and into "funds provided by profits" the amount of depreciation provided for buildings and machinery. The theory underlying this adjustment and the addition of depreciation provisions to the net profits in the statement of application of funds itself is one of the most difficult things to understand in connection with the preparation of this statement. In order not to break the continuity of the present explanation, we shall defer for a short period the explanation of this treatment of depreciation and merely call attention to the fact that entry (E) has the effect of taking out of the reserve for depreciation and adding back to the surplus the depreciation of buildings and machinery credited to the reserve during the year; entries (F) and (G) have the effect of adding back to the assets and to surplus the amounts of depreciation of tools and patents which were credited to asset accounts during the year. (Mr. Esquerré criticizes the editor for using the word "depreciation" in connection with patents; his attention is directed to the problem.)

During the year machinery which cost $7,000 was sold for $6,000. If this transaction had been the only one recorded in the machinery account during the year, that account would have shown a decrease of $7,000, but that would not have been the amount of funds provided by the sale of the machinery. (To make this point clear it is only necessary to suppose that machinery costing $7,000 had been written off during the year against the reserve; in that case no funds whatever would have been provided.) An adjustment entry (H) is therefore made, debiting the machinery account and crediting the reserve. Adjustment (I) is then made transferring out of the machinery account and to a separate line at the bottom of the statement the item of $6,000, which represents the true amount of funds provided by the sale of the machinery. Returning to the machinery line, it will be found that the original net debit increase of $10,000 has been increased by two debit adjustments totaling $7,000, and the aggregate of these items, or $17,000, is the amount of funds applied to the purchase of machinery. This item of $17,000 is therefore carried out to the "funds applied" column, which, like the net change debit column and the adjustment debit column, is also a debit column.

Adjustment (J) adds back to surplus by transfer from the reserve for bad debts the amount of the increase in the reserve during the year. The reason for this adjustment is similar to that which justifies the treatment of depreciation. (An alternative, and perhaps preferable, method would be to deduct the reserve balances at the two dates from the accounts receivable balances, and deal with only the net balances as the real values of the receivables at the two dates.)

During the year bonds of a par value of $100,000 appear to have been sold at a discount of $2,000, thus producing funds of a net amount of $98,000. The discount item of $2,000 is therefore offset, by entry (K), against the increase in bonds payable, to determine the net amount of funds provided by the additional issue.

Now that all adjustments have been made the adjustment columns are footed to see that a balance has thus far been maintained. The items in columns (3) and (4) plus or minus the adjusting items in columns (5) and (6) are then carried to their appropriate columns—(7), (8), (9) and (10). It will be noted that the item of $26,250, appearing in the "funds provided" column, represents the net amount of all surplus and surplus adjustment items.

After distributing the figures as indicated, columns (7) and (8) are brought to a balance by inserting the "increase in working capital and deferred charges" item of $66,250, and as this increase in working capital and deferred charges represents an application of funds, the amount is also entered in the "funds applied" column.

It is thought that the foregoing explanations will clarify the theory underlying the treatment of items other than depreciation, and it will be noted that the various items can be traced from the working papers to the following statements. (Reference to Mr. Esquerré's adaptation of the schedule of working capital and deferred charges will show that he included, and in a somewhat changed form, only the working capital items, omitting the deferred charge items, and thus making it appear that the total of the supporting schedule did not tie up with the main statement.)

Solution

THE HALL MANUFACTURING COMPANY

Statement of application of funds—year ended Dec. 31, 1920

Funds provided:

By net profits before providing for depreciation and bad debts:

Net profit carried to surplus.............		$8,950	
Add depreciation:			
Buildings and machinery..............	$10,000		
Tools.............................	5,000		
Patents...........................	2,000	17,000	
Add provision for bad debts.............		300	$26,250
By issue of bonds:			
Par...............................		100,000	
Less discount........................		2,000	98,000
By sale of investment in stocks...........			25,000
By sale of machinery:			
Cost..............................		7,000	
Less loss charged to reserve.............		1,000	6,000
Total funds provided..............			$155,250

Which were applied as follows:
  To purchases of fixed assets:

Buildings...........................	$55,000	
Machinery..........................	17,000	
Tools..............................	2,000	$74,000
To payment of dividends.................		15,000
To increase in working capital and deferred charges............................		66,250
Total funds applied................		$155,250

THE HALL MANUFACTURING COMPANY

Schedule of working capital and deferred charges

December 31, 1919, and December 31, 1920

	Dec. 31, 1919	Dec. 31, 1920	*Working capital* Decrease	Increase
Current assets:				
Cash..........................	$5,000	$1,800	$3,200	
Accounts receivable...............	30,000	32,000		$2,000
Raw material....................	12,000	14,500		2,500
Goods in process.................	16,000	17,500		1,500
Finished goods...................	21,000	19,000	2,000	
Total current assets..........	84,000	84,800		
Current liabilities:				
Accounts payable.................	35,000	10,000		25,000
Notes payable....................	25,000	5,000		20,000
Bank loans......................	20,000			20,000
Total current liabilities.......	80,000	15,000		
Working capital....................	4,000	69,800		
Increase in working capital...........			65,800	
			$71,000	$71,000

Deferred charges

	Dec. 31, 1919	Dec. 31, 1920	Decrease	Increase
Advances to salesmen................	$500	$1,000		$500
Unexpired insurance................	300	250	$50	
	800	1,250		
Net increase in deferred charges.......			450	
			500	500

Summary

Increase in working capital...........	$65,800
Increase in deferred charges..........	450
Total......................	$66,250

Let us now return to the question of the treatment of depreciation. To make the matter as simple as possible let us assume that a man invested $800 in business as a peddler. With $700 he purchased an automobile truck, and with the remaining $100 he purchased fruit and vegetables. He did a strictly cash business and sold his goods for exactly twice what he paid for them. At the end of the year he prepared a statement as follows:

Sales..	$10,000
Less cost of sales................................	5,000
Gross profit......................................	5,000
Less expenses....................................	1,000
Net profit.......................................	$4,000

The net profit shown by the statement is represented by $4,000 of cash deposited in bank, and he decides to buy a building with it. It is perfectly apparent that his profits have provided funds of $4,000 and that these funds have been applied to the purchase of a building. The time arrives for preparing his tax return and he calls on an accountant to help him prepare it. The accountant looks at the foregoing profit-and-loss statement and amends it as follows:

Net profit (as above)..............................	$4,000
Less depreciation of delivery truck....................	200
True net profit...................................	$3,800

Now, if we were to prepare a statement of application of funds for the peddler, it would appear as follows:

Funds provided:	
By profits:	
Net profit......................................	$3,800
Add back depreciation of delivery truck.............	200
Total..	$4,000
Funds applied:	
To purchase of building...........................	$4,000

The profits *must* have provided funds of $4,000 because a $4,000 building was purchased, and it is quite apparent that they did furnish funds of $4,000 because the depreciation charge, while reducing the profits, did not reduce the funds provided by the profits.

Mr. Esquerré appears to agree in general with this theory because, in his suggested statement, he adds back to the profits the amounts added during the year to the reserve for depreciation of buildings and machinery and to the reserve for accounts receivable. But, both in his comments and in his suggested statement, he indicates that a different treatment should be followed in regard to tools and patents. He states:

"Passing now to the source of the very funds which were applied, I find that 'tools' which must have been consumed by, and charged to, operations, since the decrease suffered by the asset has not been set aside out of profits, have produced $5,000 of cash or asset funds; that the amortization of patent value (which the editor refers to as 'depreciation') has been written off the asset, charged to operations as a profit-and-loss charge, but, nevertheless, has produced $2,000 of cash or asset funds. Whether it is cash or asset funds which the editor has in mind makes no difference whatever; in either case, he advances the theory that one of the means of providing funds is to consume assets or to write off intangibles."

The editor does not advance any such theory. The adding back of the depreciation is not based on "the theory that one of the means of providing funds is to consume assets or write off intangibles." The peddler's depreciation was not added back to the net profits because the accountant's provision of depreciation resulted in the provision of funds; it was added back because the provision of depreciation reduced the net profits below the amount of funds provided by the profits. That is to say, the funds were provided by the profits, not by the depreciation; the effect of the depreciation provision was to make the net profits somewhat smaller than the funds provided by the profits.

To this, Mr. Esquerré may be assumed to reply that his remarks did not apply to depreciation provided by setting up a reserve, but to the reduction in value of tools, which was recorded by writing down the asset instead of setting up a reserve, "because the writing off of the asset 'tools' in the amount of $5,000 is not 'depreciation' and, therefore, has not been set aside out of profits. The writing-off of tools is the result of an inventory which, when opposed to the prior inventory and to subsequent purchases, shows that the operations have actually consumed a value of $5,000 which must be considered as cost of goods manufactured, or, at any rate, as a profit-and-loss charge operating against inaccurate operating profits. The same thing is true of patents: in this case, as well as in the case of tools, a reserve was not created; the patents lost a value proportionate to the amortization of their active life, and, therefore, the loss was charged to operating profits which were too high."

The editor fails to follow Mr. Esquerré in this distinction. He can not agree that "the writing-off of the asset 'tools' in the amount of $5,000 is not 'depreciation'." If it is not depreciation, what shall we call it? Is it material as to whether the loss from wear and tear of a fixed asset due to its use in operations is computed by applying an estimated rate rather than by determining the depreciated value by means of an appraisal? Shall we say that the loss in the value of a fixed asset due to its use in operations is depreciation if it is computed by multiplying by a rate per cent, but that it is not depreciation if it is computed by appraising the property at its depreciated value? And is it material whether the charge for depreciation is offset by a credit to a reserve or by a credit to an asset account? Shall we say that the loss in the value of a fixed asset due to its use in operations is depreciation if it is recorded by a credit to a reserve, but that such a loss is not depreciation if it is recorded by a credit to the fixed asset account?

Mr. Walton, in writing of depreciation and tools, says that depreciation may be recorded "by a charge to revenue and a credit to the asset accounts themselves. This is called writing down the assets. . . . Since the tool acts directly on the material, it wears out much faster than a machine, and since the uses to which tools are put vary very greatly, it is impossible to fix any rate of depreciation that will be even approximately correct. . . . The only proper way to value them, when closing the books, is to take an inventory of them, as they stand at the time."

As to patents, let us assume that our peddler had invented a horn which was as effective in obtaining a following as that of the Pied Piper. And let us assume that the accountant had charged off $50 as amortization of the value of the patent. That would reduce the net profit to $3,750. It would appear to be necessary to add back the amortization of the patent as well as the depreciation of the truck in order to arrive at the $4,000 of funds provided by the profits.

Mr. Esquerré objects to the use of the word "funds." "The editor of the *Students' Department* uses the term 'funds' but does not say whether these funds are cash or asset funds. His terminology indicates that cash is at issue, since he says that the funds provided were applied to purchase assets and pay dividends; but it also indicates that assets are at issue, since he says that funds were applied to 'increase in working capital.' I assume, of course, that the editor did not mean to say that cash had been applied to reduce the asset cash, and above all to reduce the asset finished goods."

The criticism of the word "funds" is perhaps the most significant of Mr. Esquerré's criticisms. The term "funds" is likely to be misconstrued as meaning cash, and yet if cash were meant the statement would have been called a statement of receipts and disbursements. While the term "funds" suggests something more than cash it is not unlikely that the term "resources" is preferable.

As to the remarks about applying cash to reduce cash and finished goods, Mr. Esquerré is correct in his assumption that the editor did not intend his statements to be so construed, and it is difficult to see how any such construction could be made. The statement seems to say clearly that the new funds or resources which came into the business during the year were applied to certain purposes, such as purchases of fixed assets and payments of dividends, and have also resulted in an increase in the working capital. But since the working capital is the excess of the current assets over the current liabilities, the net increase is accounted for in detail by showing in the supporting schedule the increases and decreases in various items which account for the net increase.

It now appears to be in order to consider the statement which Mr. Esquerré regards as the "true solution."

STATEMENT OF RESOURCES AND APPLICATIONS

(a) Increase of corporate wealth:

(1) Through appraisal of land up to the market value thereof at 12/31/20— (credited to surplus)............................... $30,000

(2) Through acquisition of fixed assets:

Tools...............................		$2,000	
Buildings...........................		55,000	
Machinery:			
New machinery acquired....	$17,000		
Less old machinery sold....	6,000	11,000	68,000

(3) Through increase of operating assets:

Raw materials.......................	$2,500	
Goods in process....................	1,500	
Accounts receivable (including advances to salesmen $500.00)..................	2,500	6,500

Total, 1, 2 and 3.............. | | $104,500

507

(4) Through the retention, as an asset, of the discount lost on bond issue...............		$2,000
(5) Through the release of liens encumbering assets:		
Cancellation of bank loans..............	$20,000	
Reduction of accounts payable...........	25,000	
" " notes payable.............	20,000	65,000
		$171,500

(b) Decrease of corporate wealth:

(1) Through decrease of assets:		
Investment in bonds....................	$25,000	
Finished goods........................	2,000	
Unexpired insurance...................	50	
Cash.................................	3,200	$30,250
(2) Through consumption of assets by operation:		
Tools consumed by process..............		5,000
(3) Through amortization of intangible values- patents...............................		2,000
(4) Through loss on machinery, resulting from sale.		1,000
(5) Through distribution of surplus earned in past periods...............................		15,000
Total 1, 2, 3, 4 and 5.............		$53,250
(6) Through use of credit:		
Increase of liability for corporate bonds through issue thereof.................		100,000
Total decrease of corporate wealth..		$153,250

(c) Net increase of wealth through reinvestment of profits of the calendar year as follows:

(1) Net profits after appropriations, i.e., net profit transferred to surplus...................		$8,950
(2) Appropriated out of current earnings:		
For depreciation of buildings and machinery	$10,000	
For increase of reserve for accounts received	300	10,300
		$19,250
(3) Deduct loss of surplus previously appropriated.		
Loss of reserve for depreciation of machinery and equipment.......................		1,000
Net profits reinvested, to secure net increase of wealth.................		$18,250

In commenting on this solution which he submits on behalf of "the truth and sacredness of accounting principles" and "our beloved theory of accounting," Mr. Esquerré states:

"I beg to point out to your readers that this solution expresses a perfectly well known and eminently sound principle of business philosophy. It says that a concern obtains new wealth by:

"(1) increasing its assets,
"(2) relieving its assets of the liens which encumber them.

"It says, further, that a concern diminishes its wealth by

"(1) decreasing its assets,
"(2) using its credit,

"and it ends by saying that the net increase of wealth obtained in a period results from the net increase of assets, made possible by the reinvestment of profits, as measured by the net increase of surplus."

In regard to the heading of Mr. Esquerré's statement, it is of course a trifling matter, but the editor has had so much difficulty in impressing on the members of his various classes the importance of always showing the date of a statement or the period covered by it that he regrets the fact that Mr. Esquerré has lent the weight of his authority to the omission of this information.

An inspection of the statement shows that it consists of three main sections:

    (a) Increase of corporate wealth
    (b) Decrease of corporate wealth
    (c) Net increase of wealth through reinvestment of profits of the calendar year.

The items which appear under the first two of these captions are said to be in accordance with a "perfectly well known and eminently sound principle of business philosophy", namely that a concern obtains new wealth by:

    (1) increasing its assets,
    (2) relieving its assets of the liens which encumber them,
and that a concern diminishes its wealth by:
    (1) decreasing its assets,
    (2) using its credit.

Before this "principle" can be allowed to enter into the company of "sacred principles," it appears to be necessary to come to an understanding as to what is meant by "corporate wealth." The natural assumption is that it means net worth, and this assumption seems to be in accord with Mr. Esquerré's use of the expression, because of the fact that the balance of the third section is called both "net increase of wealth" and "net profits," and because, in the last part of his declaration of the principle underlying the statement he states that the "net increase of wealth" . . . is "measured by the net increase of surplus."

Assuming, then, that corporate wealth is to be interpreted as net worth, and increase in corporate wealth as net profit or increase of surplus, it is pertinent to inquire whether the items appearing under the captions of increase and decrease of corporate wealth really represent increases and decreases in net worth, and hence whether the "principle" is really as "eminently sound" as is claimed.

For instance, certain fixed assets have been increased, and these increases appear in the statement as increases of corporate wealth. But does it necessarily follow that a concern has increased its wealth by merely increasing its tools, buildings and machinery? Is it not more likely that the concern has merely exchanged one asset for another, or bought the property on credit? In either of these cases it can not be said that the wealth or net worth has been increased. The application of this "principle" in a statement such as suggested would appear to be very useful, however, in instances in which corporations have received fixed assets as gifts.

Also under the caption "increase of corporate wealth" there appears the following item:

"Through the retention, as an asset, of the discount lost on the
bond issue . . . . $2,000"

509

That is to say, in accordance with "a perfectly well known and eminently sound principle of business philosophy" all that a company needs to do in order to increase its corporate wealth is to sell $100,000 of bonds for $98,000, and not write off the discount.

Also under the caption "increase of corporate wealth," Mr. Esquerré shows:

"Through the release of liens encumbering assets:
"Cancellation of bank loans.......................$20,000."

That is to say, by paying your debts you increase your corporate wealth. Only the forgiveness of your debts would appear to accomplish that result. Mr. Esquerré's statement would be singularly useful to companies whose bank loans are cancelled by the bank without payment.

Showing decreases of assets under the caption "decrease of corporate wealth" does not appear to be based on any sounder theory, for the decrease in assets is usually accompanied by an increase in other assets or a decrease in liabilities, leaving the wealth unchanged except to the extent of any profit or loss on the transaction.

It will be noted that Mr. Esquerré shows the depreciation of tools and the amortization of patents as decreases of corporate wealth, while the provision for depreciation of building and machinery is shown as part of the net increase of wealth. As already stated, the editor is not convinced that two items of decrease in the value of fixed assets, caused by their use in operations, are essentially different in nature merely because one is computed by using a rate per cent while the other is computed by appraising the property at its depreciated value, or merely because one item of decrease is recorded by a credit to a reserve while the other is recorded by a credit to the asset account. Certainly there does not appear to be so fundamental a difference between two such items of depreciation as to make one a decrease of corporate wealth and the other a part of the net increase of corporate wealth.

Since the question of sacred principles has been raised, attention is directed to the somewhat iconoclastic attitude toward the relation of depreciation and net profits which seems to pervade Mr. Esquerré's communication. The accountants of the past generation, not without some struggle, finally obtained a general acknowledgment of the principle that depreciation is an expense and that the net profits are not net until after provision has been made for depreciation. And yet, in Mr. Esquerré's letter,

(Page 427) The profits are said to be $18,250, which is the sum of $8,250 transferred to surplus and the net increases in the depreciation and bad debt reserves.

(Page 429) The amounts credited to the depreciation and bad debt reserves are called amounts appropriated out of current earnings.

And the reserves are regarded as still a part of surplus, and not, as accountants usually regard them, a reduction of the value of the assets. This attitude toward the reserves is indicated by the following:

(Page 429) The loss on the sale of machinery sold during the year, which has been charged to the depreciation reserve, is referred to as a "loss of surplus."

(Page 429) The sum of the net profit of $8,250 and the increases in the reserves is referred to as "the net increase of surplus."

This attitude toward depreciation and bad debt reserves as still constituting a part of the surplus seems to be diametrically opposed to the theory usually accepted that such reserves represent an estimated decrease in the value of assets. Are we being asked to go back twenty, thirty or forty years to the time when depreciation was not recognized as an inevitable expense—to a time when "net profits" were computed without regard to depreciation; and when the amount of the depreciation to be "appropriated" was determined after ascertaining how much depreciation the profits of the year could bear?

Finally, the editor desires to reiterate his statement that the columns of this department are open to any contributions which will tend to the improvement of the form of the statement of application of funds; but he cannot rest gracefully in the position in which Mr. Esquerré's letter seems to place him, of being responsible for the form of the statement now in somewhat general use. The honor of evolving that statement belongs to an accountant of some previous generation. If blame attaches to any one for its defects, that blame must attach to all of us who have used the statement, recognized its limitations and yet not bestirred ourselves to improve it. The editor accepts his due proportion thereof and he recognizes that Mr. Esquerré has now done what he can to absolve himself from his portion of the general censure.

SPECIAL BULLETINS
OF THE AMERICAN INSTITUTE
OF ACCOUNTANTS

SPECIAL BULLETINS

When the library of the American Institute of Accountants opened in April 1918 it included a bureau of information to answer inquiries from members. The Special Committee on Administration of Endowment reported to the annual meeting in 1920 that it had authorized the librarian to issue special bulletins concerning questions and answers that passed through the bureau of information. The following thirty-three bulletins were published under this authorization:

American Institute of Accountants

Library and Bureau of Information

January, 1920

SPECIAL BULLETIN No. 1

The special committee on administration of endowment believes it would be well to publish from time to time bulletins containing questions received and answered by the Institute through the Library and Bureau of Information.

Three purposes are chiefly in view in making this decision.

First, the bulletin will give members and associates an idea of the value and importance of the services which are being rendered through these agencies.

Second, it will serve to encourage members and associates to ask questions and otherwise avail themselves of the facilities provided by the endowment fund.

Third, it will give members and associates an opportunity to criticise the answers sent in response to inquiries.

This last purpose appears to the committee to be most important. In sending out answers the Bureau of Information does not claim to be presenting the last word on any subject. The opinions expressed are those of one, two or three accountants of good standing who have set forth their views in response to request from the Bureau of Information. The opinions are transmitted under the distinct understanding that they are purely advisory and in no sense intended to be dictatorial.

The committee hopes that all who receive these bulletins will take the time and trouble to read the questions and answers, and if there is any point in the latter which appears unsound or not in accordance with the best practice, it is urgently requested that constructive criticism be frankly made.

The bulletins will appear at irregular intervals, but it is suggested that members retain them all, as it is believed that they will constitute a valuable addition to accounting literature. The value is accentuated by the fact that the questions answered are chiefly not answerable through any known text-book or other written authority.

The questions and answers presented herewith are chosen as representative of the services which the Bureau of Information has been called upon to perform.

L. S. MILTIMORE,
Librarian

1

TOBACCO MANUFACTURE

Q. A tobacco manufacturer buys leaf by the hogshead at various prices per pound, grades it into several grades and uses the different grades for different brands of tobacco.

For cost purposes, how should graded leaf be priced? Should grade #4 be treated as of the same price as grade #1 provided it came from the same hogshead? If this is done, it will happen that a month when the factory works chiefly on low grade tobacco may show a loss while a month when it works chiefly on high grade goods will show an abnormal profit. If the grades out of the same hogshead are treated as of different prices, how should those prices be determined?

A. We should assign differing prices to the several grades, based on the scale of selling prices of the various brands into which the several grades enter, although this might not be necessary for a small business:

Illustration:

$$\text{Hogshead cost} \ldots\ldots\ldots\ldots\ldots\ldots\ldots\ldots a$$

$$\text{Grade 1—lbs. @ } \frac{e}{h} \times a = b$$

$$\text{Grade 2—lbs. @ } \frac{f}{h} \times a = c$$

$$\text{Grade 3—lbs. @ } \frac{g}{h} \times a = d$$

etc., etc., etc.

$$\text{Total} \ldots\ldots\ldots a \qquad\qquad a$$

Average selling price of brands:

$$\text{Into which grade 1 enters} \ldots\ldots\ldots\ldots e$$
$$\text{"} \quad \text{"} \quad \text{"} \quad 2 \quad \text{"} \quad \ldots\ldots\ldots\ldots f$$
$$\text{"} \quad \text{"} \quad \text{"} \quad 3 \quad \text{"} \quad \ldots\ldots\ldots g$$

$$\text{Total} \ldots\ldots\ldots\ldots\ldots\ldots\ldots\ldots h$$

Prices of grades:

$$\frac{e}{h} \times a = \text{price of grade 1}$$

$$\frac{f}{h} \times a = \text{price of grade 2}$$

$$\frac{g}{h} \times a = \text{price of grade 3}$$

etc., etc., etc.

TAXES

Q. Depreciation charges, deducted from income, reduce the amount of income tax. At the same time, they reduce the "invested capital," and thereby increase the excess profits tax for the subsequent years.

At what point, in any given set of conditions, is a reduction of income tax, by means of depreciation, offset by an increase in the excess profits tax, over a series of years, based on 1917 rates of taxes?

A. We are furnishing a table which, under certain stable conditions, will answer the question.

The conditions assumed are:

1. That any dollar deducted from the income tax return will con-

2

tinue to be deducted in future, (which assumption involves the continuity of life of the object, and a flat rate of depreciation.)

2. That the invested capital will not vary from year to year except in so far as it is reduced through depreciation.

3. That the net taxable income will not vary from year to year.

4. That the rates of taxation will continue to be those in effect in 1917.

5. That the percentage of invested capital allowed as a deduction will be 8.

Under the above conditions, the problem admits of an arithmetical solution.

In column 1, there are set forth the years which would elapse before the yearly increase in income and excess profits taxes, due to the decreasing capital, resulting from depreciation charges, would equal the decrease in income and excess profits taxes, due to deductions for depreciation.

In column 2, there are set forth the years which would elapse before the total increases in income and excess profits taxes, as above, would equal the total decreases, as above.

WHEN THE INCOME SUBJECT TO EXCESS PROFITS TAX IS	COLUMN 1	COLUMN 2
Less than 15% of invested capital	17.4	33 8
From 15 to 20% of invested capital	14.3	27.6
From 20 to 25%	10.5	20.
From 25 to 33%	8.5	16.
Over 33% of invested capital	6.6	12.2

It must be emphasized that the conditions assumed are purely theoretical and would in all probability never occur in actual practice. A formula applicable to all conditions and controlling all variables would be exceedingly difficult, if not impossible, of preparation.

AUTOMOBILE TIRE FACTORY

Q. What units of cost in an automobile tire factory are customarily obtained?

What segregation is desirable for prime costs?

What special features should be provided for?

A. With the exception of the finished products and of the curing room operations, the unit of cost is usually per pound. The unit for the finished products is per casing and per tube respectively, while for the curing room operations, which are strictly a process, the cost unit is per heat hour.

The main ingredients entering in the manufacture of automobile inner tubes are rubber and chemicals. The casing consists mainly of rubber, chemicals, fabric and beads. Such miscellaneous materials as cement, valves, etc., need not be shown separately in preparing a statement of prime cost, but may be grouped under the heading of miscellaneous materials. Of course, all productive labor should be shown preferably by processes.

The features that should receive special attention are recutting of moulds, treatment of cloth wrappers, shrinkage in weight of rubber after

3

drying, the accumulation of compounds and the stabilizing of raw rubber costs.

A. The following suggestions are made in answer to an inquiry re cost-finding for an automobile tire factory. However, we would like to caution the inquirer that the question is so vague, and that there is such a wide range in the methods used in large and small tire factories, that it is rather hard to give other than the most general answers.

We are assuming that the factory under consideration is a small one and will treat the problem accordingly.

Units of cost:

1. WASHED RUBBER. As a general rule the crude rubber is received at the plant in two conditions: one ready for immediate compounding and milling; the other requiring washing in order to take out the dirt and foreign substances before the rubber can be milled.

It will generally be desirable to keep a separate classification for washed rubber, which of course would represent the cost of the crude rubber plus the expense of washing. There will be a loss incurred in this process which will further increase the unit cost. Rubber, after being washed and given a cost per pound determined by the resulting weight, would then be similar for manufacturing purposes to rubber received which does not require washing.

2. MILLED PRODUCT. This is the result of mixing the crude with the various chemicals in order to produce the desired compounds. This classification should be divided according to the various compounds resulting from the milling process. There will also be some loss in weight during this process, which must be considered as further increasing the unit cost.

3. CALENDERING. In some cases calendered stock would be pure rubber which has been milled only to the extent of preparing it for the calenders. In most cases, however, it would consist of compounds which were being rolled down to the required weight and thickness for tubes or treads. The calendering will also produce what is commonly known as friction fabric, being the result of passing the fabric through the calenders and covering it with the compounded rubber. A separate classification should be kept for each different product resulting from this process. In some cases this calendered product is cut to size at the same time it is rolled to the required thickness. When this is done, it might be advisable to keep the records according to the size of casings or tubes which were to consume this cut product.

4. CASINGS. Casings would naturally be kept according to the various sizes and styles of casings.

5. TUBES. Tubes would naturally be kept according to the sizes and kinds of tubes

Segregation of prime costs:

Prime costs will naturally follow the same groupings as outlined above for the units of cost in the case of the washing, milling and calender departments. Prime costs are generally kept according to the kinds of stock handled, because the stock resulting from these operations may be used for various kinds of tubes or tires to be determined after the stock has

4

left the department. These groupings would result in unit costs including the material, labor and factory overhead. When this material is sent to the tube and casing department, the simplest way would be to carry it into these departments at these unit costs in the same manner as though it were raw material.

The costs of tubes and casings can very easily be separated according to the kinds and sizes produced.

Special features:

Providing for special features is the hardest question of all to answer because it depends so largely upon both local conditions and the experience of the accountant installing the cost system—and probably more upon the experience of the accountant than anything else.

One generally recognized difficulty in cost accounting for rubber factories is that caused by the fluctuations in the price of raw material. It will probably be understood that purchases, especially of crude rubber, are made from day to day according to the market quotations in much the same manner that wheat is purchased for a flour mill. Skillful buying on the part of a rubber manufacturer often has as much to do with success as does economical manufacturing.

It is obviously necessary to charge the cost at some more or less fixed price for raw material if any uniformity and possibility of comparison is to result. This is generally done by establishing a price which represents what the company expects to pay for these materials during a certain period and charging costs at this established price. A ledger account can be carried which might be termed "Fluctuation in raw material," which would take care of the difference between the established prices and actual market prices. Of course this account would be a profit and loss element which should be taken care of not only when the books are closed but when making monthly statements.

Another thing that will require special attention is the loss in the weight of raw materials, and more especially in the weight of the rubber during the washing process. To get accurate results, it is generally necessary to weigh the rubber both before and after washing, so that a correct cost may be obtained which can be carried forward into the succeeding processes.

The compounding room should not present any special difficulties because all compounds are the result of very exact formulas which in a well-regulated factory would furnish a satisfactory basis for crediting the raw material accounts and charging costs.

There will naturally be an amount of scrap produced in cutting the calendered material for the use of the casing and tube departments, but this should present no difficulty if credited to the costs at the scrap value of this material.

PROFITS

Q. Company "A" makes an operating profit of $250,125.50.

Company "B" is entitled to 50% of that operating profit provided that in making the division Company "B's" proportion shall be reduced by bearing an equal proportion with Company "A" of the war profits tax

5

(80%) plus income tax, which shall be levied on the operating profit less the war profits tax.

How much does each company get? What is the algebraic formula?

A. *Premises.*

(1) Company B is entitled to one-half of Company A's operating income less income and war profits taxes.

(2) B's share of such profit when paid or accrued becomes a deductible expense to A.

(3) A is subject to war profits tax of 80%.

(4) The income of Company A during the pre-war period (1911-1912-1913) is less than 10% of its invested capital for such period or Company A was not in existence during the whole of any one of the years 1911-1912-1913.

Formula.

a= Net income before taxes.

b= War profits tax computed before considering B's share of profits as an expense.

c= Income tax computed before considering B's share of profits as an expense.

d= B's percentage of profits.

x= Net income on which B's percentage is to be computed.

a-b-c=x—.824 dx.

DEPRECIATION

Q. Please be kind enough to inform us what are the standard rates of depreciation on machine shop equipment of the various classifications such as

> Boilers
> Engines
> Motors
> Lathes
> Automatic screw machines and other automatic machines of a
> > similar nature
> Shafting and power transmission
> Special tools, including patterns, etc.

The equipment in question is used by a machinery manufacturing concern which manufactures machines of an average weight of about fifty pounds. The motors consist largely of one-half to one horse-power equipment and many of the lathes and automatics are Browne & Sharpe equipment.

A. Subject to variations which may be called for by particular conditions of which we have no knowledge, we suggest depreciation rates as follows:

1. Boilers. If water tube boilers, use a rate of 5%, and if fire tube boilers a rate of 7½% per annum.

2. Engines. If low speed engines, use a rate of 5%, and if high speed engines 7½%.

3. Motors. Inasmuch as the motors are stated to be largely from one-half to one horse-power, a rate of 10% is recom-

6

mended. For large motors, a rate of 5% is probably sufficient and for motors of medium horse-power a rate of 7½%, but for small motors such as those indicated a rate of 10% is advisable.

{
4. Lathes.
5. Automatic screw machines and other automatic machines of similar nature.
}

We note that these are Browne & Sharpe machines and therefore of good construction. Nevertheless a rate of 5% is recommended for the lathes and 7½% for the automatic screw machines and other automatics.

6. Shafting and power transmission. 7½%.

7. Special tools, including patterns. Write off any expenditure on these as it is incurred unless their future use is practically assured. In the latter case, write off at least in the proportion which the present use bears to the assured future use.

All the above rates are intended to be computed on the original cost and not on the decreasing values from year to year. They also call for the charging of all repairs and renewals to expense and not to depreciation reserves.

BONUS AND INCOME TAX

Q. Should income and excess profits tax be deducted before computing a bonus when the manager of a company is to have 25 per cent of the profits and the company 75 per cent?

A. We have received the following answer in regard to your letter.

"In my opinion income and excess profits taxes should not be deducted in such a case unless there is a provision in the agreement with the manager which specifically directs that such taxes shall be deducted. In levying taxes of this character, especially the excess profits tax, it is apparently the theory of the government that it is taking a part of the profits, or in other words, that it is asking the taxpayer to share his profits with the government. These taxes, therefore, are not ordinary expenses, such as would be deducted as a matter of course determining the profits in which the manager of the company would share."

RESERVE FOR RELINING FURNACES

Q. Will you kindly advise us as to the rate per ton on production of pig iron used by furnaces in setting up a reserve for relining furnaces.

A. We find that about 30 cents per ton is the average rate used by steel companies as a provision for relining blast furnaces. The rates before the war were very much less than this and probably averaged 15 cents per ton. The increase in the past few years has arisen on account of the high cost of refractories, labor, etc.

7

American Institute of Accountants

Library and Bureau of Information

SPECIAL BULLETIN No. 2

March 1920

[*The Committee on Administration of Endowment authorizes the publication of special Bulletins, of which this is one, on the distinct understanding that members are not to consider answers given to questions as being official pronouncements of the Institute, but merely the individual opinions of accountants to whom the questions were referred.*

It is earnestly requested that members criticise freely and constructively the answers given in this or any other Bulletin of this series.]

Attention is drawn to a plan of partnership agreement which has been printed as a separate pamphlet and is available for distribution to members who are interested.

The agreement covers a plan of goodwill and non-goodwill partnership, and should be of interest to many accounting firms. Single copies may be obtained from the office of the Institute without charge.

The following is reprinted from the Bulletin of Haskins & Sells, January 15, 1919.

L. S. MILTIMORE, *Librarian.*

SUGGESTIONS FOR PROFESSIONAL CONDUCT

These pages are intended as a source of information and general guide to the members of the staff in the matter of professional conduct. Confidential matters relating to professional conduct and technique are embodied in a volume entitled "Confidential Instructions," which is on file in the library. All instructions should be consulted frequently until the accountant is entirely familiar with them.

It is considered desirable that all members of the staff learn as quickly as possible the ways of the firm, grow into harmony with its ideals and traditions, and absorb its technique. It is important that each one have the proper point of view, assume the proper attitude toward his work, and appreciate the responsible function which is delegated to him as a representative of the firm. The file of the monthly Bulletin, which is in the library and which gives something of the history and development of the firm, will be found helpful in this respect. It is the desire of the firm that members of the staff confine their attention exclusively to the work of the firm and concentrate thereon with the purpose of coöperating in the rendering of effective service to clients.

The department for professional training has the function of acquainting new members of the staff with their professional relations, duties, and responsibilities; in serving them subsequently in the matter of advice and information, professional, technical, and personal; in looking after their comfort; and in planning and directing their educational development.

The library is provided as a comfortable and attractive place in which the members of the staff work and spend their time when not engaged in accounting work. A suggestion box located therein offers an opportunity for communications relating to the accountant, his work, the work of the firm, conditions, relations, methods, or what-not.

The books in the library are for the use and information of the staff and as well all other members of the organization. They may be

1

withdrawn from the shelves for use in the library without consulting anyone. After having served the purpose of the reader they should be left on the library table in order that the librarian may return them to their proper places on the shelves. Books desired for home reading or outside use may be obtained after the mere formality of registering them with the librarian. Suggestions as to reading will, if desired, be furnished by the director of professional training.

EQUIPMENT

All equipment, such as working bags, folders, papers, pencils, erasers, etc., are provided for the use of accountants. The only exception to this rule is a fountain pen, which the accountant requires for certain of his work and with which he should provide himself.

HOURS

When engaged on work in the offices of the firm the hours to be observed are those prescribed for the respective offices.

When engaged on work for clients outside of the office of the firm, accountants should within reason observe the hours of the offices in which they are working. Any substantial extension of the usual time either at the beginning or end of the day, so that the total becomes more than eight hours, may be ignored, or if observed should be reported as overtime.

In starting an engagement time should be charged from the hour of departure from the office.

Fractions of days should be reported as eights or multiples thereof, reducing the fractions in the summary where possible to quarters or halves.

When working in the evening the supper hour should, for the information of the bookkeeping department, be shown. Reimbursement for supper expense, in an amount fixed by the respective offices, may, where the work extends beyond seven o'clock in the evening, be obtained from the cashier on a petty cash slip.

Where the office of a client closes on Saturday at noon, or at one o'clock, so as to prevent the accountant from working in the afternoon, a full day should be charged. The circumstances in such cases should be noted on the time report.

Days spent in traveling, including Sundays and holidays, should be charged. In such instances the time should be limited to the usual office hours.

It is the desire of the firm that work unreasonably beyond the regular hours of clients and as a regular matter be avoided whenever possible. This does not mean that an accountant should display over-anxiety to get away from his work. It does mean that time in addition to office hours as a regular thing until it becomes a habit is undesirable.

Where the client presses to have work finished within a certain time it is the policy to meet the desires of the client. In such instances, or where the circumstances are such as to make necessary the extension of the work beyond the regular hours, it is hoped that accountants will accept the situation as being an incidence of the profession. Overtime should invariably be reported.

COMPENSATION

Salaries are paid semi-monthly. Where so requested checks will be sent to the bank for deposit.

It is the policy of the firm not to pay for overtime or extra work. This is partly on the theory that such practice tends to discourage unnecessary work beyond the usual hours and partly that the range of salaries paid to members of the staff who continue in the service of the firm is sufficiently high to compensate them for such encroachment on their time. Where the conditions surrounding an engagement are unusual

2

and result in extraordinary demands on the accountant, allowances are sometimes voluntarily made by the firm.

PERSONAL REPORTS

This section refers to reports rendered by members of the staff to the office and not reports by the firm to clients. The former embrace time and expense reports (form 110a), and the miscellaneous informal reports which from time to time are necessary.

Time and expense reports are required of members of the staff on the 10th, 20th, and last day of each month. No duty of the accountant is more imperative than the prompt rendering of this report. When it is appreciated that the report is the basis of the charge to clients the importance of promptness in this respect will be apparent. Accountants when out of town should appreciate especially the fact that all reports are necessarily some time in transit and be governed accordingly.

Accountants who are assigned to out of town engagements should advise the office of the hotel at which they plan to stop. If subsequently a change is made the office should be advised promptly.

Accountants should keep the offices to which they are attached advised of their whereabouts at all times, using the wire if so far distant that mail cannot reach the office within twenty-four hours.

When accountants are unable, on account of illness or other reason, to report at the office, or at the client's office, they should have the office immediately notified by telephone or telegraph in order that the client may be notified. When accountants are on engagements in places other than cities in which offices of the firm are located the clients' office should be notified direct.

Accountants whether in town or out should notify promptly the office to which attached of any change of address or telephone number.

EXPENSES.

It is the desire of the firm that members of the staff shall travel and live while on out of town engagements in a manner befitting their professional standing. At the same time, since expenses are incurred for account of clients, it is necessary that the expenses be kept at the minimum consistent with such status. The accountant should live comfortably and well without being extravagant.

In order to facilitate the bookkeeping it is preferable that the accountant in charge pay all traveling and subsistence expenses of his assistants. This rule need not be adhered to where circumstances, such as the comfort or convenience of members of the party, make it desirable that each individual pay his own expenses.

Accountants previous to departing on out of town engagements are provided with funds for expenses. These funds should be accounted for, supporting the disbursements, with vouchers wherever practicable, at the time of rendering time and expense reports.

The following indicates the character of the expenses which may be incurred:

Traveling:

Railroad fare (lowest first class through rate).
Sleeping and chair cars (one berth or seat).
Transfers (personal and baggage).
Gratuities (porters in Pullman cars at about the usual rate of 25 cents per trip of twelve hours).

Subsistence:

Rooms and meals.
Gratuities, laundry, clothes pressing, car-fares, and such things as are usual to include in expense—depending on locality and conditions—from $1.00 to $1.50 per day.

3

Miscellaneous:
    Telegrams and telephone.
    Stationery.
    Other (to be itemized).

The allowance for subsistence, including gratuities, laundry, and pressing, will be limited to reasonable amounts depending on locality and circumstances. Such amounts might perhaps be $4.00 per day in towns and smaller cities, and run as high as $7.00 in some metropolitan cities.

Consideration should be given to the probable length of time that will be required to complete an engagement wth a view to making hotel arrangements by the week instead of by the day in order that a better rate may be obtained if possible.

When accountants are engaged away from home, in cities where the firm has offices, the daily allowances for subsistence, gratuities, and laundry, etc., will be left to the discretion of the partner or manager under whom the accountant is engaged.

In cases where, owing to pressure of work, the accountant has not had time to find a suitable place at which to locate, actual expenses, in reasonable amounts, will be allowed for a period sufficient for this purpose.

When an accountant who is on a prolonged engagement is accompanied by a member of his family, an allowance, depending on location and circumstances, will be granted if desired in lieu of subsistence expenses.

Accountants who are about to undertake engagements involving expenses which are to be sustained by any division of the government, should ascertain the specifications and requirements thereof, with regard to expense allowances and vouchers. Travel regulations of the United States Treasury Department containing information of this character may be consulted upon application to the librarian.

TIME AND EXPENSE REPORT BOOK

This book is intended to afford a convenient place in which the details of time and expenses may be recorded, and to facilitate the rendering of time and expense reports.

The sheets are of two kinds, those which are ruled for expenses and a daily cash account, and those in blank which are for the time spent on engagements. The former need be carried only by accountants who are on out of town engagements.

In this book, on the blank pages, should be noted daily, the date, the hours engaged, the engagement and the particulars relating to the work of the engagement. For example, "October 15, 1917, 9-12: 1-5, Warburton Desk Company, Counting cash and reconciling bank account."

The information relating to an engagement should be entered in the time book very explicitly but concisely, and so transferred to the time report. It should be remembered that the latter record is the only one upon which the firm may depend when discussions with clients relating to the work become necessary. Reference to the accountant who did the work is not always possible, as he may be out of town or otherwise out of reach. The time report should be so full and clear as to make this unnecessary.

Particular attention should be given to showing clearly, where there are subsidiary or otherwise related companies or branches, the work on each company or branch.

In the case of monthly audits the month to which the work applies should be supplied.

If the work is performed at a place other than that indicated by the memorandum of engagement the fact should be shown, as should work performed for clients in the offices of the firm.

While the loose-leaf binder permits replacing used sheets with new ones, the former-should be preserved by the accountant. They are sometimes useful long afterward in refreshing one's memory as to precisely

4

what was being done at a given time. They w⋅ll if desired be filed in the office of the firm.

PERSONAL CONDUCT

Each accountant is a representative of the firm. It is therefore desirable that his conduct be a credit to the firm. Many little things, such as personal appearance, personal habits, behavior, attitude toward client and employes, go to form the impression which the accountant conveys. It is important, therefore, that care be exercised at all times to avoid anything which will result in placing our representative in disfavor.

Smoking in offices, for example, frequently proves objectionable. Accountants are therefore requested to refrain from smoking while engaged in the offices of clients where the clerical force is not permitted to smoke or without first ascertaining whether or not there is any objection to such indulgence.

Since all our engagements are of a confidential nature the name, or address, or telephone number of a client should not be disclosed. The use of the client's telephone for personal matters is not desirable and should only be indulged in where unavoidable. In cases of necessity communication may be had with accountants through the respective offices of the firm.

Money or gratuities should not be accepted from clients, and any such offers should be reported to the firm. Personal checks should not be cashed at (client's) offices and only in cases of emergency will exception to this rule be permissible. The necessity of having a rule to the effect that money must not be borrowed from clients or employes of clients will undoubtedly be apparent. While the firm does not desire to encourage borrowing on any scale it much prefers that if an accountant finds it necessary to borrow small sums the application be made to the firm.

It is undesirable that accountants become too intimate with clients and their employes. The attitude of the former should be one of dignified friendliness. Any association which requires more than this should be avoided. This does not mean that accountants may not with propriety accept reasonable entertainment. It does mean that the relations should not be carried so far as to make possible subsequent embarrassment.

Clients and their employes should not be antagonized. They should be accorded courteous, dignified treatment under all circumstances. This may at times be difficult, but is the proper position to take. The test of an accountant's calibre frequently is his ability to maintain his equanimity and dignity under trying circumstances.

PROFESSIONAL ETHICS

Accountants should not discuss clients, their work, or any feature thereof; with anyone, under any circumstances, except members of this organization. When it is realized that all the work of the public accountant is necessarily the private business of someone else everything which comes to his attention should be treated as strictly private and confidential.

The bookkeeping or accounting system of the client should not be criticised or discussed with the client's employes.

The business, work, or characteristics of other public accountants should not be commented upon, criticised, or discussed.

It is not considered good form to discuss with the client or his employes such matters as the length of time the accountant has been with the firm or the amount of his compensation.

It is considered unethical for a member of the staff to solicit or to arrange for employment with a client or other accounting organization without first discussing the matter with the firm.

PROFESSIONAL REPORTS

Accountants should obtain from the files copies of reports which have been rendered and familiarize themselves with the form and content

5

thereof. The working papers accompanying such reports should also be studied. The director of professional training will, if desired, make suggestions with respect to the selection of such reports.

The accountant should place his signature on the first page of the comments and each page of the exhibits and schedules of all reports and statements which he prepares. If some other accountant checks the statements, he also should sign them, indicating the fact that he has checked them.

Abbreviations should not be used and special care should be taken to see that names are legibly written.

Accountants should bear in mind the fact that their working papers frequently have to be referred to by the office, consequently such papers should be complete and clear. The name of the accountant doing the work should appear on the upper right hand corner of all working papers. As far as practicable, standard size journal and analysis paper should be used. Each statement should be properly headed with titles and dates, and, if folded, should be properly endorsed. Superseded statements should be so marked on the outside as well as across the face. The trial balance should have notes opposite each item as to its character, if not analyzed, and how verification was made. If analyses are made, they should be referred by numbers to the trial balance. All differences between book figures and figures which we are to present should be clearly set forth in journal entry supporting the working sheet. Working papers for consolidated balance sheets and income statements should show clearly in a separate column all eliminations as among component companies, and such eliminations should be supported by a detailed statement giving a description of each item eliminated.

All work connected with an engagement should be completed, as far as possible, at the office of the client.

BREWERIES

I write to ask if you can secure for me figures applicable to the rate of depreciation chargeable on brewery machinery and which have been, or are likely to be, approved by the income tax inspector. They are needed in a case concerning which the conditions are as follows:

A brewery began operations in 1913 and prepared its annual statements so far as we know, without any expert assistance until the end of 1917, when they engaged us to prepare their balance sheet and income tax return, work which has remained in our hands since that date.

When we closed the books for 1917 we found that depreciation had not been written off to an extent which we thought proper and we, therefore, set up a depreciation reserve, accretions to which have since been made from year to year.

The returns of the brewery have recently been inspected by the Treasury Department and the inspector insists, not without reason, that the depreciation should have been written off from the beginning and has prepared a fresh set of statements on this basis. The result is that while the brewery could obtain additional credits and return of taxes for the years 1914-15 and 1916, the effect is to reduce the value of their brewery plant and therefore of their invested capital, so that in 1917-18 and 1919 their taxes will be increased by a good many thousands of dollars.

The following schedule sets forth the classification which our clients have adopted and shows the rate of depreciation suggested by the income tax inspector.

6

	Inspectors	(- - - -)
Building brick and concrete......	2½	2½
Boiler and furnace...............	10	10
Machinery	10	10
Piping	10	10
Tools	25	25
Brewhouse equipment............	10	10
Cellar equipment...............	10	10
General equipment..............	10	10
Saloon equipment...............	20	00
Office furniture and fixtures......	10	25
Autos and trucks.................	30	10
Bottling plant...................	15	33⅓
Floating cooperage..............	15	33⅓
Warehouse	50	—

In addition to this depreciation, we charged off rather heavily for obsolescence for 1918 in accordance with the special instructions issued in connection with breweries.

A. We have received the following answer to your question.

Replying to the query regarding depreciation allowed by the Treasury Department in connection with accounts of breweries, I beg to advise that in one instance the rates of depreciation as allowed to your correspondent practically agreed with those which we in our regular practice have set up as depreciation reserve, but which were in three cases lower than those allowed by the inspector in the case stated, namely, tools set up by us at 20 per cent. allowed 25 per cent. in the question submitted, autos and trucks 25 per cent. allowed 30 per cent. The floating cooperage stood very low on the books of this company, so that we had deemed 5 per cent. ample depreciation on the values appearing by the books. It has been our practice, however, to write off 15 per cent. on quarters and 40 per cent. on half barrels, but so far we have not had any examination made where this depreciation has been provided.

In the main we think the rates of depreciation allowed by the department are well within or above depreciation rates which would be used in the ordinary way of business.

MINING COMPANY

Q. An accountant is called upon to audit the books of a tungsten mining corporation. He finds that the trial balance as of December 31st, 1917, is as follows:

Debits

Mining lands................................	$1,000,000.00
Buildings	10,500.00
Machinery and equipment......................	18,000.00
Tunnel construction...........................	20,000.00
Accounts receivable...........................	2,000.00
Cash in bank.................................	500.00
Profit and Loss.......................	10,000.00
	$1,060,000.00

Credits

Capital stock....·..............................	$1,000 000.00
Notes payable to bank.........	10,000.00
Accounts payable.................·...........	10,000.00
Reserve for working capital from treasury stock sales	40,000.00
	$1,060,000.00

7

-63-

The company was organized six years ago. The minutes show that the land was taken over for the entire issue of 1,000,000 shares of capital stock, at par value of $1.00 each, and that 500,000 shares were donated back to the treasury to be sold for the purpose of raising working capital. Of this treasury stock 160,000 shares have been sold at an average price of 25 cents per share, and 360,000 shares remain in the treasury unsold.

The first four years of operation showed a small profit each year, the last two years were at a loss and operations are now at a standstill. No positive value can be placed upon the land, but it consists of 800 acres in the best part of the tungsten district. Buildings and machinery are conservatively valued. The tunnel has been driven about three-fourths of the way to the objective. No paying ore has been crossed, but it is expected to connect with one of the paying mines and cheapen the cost of production.

The stock has no definite market value. Treasury stock has been sold through circulars, at an arbitrary price, in the usual way of wild-cat promotion. The company is managed by men who stand well as to business and character, and who have staked their all on the success of the company. The conditions as a whole are typical of a considerable number of mining companies in the west, standing midway between the purely wildcat schemes and the paying mines.

What would be an approved form for setting up a balance sheet? Should treasury stock for such indefinite value be shown as a part of the balance sheet, and if so, how? What sort of a certificate of audit is it possible for an auditor to write for such a business?

A. We are of the opinion that, all things considered, it would be proper to show the treasury stock on the debit side as an item, expressing the number of shares with a nominal value of say $1.00, which should be credited to Profit and Loss.

As a protection against a misunderstanding, the capital stock caption should be followed with a bracket, showing the number of shares issued and those on hand in the treasury. If it were not for the statement that the minutes show the land to have been taken over in exchange for the capital stock at par, I would prefer to have shown the land at a nominal value and the capital stock in shares, at the par per share, without extending the amount.

It might be well to set in the balance sheet an explanation of the credit of $40,000, proceeds from sale of treasury stock, thus:

Treasury stock donated........	$500,000.00
Deduct—Treasury stock unsold..................	340,000.00
Sales of treasury stock..........................	$160,000.00
Less—Discount on sales of treasury stock........	120,000.00
Surplus, from sales of treasury stock.............	$ 40,000.00

The certificate should not be given at all if it is likely to be used for promotion purposes, and even for proprietary purposes should be so qualified as to show that the stockholders or directors, or perhaps both, giving reference to the date, had, as shown by the minutes, appraised the land and authorized it to be taken up at a million dollars.

The other transactions appear to be in order and need no qualification.

8

American Institute of Accountants

Library and Bureau of Information

May, 1920

SPECIAL BULLETIN No. 3

[*The Committee on Administration of Endowment authorizes the publication of special Bulletins, of which this is one, on the distinct understanding that members are not to consider answers given to questions as being official pronouncements of the Institute, but merely the individual opinions of accountants to whom the questions were referred.*

It is earnestly requested that members criticise freely and constructively the answers given in this or any other Bulletin of this series.]

MOVING PICTURES

Q. We wish, if possible, to obtain depreciation rates on moving picture properties that would be likely to be allowed by the Treasury Department for tax purposes.

The specific items on which we desire to obtain rates are:

1. Studio building.
   Theatrical properties (furniture, special staging, etc.).
2. Scenery.
3. Wardrobe.
4. Manufacturing equipment.
   (Machines used in producing films, printing machines, chemical vats, etc.)

A. We have received the following answer to your question:

We feel that we are not in a position to give you a definite reply as to depreciation rates on moving picture properties that would be likely to be allowed by the treasury department for tax purposes, without being in possession of further facts in regard to the particular properties about which the question is raised.

As you are aware, the activities of different moving picture producers vary considerably. In some instances a company is formed to produce one or two large productions, and in other cases companies produce a certain class of pictures continuously. It is obvious that in the former case the properties might be of temporary construction, and that such items as costumes, etc., would have a useful life extending only over the life of the picture or pictures produced. On the other hand, for example, a company

I

-65-

or a particular branch of a company that devotes its entire time to the production of, let us say, comedies, would undoubtedly have a studio of permanent construction and have properties, scenery, wardrobe, etc., that might possibly be used for a considerable number of the productions.

Referring to the specific items mentioned in your letter:

Studio Building: This building may be of steel construction, raised on a substantial foundation, with glass roof and sides. If the cost of breakages in the glass due to rainstorms, accidents, etc., is charged against current operations, the depreciation allowable by treasury department would not, in our opinion, exceed 2 per cent, and would more likely be confined to 1 per cent. If, on the other hand, the studio building is of temporary wooden construction, as in fact is very often the case, a depreciation rate as high as 10 per cent or 15 per cent might be allowed, especially if the company had intentions of only producing a limited number of features.

As to theatrical properties, we can only advise you that the depreciation will depend entirely on the use to which they are put. It would seem that a physical inspection of such properties used in each production should be made after the picture is finished and depreciation figured on a basis of the wear and tear caused during the course of the production charged against such production. For example, a piano or a suite of furniture that under ordinary circumstances would be of practical use for ten years might be wholly destroyed or damaged to an extent that renders them useless for further productions. In this case, of course, the entire cost of these articles should be absorbed in the cost of production.

Scenery: In most cases the cost of scenery is chargeable entirely against the cost of production of the picture for which it is manufactured. Of course, it will happen that scenery that has been once used and placed in the storeroom will be again brought into use in the production of a later picture, but unless the programme of the studio calls for the production of more than one picture in which this scenery can be used, we are of the opinion that the entire cost of scenery painted for any one production (less, of course, its scrap value) is chargeable against that production.

Wardrobes: The larger part of these assets are subject to obsolescene rather than depreciation. The same costumes are rarely used in more than one production. Costumes for a picture depicting home life may be subject to very little depreciation during their use for that one production, but, on the other hand, unless it is definitely known that they can be used for a future production, we cannot see any good argument why they should be carried as capital item. On the other hand, a wild west costume used by a cowboy may be of very little value after a fairly large production.

Manufacturing Equipment: In our opinion, the treasury department will require any company to substantiate its theory as to the life of manufacturing equipment before passing the rate of depreciation charged by it.

It is notorious that moving picture directors are more or less careless as to equipment of all sorts. In our opinion it is not possible for a moving picture producing company to capitalize all expenditures for equipment, etc., and adopt a reguar rate of depreciation. In practically every case you

2

mention outside the studio building, inventories should be taken at frequently recurring periods and depreciation on the properties used, based on the actual wear and tear, charged against each production in which these properties have been used.

We regret that we are not in a position to give you definite information on the inquiries raised, for the reason that, as previously stated, it is impossible for us to suggest definite rates of depreciation on any particular class of properties, without giving due consideration to the circumstances surrounding each case.

CATTLE INDUSTRY

Q. For several years past this state has been recognized as offering a field for stock raising, but it is only recently that efforts have been made to conduct this business on a scientific basis, and while we have several clients who raise stock, we have none whose accounts are kept in a proper or scientific manner.

One of the largest concerns has lately added to its various interests that of cattle raising, and has invested considerable sums therein. We are now engaged in making their annual audit, and it will be of assistance to us if we have the benefit of the experience of similar concerns which have been operating elsewhere.

The questions presented to us do not raise any theoretical difficulties in the matter of accounting, but figures should, of course, be based on experiences elsewhere. We should, therefore, be glad to know what is considered the best way of treating with the general questions, particularly such

It is not practicable for our clients to take stock of their cattle every year. They propose running, therefore, for five years before taking an inventory of their live stock. They do, of course, keep a record of the number of calves branded each year and of the number of animals bought and sold, together with some record of losses from death, etc. At what figure should the value of the calves be taken in, and how should this figure be increased year by year, until the animals reach their full market value— say in three years?

Are any uniform figures obtainable as to depreciation in value of blooded bulls belonging to the herd? Are there any reliable figures obtainable as to the proper percentage to allow for unknown deaths and losses? These figures will doubtless vary so much under different circumstances that probably no definite reply can be made.

We presume the total expense of caring for cattle should be charged off each year, although a portion of this expense might be chargeable to calves for instance and carried in the nature of prepaid expense.

The specific points mentioned above are intended to be suggestions only, and not to cover the entire question.

A. Your correspondent presents one of the most difficult problems of the stockman, and the information given is of such a vague nature and the questions are so general that I am afraid no definite usable information can be given on the specific points mentioned.

1. It is, of course, important before making any definite ruling upon the subject of inventory of stock, the treatment of natural increase and losses, to know whether or not the project is a "range" proposition or a "feeder" proposition. By this is meant whether or not the cattle-man buys cattle to feed for market or whether he raises cattle to sell to feeders.

3

2. Whether or not the cattle are run as a cattle "deal" and are segregated and settled for in the books of the stockman as "deals."

3. Your correspondent does not state whether the information required is for the purpose of making a federal income return. This is important, for a stockman may adopt any method which suits his convenience, and as a matter of general practice he does this very thing, but in making his income return, he is restricted to certain rulings of the internal revenue department or treasury department as well as the law.

As far as accounting methods are concerned, the course most generally pursued by western stockmen in the past has been to treat natural increase and death losses as financial profit or loss only when sales of natural increase are made. In other words, the stockman records upon his financial books only the original cost of his herd. If any sales are made of animals originally purchased, the recorded cost of such animals is deducted from sales proceeds to find gross profit. Natural increase is not recorded upon the financial books until sold, when, there being no recorded cost of such increase, the entire proceeds of such sales represent gross profit. It will readily be seen that by this method it is unnecessary to account for death loss of any animals except those from the herd as originally purchased. All expenses of operation and upkeep were charged off in the year in which they were incurred.

In our experience the above cited method was almost predominant in the West and Northwest until federal revenue legislation showed the stockman the practical and theoretical incorrectness of his bookkeeping methods. The stockman found under this method that in years of heavy selling of natural increase he had a disproportionate taxable profit, and in years of heavy breeding but small sales his books showed him to have experienced a loss in spite of his increased wealth through natural additions to his herd.

One of our clients recently made a special trip to Washington to consult the internal revenue and treasury officers and obtain their recommendations as to accounting methods. Upon our advice he presented to them an inventory method, submitted hereinafter, and in his conversations obtained both favorable and unfavorable comment thereon. In our opinion, and from our practice in the live stock industry, it would appear essential that the live stock breeder and feeder adopt an inventory method of ascertaining profit and loss if he is not to be discriminated against in federal revenue tax levies.

The inventory method we are recommending to your client is as follows:

The stockman should take periodical inventories of his herd, preferably semi-annually. The beginning or first inventory should be based upon cost of the animals purchased, and fair market price at the date of the inventory as to natural increase, graded as to ages and weights and condition. Each succeeding inventory should be made upon the same basis. Natural increased calves should be taken into the inventory at the market price of such calves at the date of the inventory; last year's calf crop still remaining on hand should be taken into the inventory at their fair market value at that date as yearlings, and so on with all grades of animals in the herd, using the market value of the animals as the basis of extension. If the fair market value of

4

any animals has depreciated, such as breeding cows gone dry and fit only for feeders, then the new inventory should grade such animals at their then fair market value, offsetting such inventory losses against inventory gains through calves and yearlings obtaining age and weight with its consequent greater market value.

The inventory method is to be criticised chiefly from the standpoint that there may be accruing to the stockman large profits due to natural increase of one year and the aging of natural increase of other years, which are not liquidated but upon which the stockman will be taxed. A number of our larger clients have found, however, that in the case of this latter contingency a conscientious inventory will disclose offsetting losses through breeding cows and bulls depreciation.

Just how the clients of the accountant making the inventory could fit this inventory method into their business on five-year periods I haven't had the time or inclination to study out. But if they keep a careful record of calves branded each year, animals bought each year, animals sold and death losses, it would seem that a perpetual stock inventory method might be utilized for inventory purposes.

In answer to the question in respect to blooded bulls, we have found that most breeders of thoroughbred stock keep the most careful stock records or perpetual inventory records of the animals, even to the extent of putting nickel tags in the calves' ears at birth, indicating registry number so that lineage may be traced. Therefore registered thoroughbred herds are really the easiest to which to apply the suggested inventory methods. It is often the practice of thoroughbred stock breeders to depreciate the cost price of a bull by charging the initial value of each offspring with an ascertained market stand of such bull. When the entire cost value of such bull has been written off, no further depreciation is taken.

We note that your inquirer also speaks of carrying forward each year a proportion of the total operating expenses of such year as prepaid expenses or as chargeable to inventory value of natural increase of such year. We have heard this method much discussed, and offhand it would appear equitable and practical. Investigation of the theory, however, will show it to be entirely impractical, inasmuch as it would be necessary to reduce total operating expenses to a definite operating cost per head in order to know what proportion of said expenses to defer. Such reduction to unit cost per head is manifestly impossible or arbitrary at best, and will take the investigator into the devious ways of determining how much a calf eats in comparison with a full-grown bull or cow or steer.

It is my opinion that any method is dependent entirely upon the rulings of the commissioner of internal revenue or the treasury department.

———

A. 1. Usually what is known as the "tally" inventory is not taken oftener than every three years; this inventory means that every calf branded receives an additional mark known as a "tally brand," in addition to which all of the old cattle are put through a corral and receive the identical "tally" mark, so that an actual count may be made in order to verify the percentage of

5

depreciation for death loss previously taken, which, as a rule, in a large herd will approximate about 3 to 5 per cent, depending, of course, upon conditions surrounding the care of the herd during the year.

If small brood herds are kept separate and apart from the main herd, they are usually counted in detail by putting them through a corral.

2. The whole herd should be placed upon the books at the average cost value of the original herd, and each year thereafter the new-born calves should be taken at the flat price established for the main herd, in which event, the increase will be reflected in the revenue statement for the government as well as the books.

In this case you would not pay any attention to the price of high-grade male and female stock bought to replenish the herd, but allow them to take the flat price already established for inventory purposes.

3. The total expense of caring for the cattle should be charged off each year as operating expense.

Cattle and horse tally sheets, viz. :

Debits. Begin with the inventory followed by the purchases made during the year.

Credits. Begin with sales made during the year and close with the inventory.

Special. The inventories are classified as of May 1st, the date when calves begin to drop. Calves at the close of the season become yearlings (May 1st next whether your books are closed November 30th, December 31st, or later), and likewise yearlings become two-year olds, etc. After two years heifers pass to cows, and after three years geldings and broncos pass to saddle horses. Work and brood stock are handled as specials in some cases.

Conclusion—The foregoing suggestions are based upon actual experience from one of the largest ranches in America, which is as well conducted as any business in America.

The same plan is also in vogue for one of the giant ranches in South Africa and another giant ranch in Brazil, each modeled after the plan of the American ranch.

TOBACCO MANUFACTURE

The first question, Special Bulletin No. 1, page 2, on the subject of tobacco manufacture, might, I think, have been more clearly put. The general principle laid down, namely, that the total cost should be apportioned over the various grades so that the total cost of all grades is equal to the total cost of the entire lot, is a sound one, but the formula given for arriving at the price of each grade will hardly bring out the desired result.

It would be clearer, I think, to lay down the rule that the total cost of the entire hogshead or lot of goods should be apportioned over the various grades in proportion to their respective selling values. Take, for instance, a hogshead of tobacco weighing 1,000 pounds and purchased at a total cost of $280. The apportionment of the cost might be worked out as shown in the example at the top of page 8.

6

DEBITS

RANCH HORSE AND MULE TALLY FOR THE YEAR ENDED NOVEMBER 30, 192___ AND PURCHASES AND BRANDING TO ___ 192___ 1920

HORSES AND MULES ON HAND AT

Breeding Mares	Saddle Horses	3 Year Old Geldings	2 Year Old Mares	2 Year Old Horses	1 Year Old Mares	1 Year Old Horses	Stallions	Work Horses	Mules	Total Grown	Colts Branded	Amount of Purchase	FROM WHOM PURCHASED	REMARKS

CREDITS AND KNOWN AS ___ 192 ___ TO ___ HERD 192___

BRANDED SALES AND LOSSES FROM

Breeding Mares	Saddle Horses	3 Year Old Geldings	2 Year Old Mares	2 Year Old Horses	1 Year Old Mares	1 Year Old Horses	Stallions	Work Horses	Mules	Total Grown	Colts	Amount of Credits	TO WHOM SOLD	REMARKS

DEBITS

RANCH CATTLE TALLY FOR THE YEAR ENDED NOVEMBER 30, 192___ AND PURCHASES AND BRANDING TO ___ 192___ 192

CATTLE ON HAND AT

Cows	BEEF		TWO YEAR OLD			ONE YEAR OLD			Bulls	Total Grown	Calves Branded	Amount of Purchase	FROM WHOM PURCHASED	REMARKS
	Steers	Spays	Steers	Heifers	Spays	Steers	Heifers	Spays						

CREDITS AND KNOWN AS ___ 192 ___ TO ___ HERD 192___

BRANDED SALES AND LOSSES FROM

Cows	BEEF		TWO YEAR OLD			ONE YEAR OLD			Bulls	Total Grown	Calves	Amount of Credits	TO WHOM SOLD	REMARKS
	Steers	Spays	Steers	Heifers	Spays	Steers	Heifers	Spays						

7

		⌐Selling or Market⌐ Value			⌐Apportionment of⌐ Cost	
Weight	Grade	Price	Amount		Price	Amount
300 lbs.	No. 1 @	40c.	$120		32c.	$ 96
500 "	" 2 @	36c.	180		28.8c.	144
200 "	" 3 @	25c.	50		20c.	40
1,000 "			$350			$280

The total selling or market value of the tobacco after it is graded comes to $350, and as the cost, or $280, is just 80 per cent of the graded value, it follows that the cost of each grade is 80 per cent of the arbitrary price placed upon each grade.

This problem is of very frequent occurrence in many lines of business, and in some instances arbitrary values must be placed on the various grades for the purpose of calculating the respective costs. What arbitrary prices are used is of little importance so long as they are relatively fair as between grades.

BONUS AND INCOME TAX

I would like to criticise the answer to the bonus and income tax question (Special Bulletin No. 1, page 7), stating that it seems to the writer that this income tax should be deducted before determining the amount divisible between the manager and the company, as otherwise the company would have to pay the whole amount of the income tax out of their portion of the profits. If this criticism does not seem adequate I should like to hear in regard to it.

Reply:—When a manager has an agreement in accordance with which he receives a share of the profits earned by the company by which he is employed, it is recognized that the payment to the manager is in the nature of extra compensation and not a division of the profits. The manager receives extra compensation and the stockholders receive the profits.

In the first instance, since it is additional compensation, there is no reason why that compensation should be reduced by a payment which the company has to make to the government out of its profits. In dividing the profits with the stockholders, obviously the tax has to be deducted, because the government claims part of the profits and allows the owners to retain the remainder.

The manager, however, who is an employee, is not concerned with the apportionment of profits in the shape of excess profits taxes, and he would, of course, not be charged with any part of such taxes if his remuneration were in the form of a straight compensation instead of a salary plus a percentage of profits.

The average man having an arrangement of this kind looks upon the profits as the sum remaining after the deduction of all ordinary and necessary expenses. He considers the extraordinary federal taxes which have been in force not as an ordinary and necessary expense, such as was contemplated when his arrangement was made with the company, but as an extraordinary item not contemplated either by him or by the corporation at the time the agreement was made.

Of course, in some cases it has been agreed that the taxes shall be considered an item of expense, but this has been true, as far as we know, only of agreements entered into since the heavy taxes have been in force.

8

American Institute of Accountants

Library and Bureau of Information

SPECIAL BULLETIN No. 4

July, 1920

[*The Committee on Administration of Endowment authorizes the publication of special Bulletins, of which this is one, on the distinct understanding that members are not to consider answers given to questions as being official pronouncements of the Institute, but merely the individual opinions of accountants to whom the questions were referred.*

It is earnestly requested that members criticise freely and constructively the answers given in this or any other Bulletin of this series.]

MOVING PICTURES

Referring to Special Bulletin No. 3—Moving Pictures, the following comment is offered:

STUDIO BUILDING:

The memo in Bulletin No. 3 states that if "of steel construction raised on a substantial foundation, with glass roof and sides," the annual rate of depreciation allowable would not be over 2 per cent, probably not over 1 per cent. Cost of breakage is too small to consider; very little occurs.

As studios become obsolete within a short period, as the mechanical work for changing lighting (which is part of the building) is soon worn out, as the establishment of a studio does not raise the value of land and surrounding property as a factory does, as no moving picture studio has ever remained in use for fifteen years, as a studio building is almost valueless for any other purpose, as changes in studio buildings are invariably made upon the engagement of a new general director of production, and as the rate given indicates a probable useful life of fifty to one hundred years, it needs correction. A moving picture studio one hundred years old is imaginable only to one who has no knowledge of the business. At least 3 per cent should be allowed.

Wooden studios are given 10 per cent to 15 per cent. But none has ever lasted ten years.

Finally, there are now only five or six film companies in the U. S. A.

I

that have been producing negatives for ten years. Others have gone out of business, their studios destroyed or rebuilt for new owners.

The treatment of scenery cost advocated in Bulletin No. 3 is correct.

WARDROBES:

Wardrobe should ordinarily be charged against the production for which it is purchased. Occasionally a large quantity of uniforms may be got for a great spectacular picture, and there may be a considerable residual value. In such cases, charge to the production the whole cost, have a survey of what is left when the picture is finished, credit the value of the residue to the cost of the picture and charge to wardrobe account. This is the origin of the asset account "Wardrobes."

At the end of each year a survey of wardrobe on hand should be made and an adjustment of value set up for it, debiting or crediting the wardrobe account according to whether wardrobe on hand exceeds or falls short of book value. Furniture bought for specific negatives should be treated in the same way as the costumes. Such furniture is radically different from ordinary furniture purchased for regular use.

MANUFACTURING EQUIPMENT:

Directors never have anything to do with manufacturing equipment, as defined in the question. The life of the machines principally in use are, approximately, as follows:

Perforating machines............... 5 years
Printing and developing............. 8-12 years
Tanks (chemical vats).............. Not much used in modern plants. If wooden, 8-12 years. If slate, will not be physically worn out within any reasonable period

Automatic printing and developing machines, built in, need occasional renewal of parts. Main machine may last........................ 20 years

Generally a rate of 10 per cent per annum on light machinery and 6 per cent on heavy machinery has been found proper; the light machinery referred to being perforating machines, printing machines, small developing machines and the wooden frames and tanks used in small factories for developing.

Heavy machinery includes power plant, pumps, slate tanks and the larger developing machines.

The equipment with which directors have to do, and which seems to have been contemplated in the answer in Bulletin No. 3, consists principally of lighting apparatus, cameras, ladders, automobiles, properties and other articles used in the studio but not in manufacturing. Properties are not to be charged off by depreciation. The amount charged off should appear as "cost of props," classified in the same way as cost of wardrobe. The

2

remaining articles of equipment are best treated as outlined in Bulletin No. 3. By "properties" is understood—guns, swords, spears, clubs, badges, fishing rods, torches and similar articles which are not "wardrobe." The "swan" in Lohengrin is a property. If a film of Lohengrin were made, the swan would probably never be of use again, although mechanically perfect. Hence the propriety of considering its cost as part of the cost of the picture.

———

Reply:—The opinion of your correspondent is, it would seem, substantially in agreement with our views in the matter except in the case of the depreciation of the studio building and of manufacturing equipment.

STUDIO BUILDING:

Your correspondent has apparently overlooked the fact that the question asked was as to what depreciation would be allowed by the internal revenue department on moving picture properties. I quite agree that provision should be made for obsolescence where obsolescence actually exists.

I do not, however, believe that the facts that the establishment of a studio does not raise the value of the land or surrounding property, that no moving picture studio has ever remained in use for fifteen years, that a studio building is almost valueless for any other purposes, or that changes in studio buildings are invariably made upon the engagement of a new general director, will be considered by the government as good and sufficient reasons for granting an allowance for what, in my opinion, is economic obsolesence.

It is true that there are no moving picture studios which have been in existence one hundred years at the present date, but your correspondent has evidently lost sight of the fact that the moving picture industry is only in its infancy, and the same statement might correctly be made with reference to numerous other manufacturing industries of the present time.

Many manufacturing plants are to-day depreciating equipment over a normal life of ten years, although there is every probability that such equipment will be discarded long before the period of its useful life due to obsolescence resulting from modern inventions ends. Yet the government will not allow additional depreciation on such equipment based on such probabilities.

MANUFACTURING EQUIPMENT:

The depreciation suggested by your correspondent is, in my opinion, reasonable. As stated, the equipment which I contemplated in my answer in Bulletin No. 3 was such equipment as is used in the studio, to which I understood the original question more particularly applied.

MINING COMPANY

In accordance with your request for criticism on any answers given in your bulletin, I write to object to the treatment of the mining problem in Bulletin No. 2, page 7.

If the capital stock and the mining lands are correctly shown at $1,000,000, respectively, as is undoubtedly correct, the treasury stock should also be shown at its nominal value of $500,000. The value of the treasury stock per

3

share is no more and no less than the value of the original issue. The proper entry should have been to debit treasury stock $500,000, and to credit working capital with the same amount. The reason for this is that the stock was donated for the purpose of raising working capital.

If the treasury stock had sold at par, the working capital would also have represented par. As it sold at a discount, the discount is a diminution of the working capital. The result of this is that on December 31st, 1917, the balance-sheet would show capital stock "short" $1,000,000 less treasury stock $340,000, the net outstanding stock being $660,000; working capital would show a credit balance of $380,000. Reference to the figures published in the problem discloses outside liabilities of $20,000. These credit balances amount to $1,060,000, which is the total of the debit balances.

The balance of working capital account is made up of the treasury stock unsold, $340,000, and the $40,000 of cash received for the stock sold. When all the stock is sold the working capital account will represent exactly the amount of money received from the sale of treasury stock. The final disposition of this account is in the hands of the board of directors. The logical procedure would be to charge against it the items of pure expense incurred during the development work, and to credit the remainder to mining land account.

If the item of profit and loss, $10,000, is meant to be the amount spent for necessary expenses during the development of the mine, the amount should be charged to development expense, which should be carried as a deferred charge, to be eventually written off against working capital.

———

In reply to your letter of April 20, enclosing a criticism of the solution of the mining problem, as given in the Institute's Bulletin No. 2, we submit the following:

The objector bases his criticism largely upon the hypothesis that the value of the stock is definitely fixed at par by reason of the valuation of the property by the directors, stating that, therefore, the treasury stock must be valued at par. In the controversion to this assertion it may be stated that the directors, in placing a valuation on the property equivalent to the par value of the stock issued therefor, do not put themselves in the position of declaring the cash value of the stock, and it is well recognized in practice that there may be no direct relation between the valuation of property for stock-issuing purposes and the cash value of stock thus issued. The obvious purpose of the issue of such stock for property, the value of which has been fixed by the directors, is to make the stock full-paid and non-assessable, so that it may, if donated to the company, be sold at any price, or given away, without making the holders liable for any assessment.

The second fallacy in the solution proposed by the objector is, that until such time as the entire amount of donated stock is disposed of, the company would be shown to have an inflated "working capital." As a matter of fact, the term "working capital" is well understood to be synonymous with net current assets; and certainly no one would regard as a current asset 340,000 shares of treasury stock valued at $1.00 a share when the maximum price at which such treasury stock has been sold is twenty-five cents a share.

In the report of the special committee on accounting terminology of the American Association of Public Accountants, published in the 1909 year book, appears the following definition of working capital:

"That portion of capital used in the active operations of a business. It may consist of (a) capital stock subscribed and paid. (b) Capital stock sold to stockholders to raise cash. (c) Dividends or surplus undistributed. (d) Part of purchase money of business allowed to remain unpaid. (e) Loans from bank or otherwise. (f) Proceeds of accommodation notes.

4

(g) Proceeds of sale of bonds. (h) Assessment on stockholders. **Am. Enc.**"

This idea regarding the meaning of working capital prevails in virtually all discussions of the subject. Mead, in his book on "Corporation Finance," states, "Every new enterprise needs working capital, and the financial plan must provide for this. A portion of the proceeds of the securities of the new company must be put in the treasury to serve the current needs of the corporation," and again, "The working capital of the company, its cash, materials and bills receivable, varies with the volume of its business."

The objector is attempting to give financial significance to the term "working capital," when as a matter of fact any term so employed should only be considered a title for an account, which may be carried on the books as an offset to a treasury stock debit account.

To sum up, regardless of whether unsold treasury stock be carried as an asset at par or be deducted from the stock issued, the effect would be to inflate the assets; it makes no difference whether the offsetting credit account be entitled surplus or working capital. In such cases there is no good reason for, and there are many reasons against, valuing donated stock at a figure in excess of the price for which it can be sold.

MERCHANDISE IN TRANSIT

Q. A wholesale house, located west of New York, deals largely in wearing apparel manufactured in the East. Purchase terms are F. O. B. shipping point. The fiscal year closes on December 31st, and the company has steadily followed a practice more or less prevalent in the trade of not taking up in its inventories and, per contra, in its liabilities, the goods purchased for the following spring season. In past years this has not been especially important, as only a comparatively small proportion was in transit and few goods were actually received and on hand. On December 31st, 1919, however, the purchases in transit, or actually received, amounted to $121,000, whereas the trade creditors' accounts per books amounted to only $3,000. In a certified balance-sheet which we prepared we included both the asset and liability, and as a result the ratio of current assets to current liabilities was 1.77 to 1.00 instead of 3.00 to 1.00, the usual showing for this corporation.

We were then asked by the note brokers handling the paper of the company to exclude the $121,000.00 from the figures and show it as a foot-note on the balance-sheet. They stated that this was the usual manner of treating items of this nature. This we refused to do, our reasons being: (1) that part of the goods had been received and were actually in the company's premises, although still in original cases, and (2) that the goods not received were nevertheless the property of the company, subject only to the remote possibility of the rejection upon receipt and examination.

We are aware of the fact that some large accounting firms treat liabilities of this nature as foot-notes, and this undoubtedly influenced the note brokers, but we feel that our position was proper. However, we do not wish to lean backward in our anxiety to prepare statements according to the best practice, and we should like very much to receive an opinion from the Institute. We have no doubt as to the correctness of including the liability for goods received, and we are of the opinion that goods in transit purchased F. O. B. shipping point should likewise be included as the only reason for not taking up the latter (that the goods have not been examined) can likewise be advanced in connection with the former when still in original packing cases.

A. In the case of a strictly seasonal business, in which it is the practice to clean up, as far as possible, the merchandise of one season before becoming actively engaged in the operations of the following season, it would seem, from a practical standpoint, that the banker or other creditor would

5

be furnished information regarding the accounts in the most useful form, if the statement showed the condition that obtained at the end of one season before introducing factors which affect the season about to begin.

Very frequently, as appears to have been true of the company mentioned, the receipt of merchandise for the spring season does not take place until after the merchandise of the fall season has been disposed of and the books have been closed. In such a case, there would be little merchandise in transit and few goods actually received and on hand at the closing of the books, if the date selected for closing occurred midway between the two seasons.

A statement from the books as of that period would therefore be most informing to the banker or other creditor, because it would show the extent to which the company was able to clean up at the period of lowest stock and presumable least amount of liabilities.

Owing to the extraordinary conditions which have prevailed during the last few years, both as respects the manufacture and delivery of merchandise, it has frequently been necessary to contract for and receive the merchandise in accordance with the desires of the seller and not the immediate needs of the purchaser. This was apt to cause a condition such as obtained in the case mentioned, in which a company ordinarily having little merchandise in transit or on hand at the close of its season, found itself with a large volume of merchandise bought for the season to follow.

In a case of this kind it does not seem to me that, from a practical standpoint, it is reprehensible or bad accounting practice to show the merchandise bought for the spring season as a foot-note, assuming that the character of the item and the amount involved are stated clearly. It should be done as a rule in the case of seasonal businesses only where such a condition would ordinarily not obtain and would be justified on the ground that by presenting the statement in this manner it conveys the information regarding the company's accounts to the banker or other creditor in a form comparable with what they had been receiving before, and stated in a manner which, in effect, represents the true status as to the ratio of current assets to liabilities under any conditions except abnormal ones.

In prior years, even though the merchandise had not been received, it doubtless had been ordered, and while, theoretically, there may not have been a present liability there was, as respects the purchase orders, practically the same liability as in the later years except that as to the latter period the liability was expressed in terms of the actual purchase invoices. It might also be pointed out as to goods in transit, that while they may be, in effect, the property of the purchaser, there is, I believe, some legal procedure possible whereby delivery may be stopped and they may be reclaimed by the seller. They are therefore not in precisely the same class as merchandise actually on hand.

I recognize that from a purely theoretical and technical standpoint it might be claimed that if the title to the merchandise has passed to the purchaser, then the merchandise should appear as an asset, and if not paid for the equivalent amount should be included among the liabilities. I be-

6

lieve, however, that the present requirements of correct accounting practice are complied with, if in special cases a notation is made showing clearly the character of the items and the amount, if this information is stated on the balance-sheet in such a manner that it cannot possibly be overlooked or its significance fail to be appreciated by anyone who scans the statement.

I might say that generally it is our practice to add the amounts to both sides of the balance-sheet, in each case not merging the items with similar items on the balance-sheet, but stating them separately. Only where the business is virtually of a seasonal character do we consider it good practice to deal with such items in the form of a notation on the balance-sheet.

COTTON MILLS

Q. We are anxious to obtain some information regarding the fixed investment of cotton mills, also the average rates of depreciation.

We should like to have, if possible, the cost of the land separately from the cost of the buildings, machinery and equipment.

The information, both as to cost and depreciation, should be shown separately for:
Mills operating spinning plants only.
Mills operating spinning and weaving plants.
Mills operating spinning, weaving and dyeing plants.

A. It is practically impossible to return any but a very general answer to these questions, and the replies that I give are based upon my observation of the records of mills already built and operating. Taking them as a type, a spinning mill running on 25's yarn, the fixed investment of land, buildings and machinery and equipment at a 100 per cent, the machinery and equipment, etc., would be about 50 to 60 per cent of the total, the buildings about 40 or 50 per cent of the total and the land value almost a negligible percentage.

If this mill were a spinning and weaving plant the percentages would not differ very radically.

There is no direct relation, or not necessarily so, in the cost of a bleachery and dye works to the fixed investment of a spinning and weaving plant. It should be considered, and generally is, as a separate investment. Some mills operating bleacheries and dye works, bleach and dye the product of other mills as well as their own.

In considering land values of cotton mills it must be remembered that the actual area occupied by buildings is very small. Five acres perhaps would provide space enough for all the buildings necessary to house the machinery equipment, supplies and materials of a large plant. Many mills have much larger land holdings upon which one- or two-story tenements are erected for the mill operatives. This, however, is not considered as mill buildings. While perhaps a necessary investment to provide homes for the operatives, it is almost always a separate investment and generally brings in a fair return in profit, through rentals charged and invariably collected by deductions from payroll.

A large proportion of cotton mills in the southeastern states are situated in rural sections. When they were projected, as an inducement to locate in certain sections, land was given them. Or if not given them, the price

7

paid was very low, and as stated previously, the percentage to the total plant value is negligible. When this is not so, it will generally be found that the mill is located in or near some larger center of population. As an indication of low original land values, particularly in rural districts, there is hardly a cotton mill in the southeastern states which has been operating for the last five years whose land values have not sharply appreciated. Land has risen in value all over the southern states, but the greater percentage of increase in mill land is due to reasons stated. There are other reasons which have to do with the great increase in cost of some types of machinery over others manufacturing different kinds of cotton textiles, which, while taking about the same or less ground space, would tend to throw out of any fixed proportion the relative value of land to buildings and machinery and equipment.

AUTOMOBILE INSURANCE

Q. What is in your opinion

(1) the rate of percentage, based on the net premium income, of unearned premium for

(a) premiums on risks running one year or less;
(b) premiums on risks running more than one year?

An eminent British authority on insurance, Mr. Tyler, says: "Amongst insurance offices generally (other than life offices) there has for long been recognized a description of 'rate by common consent,' that the minimum necessary is 33⅓ per cent of the net premium income, i. e., the premium income after deduction of the sum paid away for re-insurance protection.

"Hence the adoption of a minimum reserve of one-third of the premium income, for the purpose of a general rule, is probably not so far removed from what it should be as at first sight might appear."

Thus Mr. Tyler believes that one-third of the premium income on annual insurance is sufficient approximately for unearned premiums.

Another British authority, Mr. Young, arrives at a reserve of 42.79 per cent, say, 43 per cent of the premium income on annual insurance.

In your opinion, would 33⅓ per cent be a fair rate? My clients claim it is too high.

A. It has been our experience that companies doing business in New York state reserve 50 per cent of the premium income after deduction of return premiums, cancellations and re-insurance, but before deduction of broker's commission.

The requirements of the state of New York call for a reserve of 50 per cent, say 43 per cent of the premium income on actual insurance.

premium income, no deduction is allowed for re-insurance in respect of those companies which are not "admitted" by the state department as doing business within the state.

8

American Institute of Accountants

Library and Bureau of Information

September, 1920

FILM EXCHANGES

Q. 1. Which is the more practical way to keep books in a film exchange, cash basis or accrual basis?

2. When do you consider the rental of film earned, when contract signed or picture played?

3. What would you consider the average percentage of income aggregating in eight months received in the first, second and third months, if such an average percentage could be established for say, one star picture, two star picture, etc.?

4. Which is the better method of depreciating picture when books are kept on accrual basis? By spreading the cost in uniform amounts over a period of one year, nine months, eight months, or by spreading the cost in uniform amounts and judging each picture on its merits?

5 In cases where pictures are written off in equal periodical terms is it advisable to apportion the income received in the same ratio; for instance, if a picture is written off in eight months on equal amounts, would it be advisable to take in the income one-eighth of the income received as earned, next two months two-eighths, etc.?

I would appreciate very much to have the opinion of fellow accountants as soon as possible and not have to wait until it is printed in the official bulletin, as it is a case of urgent call with me.

A. (1) In a film exchange the customers pay in advance with very few exceptions. This advance takes two forms, one being treated as a deposit to be absorbed at the conclusion of a contract for one or more months, and these are set up as customers' deposits. The other form of advance payment is payment at the beginning of the week for specific pictures to be used in that week, and the customers are usually debited with those pictures at the beginning of the week at the same time the cash is

I

received. Accounts receivable from exhibitors are practically worthless in most cases.

(2) We consider the rental of film earned when the service is rendered; it is stated above that payment is received at an exchange at the beginning of the week for film to be used during that week, but it is only at the end of the week that the exchange reports to its head office and the rentals are taken up as earnings.

(3) The question is not clear, but if it means that of the income received in the eight months, what percentage is received in the first two and three months, this can be stated positively only for pictures that are released in series and are of the ordinary five-reel kind. The figures are given below.

If, however, only one or two pictures are to be released as mentioned in this letter, the resulting earnings cannot be forecast.

(4) The accrual basis is clearly academic in this case; the cost should be written off at the rate that the earnings are received, that is to say, that if the earnings for the first month are 29 per cent of the total earnings that the picture may be expected to get, then 29 per cent should be written off in the first month. The table below shows that it is a matter of very little consequence whether a picture is spread over one year, eight months or eight years, inasmuch as the 95 per cent of the entire value is absorbed in the first year.

(5) The manner of writing off suggested here is so incorrect that it would be useless to attempt to find any method of distributing earnings to correct the error.

Weeks in Use	Residue	Exhaustion
4	68	32
8	49	51
12	39	61
16	33	67
20	29	71
24	25½	74½
28	20½	79½
32	16½	83½
36	13½	86½
40	11	89
44	9½	90½
48	8½	91½

MERCHANDISE IN TRANSIT

Referring to Special Bulletin No. 4, page 5, in regard to merchandise in transit, the library has received the following comment:

We concede that it is unnecessary to include in the balance sheet the purchases still in transit and the per contra liability, but we cannot agree that goods actually received should be entirely omitted from the balance sheet.

———

I feel that the point raised is quite a technical one and does not call for a special reply.

Your correspondent evidently considers the reference to the item in a

2

special comment on the balance sheet, instead of including it among the figures entering into the balance sheet totals, as an exclusion from the balance sheet. We do not so view it, however, as we feel that the important thing is to have the information brought to the attention of those receiving the balance sheet. In fact, viewed from one standpoint, it really comes out more definitely and intelligently by stating it in the manner suggested than it would if simply merged with the other balance sheet items.

The essential thing is to have the facts stated, and this the treatment of the item in the way suggested certainly accomplishes.

DEPARTMENT STORE PERCENTAGES

The following table was sent to the library:

	Mark Up	Selling Expense	Gross Profit	Turn Over
Silks and velvets..........	43.05	5.59	36.13	1.58
Linings	43.15	7.78	34.69	1.56
Ready to wear.............	54.54	4.33	27.72	5.30
Waists	36.00	4.93	31.51	6.49
Wash goods	46.76	9.81	35.89	1.50
Draperies	44.58	9.12	42.51	.85
Linen	42.50	5.90	36.90	1.29
Misses' clothes	40.21	6.33	21.51	4.15
Petticoats	35.20	4.26	28.07	3.66
Hosiery	36.55	6.13	33.85	2.03
Rugs	40.14	9.52	30.88	1.61
Bedding	40.53	8.34	38.85	1.19
Knit underwear	40.45	5.46	36.12	1.39
Gloves	37.00	7.95	36.27	1.44
Corsets	42.63	9.75	39.80	2.46
Laces	50.44	12.01	49.23	.62
Chiffons	45.78	4.98	43.33	1.91
Embroideries	60.00	17.45	40.42	.40
Neckwear	46.58	8.11	48.31	2.31
Trimmings	60.00	9.29	46.99	1.06
Veilings	48.19	7.94	46.39	2.41
Handkerchiefs	36.64	7.90	36.09	1.68
Drugs	41.98	7.63	40.15	1.44
Leather goods	42.31	7.03	37.51	1.64
Stationery	43.19	14.11	44.99	1.70
Jewelry	50.00	7.69	35.61	1.24
Parasols	39.89	12.01	36.74	1.91
Woolen dress goods	50.39	7.77	44.13	1.30
Millinery	55.85	7.89	41.24	3.20
Ribbons	49.56	11.49	43.01	.95
Paper patterns	43.56	18.31	40.74	1.11
Toys	42.59	12.55	40.07	1.08
Notions	40.66	10.70	40.95	2.46
Boys' and men's clothing.....	36.93	5.95	20.19	1.84
Art needlework	50.00	7.75	44.07	1.60
Hair ornaments	50.00	7.41	39.55	.99
Men's furnishings	39.13	6.89	33.81	1.78
Muslin underwear	39.50	5.82	29.70	2.16
Sweaters	42.22	5.56	35.97	2.43
Infants' wear	41.10	5.09	31.31	1.41
Art goods and pictures......	44.53	8.72	34.80	1.26
Hairdressing parlors	53.14	41.52	82.06	1.33
Barber shop	....	57.38	100.00	....

3

Suits	49.79	....	28.58	1.40
Coats	32.01	....	24.93	1.95
Skirts	34.98	....	25.73	1.20
Dresses	39.10	....	24.95	1.83
Furs	50.00	1.69	39.29	1.12
Millinery	51.08	32.82	45.44	7.04
Suits	45.51	....	12.05	3.65
Coats	46.03	....	22.15	2.14
Skirts	38.76	....	20.60	2.08
Dresses	46.72	....	26.95	3.40
Book average	43.19	7.26	35.98	1.84

MOTOR BUSES

Q. A client of ours is establishing a line of motor buses between this city and one about 40 miles away. They propose to charge on a mileage basis and to pick up passengers at any point, and it is their intention to handle all their own repairs.

As they have asked us to install a system which will enable them to get a good vision of their business, we thought the Bureau of Information might be able to furnish us with some general information that might be of assistance.

A. The accounts which need to be established in order to show the operations of motor buses are comparatively simple.

Assuming that the company has its own garage the principal division of the accounts would be substantially as follows:

Garage operations
Vehicle operations
Maintenance
Other expenses

Under garage operations the following subdivisions might be made:

Salaries garage office
Wages garage
Light, heat and power
Garage supplies

Under vehicle operations the following subdivisions are suggested:

Salaries operating office
Drivers' wages
Starters' wages
Gasoline
Lubricants
Tires

Under maintenance, if the work is done by the company, the accounts can either be kept so as to show repairing each particular vehicle, or they can be kept under general classifications of labor, materials and expenses, and each of these accounts can be subdivided to whatever extent is advisable.

Other expenses that will probably be incurred will be rent, insurance,

4

liceuses, injuries and damages and general expenses, such as salaries of officers and office force and all of the expenses incident to the administration of the business.

Accounts will need to be established, of course, to cover reserves for depreciation and obsolescence.

The usual general accounts showing the financial condition of the company would have to be provided, but, as heretofore noted, the reports showing statistics of various kinds are the most vital features of the accounting system. If cars of different makes are used it is very desirable to know the cost of repairing the various kinds of cars, the consumption of gasoline per mile, the time laid up for repairs and other information along such lines.

There must be a system of reports covering the starting of the cars, the collection of fares, the hours worked by the chauffeurs, care of equipment, etc. For this data see London's Tubes and Buses, by Walter Jackson, in the *Electric Railway Journal*, Oct. 11, Nov. 1, 1919, pp. 708-14, 816-23.

DEPRECIATION—ICE INDUSTRY

The following percentages to cover wear-out depreciation (not obsolescence) have been accepted by ice manufacturers. These figures are based on first cost of the property:

	%
For wooden natural ice houses and wooden storehouses............	6.4
Ice house and harvesting and hoisting machinery, including conveyors, hoists, merrimacs, basin saws, etc., and power plants for same, elevators..	9.5
* Machinery of steam-driven manufacturing plants...............	7.1
Machinery of electric-driven manufacturing plants................	7.3
Frame buildings	5
Brick buildings	2.5
Concrete buildings	2
** Horses	15.4
Harness	16.2
Wagons and other horse-drawn vehicles.........................	14.3
Automobiles	22.5
Motor trucks	22.2
Sundry delivery equipment	15

MOTOR TRUCKS

Q. It is desired to know what the best practice is in respect of burden distribution in automobile manufacture.

The particular business I am interested in is motor truck manufacture.

It is largely an assembling plant, the principal units being purchased outside. The present output is 15 or 20 trucks per month.

There is a complete machine shop connected with the plant, but no foundry. Castings are purchased outside and completed in the machine shop.

---

* In case of bad water this figure to be increased up to 7.6 per cent as a maximum.
** In case of the Southern States, where a different grade of vehicle and horse is used, these figures become 20 per cent for horses and 20 per cent for vehicles.

5

Machine shop work is done on many of the purchased (semi-finished) parts. Also the plant comprises a wood-working shop, the principal uses of which are pattern making and cab manufacture.

The preponderance of labor is in the machine shop—say 4 to 1 as compared with the assembly department. The per hour rate is at present in use throughout.

The output consists of several models varying in price, say from $2,500.00 to $4,500.00 (selling prices).

What methods would be advised in connection with the following:

1. Basis for distribution of departmental burden
2. Basis for distribution of general factory burden
3. Basis for distribution of administration expenses, etc.
4. Basis for distribution of selling expenses?

A. The library has received the following replies to your inquiry in regard to recommendations for distribution of the overhead expenses of a motor truck manufacturer:

1. BASIS FOR DISTRIBUTION OF DEPARTMENT BURDEN:

This distribution may be made upon the direct labor values or upon the cost of direct labor, preferably the former.

2. BASIS FOR DISTRIBUTION OF GENERAL FACTORY BURDEN:

The general factory burden should be distributed directly, where possible, and indirectly by prorating to the several productive departments, and adding to the product on the basis of the hours of direct labor or cost of direct labor.

3. BASIS FOR DISTRIBUTION OF ADMINISTRATION EXPENSES, ETC.:

If these expenses are of a strictly administrative character, and have no direct bearing upon the manufacturing processes, it is not customary to include them in the cost of the product, but to deduct them from the gross profits of the month or period in which the expenses are incurred.

4. BASIS FOR DISTRIBUTION OF SELLING EXPENSES:

The same remarks apply to this group of expenses as to the administration expenses. ————————

1. BASIS FOR DISTRIBUTION OF DEPARTMENT BURDEN:

A. In the automotive industry—motor car, truck, tractor and airplane engine building—the direct labor is a large and constant factor of the prime cost, and the best results appear to have been obtained by distributing the departmental burden upon the direct labor percentage method. The direct labor is considered a good index to the final cost of the job. It is used frequently by the administrative management in contract bids, estimates, etc., even where time studies rather than labor cost records are taken as a basis for predetermined cost. The large number of bench operations and hand assembly work in an automobile machine plant usually make the use of the machine rate burden distribution impracticable. Ordinarily, and especially where the wood-working shop is under the same management as the machine assembly shops, the direct labor percentage method can be used advantageously.

6

2. DISTRIBUTION OF GENERAL FACTORY BURDEN:

The general factory burden should be distributed directly to the departmental burden accounts whenever possible. The distribution to departments can be made upon a special basis for each classification or kind of general factory burden, i. e., general supervision charges according to direct labor totals in departments; rent, light and heat according to the amount and advantage of location of the floor space; depreciation and insurance according to the volume of the assets in the departments, etc., etc.

3. DISTRIBUTION OF ADMINISTRATIVE EXPENSES:

Administration expenses are most frequently distributed over the total factory cost of each job upon the theory that the plant management should be charged with the cost of operations only to the extent of the operations under their control.

4. DISTRIBUTION OF SELLING EXPENSES:

Selling expenses are quite generally distributed to the various products upon the basis of relative sales value. In the automobile industry this basis appears proper and fairly accurate, because much of the selling expense is comprised of commissions and salaries paid salesmen, and is based upon the money value of the sales.

BREWERIES

Q. We are desirous of obtaining information relative to the proper amount of depreciation to be written off on the buildings and equipment of a brewery, and are taking the liberty of writing to you to ask if you can advise us where this information may be obtained.

Perhaps if we stated the problem with which we are confronted it might give a better idea of the exact information desired. A corporation was organized in 1913 for the purpose of taking over and consolidating five small independent breweries. A new plant was constructed which commenced operations in 1914, at which time three of the small breweries were shut down, two of which were subsequently wrecked and the buildings and machinery sold. The remaining one of the three plants, after standing idle for a number of years, was rented to a rice milling company, the equipment having been removed and sold for scrap. The remaining two plants were operated for a short time but, on account of the higher manufacturing costs, were finally closed with the exception, however, of portions of the plant, which were used simply as a storehouse for the distribution of the beer manufactured at the new plant. The rates of depreciation on these abandoned plants and the amortization of certain of the properties have been disallowed by the internal revenue department in connection with an income tax investigation.

We are desirous of obtaining any information available which can support the practice adopted by this company of increasing the rates of depreciation on these abandoned properties over the normal rate previously in effect.

Briefly, the information which we desire is as follows: first, the rates of depreciation which are ordinarily used in connection with the buildings and equipment of breweries; second, the rates of depreciation which should be used in connection with the plants which have been abandoned and which in some instances were subsequently wrecked and the property sold, i. e., the approximate increase over the normal rates which should be allowed

7

for abandoned properties; third, the effect which the passage of prohibition laws would have upon the amortization of the old properties used as storehouses.

A. The library has received the following answer to your question:

I am in receipt of your letter asking for certain information relative to the proper amount of depreciation to be written off on brewery buildings and equipment. It seems to me that the following schedule should be about correct under normal conditions.

RATES OF DEPRECIATION—BREWERY BUILDINGS, MACHINERY AND EQUIPMENT

Buildings, brick construction.................................2% to 3%
Plant and machinery 10
Plant and machinery, bottling department..................... 20
Vats, casks, etc... 10
Barrels and kegs 25
Wagons 12½
Auto trucks 20
Automobiles (small cars used by salesmen, solicitors etc.)........ 33⅓
Live stock 10
Harness 10
Office furniture and fixtures 10
Storage houses, frame construction........................... 10
Brick construction 3
Bottles and boxes—the loss on bottles and boxes under normal conditions averages out about $1.00 per barrel, but local peculiarities may make it necessary to increase or decrease this figure.

Regarding the depreciation in connection with plants which have been abandoned it would seem that the salvage value should be worked out, and the difference between the original cost of the property less the depreciation to date and the salvage value ought to be written off as a loss.

There is really no question of rate of depreciation in this case, but rather the determining of the value of the equipment at the time it was abandoned.

Where the property has been sold there should be no difficulty in determining this and getting the treasury department to agree to write off the loss, because scrap or salvage value is definitely determined by selling price.

Where the property is abandoned and no sale made the treasury department might take the stand that there is no way of determining the salvage value until the sale is made. Each question of this kind would certainly have to be considered separately on its own merits.

Regarding the effect of the passage of the prohibition law upon the amortization of the old properties used as storehouses, the parts of the properties that were used for storage purposes were certainly not abandoned, and the difference in the use they were put to probably did not affect the depreciation, but if the beer stored there was not salable after the passing of the prohibition law, it would seem that these buildings could be considered abandoned just like any other parts of the property.

8

American Institute of Accountants

Library and Bureau of Information

SPECIAL BULLETIN No. 6

November, 1920

[The Committee on Administration of Endowment authorizes the publication of special Bulletins, of which this is one, on the distinct understanding that members are not to consider answers given to questions as being official pronouncements of the Institute, but merely the individual opinions of accountants to whom the questions were referred. It is earnestly requested that members criticise freely and constructively the answers given in this or any other Bulletin of this series.]

FIRE LOSS

Q. We desire to place before you the following query for your consideration:

An employee has a three-year contract with his employer whereby the employee receives a stated salary, plus 15 per cent of the net profits, at the end of each accounting period. During the first year a fire loss occurs, and on account of insufficient insurance the firm becomes a co-insurer and suffers a loss of $50,000.00.

Question 1: Is this net fire loss of $50,000.00 chargeable to operations of the business, thus reducing the profits of the business before determining the 15 per cent interest in the profits of the employee, or

Question 2: Is this amount really an impairment of capital, and therefore chargeable against capital, or

Question 3: Is it advisable to spread the amount over a period of years, or over the three-year period as per the contract existing between employer and employee?

A. The library has received the following answer to your question:

As details of the agreement between the employee and his employer are not stated, we shall have to assume that no stipulation was made regarding extraordinary profits or extraordinary losses. Doubtless it was intended that the employee should take his chance with the employer, and if there were any net profits he would be paid 15 per cent of them, and if there were no net profits obviously he would receive no additional compensation. No mention is made of losses, as to whether the employee is to reimburse his employer to the extent of 15 per cent of such losses, or whether the loss would be deducted from profits of subsequent years.

Answering question number 1, in my opinion the loss would have to be charged against operations before determining the amount on which the employee would be entitled to 15 per cent. If, instead of a loss, it had happened to be an unusual profit due to peculiarly favorable circumstances, the employee would certainly have expected to share in such profit. Conse-

I

quently it would seem to be fair that he should share in any business loss. As it is expressed in golf it is the "rub of the green."

In answer to question number 2, I would say that it is not a charge against capital, although in the case of a corporation it might result in an impairment of capital if it exhausted all of the surplus. In the accounts of the firm it would naturally decrease the amount invested in the business or capital, just as would be true of any other loss.

As to question number 3, I see no reason why the amount should be spread over a period of years. It is not in any sense a deferred charge, but is a loss which must be absorbed during the year in which it occurred. Also there would not seem to be any warrant for spreading it so far as the contract between the employer and employee is concerned. It is a loss of that particular year, and if the employee does not share in net losses of any one year, then he simply does not receive any additional compensation during that one year, but if during the succeeding two years profits are earned, he would be entitled to 15 per cent of such profits.

BREWERIES

Referring to Special Bulletin No. 5, pages 7-8: After writing our letter to you the internal revenue department refused to recognize the method employed of writing off as a loss the difference between the original cost of the properties which had been abandoned less the depreciation accrued and the salvage value of the same. Instead, the rates of depreciation were materially increased over the usual rate during prior years, resulting in practically no loss to be sustained at the time the properties were abandoned.

TURPENTINE LEASES

Regarding the rate of depreciation allowable upon what we know as turpentine leases, made upon standing timber for the purpose of allowing lessees to manufacture turpentine and rosin, the following table is in general use by some of the best informed companies in the business:

DEPRECIATION FOR TURPENTINE LEASES

Five-year lease:

First year	30%
Second year	25
Third year	20
Fourth year	15
Fifth year	10
	100%

Four-year lease:

First year	40%
Second year	30
Third year	20
Fourth year	10
	100%

2

Three-year lease:

First year	45%
Second year	35
Third year	20
	100%

The leases usually run for 3, 4 or 5 years.

SEED BEANS

Q. I would appreciate your opinion in regard to the valuation of an inventory of seed beans planted on contract under the following conditions:

The seed company for which the beans are planted furnish the seed, which is returned to them when the crop is harvested. The balance of the crop is paid for at a price stipulated in the contract, which for 1920 averaged approximately six cents per pound. The seed company correctly maintains that the cost of the seed planted, including freight, preparation and distribution, was ten cents per pound.

Will you please advise me as to the correct method of valuing the beans planted and the stock reserved for planting on next year's contracts?

A. Assuming the inquiry to have reference to the inventory value of seed beans in the accounts of the dealer, it would seem that as the dealer is able to purchase his seed from the grower at six cents a pound for 1920 this price would be proper for use in the inventory, say of 31st May, 1921, of seed in the ground.

To value the reserve stock for the next year's planting at ten cents a pound, when in all probability the next crop may be purchased by the dealer for less, would not be conservative accounting.

BOLTS AND NUTS

Q. We desire to obtain any information available regarding the proper form of manufacturing or operating statements for a business manufacturing bolts and nuts and similar products. Also the vital statistics relating to this line of business. In other words, what is the approved form of presenting the results of this line of business, both the operating figures for a given period and the vital comparative figures or percentages against former periods?

A. Plants such as you refer to are usually equipped with steam hammers, bulldozers, forges and anvils, cutting-off and heading machinery, small tools, such as pokers, rakes, shovels, tongs, etc., all of which are closely analogous to the ordinary equipment of a machine shop. The principal items of raw material are bar iron and steel, which are re-worked into different shapes and sizes, principally through heat treatment. The various labor functions— heating, drawing, cutting-off, shouldering, upsetting, offsetting, annealing, etc., can be reflected in the accounts in a manner similar to boring, turning and drilling operations in a machine shop.

No important differences exist between the proper form of operating statement for a business manufacturing bolts, nuts and similar products and that used for showing the results from operations of a machine shop or metal working plant.

The gross and net sales, costs of sales and gross profits are shown for

3

each of the various types of nut, bolt washer, etc., and in addition thereto I believe it is desirable to show the number of pounds of each product sold.

Interesting comparative figures and percentages between corresponding periods should be found in a comparison of the quantity and money value of the sales of various classes of product, and of the elements comprising the manufacturing cost of such sales. The comparative percentages of gross profit to sales, and the gross profit per pound should also be ascertained.

NEGLIGENCE

Syllabus:

1. One who holds himself out as an expert accountant, and accepts employment as such, impliedly represents that he possesses the ability and skill of the average person engaged in that branch of skilled labor.

2. An action to recover damages arising from the negligence of an expert employed to audit certain accounts is founded on breach of contract, and not in tort. The cause of action is the breach of the contract, and the different items of damage resulting therefrom do not constitute separate causes of action.

3. If from lack of proper skill, or from negligence, an expert accountant fails to disclose the true status of accounts he is employed to audit, he is liable for the damages naturally and proximately resulting from such failure; but losses resulting from a subsequent embezzlement by a city officer, or from the subsequent bankruptcy of a surety for such officer, in the absence of any circumstances tending to show that such contingency was in contemplation of the parties at the making of the contract as likely to occur, are too remote to be recovered as a consequence of such default.

4. Compensation paid an expert accountant in reliance upon his report that he has made a complete and correct audit may be recovered back, on proof that through his negligence the audit is in substance false.—121 Minnesota Reports, 296, May 2, 1913.

DRAFTS

Q. In a certificate to a balance-sheet of a seed house we included the following paragraph:

There were contingent liabilities existing in respect of drafts and acceptances on customers, discounted in the ordinary course of business, and in process of collection by the banks at June 30, 1920, as follows:

Acceptances, not due..........................	$ 9,186.27
Drafts	42,341.11
Total	$51,527.38

Some of these drafts were drawn with bills of lading attached, and some were drawn against the customers' open accounts as a method of collection. We, of course, have the bank's certificate that these drafts and acceptances were unpaid as at the above mentioned date.

We are just in receipt of a letter from an eastern brokerage firm, which is handling notes for our client, requesting us to omit from our certificate any mention of the contingent liability existing on account of drafts with bills of lading attached, which have been sold and remain unpaid. They state that they have taken this matter up with leading accountants, and find that it is the practice of these accountants not to include drafts sold against shipments of merchandise as a contingent liability.

We cannot agree with the view set forth above. We are of the opinion that all drafts with bills of lading attached which have been sold to banks would remain a contingent liability of the drawer until such time as they were actually paid.

If this were not so, any firm with a seasonal business could clean up its balance-sheet at the end of every season, simply by means of an arrangement whereby it could exchange drafts with some friendly house.

A. Answering your query regarding the showing as a contingent liability drafts attached to bills of lading which have been sold to banks:

It is my opinion these should be so shown, as until the bank has collected the drafts the contingent liability exists. Your correspondents are, in my opinion, correct in taking the stand that these contingent liabilities should be shown on the balance-sheet.

DEPRECIATION

Q. Will you kindly give me your opinion as to whether depreciation in the sense of normal physical wear on a manufacturing plant would be included or excluded as a manufacturing cost in a contract between a lessor and lessee for the operation of a property where the following language is used: "I will for the period of one year operate the properties of the company on my own account and at my expense. If the operation results in profit, that profit will be divided equally between myself individually and * * * company—one-half of the profit to each. I will pay all taxes of every character due and payable during the year, the amount thereof to be charged and deducted as an expense of operation * * *. All expenditures of every kind made in the operation of the properties will be treated as an expense of operation. I will keep the property in as good condition as turned over to me, natural wear and tear excepted."

The question, as you will see, turns upon the phrase natural wear and tear excepted. This is quite a common expression in these contracts, but just what does it cover? Natural decay through a property standing idle is one thing, wear and tear through the operation of the property is altogether different.

I am very much interested to learn the strictly correct application of this provision, and as to whether it would result in the lessor being obliged to maintain the property so far as depreciation is concerned.

A. We have received the following answer to your question: It seems to be clear that depreciation does not enter into the accounts under the contract quoted. The intent of the contract seems to me to be that all expenditures reasonably necessary for the up-keep of the properties will be made as part of the operating cost. Natural wear and tear seems to me to cover that exhaustion of physical life which, though continually going on, does not, during the term of the contract, reach a point at which proper practice would require an expenditure which would restore or prolong the physical life.

To sum up the situation briefly, it seems to me that under the contract depreciation is not to be considered, but expenditures made to arrest or restore depreciation are operating expenses.

5

•Q. In the shipbuilding industry, what is the percentage of scrap to the finished weight of steel in a steel vessel?

A. Scrap percentage may vary from 9% to 20%. The average is 12%.

TIME KEEPING AND PAY ROLL DISTRIBUTION

Q. Will you kindly send me an outline of a plan for time keeping and payroll distribution adapted to a chemical plant employing five hundred men?

A. The principal mechanical devices and records which are ordinarily used for recording working hours and distributing labor costs are as follows:

1. Time clocks located at the factory entrances and used in registering exact time at which each employee enters and leaves the plant.

2. Addressing machine for printing the employees' names and numbers on the weekly clock cards, payroll sheets and pay envelopes.

3. Adding machines for use of the payroll department.

4. Weekly clock card for each employee which shall be registered in the time clock as the employee enters and leaves the plant, and which shall be filed in visible "In" and "Out" racks on either side of the time clocks.

5. Daily labor ticket for each employee on which record is made of the time spent on each manufacturing process and non-productive task on which the employee is engaged during the day.

6. Permanent index card for each employee, showing his or her full name, address, date of employment, rates of pay with dates of changes, and other particulars.

7. Payroll sheet on which is summarized the amount of wages earned during a week by each employee and any deductions for Liberty Bond installments or other charges.

8. Labor distribution sheet for summarizing the charges to the different processes and expense accounts as indicated on the daily labor tickets.

ADDRESSING MACHINE:

The addressing machine should prove a time and expense saver in the printing of the employees names and numbers. The use of this machine also insures accuracy. An attachment can be secured which will automatically space the different names so that they will print on the cross lines of the payroll sheets.

ADDING MACHINES:

We could not advise whether a listing or non-listing type of machine would be best suited to your requirements. The key operative non-listing machine is most rapid in the hands of a skilled operator, but should not be used unless a skilled operator is available.

DAILY LABOR TICKET:

The choice of a proper form of labor ticket depends upon operating con-

6

ditions. If employees are ordinarily engaged on only one process during the day a simple form of ticket would be satisfactory.

If employees are usually engaged on two or more operations during the day a special form of ticket would be required. Two types of forms are suggested for your consideration:

(a) The ticket or card may be designed with a scale of units representing each hour and quarter hour of the working day. If the working day is ten hours there would be forty spaces, each representing a quarter hour, or one unit of time. As a workman is assigned to a new job or non-productive task, the job number or expense account number should be written on the line opposite the quarter hour corresponding with the time at which the work is started. The number of quarter hour spaces between the entries of any two job numbers would measure the elapsed time of the first job.

(b) An alternative form of labor ticket is a card with coupons. A coupon would be used for each job or non-productive task worked on during the day and would indicate the starting and finishing time.

Whatever form of labor ticket is used, the foreman should be held responsible for the accuracy of the starting and finishing time. It is feasible in many plants for the foreman's clerk to make out the time tickets. That plan is preferable to requiring the workmen themselves to write their own time cards. Mechanical clocks may also be used within the works for recording the time of starting and finishing each job.

Piece work records would have to be controlled through the inspection department, and we assume that little if any piece work would be in existence at a chemical plant employing five hundred men.

PERMANENT INDEX CARD:

This card is for reference purposes. It should be looked upon as the authentic record of the rates of wages. No changes should be made in rates of wages without the written approval of the proper official. A 3 x 5 card is the size ordinarily used for this record.

PAYROLL SHEET:

In most factories it is feasible to use one set of payroll sheets, containing the employees' names, numbers and rates of pay for a period of three months. A separate set of slip sheets can be used each week to record the hours, earnings, deductions and net payroll amounts.

The weekly clock cards should be arranged in the same order in which the employees' names appear on the payroll sheets. Before the number of hours of each employee is entered on the slip sheets, however, the weekly clock cards should be checked with the daily labor tickets. Any discrepancies between the number of hours registered on the clock card and the number of hours distributed upon the daily labor tickets for the week should be investigated and adjusted before the earnings are calculated on the payroll sheet.

7

RATE..............

EMPLOYE'S WEEKLY PAY ROLL RECORD.

DEPARTMENT........   WEEK ENDING.................EMP. NO..........

EMPLOYE'S NAME................................

DAYS	DIRECT LABOR			Indirect Labor	Hours Day Work		Total Earnings	Remarks
	Product for Sale		Product for own use	Day Work				
	Piece Work	Day Wo k	Day Work	Day Work	Reg.	O.T.		
Mon...								
Tues...								
Wed...								
Thurs..								
Fri....								
Sat ...								
Sun. ..								
TOTALS								

LABOR DISTRIBUTION SHEET:

This form should provide spaces for all the processes and expense accounts to which labor costs may be charged from daily labor tickets. The total amount of money entered on the labor distribution sheet against the various processes and expense accounts should equal the total amount of earnings each week as shown on the payroll sheet. The labor distribution should be reconciled with the payroll as soon as possible after the end of the pay period.

8

American Institute of Accountants

Library and Bureau of Information

SPECIAL BULLETIN No. 7

December, 1920

INVENTORIES, COMMITMENTS AND FOREIGN EXCHANGE

Q. I should be much obliged if you could give me the views of some leading New York accountants on the treatment of inventories and contracts for forward delivery at the end of the year.

A. By the courtesy of a New York firm of accountants we are able to present as an answer to the above question a memorandum of a discussion prepared by the firm for the use of its own offices dealing with the questions of inventories, commitments and foreign exchange.

The problems of inventories, commitments for purchases of goods at prices in excess of market and foreign exchange, which were recognized as to some extent inter-related, were discussed at length.

The subjects were considered in relation to

(a) Treatment in books.
(b) Treatment for tax purposes.
(c) Statement in published accounts.
(d) Form of certificate to be given.

Inventories:

The question was discussed at length whether the present reduction of prices was likely to be temporary. It was agreed that prices were in many cases below cost to some producers. It was felt though that there must be a reduction in the standard of living in some parts of the world for some years, and this must mean that until reduction of production takes place there would be excess supply, so that prices would not be governed by cost until some of the higher cost producers, being eliminated, production and demand should be more nearly equalized.

It was agreed, therefore, that it would not be sound to treat present declines as purely temporary.

It was agreed that it would be in order to show operating profits on the basis of inventories at cost (less usual provisions for obsolete stocks, etc.), and the adjustment from cost to market as a special charge either against profits or surplus, provided that the procedure adopted was clearly disclosed. In point of fact, the loss from the decline of prices is an offset to the extraordinary profits from increasing prices realized over a series of years and not an operating loss of the year. But as the extraordinary profits in past years have been included in the ordinary profits, any statement this year must either similarly absorb the corresponding decline or show clearly that this decline has not been absorbed in the operating results.

It was considered that clients generally should and would agree to the cost or market, whichever is lower, basis for their published accounts. It was pointed out that the Internal Revenue Department permitted this principle to be carried to the length of taking goods in process and finished goods at values based on current values of basic raw material. It seemed that in principle this could be supported only on the theory that a specification cost based on current costs in all respects represents the present market value on a reproduction basis. It was not felt that the department would be prepared to go this length or that clients generally would wish to do so, but as the logical result of the department's rules it seemed permissible. It was felt that clients practically had an option whether they would or would not adjust basic raw materials in work in process and finished goods in making cost or market adjustments.

The question of goods purchased in foreign markets was considered. Persian carpets were taken as an illustration. The market in Persia has declined slightly, and the value of the Persian kran has declined about 50 per cent. It was agreed that market in such cases means to importers the present Persian price converted at the current exchange rate.

The treatment of inventories by companies having contracts for sale of goods at prices yielding a profit above cost was considered. It was agreed that where goods have been bought specifically for such contracts, they should be taken at cost even if that be higher than market, both for general accounting and tax purposes. This should apply only if the contracts are enforceable contracts with responsible people—not in cases where enforcement would involve such risk of a bad debt as to be unwise. It was recognized that the question as to applying goods on hand to such contracts where they were not earmarked was difficult, and the firm should not be disposed to question any reasonable course adopted by any client in this matter.

The question whether cost cards should be adjusted was discussed. It was felt that clients should have something in the nature of a detailed inventory in which individual items would be reduced to market, so as to produce it to the Internal Revenue Department, but that subject to this requirement it was not necessary, nor probably desirable, to adjust inventory cards. In some cases, however, it might be convenient to make adjustments as at the close of the year and reverse them in the new year.

For tax purposes clients might be well advised to adhere to cost, if adjustment to market would mean converting small profits into losses or increasing losses. In such cases adjustment to market for general purposes could be effected by reserves. It was agreed that there was little prospect of legislation permitting recovery of 1919 taxes on account of 1920 losses, but a fair chance of the enactment of provisions permitting losses to be carried forward and applied against future profits in some way.

Commitments:

It was agreed that disclosure of the fact that a concern has commitments for future purchases at a cost substantially in excess of present market values is a material factor in its financial position unless it has offsetting sale contracts with responsible purchasers. The treatments were considered in order of preference:

(1) A reserve for loss on such commitments, which, if earmarked, may be included in reserves and not treated as a current liability.

(2) A footnote showing the difference between purchase cost and market value of such commitments.

(3) A note that there has been no provision for such difference.

In cases 1 and 2 an unqualified certificate can be given. In case 3 the certificate should state that *"subject to the fact that as stated in the balance-sheet no provision has been made,"* etc. This qualification seemed necessary, since the amount of the difference is a material fact and is not disclosed.

For tax purposes it is clear that no deduction in respect of the difference between market values and the purchase price of goods contracted for but not delivered can be made. Where, therefore, companies face a loss, and desire to take it in 1920, they must take appropriate action before December 31st. This can be done in various ways, including

a. Expediting delivery of the goods so as to bring them into the inventory at December 31st.

b. Making a payment to secure a cancellation.

c. Transferring the contract or selling firm for future delivery an amount equal to the amount for which contract has been made.

It was thought the second method mentioned could not be objected to even if contemporaneously the contractors should enter into new contracts for similar goods at lower prices.

It was pointed out that while methods 1 and 2 might be attractive to companies which had large profits and wished to bring in losses to offset them, the other parties to the contracts might also in some cases have large profits and be unwilling to bring additional profits into 1920. It was suggested that this would be particularly true in regard to sugar contracts. It was felt that the third alternative would meet such a situation adequately.

The question was raised whether there was any moral objection to the course suggested, and it was considered that as there was a loss to be faced on the goods, and as the cause of that loss was the action of buying in 1920, there could be no moral or legal objection, provided that the company established the loss by action of a definite and final character in 1920.

It was recognized that with many companies the tax consideration and the financial or credit considerations would operate in opposite directions, but it was felt that on the whole the companies would be well advised to take their losses and save the taxes, especially as all credit granting institutions would be sure to inquire very closely into the question of obligations in respect of such commitments.

Foreign Exchange:

In regard to the question of exchange it was agreed that the soundest conclusions would be reached by regarding foreign currencies as commodities. When an American concern sells a product that has cost a certain amount of dollars for a certain amount of, say, marks, it exchanges one commodity for another, and the ordinary way of determining the profit is by taking the commodity received (the marks) at its face value at the date of acquisition. Once the marks are in stock they must be carried in accordance with the ordinary inventory practice at cost or market, whichever is lower. Viewed from this angle there can be no question of loss on exchange at the time of sale. On the contrary, to take the marks in at par would obviously be to take up an unrealized and improbable profit. The only question of exchange loss is in relation to the decline in value between the date of the original sale and the end of the year.

On the whole it was agreed that current assets and current liabilities must be treated in a consolidated balance-sheet, or for purposes of valuing foreign investments at current rates of exchange at the close of the year. It was agreed that in some cases it might be permissible to show an extraordinary loss on exchange as a separate item in the profit and loss account, but that the amount so to be shown would require to be very carefully considered.

It was pointed out that great care should be taken in adopting the above principles not to apply them to foreign currency items which represent conversions of American dollar values, such as the f. o. b. value of goods of American origin. Obviously this item should be converted back into dollars at the same rate as was applied to the original conversion.

Foreign Drafts:

The New York partners mentioned that cases on a large scale had arisen in New York where exporters had shipped goods with sight drafts attached to territories such as Cuba and South America, and the consignees had refused to accept either the goods or the drafts. It was agreed that in such cases the sale was not completed and no profit should be taken for tax purposes, but the goods treated as inventory and valued at cost or at their market value on the spot where they happened to be. It was agreed that this treatment should also apply to goods in transit as to which the time had not arrived when the consignee would be called upon to accept the draft or the goods. The view was expressed that comparatively few of these cases would arise at other offices than New York, and it was suggested that any offices encountering such cases should communicate with New York in regard thereto.

American Institute of Accountants

Library and Bureau of Information

SPECIAL BULLETIN No. 8

February, 1921

A METHOD OF ASCERTAINING PIANO MANUFACTURING COSTS

Q. Would you be so kind as to furnish us with data bearing on the method of ascertaining piano manufacturing costs?

A. Preliminary to the introduction of any comprehensive method of cost accounting into a piano factory, three conditions are requisite: first, that continuous control is maintained over raw materials, parts and supplies through the maintenance of storerooms throughout the factory under charge of responsible employees whose primary duty is to see that materials are withdrawn only upon presentation of duly authenticated requisitions; second, that the factory is divided and organized into logical and distinct departments so that the production of each department be accurately ascertained; and, third, that detailed, written manufacturing instructions and specifications are prepared for all products required to be manufactured. The system described in this memorandum is based on the use of predetermined or standard costs. Briefly stated the method provides that careful, detailed estimates of the cost of each product be prepared preliminary to manufacture and that the subsequent actual costs of manufacture be systematically compared with the predetermined standard costs. A suitable form of Standard Cost Sheet is as follows:

I

Form No. I

Standard cost of ....   No. ....

Date compiled .... By .... Revised ....

Particulars (Arrange by operations and departments)	Materials and Supplies			Mfg. Parts			Dir. Labor			Burden Exps.		Total
	Qty.	Pr.	Amt.	Qty.	Pr.	Amt.	Qty.	Pr.	Amt.	%	Amt.	Amount
Total cost												
Cost per unit												

2

-102-

The functions of the standard costs are threefold:

(1) To arrive at the approximate departmental efficiencies from month to month: This is accomplished by charging against each department its operating cost and crediting it with its production valued at standard costs. The variation in the ratio of actual to standard costs from month to month will be an index to the efficiency obtaining in each department. It will be noted that the standard costs are divided into the cost components of Materials and Supplies, Manufacturing Parts, Labor and Burden, the idea being that all charges and credits to Production Accounts will be classified under these captions, so as to more readily account for the variations between actual and standard costs.

(2) To ascertain current unit costs: After ascertaining the ratio of actual costs to standard costs, obtaining in each department as outlined above, approximate current manufacturing costs may be obtained by applying the ratio to the standard or predetermined cost of the part under consideration. It is obviously important to know that the ratio between the actual and standard costs within a given department applies ratably to all products manufactured by that department, and if not, to know the approximate variations in the ratio between products or classes of products.

(3) To ascertain monthly profits and losses: This function is merely an application of function number 2. The cost of each month's shipments is arrived at by valuing the quantities shipped at their respective standard costs and then converting the standard costs of shipments to actual costs by applying the ratio found to exist between the actual and standard cost of production.

So that the cost figures may form part of and be controlled by the general accounts, they should be recorded under the double entry system of bookkeeping in a Cost Ledger. The Cost Ledger should be subsidiary to the General Ledger and should be charged with all expenses incident to manufacturing and credited with the cost of pianos shipped and billed to customers, the balance remaining in the ledger representing, of course, the cost of materials and products remaining on hand. The principal entries made on the General Ledger each month affecting the Cost Ledger Controlling Account would be as follows:

Cost Ledger Controlling Account,   Dr.
> To Vouchers payable (for materials, payrolls, etc.)
> Prepaid expenses (insurance, taxes, etc.).
> Accrued liabilities (taxes, etc.).
> Reserve for depreciation (depreciation of manufacturing properties).
> To charge the Cost Ledger with expenses for the month of .... incident to manufacturing.

Cost of Sales,   Dr.
> To Cost Ledger Controlling Account,
> To relieve the Cost Ledger of the manufacturing cost of shipments made during the month of ....

3

The accounts maintained in the Cost Ledger would fall into five divisions, namely, those with—

1. Raw materials and supplies.
2. Productive departments.
3. Auxiliary departments.
4. Manufactured parts and pianos.
5. Manufacturing profit and loss.

The accounts under each division would be classified as follows:

I.—*Raw Materials and Supplies:*
* Lumber.
* Veneer.
* Glue.
* Sand and Garnet paper.
* Hardware supplies.
* Boxes and shooks.
* Coal.
* Piano materials.
* Etc.

II.—*Productive Department Accounts (Work in Progress):*
Mill Dept.
Case Dept.
Machine Shop.
Piano Dept.
Finishing Dept.
Etc.

III.—*Auxiliary Department Accounts:*
Power.
Receiving, Shipping and Stock.
General expense.
Etc.

IV.—*Finished Parts and Pianos:*
* Manufactured Parts.
* Uprights.
* Grands.
* Etc.

V.—*Manufacturing Profit and Loss Accounts:*
Materials and Supplies.
Manufactured Parts.
Direct Labor.
Burden Expenses.

NOTE.—Subsidiary records are to be maintained for accounts marked with an asterisk (*).

The procedure in connection with each of the five classes of accounts is as follows:

Form No. 3			Cost Ledger			Debits	
Date	Particulars	F.	Materials and Supplies	Manufactured Parts	Direct Labor	Burden Expenses	Total

4

Form No. 2

Standard Cost Value of ....

Month of ...., 192..

Dept. Production

Products	Qty.	Materials and Supplies		Mfg. Parts		Dir. Labor		Burden Expenses		Total	
		Per Unit	Amt.	Per Unit	Amt.	Per Unit	Amt.	Per Unit	Amt.	Per Unit	Amt.

5

The raw material and supply accounts are charged with the cost of materials purchased and credited with the cost of materials withdrawn from storerooms by manufacturing departments. Subsidiary records containing individual accounts with each kind of material and supply are maintained in support of these accounts. The productive department accounts are kept on such a form as follows: (Form No. 3.)

Each department is charged with its operating costs and credited with the standard value of its production, the standard value of production being ascertained by pricing the quantities produced at the predetermined or standard costs. For this purpose a form arranged as follows is provided: (Form No. 2.)

It is necessary to make physical inventories of the Work in Progress remaining in each of the productive departments at the close of each month and to value the inventories at standard costs. The balances in the accounts, representing the manufacturing profit and loss (i.e., the difference between the actual and standard costs of the departments' productions) is transferred to the manufacturing profit and loss, so that the balances remaining in the Productive Department accounts represent the inventories of Work in Progress valued at standard costs. The auxiliary departments are charged with the cost of operating the respective departments. At the close of each month the accounts are closed out by transfer to the Productive Department accounts, the apportionment to the Productive Department's accounts being made on the basis of service rendered to each of the productive departments. The Manufacturing Parts and Pianos accounts are charged respectively with the standard cost of parts and pianos produced and credited with the standard cost of parts requisitioned and pianos shipped, the balances in the accounts representing the standard cost of the inventories of parts and pianos on hand. The manufacturing profit and loss account is charged with the excess of the actual cost of the departmental productions over standard costs. Both the actual and standard costs should be entered in memorandum in this account and the account should be relieved each month of an amount equivalent to the product of the ratio of the net cumulative actual and standard costs and the standard cost of shipments.

The operation of each of these five classes is further shown by the following pro forma journal entries required to be taken up on the Cost Ledger each month:

Sundry Raw Material and Supply Accounts.
Productive Department Accounts—
  Direct labor.
  Indirect labor.
  Burden expenses.

Auxiliary Department Accounts.
  To General Ledger Controlling Account.
    Voucher Register distribution.

6

Productive Department Accounts—
Materials and Supplies.
Auxiliary Department Accounts.
To Raw Material and Supply Accounts.
Materials and Supplies requisitions distribution.
Sundry Productive Department Accounts.
To Sundry Auxiliary Department Accounts.
Clearing Auxiliary Department Accounts.
Productive Department Accounts.
To Manufactured Parts.
Parts requisitions distribution.
Uprights.
Grands.
Manufactured Parts.
To Productive Department Accounts—
Materials and Supplies.
Manufacturing Parts.
Labor.
Burden.
Departmental productions at standard costs.
Manufacturing Profit and Loss Accounts—
Materials and Supplies.
Manufacturing Parts.
Labor.
Burden.
To Productive Department Accounts.
Balances in department accounts after bringing down inventories of
work in progress valued at standard costs.
Cost Ledger Controlling Account.
To Uprights.
Grands.
Manufacturing Profit and Loss Account—
Materials and Supplies.
Manufacturing Parts.
Labor.
Burden.
Standard cost of shipments together with proportion of manufacturing
profit and loss accounts.

The results of the system are embodied in the following financial and
cost exhibits prepared each month from the General and Cost Ledgers:

Exhibit I—Balance Sheet.
"   II—Profit and Loss Statement.
"   III—Analysis of Sales.
"   IV—Statement of Inventories.
"   V—Summarized Manufacturing Statement.
"   VI—Analysis of Department Profit and Loss by Cost Com-
ponents.

7

Exhibit VII—Analysis of Burden Expenses (Auxiliary Departments).

" VIII—Analysis of Burden Expenses (Auxiliary Departments).

Exhibits I to III are common to all businesses. Drafts of Exhibits IV to VIII are appended hereto.

STATEMENT OF INVENTORIES—EXHIBIT IV

MONTH OF ...., 192

PARTICULARS	Balance on hand beginning of month	Purchased and manu- factured during month	Requisi- tioned and shipped during month	Balance on hand end of month
Raw materials and sup- plies (actual cost):				
Lumber				
Veneer				
Glue				
Sand and garnet paper				
Hardware supplies				
Boxes and shooks				
Coal				
Piano materials				
Etc.				
Work in progress (stan- dard cost):				
Per Exhibit V				
Manufactured parts (standard cost):				
Cases				
Keys				
Hammers				
Backs				
Bridges				
Strings				
Etc.				
Pianos (standard cost):				
Uprights—				
Unboxed				
Boxed				
Grands—				
Unboxed				
Boxed				
Manufacturing profit and loss:				
Materials and supplies				
Manufacturing parts				
Direct labor				
Burden expenses				
Total, per Exhibit I				

8

SUMMARIZED MANUFACTURING STATEMENT—EXHIBIT V

Month of ...., 192..

| Departments | Cost Components | | | | | Deduct—Inventory of work in progress at close of month | Balance—Actual cost of month's finished production | Standard value of month's production | Manufacturing profit or loss | % of manufacturing profit and loss | |
	Materials and supplies	Manufactured parts	Direct labor	Burden expenses	Total manufacturing cost					Current month	Previous month
Mill											
Case											
Machine											
Piano											
Finishing											
Etc.											

ANALYSIS OF DEPARTMENTAL PROFITS AND LOSSES—EXHIBIT VI

Cost Components

Month of ...., 192..

DEPARTMENTS	COST COMPONENTS														
	MATERIALS & SUPPLIES			MANUFACTURED PARTS			DIRECT LABOR			BURDEN EXPENSES			TOTAL		
	Actual	Standard	Difference	Actual	Standard	Difference	Actual	Standard	Difference	Actual	Standard	Difference	Actual	Standard	Difference

10

ANALYSIS OF BURDEN EXPENSES—EXHIBIT VII
(PRODUCTIVE DEPARTMENTS)
Month of ...., 1920..

Particulars	Departments						
	Mill	Case	Machine	Piano	Finishing	Etc.	Total
Supervision							
Indirect labor							
Heat, light and power							
Supplies							
Insurance and taxes							
Spoilt work							
Repairs							
Depreciation, etc.			Similar	form for	Exhibit	VIII	
Propn. auxiliary:							
Power							
Rec., Sh. and store							
General exp.							
Miscellaneous							
Etc.							

SHIPBUILDING

Q. In the case of a shipbuilding company constructing steel ocean-going vessels and operating with normal efficiency, should the ratio of manufacturing overhead, as defined below, be about 50% of direct labor or more or less than that figure? Should the ratio of administrative expense to total manufacturing cost be about 5% or more or less?

Definition of manufacturing overhead: Manufacturing overhead as used in the above query is composed of

(a) Indirect labor (salaries of shop managers, superintendents, clerks, inspectors, cleaners, etc.)

(b) Manufacturing expense (repairs, supplies, fuel, water, insurance, etc.)

A. Taking the definition of manufacturing overhead given by you, my view, based on the experience of my firm with shipbuilding accounts, is that manufacturing overhead should be less than the 50% you mention on the direct labor.

Operating with normal efficiency, it is probable 35% would be nearer the correct figure, possibly 40% in certain cases.

It is hard to determine the ratio of administrative expenses to total manufacturing cost, but the percentage is in any case quite small.

The 5% you mention is not unreasonable, though probably if the definition of administration expense is confined within the strictest limits, the 5% would be a somewhat generous figure.

II

SECOND-HAND MACHINERY

Q. In a system of accounting in which a liability for accrued depreciation is set up against plant inventory maintained at its original cost, what is the proper accounting method of entering original purchases of second-hand machinery?

The point of the inquiry is that our client has been accustomed to maintain his plant inventory at its original cost, setting up an increasing depreciation liability item contra. In a number of cases he has bought second-hand machinery at from one-half to two-thirds of its original cost price new. Is it correct accounting for him to enter in his plant inventory the cost price of this article new, setting up immediately on the other side the depreciation accrued on it to date as represented by his decreased purchase price? He points out that this is the only correct way for his statement to reflect his true inventory value, and wishes to know whether this method follows accepted accounting practice, or if not, if it can be defended.

A. I am of the opinion that the plant inventory account should be charged with the cost to the client of the machinery purchased, whether it be new machinery or second-hand machinery.

It is not unusual, however, where an appraisal of a plant has been made for the machinery to be appraised at its replacement value new, with a contra item for the depreciation accrued on that value to the date of the appraisal. On the same basis, it might not be improper for the second-hand machinery referred to to be appraised on the basis of its original cost and the difference between such cost and the amount paid for the machinery when purchased second-hand credited to a depreciation reserve account. Of course, any such adjustment should be reflected by a journal entry giving full explanation of the transaction.

I say this procedure might not be wrong, because, in my opinion, it would depend in large measure upon the question of the amount involved and the purpose for which the adjustment was made. If the amount represented only a small proportion of the total machinery in the plant, and the adjustment was made for the purpose of merely having the books record the original value new of the machinery in the plant, I can see no harm in the method suggested; but if, on the other hand, it constituted a large proportion of the total charged to the machinery account, and would therefore materially misrepresent the amount invested in the plant, or if the adjustment was made with the intention of in any way presenting misleading statements, or in causing anyone who saw such statements to form erroneous conclusions, then I would say that the method proposed was wrong.

ANONYMOUS LETTERS

Unsigned communications will be ignored.

12

American Institute of Accountants

Library and Bureau of Information

September, 1921

SPECIAL BULLETIN No. 9

[The Committee on Administration of Endowment authorizes the publication of special Bulletins, of which this is one, on the distinct understanding that members are not to consider answers given to questions as being official pronouncements of the Institute, but merely the individual opinions of accountants to whom the questions were referred. It is earnestly requested that members criticise freely and constructively the answers given in this or any other Bulletin of this series.]

DEPRECIATION FOR BRICK MANUFACTURE

Q. Kindly forward any data you may have in connection with prevailing rates of depreciation of equipment and plant used in the manufacture of bricks.

A. The library has received the following answer to your question:

In reply to your letter would say that, recently, the following rates were used by us after consultation with and the approval of the president and superintendent of one of the largest construction companies in the country. Both these men had extensive experience in the manufacture of bricks.

Machinery and equipment:

Pugmills, grinding pans, brick machines, etc.	10%
Engine and boiler house machinery	7½
Steam shovel and quarry machinery	10
Trucks and loading equipment	20
Loose tools, etc., to be inventoried.	

Buildings:

Periodic kilns, subject to the strain of continuous reheating and cooling off	10%
Continuous heat kilns	7½
Drying tunnels	5
Sheds and outbuildings	20

The above rates were, of course, based on the actual conditions encountered and these would not necessarily be found in every plant. I believe, however, that they may be taken as a fair guide.

The machinery and buildings peculiar to a brick plant will be found to be of a rapidly depreciating nature. Periodic kilns especially, owing to the repeated heating and cooling off, soon get into a state where their residual value is negligible and their usefulness is only maintained by heavy repairs. Such repairs or the repairs of small or rapidly wearing parts of machines are not included in the above rates.

An accurate rate, however, can only be decided upon after a study of local conditions. In another plant a straight rate of 10 per cent. was used on all plant and equipment, including building, but this is not considered a proper method.

I know of no approval that has been officially given by the commissioner of internal revenue to rates of this sort.

WHOLESALE BAKERIES

Q. Can you furnish me with information which will show the methods used in distributing the labor cost in a large wholesale bakery making a line of cakes and various kinds of pastry, some of which will be made in large batches and some in very small batches, in some instances only one cake of a kind constituting an order?

There is no feasible way that I have discovered of collecting the labor cost of the work being done, because the employees change frequently from one job to another, in many cases not being on a given job for more than five or ten minutes.

The material used does not seem to suggest any feasible basis of distribution because some large and costly mixes can be prepared in the same length of time as is required for small and inexpensive mixes.

Our client very earnestly desires to obtain a practical cost on all of the important items coming from the bakery. He informed us that whenever this has been tried, the question of labor distribution has proved an obstacle which could not be overcome.

If you can give me any information out of the experience of others who have had such a problem, it will be very much appreciated.

A. On receipt of your letter we referred it to one of the best bakery accountants of whom we have knowledge, and are today in receipt of his advice as follows:

I am afraid that the person seeking to get detailed labor costs on bakery products is doomed to disappointment, that is, if he wishes to distribute the payroll over each of the varieties of goods made.

As an illustration, I cite one of our plants, employing about twenty men in the bakeshop. This plant manufactured some 250 varieties of cakes, pies, tarts and doughnuts daily. Take the question of labor cost on fillings alone; some fillings are almost ready for use when bought, others are prepared almost entirely in the shop. Usually a quantity is prepared at one time. This particular filling may be used in thirty or forty varieties of goods in different quantities. Part of the filling may be used in preparing some other kind of filling. Again, a pie dough is mixed. It may be used on a dozen kinds of pies and several different sizes of each kind; or, part of it may be used for an entirely different purpose, such as dough for tarts. The work is so interrelated that time accuracy cannot be obtained.

Most shops making a full line divide their payroll as between bread, cake, pie and fried goods workers. In the bread shop a further distribution is possible between superintendence, mixers, bench hands, ovenmen and general helpers. Except in large shops, however, bench hands or helpers are apt to be used on the oven as well as on their own work.

The only way to determine the cost of an individual batch is to actually time the work expended in mixing, moulding, filling and baking the goods. Even this is more or less approximate, as in a sanitary shop

2

cleanliness is next to godliness, if it does not even precede it, and the cost of keeping the floors, machines, pans and equipment clean must be estimated. To get exact costs on each batch of goods would be so difficult that it would cost more than it was worth.

If I had reason to believe that an article was not properly priced, the test made was to actually superintend the weighing of the raw materials entering into the batch (although we had control of this in another way), time the labor by kinds of labor, add the estimated indirect labor, estimated cost of operation for coal, light, rent or shop space and depreciation of machinery, and the cost of wrapping, the total of which would give me the cost of the batch of goods delivered to the shipping room. I usually made at least three such tests before using the figures. Percentage cost of delivery and general overhead was always known, so that these figures would give me approximate results.

I believe this is about the best that can be done with the matter. I have never heard of anything further than this being attempted with sweet goods, although with bread it is in some cases possible to approximately separate different kinds.

TAXICABS

Q. What is the depreciation on taxicabs?

A. The opinion we have received regarding the rate of depreciation for taxicabs is 33⅓ per cent.

STEAMSHIP COMPANIES

Q. I should be obliged if you will kindly give your advice on the following question:

A steamship company keeping its accounting costs with a voyage as a unit, dry-docks its vessel for annual overhaul and distributes the cost of repairs over the voyages since the previous overhaul, on the basis of the time occupied on each voyage.

In addition, the vessel is frequently laid up for extraordinary repairs between the annual overhauls. It has been the practice of the company to charge such repairs to the voyage during which they were made, despite the fact that part or the whole of the damages may have accumulated during prior voyages. This results in an unfair distribution of this expense and upsets the comparison desired in keeping the accounts on the voyage unit basis.

A. It probably is the case that most steamship companies follow the practice of charging the voyage accounts only with those expenses which pertain directly to the voyage operations. For statistical purposes extraordinary expenses and the cost of overhauls may be spread at a later date.

If it were feasible to do so, it would be more scientific to charge to each voyage a reserve which would be sufficient to cover that voyage's proportion of annual overhaul.

It would be better still if a rate of depreciation could be arrived at which would be sufficient to cover obsolescence as well as actual depreciation and to apply a proportionate amount of this depreciation against the voyage account. If the rate could be fixed with a sufficient degree of accuracy so that it would cover extraordinary repairs and overhauls

3

which, presumably, would have the effect of prolonging the life of the vessel, then such charges might be made against the reserve account.

FUNDED DEBT

Q. Excluding from consideration the obvious definition that the funded debt of a company represents its obligations maturing at a date more than one year subsequent to the date of the balance-sheet, can you give me a real definition of funded debt?

On a balance-sheet as at Dec. 31, 1920, is it not proper to include under the "Funded Indebtedness" caption, mortgage bonds maturing June 30, 1921, providing the date of maturity is plainly indicated on the balance-sheet? To class such obligations as current liabilities might conceivably result in misunderstandings as to the company's financial situation.

In the case of serial equipment notes secured by a chattel mortgage on the property which is being acquired under a three-year rental contract, under what caption should these notes be stated on the balance-sheet? The notes are of equal amounts and mature monthly over a period of 3 years and the equipment remains the property of the mortgagee until the last note is paid. I took the position that these notes were neither funded nor current indebtedness in the ordinary sense and placed them on the balance-sheet between the funded indebtedness and current liabilities under the caption of "three-year serial equipment notes." In the case in question I was dealing with a public utility and the matter of the ratio of current assets to current liabilities was relatively unimportant. I have been advised that had I met with such a situation in the audit of an industrial, it would have been desirable to split the serial note issue into two parts and to show as a current liability the equipment notes maturing within twelve months from the date of the balance sheet.

A. The library has received the following answer to your question:

In my opinion, even though the bonds mature June 30, 1921, they should nevertheless be carried under the caption of funded indebtedness in the balance-sheet as of December 31, 1920. It is sufficient if the date of maturity is stated plainly. The amount is no less a funded debt because the date of maturity happens to be near at hand. On or before becoming due provision may be made for refunding it so that it may never be a current liability.

As to the three-year serial equipment notes, I believe it to be entirely proper to state them in the manner described in the qustion, i. e., to place them after the current liabilities under the caption, "three-year serial equipment notes." In this case also, it is obvious that the terms of the notes should be stated in such a manner that the amount payable in the near future will be indicated clearly. As a practical matter, it seems to me preferable to set them forth in one item rather than separate them into two accounts, one the early maturities which would be included in current liabilities, and the remainder which would be carried under the note caption.

It is nevertheless true that some accountants might consider it necessary to enter those which will mature at a comparatively early date in with the current liabilities. Reserves for federal taxes, for instance, are usually carried with the current liabilities, although no part of the amount is payable until 2½ months after the close of the fiscal year.

Such seeming inconsistencies as this, viz., including reserve for taxes in current liabilities and allowing notes, which will mature within six or

4

-116-

twelve months, to remain under the equivalent of a funded debt caption, are met with in accounting. The factor of more vital importance than exact uniformity or consistency to my mind is the disclosure of full information. If the balance-sheet cannot be criticized from that point of view, I believe all the essential requirements are complied with, even if, as in the case mentioned, all the notes remain under the one caption, even though part of them may be due within a comparatively short time.

I see no reason why they should be dealt with differently in an industrial balance-sheet as distinguished from that of a public utility. In a consolidated balance-sheet, in which there were long-term notes in some companies and bonds of a more or less distant date of maturity in others, I have entered them all under the general heading of "funded and long-term debt." Under this general caption were stated, of course, the various issues showing the character of the obligation and its maturity.

BY-PRODUCTS

Q. We desire to secure some information as to the usual accounting procedure adopted by recognized accounting authorities in recording the cost of net profit of by-products, particularly as they affect the soap manufacturing industry which produces the by-product of glycerine.

It is desired to secure in full, and if possible, a statement from recognized authorities, as to whether in a case where it is impossible to properly allocate the actual cost of producing a by-product as against the cost of producing the soap, the sales of the by-product should be recorded in the year in which they are actually sold, as it is possible, in some instances, that although the soap as manufactured is sold within a reasonable period after manufacture, owing to the steady demands for soap, the by-product would be compelled to await future demand, which is very unsteady, and cannot be ascertained or anticipated with any degree of correctness.

The main point on which we desire enlightenment is as to whether the income on the by-product should await the sale of the by-product or as to whether the by-product on hand at the end of each year should be inventoried at an estimated cost (the actual cost being indeterminable) and the cost of the main product be credited with the estimated cost or market value of the by-product.

A. Some by-products, so-called, are of such minor importance and value that the amount realized from them is deducted from the cost of producing the major product. In other cases, the by-product becomes a greater factor by the introduction, perhaps, of other ingredients and in that event may be of sufficient magnitude to warrant its being treated as a product standing by itself on which its own profit or loss would be determined. In that case, the cost, as nearly as it can be determined, of the element derived from the manufacture of the major product will be credited to that product and charged against the by-product account.

It really makes very little difference, however, whether the by-product is of greater or less importance as respects the cost of the major product, except that in one case the cost would be deducted from the cost of the major product, and, in the other case, the realization from the sale of the by-product would be deducted from the major product cost.

In the latter case it would seem that there would be no difference in treatment between such a by-product and scrap that might accumulate as a result of manufacturing process. In some operations, such as

5

stamping out articles from brass sheets, a comparatively small part of the metal remains in the finished product and the scrap accumulations are very large. Obviously, the cost of the product cannot be determined until credit is allowed for these scrap accumulations.

The same principle would seem to be true of by-products. The cost of the major product cannot be determined accurately until credit is given for whatever value the by-product may have. There seems to be no reason why the reduction in cost, or so-called income from the by-product, should await its sale any more than credit would not be allowed on scrap until it is sold. If any is on hand at the end of the year, in our opinion, it should be inventoried at a fair market value as nearly as that can be determined. If it is to be sold, it should be inventoried at cost, if that is less than market value, if the cost can be determined, and it is to be used with other ingredients in making a minor product to be marketed in due course.

NON-PAR VALUE SHARES

Q. I would appreciate it very much if you would advise me what experience members of the institute have had in regard to the proper handling of non-par value shares for a corporation.

We have a client who has had one thousand (1,000) shares of stock, par value $100.00 outstanding, and a surplus of approximately $150,000.00. The company is reorganizing, changing to non-par value stock. Should the surplus of $150,000.00 be closed into the capital account?

We are of the opinion that it should be unless the client has a reason to the contrary. We are also of the opinion that the profits for subsequent years should be carried into a surplus account so as to be a guide to the management and in this way avoid impairing the original capital stock by declaring dividends in excess of accumulated earnings since the reorganization. If the client desires to declare a dividend at the time of reorganization, this amount should be held in the surplus account and not closed into the capital account.

A. It is optional whether or not the surplus in question be transferred to the capital account.

There is no particular advantage in so doing.

On the contrary there is the possible disadvantage that if profits after the change in form of stock are not sufficient for dividend requirements and the previous surplus has been transferred to capital and such amount stated in the certificate as the capital with which the corporation will carry on business, the corporation presumably may not then use any of such former surplus without violating section 20, paragraph 2, of the New York Stock Corporation Law, as follows:

> "No such corporation shall declare any dividend which shall reduce the amount of its capital below the amount stated in the certificate as the amount of capital with which the corporation shall carry on business."

If the corporation desires to declare a dividend at time of reorganization or has reason to believe the surplus at time of reorganization will be required for future dividends, the amount of the surplus should be allowed to remain in the surplus account.

Profits subsequent to reorganization should be closed into a surplus account against which dividends should be charged.

6

DIVIDENDS

Q. A corporation expected to go into a proposed consolidation about ten years ago. The deal did not go through. This corporation had had an appraisal made which showed the value of the building and machinery as being $200,000 in excess of the book figures. This appreciation was placed upon the books at that time. This amount cannot be included in computing invested capital under the federal income-tax laws.

Owing to the heavy slump in prices at this time, it appears that the surplus account may be cut down below the amount of appreciation, viz., $200,000.

Now then; what New York state laws govern whether dividends may, or may not, be paid out of this unearned profit in the surplus account?

Since that time a stock dividend has been declared which dividend was over the amount of the $200,000. How would that affect the situation?

A. In reply to your letter, in which you recite a question as to the legitimacy of drawing upon surplus created through recording the appreciation in value of buildings and machinery to the extent of $200,000.00. In our opinion—which may not, however, be the opinion of lawyers—the distribution of such a surplus fund, the earnings of the business having previously been distributed, would constitute an impairment of capital such as is in violation of the generally accepted fundamental principle that dividends may not be paid except out of earned profits, and in violation particularly of section 28 of the Stock Corporation Law of New York State, the first sentence of which reads as follows:

> "The directors of a stock corporation shall not make dividends, except from the surplus arising from the business of such corporation, nor divide, withdraw or in any way pay to the stockholders or any of them, any part of the capital of such corporation, or reduce its capital stock, except as authorized by law."

In the case you cite, however, a stock dividend has been declared in excess of the amount of the $200,000.00 appreciation and it is only logical to assume that the stock dividend was first intended to capitalize the accretion in value of the capital assets. If the directors in their declaration designated the appreciation as the source from which the stock dividend was drawn, there could have been no question about it, as the intention of the company would be controlling in this matter, but even without such a specific declaration we think it would be generally admitted that the appreciation had been converted into capital stock through the stock dividend—if for no other reason because it could not be distributed.

It, therefore, appears that in the question proposed the company is not obliged to maintain a surplus equal to the amount of the appreciation of property accounts previously written up, but may distribute the remaining surplus below the amount of such appreciation.

MORTGAGES

Q. A second mortgage company buys $1,000.00 mortgage for $800.00, due in two years from date of purchase, thereby earning $200.00, the payments to be made on a monthly basis.

From a good accounting standpoint, as well as a federal income-tax standpoint, we desire to obtain your opinion as to how this should be entered on the books, that is

(a) Should it be set up at a cost in the mortgage account of $800.00, the monthly payments being applied against the principal until the full $800.00 is paid and the last $200.00 being all earned and recorded on the books as an earning the dates upon which the last $200.00 is actually paid?

7

(b) Should the mortgage be set up at net cost, namely, $800.00, a proportion of each payment upon principal being considered a proportion of the earning of $200.00, thereby evenly distributing the earning as the payments are made?

(c) Should the mortgage be set up at gross, namely, $1,000.00, and set forth a $200.00 earning in a deferred account, applying a proportion of that earning equally over the period of two years according to the payments being made or regardless of how the payments are made?

Are any of the three methods given above commendable, practical, and advisable to put in use. If you have other suggestions as to the proper procedure for a second mortgage company, we would greatly appreciate your advice as to the best method of maintaining that class of records.

A. All three of the alternative methods suggested in the question of your correspondent have been used in cases similar to that stated in the question.

Procedure A is similar to that commonly approved by the probate courts for use in the case of estates. The general practice in the case of estates, or trust funds, is to treat as an investment of principal the amount actually paid for an investment, in the present instance $800 for the $1,000 second mortgage, and when the liquidation of the investment is completed, to treat the realization of the discount as a profit at that time. Of course, in the case of estates or other trusts, this profit is added to the principal account, whereas in the case of a mortgage company it would naturally merge with other earnings and find its way to surplus.

Procedure B is that which would appear to be most in accord with the intent of the treasury department regulations. On the other hand, we doubt whether the treasury would object to procedure A in the case where a second mortgage company pursued a consistent policy of taking up as an earning a discount only at the final liquidation of each mortgage. Of course, if the full amount of the investment were returned prior to the last payment, naturally as soon as the $800 had been repaid the company would begin reporting the remaining collections of principal as taxable income, as well as profits for its earning statement.

Procedure C is analogous to that now followed by most banks in their treatment of discounts on notes receivable discounted. The face amount of the note is entered among the assets, and the discount is treated as a deferred earning, a part thereof being taken up as income in each fiscal period so that the discount has all been absorbed in the earning accounts by the time the note matures.

While under procedures B and C the statement of the transaction differs slightly from a balance-sheet standpoint, the effect on the statement of earnings and the tax returns is identical under the two modes of procedure. From the earnings standpoint it is, in effect, that which is also followed by insurance companies using the amortization basis of bond valuation which is permitted by the insurance department of various states.

Procedure A is, of course, the most conservative of the three, and since the investments for which the procedure is being determined are not gilt-edged securities, but investments of a more speculative character, as is indicated by the amount of discount used in the illustration, the most conservative manner of treating the subject in the accounts would seem preferable.

8

American Institute of Accountants

Library and Bureau of Information

SPECIAL BULLETIN No. 10

October, 1921

CASH COMMISSIONS

Q. The corporation I have in mind is selling its own capital stock through agents, paying the agents a cash commission on the sale. To my way of thinking, the commission, if it amounts to any considerable sum, could be capitalized, and the expense prorated over a number of years or carried indefinitely, since it is incurred for the purpose of expansion. I find no authority covering this point. It is not the same as discount on bonds since the stock has not a certain maturity date.

A. The cash commission paid or other expenses incurred in connection with the sale of the capital stock of a corporation could very properly be charged to organization expenses. It was generally the practice in the past either to charge off the entire amount of the organization expenses the first year, although sometimes they were spread over two or three years or more. Unless there are very good reasons to the contrary, we always advise disposing of the organization expenses the first year, since if carried as an asset they add nothing to the strength of a financial statement.

While in the past it has been the custom to actually charge off such expenses, it is desirable in view of the present tax laws to now deal with them in a little different manner. They cannot, of course, be applied as a deduction in determining the amount of taxable income, but they do form part of the invested capital. Even if they were charged off they could be added back to the surplus in calculating the amount of invested capital, but in order that they may not be overlooked, it is preferable, in absorbing them in the current year's operations or in several years' operations, to credit the amounts so charged off to a reserve for organization expenses rather than to the account organization expenses itself.

If this method is adopted, the organization expenses disappear from the balance-sheet, but at the same time there is no danger of the amount being overlooked because the title to the reserve account indicates that it is of such a nature that it should be included in stating the invested capital.

1

CONSOLIDATIONS

Q. Five corporations, all of whose stocks and bonds are owned by a holding company, are to be consolidated into a new corporation. The bonds are to stand unchanged and the stock of the new or consolidated company is to be issued to an amount equal to the total of the stocks of the consolidating companies. All this stock will be owned by the holding corporation and the result will be an exchange only by the holding corporation of the stocks of the five corporations for an equal amount of that of the new corporation.

I would like to know whether it is proper for the new corporation to set up the total of the surplus of the consolidating corporations as surplus in its opening entry, and whether it can declare dividends out of it to the holding company. By virtue of the ownership of all the securities of the constituent companies in the first place and the ownership of all the securities of the new corporation in the second place, there is no real change in the corporate relationship, as the companies were and remain one earning proposition.

A. The library has received the following answer to your question:

In my opinion, the consolidation of the five subsidiary corporations into one subsidiary corporation, under the conditions stated in the inquiry, would not change the status of the several corporations as respects the surplus account or the propriety of using that surplus account for the payment of dividends of the holding company.

In making the above statement it has been assumed that all of the surplus of each of the five subsidiary corporations is current surplus which could be used in the payment of dividends of the holding company. If, however, the subsidiary corporations or any of them were acquired as going concerns by the holding company and at the time they were acquired had accumulated a certain amount of surplus, then that surplus at the date or dates they were acquired is capital surplus so far as the holding company is concerned and would not be available for the payment of dividends. It is probably not necessary to explain why such surplus should be dealt with as capital surplus, because the reasons for doing so can be found in numerous articles which have been published from time to time relating to the accounts of holding companies and the preparation of consolidated balance-sheets.

If the five corporations or any of them have or should have thus established capital surplus accounts in addition to their current surplus accounts, then a like distinction should be made on the books of the new subsidiary corporation and only the current surplus of that corporation would be available for dividends of the holding company.

FIRE LOSSES

Q. I will be very glad if you could give me the experience of some other accountants who may have had similar experience in reference to the following:

One of our clients had a fire. In settling with the insurance company he was reimbursed at the replacement value, this replacement refund was in excess of what the goods originally cost—in other words a profit was made on the insurance.

Should this be handled as a separate proposition showing the cost of the goods injured by fire and the refund received from the insurance company which was in excess of the cost?

A. If the property destroyed by fire was merchandise and the amount was considerable, the profit might well be stated separately. If it was

2

relatively small this would seem to be unnecessary. If the property destroyed was in the nature of capital assets any profit taken should be shown as a separate credit to profit and loss. It might, however, be preferable for the concern to take advantage of the provisions of the tax regulations in regard to replacements and credit the amount to a fund to which it would charge the cost of replacing the capital assets. In this way a saving would tend to be effected.

An insurance company undertakes to make good to the insurer the loss sustained by a fire. In other words, it is intended that the insurer shall not be in a less favorable position as respects his merchandise after the fire than he was before the fire.

In the case mentioned the amount refunded was in excess of what the goods originally cost, presumably because the market value of the goods had advanced in the meantime. If the market value of the goods destroyed had not advanced then the insurer would have received from the insurance company an amount equal to only the cost of the goods.

In the latter case it is clear that the transaction would be similar in effect to the return of merchandise to a vendor and an allowance therefor at cost. In such a case the merchandise purchase account would be credited in order that the net purchases for the year might be shown.

In the case of a loss by fire, therefore, it appears to be proper under the circumstances mentioned, to credit the merchandise purchase account or whatever account may be used to show the purchases of merchandise, with the cost of the goods destroyed and charge this amount to a separate account.

The amount received from the insurance company would be credited to this latter account and the profit, presumably due to the increase in market value, would be credited to the profit-and-loss account.

ROYALTY ON SAND

Q. What is the average rate of royalty on glass sand?

A. We have had experience with one of the largest producers of molding sand products. I do not know how that sand would compare with glass sand, but in the molding sand business the cost varies from a minimum of five cents per ton to a maximum of fifty cents per ton (with an average of about twenty-five cents per ton), depending on the grade of sand and its availability for shipping.

NON-PAR-VALUE SHARES

In Special Bulletin No. 9, for September, page 6, appears this paragraph:

"If the corporation desires to declare a dividend at time of reorganization or has reason to believe the surplus at time of reorganization will be required for future dividends, the amount of the surplus should be allowed to remain in the surplus account."

This subject was debated at a meeting of the New York State Society of Certified Public Accountants last winter. I think it was unanimously decided that accountants should not sanction balance-sheets prepared as indicated but that surplus at time of reorganization should be carefully

3

segregated from general surplus and be shown as special or capital surplus so that it would not be used as dividends even though there might be some legal sanction for the practice.

MORTGAGES

We have received the following comment on the article, Mortgages, which appeared in Special Bulletin No. 9, page 7:

The answer to the question on pages 7 and 8 ignores one of the major points in the question and that is the rate of interest. Second mortgages rarely carry a rate of interest in excess of six per cent. per annum, whereas the effective rate of interest is considerably higher. On an accrual basis, this effective rate should be taken into account; it is erroneous to treat the difference between cost price and par value as a profit at the end of the period.

BONDS

Q. A water company is required by its mortgage to deposit with the trustee of said mortgage a sum of money annually for a depreciation fund. Such fund is to be used for replacements. The trustee has purchased with a portion of this fund bonds of the company, paying for same 90 and accrued interest. If the cash in the fund at any time is insufficient to reimburse the current funds of the company for replacements made by it, such bonds in the fund will have to be sold. The question is, shall these bonds be charged into the fund at cost, or shall they be charged at face value and the difference between cost and face value credited to surplus? Furthermore, in the balance-sheet shall these bonds be included on the asset side in the depreciation fund, or shall they be deducted on the liability side from the bonds issued, so that the net figure will be shown as bonds outstanding in the hands of the public? The Public Service Commission (Pennsylvania) classification of accounts for water companies requires that the difference between face value and cost shall be credited to surplus and the face value of the bonds charged to the fund account.

A. The question does not set forth the exact terms of the mortgage requirements, and it is not therefore practicable to make a definite reply.

In the first place it would appear that the fund created by annual deposits with the trustee is a depreciation fund rather than a fund set aside for the purpose of redeeming the company's funded debt, and that there is no requirement as to accumulating interest on the fund assets. The fact that the trustee uses the assets in this fund to reimburse the company for expenditures for replacements and that the bonds purchased with the fund cash would be liable to be sold at any time to provide cash for replacements would argue that the company's bonds, which have been purchased at a price of 90 and accrued interest, should remain in the fund at cost price, or 90 and accrued interest, as a temporary investment of the fund assets.

The "Uniform Classification of Accounts for Water Companies in the State of Pennsylvania" under Account No. 112, Sinking Fund Assets (p. 25), deals with bonds acquired by a utility for the purpose of redeeming its funded debt, but in the question stated it would not appear that the bonds referred to are purchased for this purpose, and as they are subject to realization, should not be carried at their face value.

If, however, the terms of the mortgage imply that the cash deposited constitutes a sinking fund for the redemption of funded debt, the bonds purchased through this fund in ordinary practice would be canceled

4

(unless the mortgage required that the interest on the bonds be credited to the fund) and the bonded debt outstanding reduced by the amount of the bonds so canceled. The difference between the cost price of the bonds and the face value of the bonds may be credited as follows:

(a) That part of the difference which is represented by the proportionate amount of bond discount on the asset side of the balance-sheet should be credited to "unamortized bond discount account."

(b) If the bond were purchased at a lower figure than that for which it was originally issued, the difference in the price paid and the proceeds originally received from its sale could be credited to surplus account in accordance with instructions under account No. 112 of the Pennsylvania Commission. A more conservative manner in which to treat this credit would be to credit the entire difference between cost and face value to "unamortized bond discount account," as under instructions relating to account No. 131, "Unamortized Debt Discount and Expense." Bond discount and expense may, if desired, be amortized more rapidly through charges of all or any part of it, either at the time of issue or later, to account No. 711, "Other Deductions from Surplus Account."

It would appear that so long as records supporting entries are so kept that the utility can furnish information as to the nature and amount of its credit and debit made in regard to bond discount, some latitude would be allowed in setting up the accounts so long as the spirit of the regulations of the commission was not violated.

The following additional information was given:

In my report on the company involved I have stated the bonds so purchased at cost in the depreciation fund on the assets side of the balance-sheet, thus:

Depreciation fund:
Cash on deposit with trustee............ $10,000.00
Bonds of this company, $10,000 face value 9,000.00
Interest accrued, not due, on funds and
  bonds 200.00

Total depreciation fund $19,200.00

The terms of the mortgage under which the depreciation fund is carried are:

The company shall pay to the trustee on the first day of September, 1916, and thereafter on the first day of September in each year to and including the first day of September, 1925, the sum of four thousand dollars ($4,000); and beginning on the first day of September, 1926, and thereafter on the first day of September in each year to and including the year 1954, the sum of five thousand dollars ($5,000), so long as any bonds secured by this mortgage remain outstanding. The trustee shall hold the money so paid in a special fund to be known as the "depreciation fund," which shall be subject always to the lien of this mortgage and shall be paid out by the trustee only to reimburse the company for the actual cost of renewals and replacements which shall be made by it from time to time upon the property of the company.

If any portion of the sum paid into the said depreciation fund on the first day of September in any year shall remain unexpended on the first day of September of the next succeeding year, the trustee shall, if and when requested in writing so to do by the company, accompanied by a certified copy of a resolution of the board of directors requesting such action, invest such unexpended portion in outstanding bonds secured by this

5

mortgage at the lowest prices reasonably available, not to exceed one hundred and two and one-half per cent. (102½%) of the face value thereof and accrued interest.

All bonds so purchased and held by the trustee as a part of said depreciation fund shall be held by the trustee as valid outstanding bonds secured by this mortgage and entitled to all the security thereof and subject to resale upon the written request of the company, as hereinafter provided. When and as the coupons attached to said bonds respectively mature, the same shall be cut off and canceled by him to the company. All bonds so held by the trustee as part of the depreciation fund shall be delivered to the company by the trustee upon the company's request in writing from time to time, and upon the payment to the trustee of cash equivalent to the average price at which the bonds then forming a part of said fund were purchased, and said bonds, with all unmatured coupons thereto attached, shall thereafter be subject to resale by the company as and when, and at such price or prices as the company may be able to obtain therefor either at public or private sale.

If the facts submitted herewith will enable you to do so, please advise if your reply is now definite.

Following is the supplementary information relative to this question:

In my opinion the bonds are correctly set forth in the balance-sheet as sinking-fund assets at their cost price. If, however, there is any reason to believe that these bonds could not be realized at the price paid and there is no immediate prospect of recovery in price, the bonds should be carried at market. Presumably the mortgage does not contemplate the realization of a loss on the sale of the bonds, but as these are liable to be converted into cash for purposes of replacements at any time, the most conservative method of treatment would be to carry them at their market value, if they have one. Under these circumstances, any loss sustained by sinking-fund assets could hardly be put in amongst the assets and would have to be absorbed out of the company's revenues. Presumably the sinking fund would have to be maintained intact, and if so the amount of loss realized and provided for by charge against revenue would have to be replaced by an equal amount of cash from current funds.

With regard to the accrued interest paid at the time of purchase, this should be carried as a sinking fund asset up to the time when the next coupon matures and is canceled by the trustee and surrendered to the company, at which time the company should reimburse the sinking fund deposit for the amount paid. Interest accruing subsequent to the date of purchase should be charged to accrued interest receivable and credited to non-operating revenues.

DISCOUNTS

Q. Should discount on purchases in a trading concern be shown as additional revenue or as a reduction in the cost?

Should discount on purchases in a manufacturing concern having a cost system be shown as a reduction in the cost of purchases or as additional revenue?

A. Discounts are of two kinds, trade and cash. Usually trade discounts are deducted on the face of the invoice and the bookkeeping entries are made accordingly for the net amount. In regard to so-called "cash discounts," the better practice is to treat such discounts also as deductions from the cost of purchases. The net price, after deducting all discounts, represents the true cost of the goods. If the discount is not taken the

6

loss is a penalty for failure to pay promptly. This principle is recognized in public service classifications where credits to income are made separately for

Sales of (say, gas), net after discount

Forfeited discounts.

For the purposes of a cost system it is, however, scarcely necessary to adjust the individual prices on purchases in respect of genuine cash discounts, as to do so would be a degree of refinement not warranted by the value of the results.

DEPRECIATION

Q. Corporation X has been engaged in manufacturing a specialty for ten years, during which period it has had an average investment in plant and equipment of $500,000. During the first five years it consistently incurred losses which ultimately aggregated $200,000, but during the latter five years it made profits aggregating $250,000. No provision for depreciation was made during the first-mentioned period on the theory, which the corporation insists is sound, that since no profits were made there was no available source from which to provide a reserve for depreciation. During the latter period since profits were actually earned depreciation was written off at an annual rate based upon cost and probable life from date of purchase without in any way reflecting the failure to provide for depreciation in the earlier period.

Query 1. Is it sound accounting to disregard depreciation of plant and equipment in use as a charge to profit-and-loss account in periods when no profits are earned?

2. Is is proper to determine a net loss on profit-and-loss account without making provision for depreciation?

3. Is a balance-sheet prepared during years of deficits properly and correctly prepared if no provision has been made for depreciation?

A. It seems to me clear that depreciation goes on whether a company is making money or losing money. As long as the plant is being operated depreciation takes place. My answers to your inquiries would therefore be as follows:

Query 1. It is not sound accounting to disregard depreciation of plant and equipment in periods when no profits are earned.

2. It is not proper to determine profits without making provision for depreciation.

3. A balance-sheet is not properly prepared if provision is not made for depreciation.

AMOUNTS DUE FROM OFFICERS AND EMPLOYEES

Q. We have had a recent discussion with the officers of a bank in this vicinity as to the propriety of classifying amounts due from officers and employees as current assets. In our opinion such amounts ought to be considered current assets unless the circumstances are such that the amounts are not to be realized in the ordinary course of operations.

We think that it would be clearly a misstatement of fact, and an injustice to the client not to show such items as current assets where there are no peculiar circumstances, because if it is not done, it is easily possible that the client's financial condition will not show the required proportion of net current assets.

A. The library has received the following answer to your question:

In my opinion the amounts due from officers and employees should be considered as current assets, ear-marked, of course, unless they are

7

very much out of the ordinary. I do not think, however, that it is desirable to include them in the "quick assets" if such assets are specifically totaled on the balance-sheet.

OVERHEAD EXPENSES

Q. One of the leading bankers of this city has requested that we get the most authoritative opinion possible on the following problem of distributing overhead expenses:

A motor company has 16 departments, consisting of new cars, accessories, parts, tractors, tractor parts, plows, harrows, harrow parts, repair shop, etc. A number of expenses are chargeable direct to the various departments. The problem is to determine an equitable basis on which to distribute administrative salaries, rent, heat and light, and various other overhead expenses.

Some have suggested that this distribution be made on a basis of sales; others, on a basis of gross profits previously shown; and still others, on a basis of floor space, position of same, time devoted by officers and employees in the various departments.

We would appreciate it if you will turn our letter over to some member of the Institute, whom you think is well qualified to give us a scientific method of distribution from the information given above.

A. My reply to the question must be of a general nature, because any plan for distributing administrative overhead must be based upon a definite knowledge of the functional organization, plant facilities, and operating conditions of the business under consideration.

The usual procedure for distributing administrative expenses in motor companies provides that as great a proportion as possible of the general expenses should be allocated to appropriate departmental burden accounts.

A careful study of the existing conditions will usually suggest fair basis for distributing most of the administrative expenses. The rent and property taxes may be charged to the various departments on a basis of the relative value of the floor space occupied; light and power costs may be distributed upon the number of outlets and rated horse-power requirements of the department, or if greater accuracy is desired, the current used can be measured by simple instruments; fire and compensation insurance may be distributed upon the value of the insurable contents and pay rolls of each department, etc.

The unapportioned balance of the administrative expenses may be then spread upon either the direct labor cost, direct labor hour, or machine hour basis. The basis most commonly used for apportioning the residue of the administrative expenses is the direct labor cost basis. This practice appears to be most popular, principally because it is easily applied and generally understood by manufacturing executives. It is obviously inaccurate where wages for similar classes of work are not fairly uniform in the various departments. In many cases it would be more accurate to use the direct labor hour or machine hour basis.

SPECIAL BINDERS

Binders which were ordered for the convenience of members for filing their library bulletins are ready for sale at the price of $1.25 each.

8

American Institute of Accountants

Library and Bureau of Information

SPECIAL BULLETIN No. 11

December, 1921

[The Committee on Administration of Endowment authorizes the publication of special Bulletins, of which this is one, on the distinct understanding that members are not to consider answers given to questions as being official pronouncements of the Institute, but merely the individual opinions of accountants to whom the questions were referred. It is earnestly requested that members criticise freely and constructively the answers given in this or any other Bulletin of this series.]

BALANCE-SHEETS

Q. We would appreciate an expression of opinion on the following matter, with regard also to these points of view:

    1. The public accountant,
    2. The law in the matter,
    3. The banker.

A partnership operating a manufacturing business decides about December 20 that it will liquidate on December 31. One of the partners at this time contemplates buying the interest of the other partner and incorporating the business, and approaches him regarding the purchase. Various discussions take place, and in the meanwhile inventory is taken December 31. On about January 10 the deal is closed on the basis of the inventory taken and the necessary legal steps completing the incorporation of the succeeding owners are finished about February 1. The corporation assumes all of the assets and liabilities as at January 1 and responsibility for all transactions from this date.

As a basis for establishing a line of credit with the bank the corporation submits its balance-sheet. No inventory was taken after January 1 (inventory is taken at the close of the year, and only once a year, this being the customary time for stock-taking in such business). The balance-sheet submitted, therefore, is as at January 1, all of the foregoing explanations being properly added.

In the light of the above information, has the public accountant the right to present a balance-sheet for the corporation dating it "as at January 1," and supplementing it with a concise statement of the fact that the corporation, although subsequently incorporated, has assumed the business as of this date?

Is it legal in the full sense of the actual and moral or other obligations of the corporation, to practically antedate its operations in the way described (pre-organization transactions, as it were)?

A certain well-known bank objects to this procedure, taking the position that this is entirely wrong and insists that the corporation organized on February 1, 1921, cannot very well show assets and liabilities as at a prior date.

What objections has the bank a right to make when the facts are clearly stated? Both the attorney and the accountant of the corporation proffer such additional information and assistance as the banker may desire.

1

A. The question may not be decided on the basis of any right which the public accountant may or may not have. The question is entirely one of whether or not the presentation of a balance-sheet "as at January 1" when in fact the corporation, the financial condition of which the balance-sheet purports to represent, did not come into existence until February 1, would be in accordance with good accounting practice.

In our opinion from a technical point of view it would not be good practice. A balance-sheet strictly speaking should reflect a condition at a given moment of time. If the time in question were January 1, by no stretch of the imagination could it be construed as February 1 except perchance the condition remained identical until February 1, in which case it would become a balance-sheet of February 1. The statement of facts does not make clear whether or not the transactions intervening between January 1 and February 1 changed the financial condition. The difficulty would appear to be overcome by making it the balance-sheet of the co-partnership and dating it, as a matter of precision, December 31. The bank would then be on notice to inquire as to the happenings during the interval.

From a legal point of view, the proposal to offer the balance-sheet of January 1 as the statement of the corporation coming into existence on February 1 would obviously be wrong, unless as has been stated no change in the financial condition occurred between the two dates, in which case the corporation might adopt the balance-sheet and give it the date of February 1.

The bank has the right to refuse to accept any statement as a basis on which to grant credit and appears to be within such right in the case under consideration. The reason advanced by the bank in exercising its right in this case seems to be founded on a technicality and possibly may not have disclosed the real reason for having refused to consider it.

As a practical matter it would appear that the bank is not willing to rely on the integrity of the statement and is taking advantage of a technicality, since if the statement is correct and sound and the condition has not materially changed since December 31, it would make little difference as to the exact date of the balance-sheet.

ACCOUNTING FOR SPECIAL INDUSTRIES AND TRADES

Q. I would like to secure a list of the trade associations or other bodies which have studied and developed a classification of accounts for specific industries or businesses.

A. The following associations and government departments have made a study of accounting. The addresses given in this list will change frequently in view of the fact that many of the secretaries are elected for one year only. Any additions or corrections will be welcomed.

Chamber of Commerce of the United States of America, Mills Building, Washington, D. C.

Publications: What a Cost System Should Do for You; Overhead Expenses; Cost Accounting Work in Trade Organizations.

2

Illinois Manufacturers' Association. John M. Glenn, secretary, 76 West Monroe street, Chicago, Illinois.
Publications: Preparation and Use of Financial Statements; Reports of Committees on Cost Accounting Procedure; Monthly Bulletin, Illinois Manufacturers' Costs Association.

United States Department of Commerce, Washington, D. C.
Publications: Uniform Contracts and Cost Accounting.

United States Federal Reserve Board, Washington, D. C.
Publications: Approved Methods for the Preparation of Balance-Sheet Statements.

United States Federal Trade Commission, Washington, D. C.
Publications: Fundamentals of a Cost System for Manufacturers.

AGRICULTURAL MACHINERY

National Association of Farm Equipment Manufacturers, 72 West Adams street, Chicago, Illinois. Committee on Manufacturing Costs.
Publications: Uniform Cost Accounting System for Manufacturers of Implements and other Farm Operating Equipment; Cost Systems— Operating Value. These pamphlets were published when the name of this association was National Implement and Vehicle Association.

AGRICULTURE

This work has been done by the United States Department of Agriculture and the various state departments.

United States Federal Board for Vocational Education, Washington, D. C.
Publications: Bookkeeping: Farm Receipts and Expenditures in Single Entry.

ARCHITECTS

Michigan Society of Architects. William Palmer, secretary, 404 Moffat Block, Detroit, Mich.
Publications: Proposed General Accounting and Cost System for the Michigan Society of Architects, Architectural Forum, Jan., 1919, p. 13.

AUTOMOBILES

Iowa State College of Agriculture and Mechanic Arts. Engineering Extension Department, Ames, Iowa.
Publications: Cost Keeping System for the Automobile.

Motor Truck Association of America. T. D. Pratt, general manager, 1819 Broadway, New York.
Publications: Three forms; Highway Transportation, a monthly magazine.

Truck Owners' Conference, Inc. Harold P. Gould, chairman, 5 South Wabash avenue, Chicago, Illinois.

BAKERIES

Fleischmann Company, 699 Washington street, New York.
Publications: Treatise on Increasing Bakery Efficiency by J. E. Wihlfahrt.

3

American Bankers' Association, 5 Nassau street, New York.

United States Federal Reserve Board, Washington, D. C.

BARRELS

Steel Barrel Manufacturers' Association, 855 Leader Building, Cleveland, Ohio.

BELTING

Leather Belting Exchange. Louis W. Arny, secretary, 417-418 Forrest building, 119 South Fourth street, Philadelphia.

Publications: Cost Keeping in the Leather Belting Industry, by W. F. Carroll.

BISCUITS AND CRACKERS

Biscuit and Cracker Manufacturers' Association of America. Edward Griswold, secretary, 90 West Broadway, New York.

Publications: Cost Accounting System.

BOILERS

American Boiler Manufacturers' Association. H. N. Covell, secretary, 191 Dikeman street, Brooklyn, New York.

Publications: Report of cost committee.

BOTTLES

National Bottle Manufacturers' Association of the United States and Canada. C. H. Ferris, secretary, 120 Broadway, New York.

Publications: Uniform Cost System.

BOXES, PACKING CASES, ETC.

National Association of Box Manufacturers. H. L. Pease, secretary, 1553 Conway building, Chicago, Illinois. Cost Accounting Committee.

Publications: Cost Accounting Plan.

BRASS

National Association of Brass Manufacturers, suite 1813-1818 City Hall Square building, Chicago, Illinois.

Publications: How to Figure Costs in the Brass Business; Cost Accounting for Brass Manufacturers.

BRICK-MAKING

American Face Brick Association. R. D. T. Hollowell, secretary, 110 South Dearborn street, Chicago, Illinois.

Publications: Report on Cost Finding.

National Paving Brick Manufacturers' Association. Maurice B. Greenough, secretary, Engineers building, Cleveland, Ohio.

Publications: System of Uniform Cost Finding for Paving Brick Manufacturers.

4

National Association of Building Owners and Managers, Republic building, Chicago, Illinois.

Publications: Condensed Report of the Committee on Accounting and Exchange.

CANNING AND PRESERVING

National Canners' Association. F. E. Gorrel, secretary, 1739 H street, N.W., Washington, D. C. Standing Committee on Accounting.

Publications: Classification of Accounts; Standard Classification of Accounts; Cost Accounting Committee.

CANS

American Can Company, 120 Broadway, New York.

Publications: Plan of Cost Accounting for General Line Factories.

CAR WHEELS

Association of Manufacturers of Chilled Car Wheels. George W. Lyndon, president, 1847 McCormick building, Chicago, Illinois.

Publications: Uniform Cost Accounting System.

CASKETS

Casket Manufacturers' Association of America. John M. Byrne, secretary, 308 Odd Fellows' Temple, Cincinnati, Ohio.

A survey of the casket manufacturing industry was made some years ago and as a result of the survey, certain uniform principles to govern cost compilations were made. No written instructions nor descriptive matter has ever been prepared. All installations are made under oral instructions.

CEMENT

Portland Cement Association. F. L. Page, secretary, 111 W. Washington street, Chicago, Illinois.

Publications: Cost Accounting (not available for distribution).

CHEESE

Wisconsin Agricultural Experiment Station, Madison, Wisconsin.

Publications: Cheesemakers Save by Figuring Costs, by J. L. Sammis and O. A. Juve.

CLEANING

National Association of Dyers and Cleaners, 3723 Olive street, St. Louis, Missouri.

The system is still in its initial stage.

CLOTHING

International Association of Garment Manufacturers, 320 Broadway, New York.

Publications: Uniform Cost Accounting System.

5

National Cloak, Suit and Skirt Manufacturers' Association, 310-311 New England building, Cleveland, Ohio.
Publications: Cost Finding in the Cloak and Suit Industry.
United States Bureau of Foreign and Domestic Commerce, Washington, D. C.
The following reports contain chapters on cost accounting: Men's Factory-made Clothing Industry; Women's Muslin-underwear Industry; Shirt and Collar Industries.

CLOTHING TRADE

National Association of Retail Clothiers. Charles E. Wry, executive director, Brooks building, 223 W. Jackson boulevard, Chicago, Illinois.
At the last annual convention a resolution for the establishing of a research and efficiency bureau was adopted.

COAL TRADE

Chicago Coal Merchants' Association, 10th floor, Plymouth building, 417 South Dearborn street, Chicago, Illinois.
Publications: Accounting System.
United States Fuel Administration, Washington, D. C.
Publications: System of Accounts for Retail Coal Dealers, November 1, 1917.
University of Washington, Seattle, Washington.
Publications: Cost Accounting for Retail Fuel Dealers, by William E. Cox.

COFFEE

National Coffee Roasters' Association. Felix Coste, manager, 74 Wall street, New York.
Publications: Columbia University School of Business, Department of Accounting, Division of Research. N.C.R.A. Report Forms.

CONCRETE

Concrete Products Association. Wallace R. Harris, secretary, 542-55 Monadnock block, 53 W. Jackson boulevard, Chicago, Illinois.
Publications: Report of the Cost Accounting Committee.

CONFECTIONERY

Midland Club. A. H. Newman, secretary, 1306 Garland building, Wabash avenue and Washington street, Chicago, Illinois.
Publications: Official Cost Accounting and Cost Finding Plan Designed and Prepared for Manufacturing Confectioners.
National Confectioners' Association of the United States, 1921 Conway building, 111 W. Washington street, Chicago, Illinois.
Publications: Cost Manual; in cooperation with the officials of the Midland Club a more complete manual has been adopted.

6

Aberthaw Construction Company, 27 School street, Boston, Mass.
  Publications: Construction Costs, by W. N. Connor; reprinted from the
  Journal of the Boston Society of Civil Engineers, May, 1921.

COOPERATIVE STORES AND SOCIETIES

Co-operative League of America, 2 West 13th street, New York.
  Publications: Co-operative Accounting, by Ernest C. Cheel; System of
  Accounts for a Small Consumers' Co-operative, by E. R. Browder;
  Co-operative Accounting, by P. G. Ward.

United States Department of Agriculture, Washington, D. C.
  Publications: Business Practice and Accounts for Co-operative Stores,
  by J. A. Bexell and W. H. Kerr; Co-operative Organization Business
  Methods, by W. H. Kerr and G. A. Nahstoll.

COOPERS

Associated Cooperage Industries of America. V. W. Krafft, secretary,
  B20 Railway Exchange building, St. Louis, Missouri.
  Publications: Cost Charts and Distribution Sheets.

COTTON

United States Department of Agriculture, Washington, D. C.
  Publications: System of Accounting for Cotton Ginners, by A. V.
  Swarthout and J. A. Bexell.

COTTON MILLS

National Association of Finishers of Cotton Fabrics. Harry E. Danner,
  secretary, 320 Broadway, New York.
  Publications: Report on Uniform Cost Accounting; Preliminary Survey
  for a Uniform Cost System.

CREAMERIES

Iowa State College of Agriculture and Mechanic Arts, Agricultural Experiment Station, Ames, Iowa.
  Publications: Creamery Bookkeeping, by M. Mortensen.

United States Department of Agriculture, Washington, D. C.
  Publications: Accounting Records for Country Creameries, by J. R.
  Humphrey and W. H. Kerr; Classification of Ledger Accounts for
  Creameries, by G. O. Knapp, B. B. Mason and A. V. Swarthout.

CREDIT

National Association of Credit Men. John Whyte, director of research,
  41 Park Row, New York.
  Publications: Forms Adopted and Recommended.

DAIRYING

Dairymen's League Co-operative Association, Inc. H. C. Crombie, comptroller, Utica, New York.
  This association is working on a chart of accounts.

7

Harvard University, Graduate School of Business Administration, Bureau of Business Research, Cambridge, Massachusetts.
Publications: Operating Accounts for Retail Drug Stores; Operating Expenses in Retail Drug Stores in 1919.

National Wholesale Druggists' Association. C. H. Waterbury, secretary, 99 Nassau street, New York.
Publications: Forms recommended by the committee on uniform accounting.

DRUGS

American Pharmaceutical Manufacturers' Association. Ralph R. Patch, secretary, room 570, 32 Liberty street, New York.
Have a committee on costs and overhead who report at the annual meeting. This report is incorporated in the Proceedings.

DRY GOODS

Controllers' Congress, National Retail Dry Goods Association. D. E. Moeser, secretary, 27 Winter street, Boston, Massachusetts.
Publications: Committee on the Standardization of Retail Store Accounting and Practice; Reports and Digest of the Proceedings; Recommendations of the Committee.

Retail Research Association. Paul H. Nystrom, director, 225 Fifth avenue, New York.
The National Retail Dry Goods Association through its Controllers' Standardization Committee has developed uniform account classifications and practically all of the stores are following the N.R.D.G.A. classification. A manual that will prescribe the manner in which the stores will report to this office their sales figures at regular intervals is being prepared. The only other accounting data are suggestions and recommendations made by the controllers who make office and accounting studies in each store. Practically all of this work is of a confidential nature.

DYEING

National Association of Dyers and Cleaners, 3723 Olive Street, St. Louis, Missouri.
The system is still in its initial stage.

DYES

American Dyes Institute. W. R. Corwine, secretary, 132 West 42nd street, New York.
Publications: Uniform Cost Accounting Methods.

ELECTRIC AND STREET RAILROADS

American Electric Railway Association, 8 West 40th street, New York.
Publications: Proceedings; Pamphlets on Special Subjects

8

National Association of Electrical Contractors and Dealers. Farguson Johnson, secretary, 15 West 37th street, New York. Accounting Committee.

Publications: Have issued the following advertising pamphlets which are sent to members advertising the Standard accounting system: Standard Accounting System for Contractors and Dealers in the Electrical Industry, pt. 1, What It Is and How to Use It; pt. 2, Supplementary Pamphlet of Explanation with brief description handling notes, trade acceptances and work in progress account.

ELECTRIC LIGHT AND POWER COMPANIES

National Electric Light Association, 29 West 39th street, New York.
Publications: Standard Classification of Accounts; Proceedings.

ELECTRIC SHOPS

Delco-Light Company. R. D. Funkhouser, treasurer, Dayton, Ohio.
Publications: Bookkeeping System for Delco-Light Dealers.

ELECTRICAL MACHINERY AND EQUIPMENT

Electrical Manufacturers' Council. Frederick Nicholas, secretary, 522 Fifth avenue, New York.

Committee on Standardization of Accounting and Cost System for the Electrical Manufacturing Industry, S. L. Whitestone, c/o General Electric Co., Schenectady, New York.

Publications: Standard Accounting and Cost System for the Electrical Manufacturing Industry.

Machinery Builders' Society. James C. Bennett, Chairman of the Council of Accountants. Westinghouse Electric & Manufacturing Company, 165 Broadway, New York.

Publications: Copies of the standard cost system will be available about January 1st.

FLAVORING EXTRACTS

Flavoring Extract Manufacturers' Association of the United States. F. P. Beers, president, Earlville, N. Y.

Publications: Circular No. 70, Revised Cost System or Cost Committee's Report.

FLOUR MILLS

United States Food Administration, Milling Division.
Publications: Suggested Accounting System for Wheat Flour Millers.

FOUNDRIES

American Foundrymen's Association. C. E. Hoyt, secretary, Marquette building, 140 South Dearborn street, Chicago, Illinois. Standing committee on foundry costs.

Publications: Standard Foundry Cost System.

9

American Malleable Castings Association. Robert E. Belt, secretary, 1900 Euclid building, Cleveland, Ohio.
Publications: Uniform Cost Accounting Methods, by Robert E. Belt.

National Founders' Association. J. M. Taylor, secretary, 29 South La Salle street, Chicago, Illinois.
Publications: Service Bureau Bulletins.

Steel Founders' Society of America. Thomas C. Pears, secretary, 511 Magee building, Pittsburgh, Pennsylvania.
Publications: Report of Committee on Costs.

FRUIT SHIPPING ASSOCIATIONS

United States Department of Agriculture, Washington, D. C.
Publications: System of Accounting for Cooperative Fruit Associations, by G. A. Nahstoll and W. H. Kerr.

FURNITURE

National Association of Chair Manufacturers, Gardner, Massachusetts.
Publications: Uniform Plan of Cost Accounting Control.

National Association of Upholstered Furniture Manufacturers, suite 1600, 110 South Dearborn street, Chicago, Illinois.
Publications: Uniform Trial Balance upon which the accounting system has been built.

FURNITURE, METALLIC

National Association of Steel Furniture Manufacturers. J. D. M. Phillips, secretary, Engineers building, Cleveland, Ohio.
Publications: Uniform Cost Accounting for the Steel Furniture Industry, by E. W. Kath.

GAS

American Gas Association. H. W. Hartmann, secretary, 130 East 15th street, New York.
Committees: Uniform Classification of Accounts; Standard Uniform Accounting Nomenclature; Job Order Systems; Office Labor-saving Devices; Continuous Inventory of Fixed Capital; Fire-insurance Rates.
Publications: Uniform Classification of Accounts.

Natural Gas Association of America. William B. Way, secretary, Oliver building, Pittsburgh, Pennsylvania.
Publications: The Uniform Classification of Accounts for Natural Gas Companies has been adopted by the state of Pennsylvania.

GLASS

National Ornamental Glass Manufacturers' Association of the United States and Canada. Charles C. Jacoby, secretary, 2700 St. Vincent avenue, St. Louis, Missouri.
Publications: Accounting forms have appeared in the Bulletins.

United States Bureau of Foreign and Domestic Commerce, Washington,D.C.
Publications: The "Glass Industry" contains a chapter on accounting.

10

United States Department of Agriculture, Washington, D. C.
Publications: Lumber Accounting and Opening the Books in Primary Grain Elevators,' by J. R. Humphrey and W. H. .Kerr; System of Accounts for Farmers' Cooperative Elevators, by J. R. Humphrey and W. H. Kerr; System of Accounts for Primary Grain Elevators, by J. R. Humphrey and W. H. Kerr; System of Bookkeeping for Grain Elevators, by B. B. Mason, Frank Robotka and A. V. Swarthout.

GROCERY TRADE

Harvard University, Graduate School of Business Administration, Bureau of Business Research, Cambridge, Massachusetts.
Publications: Expense in Operating Retail Grocery Stores; Harvard System of Accounts for Retail Grocers; Management Problems in Retail Grocery Stores; Methods of Paying Salesmen and Operating Expenses in the Wholesale Grocery Business; Operating Expenses in Retail Grocery Stores; Operating Expenses in the Wholesale Grocery Business; Operating Expenses in the Wholesale Grocery Business in 1919; System of Operating Accounts for Wholesale Grocers; Operating Expenses in the Wholesale Grocery Business in 1920; Wholesale Grocery Business in January, 1921.

HARDWARE TRADE

Associated Advertising Clubs of the World, 110 West 40th street, New York
Publications: Business Record Systems Book of Instructions for Retail Hardware Dealers.
Harvard University, Graduate School of Business Administration, Bureau of Business Research, Cambridge, Massachusetts.
Publications: Operating Expenses in Retail Hardware Stores; System of Operating Accounts for Hardware Retailers.
National Pipe and Supplies Association. G. D. McIlvaine, secretary, 908-9 Oliver building, Pittsburgh, Pennsylvania.
Publications: Cost Distribution Sheet.

HEALTH DEPARTMENTS

American Public Health Association. A. W. Hedrick, secretary, 370 Seventh avenue, New York.
Publications: The report of the Committee on Uniform Administrative Accounting for Health Departments, American Journal of Public Health, July, 1916.

HEATING

Illinois Public Utilities Commission, Springfield, Illinois.
Publications: Uniform System of Accounts for Heating Utilities.
Missouri Public Service Commission, Jefferson City, Missouri.
Publications: General Order No. 15 in the Matter of a Uniform System of Accounts for Heating Companies.

11

National Association of Ice Industries, 18 East 41st street, New York.

ICE CREAM

National Association of Ice Cream Manufacturers, foot of White street, Rochester, New York.
Publications: Uniform Cost Accounting System for Ice Cream Manufacturers.

INSTITUTIONS

Illinois Efficiency and Economy Committee, Springfield, Illinois.
Publications: Report on Accounting Administration for Correctional Institutions, by Spurgeon Bell.

INSURANCE

United States Department of Agriculture, Washington, D. C.
Publications: System of Records for Local Farmers' Mutual Fire Insurance Companies, by V. N. Valgren.

JEWELRY TRADE

Associated Advertising Clubs of the World, 110 West 40th street, New York.
Publications: Business Record Systems Book of Instructions for Retail Jewelry Merchants.
Harvard University, Graduate School of Business Administration, Bureau of Business Research, Cambridge, Massachusetts.
Publications: Operating Accounts for Retail Jewelry Stores.
Jewelers' Research Bureau, American National Retail Jewelers' Association. H. V. Wright, director, 439 South Broadway, Los Angeles, California.
Publications: Complete Manual of Operating Accounts; The Results of the Investigations Are to Be Found in Bulletins Published by the Harvard Bureau of Business Research.

KNIT GOODS

National Knitted Underwear Association. Bernard Steuer, secretary, 321 Broadway, New York.
Working on a uniform cost classification and data.
United States Bureau of Foreign and Domestic Commerce, Washington,D.C.
The following reports contain chapters on accounting: Knit Underwear Industry; Hosiery Industry.

LAUNDRIES

Laundryowners' National Association, Department of Cost Accounting, Drawer 202, La Salle, Illinois. This association has a cost committee, the duties of which are to establish cost accounting systems in plants of the members.
Publications: Special Bulletins; Manual of Instruction for the Installation and Operation of the Standardized System of Cost Accounting. During this year they expect to issue a couple of pamphlets enlarging upon some of the subjects taken up in the manual.

12

National Council Lighting Fixture Manufacturers. Charles A. Hofrichter, secretary, 231-233 Gordon Square building, Detroit avenue and west 65th street, Cleveland, Ohio. Cost Accounting Committee.

LIME

National Lime Association, 918 G street, N.W., Washington, D. C.
Publications: Uniform Cost Accounting System for the Lime Industry; v. 1, Analysis Sheet Method for the Small Manufacturer; v. 2, Cost Ledger Method for the Large Manufacturer; sup. 1, Analysis Sheet Method for the Small Manufacturer; sup. 2, Cost Ledger Method for the Large Manufacturer.

LITHOGRAPHY

National Association of Employing Lithographers, 39 State street, Rochester, New York.
Publications: Cost Manual.

LIVESTOCK

American National Livestock Association. John W. Springer, secretary, 515 Cooper building, Denver, Colorado.
Publications: Livestock Accounting, by E. D. Newman, Proceedings, 1921, p. 60.

LIVESTOCK SHIPPING ASSOCIATIONS

United States Department of Agriculture, Washington, D. C.
Publications: System of Accounts for Livestock Shipping Associations, by J. R. Humphrey and W. H. Kerr.
Wisconsin Agricultural Experiment Station, Madison, Wisconsin.
Publications: System of Accounts for Livestock Shipping Associations, by C. N. Wilson; Wisconsin Livestock Shipping Associations, by B. H. Hibbard, L. G. Foster and D. G. Davis.

LUMBER

British Columbia Lumber and Shingle Manufacturers, Ltd., 917 Metropolitan building, Vancouver, B. C.
Publications: Lumber Production Costs in Grades, by W. R. Steer.
California White and Sugar Pine Manufacturers' Association. Stovell Smith, secretary, New Call building, San Francisco, California.
An accounting system was prepared under the direction of a committee authorized by the board of directors.
New York Lumber Trade Association. H. B. Coho, secretary, 17 West 46th street, New York. Evening classes for the benefit of members.
Publications: Extract from paper of W. S. Beckley presented to the New York Lumber Trade Association at their meeting, Tuesday, October 21, 1919.
North Carolina Pine Association. Vaughan Camp, secretary, Norfolk, Va.
Publications: Manual of Cost Reporting.
Southern Pine Association. J. E. Rhodes, secretary, New Orleans, La.
Publications: Uniform Statement of Logs Stock Accounts.

13

United States Department of Agriculture, Washington, D. C.
   Publications: Lumber Accounting and Opening the Books in Primary Grain Elevators, by J. R. Humphrey and W. H. Kerr.
West Coast Lumbermen's Association, Seattle, Washington; Portland, Oregon, Grand Central Terminal, New York.
   Publications: Uniform Cost Accounting System.

MACHINE TOOL INDUSTRY

National Machine Tool Builders' Association. Ernest F. Du Brul, general manager, 817 Provident Bank Building, Cincinnati, Ohio.
   Publications: Uniform Cost System; Preliminary Report.

METAL WORK

Mr. Richard Appel, secretary of the Rolling Steel Door Association, Hollow Metal Door Society, Institute of Electrical Contractors, National Council of Lighting Fixture Manufacturers—New York Division, Institute of Lighting Fixture Manufacturers, 103 Park avenue, New York, has issued the following charts: Graphic Presentation of a Detailed Analysis of the Cost of Goods Sold; Graphic Presentation of a Detailed Analysis of Selling Costs and Their Relations to the Selling Price.

Architectural Iron and Bronze Manufacturers. W. A. Morrison, secretary, 331 Madison avenue, New York. This association has a standing committee on cost accounting but has never adopted a uniform classification of accounts.

Metal Finishers Equipment Association. Franz Neilson, secretary, 85 Nassau street, New York.
   The committee has not completed its final report.

National Association of Sheet Metal Contractors of the United States. Edwin L. Seabrook, secretary, 608 Chestnut street, Philadelphia, Pa. Committee on overhead expense.
   Publications: Form for Ascertaining the Cost of Conducting Business or Overhead; Overhead Expense Committee Report, Milwaukee convention.

MINING AND METALLURGY

American Zinc Institute. Stephen S. Tuthill, secretary, 27 Cedar street, New York.
   Publications: 1921 Bulletin, page 30—paper by George W. Potter.

Consolidation Coal Company, 67 Wall street, New York.
   Publications: Classification of Accounts.

National Coal Association. W. B. Reed, secretary, Commercial Bank building, Washington, D. C.
   Publications: Report and Suggestions of Committee on Standard System of Accounting and Analysis of Cost of Production; Articles in Coal Review.

14

United States Bureau of Mines, Washington, D. C.
   Publications: Cost Keeping for Small Metal Mines, by J. C. Pickering;
   Report of the Committee on the Standardization of Mining Statistics.
United States Federal Trade Commission, Washington, D. C.
   Publications: Instructions for Compiling Report on Cost, Income and
   Tonnage . . . Coal or Lignite Operators . . .

MOVING PICTURES

Goldwyn Pictures Corporation, 469 Fifth avenue, New York.
   Publications: Manual of Goldwyn Branch Operations.

MUSIC TRADE

Music Industries Chamber of Commerce, 105 West 40th street, New York.
   The News Trade Service Bureau is making an inquiry into problems
   of cost figuring as applied to music merchandising. Nothing has
   been issued.

OIL REFINERIES

United States Federal Trade Commission, Washington, D. C.
   Publications: General Schedule for Refiners.

OILS

United States Bureau of Mines, Washington, D. C.
   Publications: Cost Accounting for Oil Producers, by C. G. Smith.

OPTICIANS

American Association of Wholesale Opticians. Guy Henry, secretary,
   Times building, New York. Cost accounting committee.
   Publications: A Suggested Aid for Keeping Tab on Accounts which
   Require Special Watching; Bulletins; Standard Cost Accounting
   System.

PACKING

Institute of American Meat Packers. C. B. Heinemann, secretary, 22 West
   Monroe street, Chicago, Illinois.
   Publications: Tentative Draft of Proposed Accounting Instructions on
   the Hog Business; Theory of Packing House Accounting; Suggested
   Methods of Handling Plant Operating Income and Expense Accounts;
   Tentative Draft of Proposed Accounting Instructions on the Cattle
   Business.

PAINT, VARNISH, ETC.

Paint Manufacturers' Association of the United States. George B. Heckel,
   secretary, 636 The Bourse, Philadelphia, Pennsylvania.
   Publications: Uniform Cost Methods.

15

Cost Association of the Paper Industry. Thomas J. Burke, secretary, 18 East 41st street, New York. The American Paper and Pulp Association is the parent association, while the technical and cost associations are service associations affiliated with them. All accounting matters are dealt with through the cost association of the paper industry.

Publications: A Budget Cost System for Paper Mills; Bulletins.

Newsprint Service Bureau, 342 Madison avenue, New York.

The cost keeping committee includes various officials and accountants of those companies who are members.

Publications: Cost Keeping for Newsprint Paper Mills; Grade Costs; Idle Time Cost, How Determined in a Newsprint Paper Mill.

Wrapping Paper Manufacturers' Service Bureau. A. J. Stewartson, secretary, 2 Rector street, New York.

Publications: Code of Accounts; Uniform Method of Cost Keeping.

PAPER TRADE

National Paper Trade Association of the United States. William C. Ridgway, secretary, 41 Park Row, New York.

Publications: Standard Classification of Expense.

PLUMBING

Heating and Piping Contractors' National Association, Inc. Henry B. Gombers, secretary, 50 Union Square, East, New York. Formerly the name of this association was the National Association of Master Steam and Hot Water Fitters.

Publications: Confidential Instructions, Standardized Accounting and Cost Keeping System; Overhead in Business, by W. L. Fleisher; A Brief Message for Your Conference Committee.

POULTRY

United States Department of Agriculture, Washington, D. C.

Publications: System of Poultry Accounting, by R. R. Slocum.

PRINTING

United Typothetae of America, 608 South Dearborn street, Chicago, Illinois.

Publications: Standard Accounting System for Printers; Standard Cost Finding System; Treatise on the Standard Accounting System for Printers; Report of the American Printers' Cost Commission.

PUBLIC UTILITIES

Uniform classifications of the Government and various states.

RAILROADS

Bureau of Railroad Economics, 429 Homer building, Washington, D. C.

Railway Accounting Officers' Association. E. R. Woodson, secretary, 1116 Woodward building, Washington, D. C.

REFRACTORIES

Refractories Accountants' Institute. W. J. Westphalen, chairman, Laclede-Christy Clay Products Company, Accounting Department, St. Louis, Missouri.

16

National Association of Credit Men, 41 Park Row, New York.
  Have a business service committee which takes up retail accounting.
United States Federal Trade Commission, Washington, D. C.
  Publications: System of Accounts for Retail Merchants.

ROADS AND HIGHWAYS

Oregon State Highway Commission, Portland, Oregon.
  Publications: Manual for Cost Keeping and Accounting.
Philadelphia Bureau of Highways and Street Cleaning, Philadelphia, Pennsylvania.
  Publications: Highway Report, 1914, p. 85.
United States Department of Agriculture, Washington, D. C.
  Publications: Highway Cost Keeping by J. J. Tobin and A. R. Losh.

ROLLING MILLS

National Association of Sheet and Tin Plate Manufacturers. Walter W. Lower, secretary, Oliver building, Pittsburgh, Pennsylvania. Each month blank cost sheets are supplied to members, who fill them in and return. A complete report is issued.
  Publications: Standard Card of Accounts Sheet Mills.

RUBBER-PROOFING

Rubber Association of America, Inc., 52 Vanderbilt avenue, New York. Accounting Committee.
  Publications: Recommended Plan of Cost Accounting Control for the Members of the Rubber Proofers' Division.

SCHOOLS, COLLEGES, ETC.

American Association of University Instructors in Accounting. E. J. Filbey, secretary, University of Illinois, Urbana, Illinois.
  Publications: Papers and Proceedings.
United States Bureau of Census, Washington, D. C.
  Publications: Standard Form in Reporting the Financial Statistics of Public Schools.

SHIPBUILDING

Atlantic Coast Shipbuilders' Association. Henry C. Hunter, secretary, 30 Church street, New York.
  Publications: Cost Accounting in Shipbuilding.
United States Shipping Board, Emergency Fleet Corporation, Washington, D. C.
  Publications: Cost-plus Contracts: Cost Analysis from Wooden Ships.

SHIPS AND SHIPPING

United States Interstate Commerce Commission, Washington, D. C.
  Publications: Uniform Classifications.
United States Shipping Board, Emergency Fleet Corporation, Washington, D. C.
  Publications: Classification of Accounts to be Used in Accounting to the United States for Requisitioned Vessels Operated for Government Accounts.

17

Associated Advertising Clubs of the World, 110 West 40th street, New York.

Publications: Business Record Systems Book. of Instructions for Retail Shoe Merchants.

Harvard University, Graduate School of Business Administration. Bureau of Business Research, Cambridge, Massachusetts.

Publications: Depreciation in the Retail Shoe Business; Harvard System of Accounts for Shoe Retailers; Harvard System of Accounts for Shoe Wholesalers; Harvard System of Stock Keeping for Shoe Retailers; Management Problems in Retail Shoe Stores.

National Shoe Retailers' Association of the United States of America, Inc. T. C. Mirkil, secretary, 501-503 Franklin Trust building, Philadelphia, Pennsylvania. Working with the Bureau of Business Research, Harvard University.

Publications: Bulletins.

SILVERWARE

Sterling Silverware Manufacturers' Association. Frederick S. Taggart, secretary, Silversmith's building, 15 Maiden Lane, New York.

Publications: Standardized Cost Accounting System for the Sterling Silverware Industry.

STOKERS

Stoker Manufacturers Association. J. G. Worker, secretary, Phoenix Manufacturing Co., Eau Claire, Wisconsin.

M. V. Sauter, American Engineering Co., Philadelphia, Pa., is chairman of the cost accounting committee.

STOVES

National Association of Stove Manufacturers. R. S. Wood, secretary, 508 National State Bank building, Troy, New York.

Publications: Cost Manual.

National Warm Air Heating and Ventilating Association. Allen W. Williams, secretary, Columbia building, Columbus, Ohio.

Publications: Cost Formula for Warm Air Heaters.

SUGAR

United States Federal Trade Commission, Washington, D. C.

Publications: Report on the Beet Sugar Industry in the United States.

TANNING

Tanners' Council of the United States of America. Roland H. Zinn, chief, Cost Accounting Bureau, 41 Park Row, New York. Formulating and eventually expect to adopt a uniform method of cost accounting in the various groups of this industry.

TOYS

Toy Manufacturers of the United States of America. Fletcher D. Dodge, secretary, Flatiron building, New York. Committee on Cost Accounting.

18

National Implement and Vehicle Association of the United States of America, 76 West Monroe street, Chicago, Illinois.
Publications: Uniform Cost Accounting System for Manufacturers of Implements and Other Farm Operating Equipment.

WAREHOUSES

American Warehousemen's Association. Charles L. Criss, secretary, 1110 Bessemer building, Pittsburgh, Pennsylvania.
Publications: Cost Finding for Warehousemen by Chester B. Carruth and H. I. Jacobson; Report of Uniform Methods Accounting Systems, Committee of the Household Goods Subdivision; Proceedings, 1919; Bulletins; Standardization of Basis for Rates.

Maine Public Utilities Commission, Augusta, Maine.
Publications: Uniform Classification of Accounts for Warehousemen.

Wisconsin Division of Markets, Madison, Wis.
Publications: System of Accounts for Coöperative Warehouses.

United States Department of Agriculture, Washington, D. C.
Publications: System of Accounts for Cotton Warehouses by R. L. Newton and J. R. Humphrey.

WATERWORKS

American Waterworks Association. J. M. Diven, secretary, 47 State street, Troy, N. Y.

New England Waterworks Association. Frank J. Gifford, secretary, 715 Tremont Temple, Boston, Massachusetts.
Publications: First Report to the New England Waterworks Association of the Committee on Uniform Accounting; Journal, March, 1921.

WHARVES

Maine Public Utilities Commission, Augusta, Maine.
Publications: Uniform Classification of Accounts for Wharfingers.

WOODWORK

Eastern Woodworkers' Cost Information Bureau. E. F. Hunt, secretary, 103 Park avenue, New York.
Publications: Stabilizing an Industry.

Millwork Cost Bureau. W. P. Flint, secretary, 11 South La Salle street, Chicago, Illinois. This bureau is a coöperative association of sash, door and millwork manufacturers, organized not for profit, but for the purpose of supplying the members with methods whereby they may ascertain their cost of manufacture.
Publications: Are You Applying Burden Properly?; A Review of Burden Applications Prepared by Millwork Cost Information Bureau, Chicago, Illinois, reprinted from Sash-Door-Finish, September, 1920

19

Referring to Special Bulletin No. 10, page 3, under Non-Par-Value Shares, the following comment has been received:

The answer to the question was predicated on the assumption that the reorganization constituted merely a change in the form of capital stock, namely, from stock with par value to stock without par value. On such assumption, there appears to be no reason for revising the previous answer to the question.

If, however, reorganization means effecting a new legal organization, it is probable that the answer should be amended. The successor corporation under such circumstances would probably acquire the net assets of the predecessor corporation and the value of the net assets would fix the amount of the capital with which the successor corporation would begin business.

There is considerable doubt in the minds of many accountants and lawyers as to the possibility of acquiring by purchase or otherwise the surplus of one corporation by another. It is undoubtedly possible in the case of a merger for one corporation to acquire and merge with its own, the surplus of another corporation. It is also probable that in one case, where the balance-sheet of a predecessor corporation was incorporated in and made a part of the contract of sale, the successor corporation did, in fact, purchase and acquire the surplus of the predecessor corporation. This is, of course, an unusual case and constitutes an exception to the rule.

The point is made by some accountants that a new corporation acquiring the net assets of another corporation has no earned surplus. This view probably prevails generally and if accepted, would preclude the possibility in the case of a legal reorganization of setting up a surplus account on the new books.

To sum up, it appears that where reorganization consists merely in changing the form of the capital stock, there is no reason for combining the surplus with the capital. But where a new legal organization is effected, the best practice is to combine the surplus with the par value of the capital stock or in other words, ignore any division of the net asset value and show the capital of the new corporation in an amount equal to the value of the net assets acquired. There seems to be no purpose served in the first case in restricting the surplus at the time of change from par to non-par stock or to record the surplus as special or capital surplus. The form of capital stock should have no effect upon the surplus in so far as it is available for distribution as dividends. The surplus may, however, be affected if the amount of stated capital with which the corporation agrees to carry on business is in excess of the amount of capital represented by the outstanding issues of stock with par value.

AUTOMOBILE INSURANCE COMPANIES

Q. I would like to know the most approved method of handling the accounting for and the records best adapted to an automobile insurance company, the main accounting problems of which are involved in the following data:

Risks covered:
Fire
Theft
Property damage
Public liability
Collision.

Initial fees:
A per capita and listing fee is paid with application.

20

Premiums (assessments):
    Assessments are levied monthly. The Total assessments levied are obtained by adding to the losses in each class of risks a percentage for expenses.
Method of arriving at rate of assessment:
    The value of each car insured is divided into $100.00 units.
    The rate for each class is obtained by dividing the total assessment in the class by the total number of units in that class.
Surplus:
    A surplus is to be established by an additional assessment based on horse-power without considering class of risk.

A. We are submitting herewith a list of the financial records with an explanation of the functions of each together with a chart of accounts which we have found suitable for an automobile insurance company.

We are reliably informed that it would not be possible for a company to procure permission from the insurance departments of many states to conduct an automobile insurance business employing the method of arriving at assessment rates stated in your inquiry.

The principal general ledger accounts necessary to reflect the activities of the business and to collect the statistical information required annually by state insurance departments are as follows:

Asset accounts:
    Cash in banks and trust companies
    Petty cash funds
    Premiums receivable
    Premium notes receivable
    Investment securities
    Interest due and accrued.

Liabilities and reserves:
    Reserve for unearned premiums
    "   "   losses
    "   "   reinsurance
    "   "   expenses incurred
    "   "   taxes
    "   "   dividends declared
    "   "   unadmitted assets
    Profit and loss
    Surplus

Profit-and-loss accounts:
                EARNINGS
    Net premiums written
    Earned premiums
    Interest on investment securities
    Interest on deposits
    Interest on notes receivable
    Accumulation of discount on investment securities
    Uncollectible premiums recovered
    Gain on sale of investment securities
    *Initial fees

*This account is set up on the assumption that initial fees are to be retained by the company whether or not a policy is issued.

21

LOSSES

Losses paid
General expenses
Taxes
Loss on sale of investment securities
Reinsurance premiums
Interest paid on investments
Amortization of premium paid on investment securities
Uncollectible premiums written off

It is important to note that the reserves for unearned premiums and losses are based on statutory requirements and must be computed in accordance with the law.

Unadmitted assets consist of the following:

Premiums receivable over 90 days old
Premium notes receivable over 90 days old
Accrued interest on notes taken for premiums receivable over 90 days old
Accrued interest on bonds in default
Decrease of securities from book value to values based on prices fixed by the state insurance department.
Loans to employees.

The books of record are listed below:

Policy register and premium journal
Endorsement register
Policies not taken and cancelation register
Cash receipts book
Cash disbursements book
Policy holders' ledger
General ledger
Dividend journal (mutual companies)
General journal
Statistical record

Entries to the policy register and premium journal are based upon the information furnished by the assured in the policy declaration. The left-hand page of the journal contains columns for:

Number of policy
Date of commencement
Name of assured
Initial premium

and the right-hand page contains columns for the distribution of the initial premium, viz.:

Fire
Theft
Property damage
Public liability
Collision

From the premium journal the initial premium is posted to the debit of the policy holder's account. At the end of the month the total of the

22

initial premium is carried into the general ledger controlling account by the following entry:

Premiums receivable
    Net premiums written
To record net premiums written during the month.

The purpose of the endorsement register is to record subsequent endorsements on the policy which either increase or decrease the initial premium. At the end of the month if there is a net decrease it is charged to Net Premiums written and credited to Premiums Receivable or vice versa in case of a net increase.

The title of the policies not taken and cancelation register indicates the character of the entries contained in that book. State insurance departments, however, require that the amount of return premiums from these two causes be shown separately, so that separate columns for policies not taken and policies canceled are necessary in this register. The total at the end of the month is brought into the controlling account by the following entry:

Net premiums written
    Premiums receivable
To record policies not taken, and the return premium on policies canceled during the month.

The remaining books of record are self explanatory.

The closing entries at the end of the year consist of the following:

Net premiums written
    Earned premiums
To transfer net premiums written for the year
Earned premiums
    Reinsurance premiums
To transfer reinsurance incurred during the year
Interest on investment securities
    Interest paid on investment securities
To close the latter account

Earned premiums	$(Amount unearned)	
Losses	(Amount of reserve)	
General expenses (excluding taxes)	(Amount due and unpaid)	
Taxes	(Amount due and accrued)	
Reinsurance	(Amount due and unpaid)	
Dividends	(Dividends declared and unpaid)	
Reserves	$	(Total of above)

To set up reserves as at end of year
Interest due and accrued
    Interest on investment securities
    Interest on deposits
    Interest on premium notes receivable
For interest due and accrued at end of year
Investment securities
    Accumulation of bond discount

23

For amortization of bond premiums and accumulation of bond discount

Accumulation .... $

  Less: Amortization .... _____

             $

Earned premiums
Interest on investment securities
Interest on deposits
Interest on notes receivable
Accumulation of bond discount
Uncollectible premiums recovered
Gain on sale of investment securities
  Profit and loss
To close accounts for the year
Profit and loss
  Losses paid
  General expenses
  Taxes
  Loss on sale of investment securities
  Uncollectible premiums written off
To close accounts for the year
Profit and loss
  Reserve for unadmitted assets
To set up reserve for the following unadmitted assets at the end
  of the year:
  Premiums receivable over 90 days old
  Premium notes receivable over 90 days old
  Accrued interest on notes taken for premiums receivable over
   90 days old
  Accrued interest on bonds in default
  Decrease in securities from book values to values based on prices
   fixed by state insurance departments
  Loans to employees
Profit and loss
  Surplus
To transfer net addition to surplus for the year
In addition to the records and accounts mentioned above the following
statistical information is required for the annual statements to state
insurance departments:
  Net premium by states
  Premiums by states and kinds of insurance
  Premiums by states and by policy year of issue
  Losses paid—by states
  Losses paid—by policy year of issue
  Losses paid—by states and kinds of insurance
  Amount of war revenue tax on business done in each state
  Amount of state premium tax on business done in each state
  Amount of federal income tax on business done in each state
  Cash balance in each bank on the last day of each month
  Interest income from banks and trust companies by months

24

American Institute of Accountants

Library and Bureau of Information

SPECIAL BULLETIN No. 12

June, 1922

[The Committee on Administration of Endowment authorizes the publication of special Bulletins, of which this is one, on the distinct understanding that members are not to consider answers given to questions as being official pronouncements of the Institute, but merely the individual opinions of accountants to whom the questions were referred. It is earnestly requested that members criticise freely and constructively the answers given in this or any other Bulletin of this series.]

DIVIDENDS

Q. A company engaged in drilling oil wells and producing oil appreciates its leaseholds, by reason of discovery value as permitted under the Revenue Act of 1918, and computes depletion upon the basis of such appreciation value. No profit is made from operations, after deducting depletion, and there is consequently no available surplus from operating.

It is contended that dividends which have been paid should be charged against reserve for depletion so that such dividends may be construed as a return of capital, and not a distribution of profits, and reference is made to Article 1549, Regulations 45 revised, and also to Montgomery's *Income Tax Procedure, 1919*, pages 334 and 335, in support thereof. We contend that neither of these references contemplate the existence of surplus by appreciation to discovery value and where such surplus exists, dividends paid, where no profits have been earned, should properly form a charge against such surplus. We feel that the determination as to whether dividends were paid out of earnings or paid out of capital will rest upon the facts and not upon the mere charging of such dividends to reserve for depletion, and that the charging of such dividends to the surplus reserve constitutes proper procedure where such a surplus has come into existence.

A. Is it proper to pay dividends to shareholders of a corporation out of a surplus created by appreciating the value of the natural resource owned by the corporation when such created value is comprised in the value used as a basis for computation· of depletion deductions for tax purposes, without such dividends being considered liquidating dividends?

The following facts appear in, or can be inferred from, the language in which the question is clothed:

The corporation is engaged in drilling and operating oil wells.

It increased the value of its assets by an estimated, discovered value of the oil it owns or controls.

Additional capital stock was not issued to its stockholders to represent the increased value above mentioned, but the resulting appreciation was credited to surplus account.

1

The corporation charged off annually proper quotas for depletion of the value of the resource based not only upon actual outlay therein, but upon the appreciated value of its oil body.

Not having any income in one year after such depletion had been charged off and having no accumulated earned surplus it distributed a dividend, and contends that such dividend may be charged to the created surplus.

Assuming that there is nothing in the articles under which the corporation was organized and exists, in the laws of the state in which it was incorporated, nor in the regulations and by-laws governing its operations, to prevent paying a dividend from an estimated increase in value of the property owned by the corporation;

Assuming that all the stockholders thoroughly understand that this dividend did not come from profits actually earned, and that they understand that when such moneys are paid to them that it is not impossible to have such dividends contested later, either by the creditors of the corporation or by future stockholders;

The contention of your questioner must fall, because

it defeats the purpose that the corporation set out to attain when it set up its depletion reserve.

Manifestly the only legitimate consideration that could have animated the corporation in charging against its gross income an annual pro rata proportion for depletion, was to maintain its capital investment intact, including the created surplus.

The corporation once setting out upon such a course and having it recognized by the federal government, cannot reverse its position and still have the right to deduct depletion upon the basis of discovered value.

Not being able to reverse its position the dividends so paid are unquestionably liquidating dividends, as they can only be considered as a return to the stockholders of the reserve for depletion formerly set aside.

Much might be said as to the advisability of the policy of distributing a dividend out of an unrealized (and perhaps an unrealizable) profit, but that consideration does not appear to have any place in the mind of the questioner.

CHAIN DRUG STORES

Q. I am interested in learning what method is in most effectual use among the chain drug stores of the country, for the purpose of keeping their stock in trade or perpetual inventory and the method of disbursing to the drug stores.

A. We have your letter inquiring as to the most effectual method used by chain drug stores for the purpose of keeping perpetual inventories and of disbursing to the stores.

Our stores do not keep perpetual inventories. We control the stores' stocks on the basis of purchases and sales. We have a stock standard figured at cost for every store. The store manager must operate at all times within his standard. He is privileged to go under

2

but is not privileged to go over. Should a store manager go over, it is considered that he is overstocked, and he is called upon to reduce same as quickly as possible.

Our stores forward what we term a regular order to the depot every two weeks. Practically every item our stores are permitted to carry is stocked in the depots. This does not mean items that have only a local demand and on which direct orders on the suppliers are issued for the store. In other words we carry all items in the depots that are sold generally throughout our chain.

When a store manager forwards his order to the office, he attaches a sale and purchase report showing the amount of sales since the previous order as well as the total retail value of all merchandise received since the last order, plus the retail value of the merchandise being ordered.

At the end of each month we notify the stores of the amount of purchases made during the month and the amount of sales for the month as well as the percentage of merchandise purchased as compared with the sales. This information enables the store manager to watch his stock at all times.

We take inventory of the stores every three or four months, and at that time we inform the store manager of the amount of merchandise he has on hand both at cost and at retail, and at the same time advise him of the gross and net profit that he has made for the inventory period.

We do not know whether or not you are interested in the manner of stock keeping by the depots. We simply keep stock cards of all items carried and take inventory of the items every week or ten days, according to the selling demand of each individual item. The depots keep a perpetual inventory on expensive merchandise and on items such as cigarettes and cigars that are apt to be tempting to the employees.

AGENT'S COMMISSIONS

Q. A client of mine is making contracts for the installation of certain machinery and is selling these installations. In connection with this they enter into an agreement between the company and an agent who represents that he, having had several years' experience in the manufacture and sale of instrumentalities, relating to the production and utilization of the product, is desirous of effecting a working arrangement to represent the corporation as a "sales engineer," and is to devote his time to work leading up to sales, etc. The corporation is to pay said agent commissions as follows:

      15% on sales aggregating $
      12½% on sales aggregating $
      10% on all sales thereafter

The corporation is to provide the agent with a drawing account of $500 per month, and said corporation is to be credited with the sums of money thus advanced to said agent on said drawing account against commissions earned or which may be earned during the year period up to the time of a temporary or permanent settlement. What is the best way to treat the agent's commissions?

A. The treatment of the agent's commissions on the books of the corporation assumes, obviously, that sales reports will be rendered

3

in sufficient detail to permit of the computation of the commissions due the agent. Therefore no question arises in that regard.

The corporations may adopt either of two methods in handling the commissions, viz.:

(a) The corporation may open an account on its books with the agent, for example, "John Doe, Commissions." This account will be credited and "Commission expense account" charged monthly, or periodically, for the commissions earned as computed on the agent's volume of sales. The commissions account represents an expense of the business, and should be included, in the preparation of the income statement, in the selling expense of the period.

The "John Doe, Commissions" account will be debited for the monthly advances of $500. The account, in all probability, will show a balance from month to month, which balance (whether debit or credit) will be carried along to the time of a temporary or permanent settlement, when a cash payment or receipt will balance the account in full.

By this simple procedure the operations have been charged monthly for the commissions chargeable to that month, while the payments of cash monthly in advance have been a contractual relation and do not affect the expense of operations.

(b) The commissions would be handled as outlined above, except that two accounts might be carried in the books. One of these, "John Doe, Commissions" would be credited, as above, for the commissions earned, while a second account, perhaps "John Doe, Agent's Advances" would be charged for the cash monthly payments. Both accounts would be permitted to accumulate up to the time of a temporary or permanent settlement, when one account might be closed into the other, and a cash settlement made as in method (a) above.

Either of these methods is comparatively simple, and either of them should give satisfaction.

AUTOMOBILE SALES

Q. Will you kindly let me know what is the best practice in handling the following?

A dealer in used automobiles sells cars for cash, notes, liberty bonds, or other used cars, or a combination of all. The notes received by him from customers is of course charged to notes receivable. About 80% of the notes thus received, all bearing interest, are discounted either at the bank or with some discounting company. When the notes are discounted, cash is debited and notes receivable is credited. If the maker pays the note when due, the transaction is closed, if he defaults, the car sold may be seized and forfeited by the buyer. The discounting company does not notify the automobile dealer when the notes are paid, but calls up each day on the telephone and notifies the dealer as to what notes are not paid. The dealer sometimes pays the discounting company for the notes so unpaid and sometimes simply allows the charge to him to remain as such. When a car is seized for non-payment of a note, the dealer charges "Cars Purchased" and credits the discounting company on his books for the market value of the car seized. The notes received run in a series covering a period of one year.

The point is, what is the best way to handle the above transactions, to show the total amounts of notes unpaid whether discounted or not;

4

the total amount discounted; the amount overdue and the amount not yet matured; and the liability to the discounting company for seized cars not reimbursed to them by the dealer? The method of procedure as a matter of bookkeeping would also be appreciated.

A. In replying to your letter relative to method of handling automobile sales transactions, mortgage notes arising out of them, the discounting of the mortgage notes and the repossession and resale of cars by reason of foreclosure of the mortgage, I feel that it is best to outline the various transactions in pro forma journal entries, which follow:

(1) Cash
    Other consideration
    Notes receivable
        To sales
            Discount company
      For sale of car.

(2) Discount company
        To notes receivable discounted
      For sale of note to discount company.

(3) Cash
        To discount company
      For periodic settlements with discount company.

(4) Notes receivable discounted
        To notes receivable
      For collection of notes by discount company.

(5) Notes receivable discounted
        To discount company
      For notes not paid at maturity by maker.

(6) Discount company
        To notes receivable.
      For defaulted notes subsequently paid.

(7) Cars repossessed
        To notes receivable
      For repossession of car.

(8) Cash
    Other consideration
    Notes receivable
        To cars repossessed
            Discount company
      For sale of repossessed car.

Journal entry No. 1 for the sale of the car contemplates that there may be some consideration other than cash or notes receivable. Such other consideration would in most cases be the allowance upon the used car which was traded in. In these entries sales will be credited with the sale price of the car; the discount company will be credited for the amount of charges and interest which are added to the amount of the deferred payment as consideration for extending the time of payment.

5

Journal entry No. 2—This entry is made for the purpose of charging the discount company for notes that are discounted by it and entry No. 3 records the periodical settlement with the discount company.

Entry No. 4 records the cancelation of a liability upon notes receivable by reason of those notes having been paid by the maker to the discount company. Ordinarily this entry will be made upon the day following the customary time of report by the discount company to the sales company of delinquents.

These four entries record all of the transactions in the event that the mortgagor makes payment of all of his notes when and as they become due.

If there be any lapses in payment entry No. 5 becomes necessary. This entry is made for the purpose of recording the assumption by the company of a liability to the discount company by reason of lapse in payment by the maker. Ordinarily when such lapses occur and the maker of the notes subsequently makes payment this subsequent payment is made to the discount company. In the event of such payment it is necessary upon notice from the discount company to record the transaction as shown by entry No. 6.

Should the purchaser of the car and the maker of the notes remain in default and also fail to pay some subsequent notes, it is customary to foreclose the mortgage and repossess the car. In the event of repossession an entry the same as No. 5 will be made in the amount of all the remaining notes given in connection with that particular car.

Entry No. 7 will be made charging cars repossessed and crediting notes receivable in the total amount of all of the notes which have been unpaid. When a repossessed car is sold, entry No. 8 records the consideration received for the car. This entry No. 8 is the same as entry No. 1 in every respect except that cars repossessed is credited with the sales price instead of the sales being so credited. The debit or credit balance in the account "cars repossessed" will measure the loss or gain by reason of repossessions. It is almost needless to say that it will be a very rare occurrence for a year's transactions in repossessed cars to show a profit.

In the handling of the details of the accounts it will be well to have a card record of the notes receivable so that the account for any note might be transferred from the notes receivable file to the notes receivable discounted file. This would furnish an easy method of determining whether or not the detail was in agreement with the control in these two accounts.

I note in the inquiry which you have transmitted that there is asked for, among other things, a method of recording "the liability to the discount company for seized cars not reimbursed to them." In all of the cases which are handled by my firm I find that there is no liability to the discount company by reason of seizure of a car, but that liability arises at the time of non-payment of the note by the maker thereof by reason of the endorsement of the auto sales company. While it is true that repossessions ordinarily are made in the name of the discount company this is a matter of convenience only and the ex-

6

pense and court costs of such repossessions are invariably char ed against the auto sales company by the discount company. Both parties to the transaction consider that the repossessed car is the property of the sales company and that the sales company has a liability to the discount company for all defaulted notes, interest thereon and expense in connection with repossession.

A. The proper accounting for used cars handled by an automobile dealer will perhaps best be illustrated by the following hypothetical transaction:

Assume that the dealer buys a used car for $800; sells it for $1200; charges the sale price to the customer; takes the customer's notes in a series of twelve, payable monthly; discounts the notes. The customer meets three of them; fails to meet the fourth; the car is repossessed and the discount company is credited in open account with the balance unpaid on the notes.

The transaction stated in terms of journal entry would be as follows:

Used cars purchased	$ 800.00	
Accounts payable		$ 800.00
Accounts receivable	1,200.00	
Sales of used cars		1,200.00
Notes receivable	1,200.00	
Accounts receivable		1,200.00
Cash	1,180.00	
Discount	20.00	
Notes receivable discounted		1,200.00
Cost of cars sold	800.00	
Used cars purchased		800.00
Sales of cars	1,200.00	
Profit and loss		1,200.00
Profit and loss	800.00	
Cost of cars sold		800.00
Cars repossessed	800.00	
Notes receivable		800.00
Notes receivable discounted	1,200.00	
Notes receivable		300.00
Discount company		900.00
Profit and loss	100.00	
Notes receivable		100.00

While all of the above transactions have been stated in terms of journal entry, it is obvious of course that those involving cash would be handled through the cash book. The other entries would have to be handled mainly through the general journal. However, if the volume of transactions is heavy, provision may be made for a special journal with columns to the right and left, respectively, of the descriptive section, for the classification of items relating to the discounting of the notes and the repossession of the cars.

7

STOCK WITHOUT PAR VALUE

Q. Will you kindly advise me what is the proper manner to take care of capital stock which has no value, more especially when some of the stock is sold in connection with preferred stock at varying values.

Should not the amount received for such stock be credited to surplus?

A. We find it rather difficult to reply to the question contained in your letter because of the fact that the question is not clear.

Does "capital stock which has no value" mean capital stock without par value? Does stock sold in connection with preferred stock at varying values refer to preferred stock or other stock?

It is customary to credit amounts received from sale of stock without par value to an account designated "common stock capital account" or "preferred stock capital account" as the case may be and not to surplus. Perhaps this answers the question satisfactorily.

PREMIUMS

Q. A trust company has been appointed trustee to handle a sum of money as follows: To pay the income to A during his lifetime and at his death pay over the principal to B.

During the life of A the trust company purchases a $1,000 bond for $1,100. This bond matures ten years hence for $1,000.

Should the $100 premium paid on this bond be charged against A (the life tenant) or B (the remainderman)?

The question comes from a state in which there has been no legal decision. We already have the decisions of other states. Our inquirer wishes an accountant's opinion.

A. The premium of $100 paid for the bond in the instance which you cite should in our opinion be amortized out of the income from the bond during the life of the bond and the difference between the amortization charge and the interest received credited annually to income. Thereby the premium paid on the bond would be chargeable against A (the life tenant) or B (the remainderman) on the basis of the life interest which each had in the bond.

CERTIFICATES

Q. An accountant practising under his own name, employs seniors, who make a complete audit of the client's records, prepare the report and submit the same to this accountant for his criticism prior to the same being typed. The question arose over the style of the certificate. It has been customary for the certificate to be in this form:

We have audited the books and accounts of the Jones-Smith and Brown Company for the period January 1, 1921, to December 31, 1921, and

I HEREBY CERTIFY that the accompanying balance-sheet as of December 31, 1921, and the income and profit-and-loss statement for the period January 1, 1921, to December 31, 1921, are in agreement with the books and accounts, and in my opinion, subject to the accompanying comments, set forth the financial condition of the company on that date.

The principal contention of the person criticising this certificate was that it should start "I have audited" rather than "we have audited."

A. We have no hesitation in saying that where an individual accountant is in practice on his own behalf certificates to balance-sheets issued by him should be in the first person singular, and not the first person plural.

8

American Institute of Accountants

Library and Bureau of Information

Special Bulletin No. 13

July, 1922

NEWSPAPER SUBSCRIPTIONS

Q. In auditing the accounts of a daily and weekly newspaper publication, we find that all money received from subscriptions has been credited to income in the period in which received, and we also find that the method of keeping the records makes it very difficult to arrive at the amount of prepaid circulation at any date.

In this particular case the amount of prepaid circulation is important, and it is also important to know the amount of earnings in the future on the accrual basis. We should be glad to have you obtain through the Bureau of Information opinions as to the proper and practicable method of handling income from subscriptions on the accrual basis, and give us your results.

A. We suggest that the installation of a subscription record somewhat of the following columnar arrangement may answer the purpose:

1—Date

2—Number (or other identification) of subscription

3—Subscription period

4—Amount of subscription

    Fiscal period to be credited

5— 1st quarter

6— 2nd quarter

7— 3rd quarter

8— 4th quarter

    Beyond

9—   Period

10— Amount

11—Remarks

All subscriptions should be entered consecutively and the amount spread over the fiscal periods in which they will be earned. Cancelations should be entered in similar manner but in red. At the close of each fiscal period the totals of columns 5, 6, 7, 8 and 10 should be respectively credited to the corresponding revenue accounts, a revenue account to be opened for each fiscal period. Among the earnings of the current fiscal period, say the first quarter of the year, only the balance of that particular revenue account should be taken up and the aggregate of balances of the other revenue accounts will appear on the liability side of the balance-sheet as a deferred item of "unearned subscriptions."

1

If monthly statements of earnings are required there should be a division of the subscriptions by months. If only an annual statement is desired the division of the subscriptions will be as between current and future years. Corresponding changes should then be made in the columnar arrangement of the above suggested record. The columns "beyond" will give the proportions applicable to the earnings of future years as well as the data for opening the subscription record and the several revenue accounts of the succeeding year.

DEPRECIATION ON INSULATION IN COLD STORAGE WAREHOUSES

Q. We should greatly appreciate it if you could advise the standard rate of depreciation on the insulation in cold storage warehouses.

A. The factors which determine the useful life of the insulation are quality of material and workmanship, the life of the equipment which is insulated and the conditions under which the business is operated.

The manufacturers of insulating material for cold storage warehouses agree that whether it be made of a cork, sawdust or straw base, if the material is properly made and applied, other conditions being ideal, the insulation material will last as long as the section of the building or the equipment to which it is applied. Disregarding the conditions under which the particular industry operates, the same rates of depreciation should be used for the insulation therefor as are used for the building, the flooring, the ceiling, the brine pipes, the tank or the refrigerating machinery, respectively.

The insulation material will deteriorate very rapidly if the building or the floor is subjected to shocks or jars, by reason of leaking pipes and other like causes. When these factors can be definitely computed the rates of depreciation first suggested should be adjusted thereby. For leaking pipes, unusual strains, etc., the adjustment must be determined from the experience of the particular enterprise or the necessary replacement be treated as a current expense.

BALANCE-SHEETS

Q. The company under consideration was organized in 1919 under the laws of the state of New York and was authorized to issue common stock of no par value to the aggregate of $500,000 at a minimum value per share of $5, which was the then existing law in this state in regard to capital stock of no par value. The first shares issued were to the president and a director of the corporation for goodwill and services for part of the first year. These shares were placed on the books at the minimum value of $5 per share. All other shares since that time have been issued for cash or property at the rate of $100 per share. The amount of stock issued to the president, which was given a value of $5 per share, enabled him to have the controlling interest in the outstanding capital stock. In the preparation of the balance-sheet we shall of course show the number of shares of stock outstanding and the aggregate value of the total shares. It will be obvious then that the value per share will be much less than $100 on account of the original issue to the president and a director on the basis of $5 per share. Our question is as to whether or not a specific footnote to the balance-sheet calling attention to the manner in which the stock was issued is necessary and also as to whether a succinct statement of the facts should be made as a definite part of the comments of the report.

2

We feel a duty towards stockholders and the public in preparing this report and we wish to be very technically correct in our presentation of the facts. Any opinion that you may care to procure for us in regard to the matter will be very greatly appreciated.

A. We are of the opinion the case submitted warrants a specific reference in the balance-sheet or as a footnote thereon as to the basis on which the two lots of the common capital stock of no par value have been issued. It might be contended that the stockholders who contributed property and cash on the basis of $100 per share should have had knowledge of the number of shares outstanding and the balance-sheet valuation of these shares immediately prior to their transactions, thereby recognizing that, as a result of their transactions, the value per share would really be less than $100. In the average body of shareholders, there would undoubtedly be a number who would not be sufficiently alert as to observe the effect of the transactions so far as the resulting value per share is concerned. On that account, it would seem to be well to clearly state the position. But what makes it more necessary is the wide variation in value per share between those originally issued for goodwill and services and those subsequently issued for property and cash, the fact that the shares issued at $5 per share were acquired by the president and a director and that the shares thus issued to the president gave him a controlling interest. While the statement in the balance-sheet would be sufficient, if it goes so far as to indicate the number of shares issued at $5 and the number at $100, with the values set against each, the reference necessary in the report should be made more extended.

CAPITAL STOCK

Q. It has always been my custom to make opening entries in the order of incidence of the physical conditions. Thus in the case of no par stock it seems necessary to make the entry for authorization of capital before the value of such capital has been determined. I submit the following set of entries which I am submitting for your criticism:

Opening Entries

THE BLANK COMPANY

Incorporated 1921

——————, ——————

February 25, 1921

Capital stock—common—unissued .... 2,500 shares

    Capital stock—common—authorized ......   2,500 shares

To record the authorization for issue of 2,500 shares of the common capital stock of the company without par. This is a statistical entry only for purpose of chronological record and fiscal entries will be made as shares are issued and values thereof determined from considerations received therefor.

25

Capital stock—preferred—unissued 100,000.00

    Capital stock—preferred—authorized 100,000.00

To record the authorization for issue of 1,000 shares of the preferred capital stock of the company at a par value of $100 each. See stock certificates and minute book for preference regulations.

3

Subscribers—common stock	50 shares 500.00	
Capital stock—common—unissued		50 shares 500.00

To record receipt of subscriptions for 50 shares , of common stock at $10 each. The total value thereof ($500) is declared as the amount with which the company will "begin to carry on business."

2

Capital stock—common—unissued	500.00	
Capital stock—common—authorized		500.00

To record value established for fifty shares of common stock subscribed for in preceding entry.

April 11, 1921

Cash	500.00	
Subscribers—common stock		500.00

To record receipt of cash for stock subscribed for as noted in entry 3-2-21.

11

Stock in the Blank Company of 1907	47,610.78	
Cash		500.00
Stockholders in the Blank Company of 1907		47,110.78

To record purchase of stock in the Blank Company organized in 1907. See minutes of even date.

11

Stockholders in the Blank Company of 1907	2,450 shares 47,100.78	
Capital stock—common—unissued		2,450 shares 47,110.78

To record satisfaction of obligation to old stockholders by the issuance of 2,450 shares of common stock at the entered total value.

11

Capital stock—common—unissued	47,110.78	
Capital stock—common—authorized		47,110.78

To record value established for 2,450 shares of common stock issued as per preceding entry.

April 11, 1921

Cash in bank	1,086.39	
Petty cash	89.75	
Liberty bonds	3,450.00	
Inventory	3,182.46	
Office equipment	3,093.42	
Accounts receivable	4,078.48	
Wilberite Roofing Co.	3,408.61	
Cleveland Top & Specialty Co.	204.19	
Albert G. Wade	226.79	
Bulletins—March, April, May	68.70	
Special account—customers' dollar account	28.00	
Freight claims	847.42	
Customers' and prospects' list	120,000.00	
Customers' advances		3,100.16
Freight claims—customers		98.67
Notes payable		14,763.83
Trade acceptance		5,000.00
Accounts payable		6,117.98

4

Cray Bros.		54,636.87
C. J. Krehbiel		7,652.51
Credit vouchers of 1920		178.96
Credit vouchers of 1921		36.48
Reserve for depreciation		567.97
Stock in Blank Company of 1907		47,610.78

To record receipt of assets and assumption of liabilities of the Blank Co. of 1907, and cancelation of stock therein.

28

Treasury stock—common	300 shares	
Donated stock—common		300 shares

To record donation to company of three hundred common shares by G. A. Bottger and E. D. Cray.

July 23, 1921

Notes payable	2,000.00	
Capital stock—preferred—unissued		2,000.00

Issuance of 20 shares to Wm. Whitman in payment on a note held by Excelsior Ptg. Co.

Excelsior Ptg. Co.	3,700.00	
Capital stock—preferred—unissued		3,700.00
Donated common stock	15 shares	
Treasury stock		15 shares

Above stock as indicated issued in payment of $3,700.

Cray Bros.	54,500.00	
Capital stock—preferred—unissued		54,500.00

Above preferred stock issued as indicated in payment on account to Cray Brothers.

A. In our opinion the entries covering unissued capital stock are not only unnecessary, but also burden the ledger with offsetting debit and credit items, which are of no value in the financial records, and also make the recording of the transactions covering the issue of capital stock unnecessarily complicated.

The journal should be opened with the entry recording the subscriptions to capital stock, this entry being preceded by an explanatory statement setting forth the name of the company and giving a brief summary of the articles of incorporation, including the purpose of the business, amount of capital stock authorized, etc. The credits to capital stock should only be for the stock actually subscribed for, it being of course very necessary that the records should show wherever any stock subscribed for remains unpaid. It might be well for the purpose of ready reference to make a note under the head of the capital stock account in the ledger as to the amount of authorized stock. This method will eliminate the first two entries, the second from the last on page 1, and the third on page 2, the word "unissued" being omitted from the other entries recording the subscriptions and issue of certificates.

We are not quite clear as to what is meant by the explanation given in the fifth entry "to record value established." If the company has been incorporated under the laws of the State of New York, we presume that the proper provision has been made in the articles of incorporation for the minimum value of the common stock in accordance with paragraph 3, section 19 of chapter 694, laws of 1921. If so, the amounts shown in this entry represent the asset value received in consideration of the issue of

5

the stock, the value received from the original subscribers being at an entirely different rate from that received for the rest of the stock issued.

So long as the value received for the common stock is equal to, or exceeds the value stated in the articles of incorporation, no explanation is necessary further than a memorandum that issue was in accordance with the resolution of the board of directors.

As regards the entry recording the donation of stock to the company, we are of the opinion that the proportionate part of the book value of this common stock should be recorded in this entry and upon the sale of any of this stock, the proper proportion should be transferred from the donated stock account to capital surplus to record the value of the gift to the company.

If the fifteen shares of common stock were issued as a bonus with the preferred stock, it should be so stated in the entry, the value of the fifteen shares of common stock being treated as an additional cost of liquidating the account referred to.

A. It would appear to us that no good purpose can be served by spreading so many entries upon the books where a much less number would present an equally clear and certainly less confusing record. The principal criticism we have to make with reference to opening a "capital stock-common-unissued" account, as proposed in the inquiry, is the fact that in the entries suggested, the account has been debited and credited in some cases with shares only and other instances with dollars only, and in still others with both shares and dollars. After posting the entries and closing out the account its appearance, to say the least, would be unusual. Where no-par value stock is involved in books of account it is, of course, necessary to keep a sort of dual record, the one element recording the number of shares involved in the entries and the other the value in dollars placed upon the shares. This can best be accomplished by establishing a computing column for the number of shares in the explanatory column of the ledger account or accounts affected by the transactions in the shares.

In our opinion the recording of authorized shares of capital stock of no-par value can best be accomplished by appropriately heading the account "common stock authorized." Then, in the case mentioned, this account would be credited with 50 shares (recorded in the computing column for shares) and $500 (recorded in the regular money column), charging the subscribers with the $500. Similarly, another entry would be made crediting the former account with 2,450 shares and $47,110.78, charging "old company stock" therewith. This procedure would eliminate several unnecessary entries and produce a record which could be readily understood. Furthermore, we believe that giving effect in a subscriber's account to anything but dollars and cents is an erroneous practice. Under the plan outlined in the problem, subscriber's account is charged with 50 shares and $500, but on the other hand this account is credited only with $500, leaving in effect a debit balance of 50 shares in the account, which, obviously, is improper.

6

Another point that might be subject to criticism is the fact that the treasury stock which is offset by donated common stock is only entered as to the number of shares involved, while there was a definite value established per share by the issuance of 2,500 shares for $47,610.78. We believe that the value per share, thus established, should be used with respect to recording the donated stock.

JEWELRY

Q. I am desirous of obtaining the following statistical information relative to the manufacturing jewelry business to prove certain facts to a client and if you have such figures at your command or can refer me where to secure them would appreciate it greatly.

What is the general average of percentage for materials used, miscellaneous factory expenses, factory labor, selling expenses, overhead expenses, basing the figures on the sales?

A. We have no statistical information exactly in line with your inquiry but the following may be of interest:

A concern which manufactures silver toilet articles, tea services, vases, picture frames and other articles of a like nature, shows the following results for the fiscal year ended in 1921:

Labor, material and factory overhead	70.6
Selling expenses	3.9
Administrative and general	22.7

Another concern manufacturing a cheap line of jewelry shows the following results:

Labor, material and factory overhead	67.7
Selling expenses	22.4
Administrative and general	22.1

Still another concern, manufacturing jewelry novelties, etc., the raw materials of gold, silver, copper and brass, shows

Factory cost	68.9
Selling expenses	4.1
Administrative and general	5.2

Our records in none of the above cases show the separation as between labor, materials, and general factory overhead. In our opinion the percentage of labor and materials would vary considerably depending upon the nature of the product and the kind of raw material used. In some instances the finer materials, such as platinum and gold, might be used almost exclusively in connection with precious stones, whereas in other cases a large percentage of the product might be manufactured from cheaper materials and imitation stones.

COCOANUT OIL INDUSTRY

Q. What is the average rate of depreciation for steel and concrete buildings and machinery in the cocoanut oil industry?

A. Buildings—steel and concrete ....1—1½%
   Machinery .... 10 %

DEPRECIATION ON SCHOOL BUILDINGS

Q. I am very anxious to obtain the best thought on the question of annual depreciation on school buildings and other fixed assets of school districts or municipalities.

7

In the great majority of cases these buildings are erected from the proceeds of bond issues voted especially for this purpose, and the authorities seem to differ regarding the method of handling depreciation.

It is obvious, of course, that annual provision must be made for a sinking fund to retire the bonds at the date of maturity.

Some authorities advance the idea that while depreciation should be taken into consideration as a part of the cost of operation, the charges should not be made against current revenue but should be applied against capital surplus. It appears to me that if it is to be considered as an operating expense, it should be charged against current revenue.

A. The difference among the authorities regarding the method of handling depreciation, to which your correspondent refers, is doubtless closely related to the difference of opinion as to whether capital assets and liabilities with a balancing capital surplus should or should not form part of a municipal balance-sheet. The arguments against their inclusion are presented in Oakey's "Principles of Government Accounting and Reporting." Without going into the technical counter arguments, we may suggest the practical one that the inclusion of these capital items presents in a concise form information regarding the property which the city has accumulated, and the extent to which it exceeds the outstanding funded debt—and thus, information which is unlikely to be elsewhere assembled in convenient form and sometimes quite unavailable.

School property and other fixed assets and the debt created to defray their cost of construction both enter into the capital portion of the balance-sheet, the net balancing figure of which is the capital surplus. Any adjustment of the value of the school properties must, therefore, affect to a corresponding extent the capital surplus. Depreciation in the value of the school properties goes to decrease this capital surplus.

It is desirable that the values at which city properties are carried not only should be reasonable but also should be computed according to a definable and defensible rule. Annual reduction of the asset or annual accretion to a depreciation reserve by a fair estimate of the accruing depreciation would accord with such a rule. Such provisions for depreciation are, on the argument indicated above, chargeable to capital surplus.

In municipal accounting, the provisions for sinking fund and for depreciation have no necessary relationship beyond the fact that a bond issue is sometimes limited by law to a term fixed by taking into consideration the normal term of service of an improvement of the character of that to be financed. While depreciation is a capital fund matter, sinking fund provisions must be made out of current revenues. The sinking fund itself is usually treated as a reserve fund, though in many instances it might reasonably be consolidated with the capital fund. To the extent that the provision for depreciation corresponds to the contribution raised for the sinking fund, the depreciation might be said to have been in effect provided out of current revenues.

In considering this matter we have had in mind property such as schools or other structures used for general city purposes. The principles applying to municipal utilities, such as water works, are fundamentally the same, but their application is somewhat different from that described.

8

American Institute of Accountants

Library and Bureau of Information

August, 1922   SPECIAL BULLETIN No. 14

[The Committee on Administration of Endowment authorizes the publication of special Bulletins, of which this is one, on the distinct understanding that members are not to consider answers given to questions as being official pronouncements of the Institute, but merely the individual opinions of accountants to whom the questions were referred. It is earnestly requested that members criticise freely and constructively the answers given in this or any other Bulletin of this series.]

TANNERY EQUIPMENT

Q. In connection with one of our client's income-tax returns, it has become quite important that we determine approximately what the normal percentage of repairs bears to the sound value of the equipment upon which such repairs are made. These clients carry out two distinct businesses, one of which is a tannery and the other is the manufacture of workmen's gloves. In the case of the tannery, they have the usual equipment, consisting of vats, tanks and all of the machinery which goes with a tannery. In the case of the glove manufacture, the chief machinery consists of various kinds of special sewing machines.

It would be a great assistance to us if it were possible to find out what the normal percentage is, as stated above, all replacements, however, being kept out of the calculation. It occurred to us that perhaps amongst the members of the Institute, there might be someone who would be able to give us this information, based upon the experience of some other clients.

A. In reply to your inquiry regarding a normal percentage which repairs should bear to the sound value of equipment upon which the repairs are made, it is not possible to fix a constant standard as the amount of the repairs will vary in the same industry with the kind of equipment used, and will also vary from year to year with the age of the equipment, the need of repairs increasing with each year.

Assuming that your inquirer has these facts in mind, it may be helpful for him to have some data based on experience of other manufacturers. We cannot give him anything of value with respect to the manufacture of workmen's gloves, nor are we able to give any data on tannery equipment covering an extended period of time. However, in our records we do find that tannery equipment having an average age of 15 years has incurred repairs expense as follows:

Buildings	from 6% to 9%
Machinery	from 9% to 10%
Tools	9%

1

The above percentages include the period of high prices following the war, but do not include the year 1921, in which, because of the marked depression in the industry, expenses were kept down to an absolute minimum.

In supplying the above information we have had in mind that probably others may give similar facts, possibly some of them concerning machinery which has not been used for so long a time and that from the data obtained from these several sources your inquirer may find the information which he requires.

DIVIDENDS

The Bureau of Information has received a number of criticisms of the answer to "Dividends" appearing in Special Bulletin No. 12, June, 1922. As these criticisms are similar, we are publishing only one of the letters.

The question and answer regarding dividends of an oil company that had appreciated its lease holds for discovery value and had taken depletion on that value as set forth in Special Bulletin No. 12 have been read with interest. In accordance with the request for free and constructive criticism printed at the head of that bulletin, may I venture to make a few suggestions regarding the answer to this question.

The provision in the income tax law that permits depletion based on discovery values is in the nature of a special exemption from taxation. There is no ground whatever for saying that a company discovering oil on a cheaply acquired lease and selling the oil for more than the expenses of operation and the depletion on the cost of the lease has no income. Even Congress could not enact that it had no income. What Congress did enact was that it had no taxable income, or in other words, that its income would be free from taxation.

Income actually realized may be distributed as a dividend irrespective of whether it is subject to federal income tax. If the entries setting up the appreciation and providing for the depletion are properly made, the books will show clearly the effect of the entries made to substantiate the depletion claimed for purposes of federal income tax, and the true position of the company on the basis of sound economics and business principles. The procedure by which this is obtained may best be explained by making the case concrete and showing how it works out. If the company acquired a lease for $5,000 and its discovery of oil brought the value of it to $500,000 thirty days after discovery, the books should show

Lease	$ 5,000	
Capital		$ 5,000
Appreciation of lease	495,000	
Special Surplus		495,000

If oil is produced so as to show a profit before depletion of $30,000 and if this profit is realized in cash there would appear also

Cash	$ 30,000	
Profit & Loss		$ 30,000

2

The depletion computed under the laws and regulations based on discovery value might amount to $100,000. In this case the entries should be as follows:

Profit & Loss	$ 1,000	
Special Surplus	99,000	
Reserve for Depletion		$ 1,000
Special Reserve for Depletion		99,000

The balance-sheet will then show

ASSETS		LIABILITIES	
Cash	$ 30,000	Reserve for Depletion	$ 1,000
Lease	5,000	Special Reserve for Depletion	99,000
Appreciation of Lease	495,000	Capital	5,000
		Special Surplus	396,000
		Profit & Loss	29,000
TOTAL ASSETS	$530,000	TOTAL LIABILITIES	$530,000

It will be noted that the three accounts "Appreciation of Lease," "Special Surplus" and "Special Reserve for Depletion" will always exactly offset each other. To see the true financial position of the company it is necessary simply to eliminate them. The other accounts show the true conditions from a sound economic and business standpoint. These three accounts are merely a record to substantiate the subsidy which Congress saw fit to grant to oil producers. The company has no taxable income but it has realized profits which may be paid as dividends. When such dividends are paid the stockholder is subject to the same surtax as on any other dividends.

IMPREST FUND

Q. I would be obliged if you would supply me with the definition of "Imprest Fund," telling me the derivation of the word "Imprest."

I was recently asked by one of our clients the meaning of the word "Imprest" as he could not locate it in the dictionary after he had observed it on my papers.

I told him it was a technical term applied to a specific sum of money which is periodically reimbursed for its disbursements.

After consulting my dictionary I realized the logical source of information would be the Terminology Department of the Journal of Accountancy.

A. In modern parlance the word "Imprest" is used only in the phrase "Imprest System." This is a system of disbursing by means of advances, the use of which is generally confined in this country to a Petty Cash fund, although it is used in certain departments of the British Government. The Cashier of the fund is given a definite "round" sum of money, which he disburses as necessary and usually for sundry petty expenditures, and of which he keeps a record, frequently in a columnar book. Either at fixed periods—such as a week or a month—or when the fund approaches exhaustion, a statement is made showing the disbursements and the accounts to which they are chargeable. A cheque is then drawn for the total amount of such ex-

3

penditures and is charged to the accounts shown in the distribution, the proceeds of the check being placed in the fund, which is thereby restored to its original amount.

The derivation of the word is interesting for it carries us back for some hundred of years and gives us glimpses of the methods of our fore-runners. It aids us to picture them at their work, beruffed, be-cloaked and trunk-hosed and reminds us of those happy times when clients were both willing and able to care for the physical comfort of their auditors for we find that in 1552, the Auditors of Lanark were allowed 6s. 8d. for that they "dranc" and in 1568, one item reads—"Ten shillings given to the Audetour is in drink."

The word is made up of the preposition "In"—which is common to the Latin, French and English language and which before a labial usually takes the form "Im"—"Prest."

The prefix has no definite modern significance and originally was frequently merely intensive. The "prest", however, is interesting for it brings out the original meaning of the word. It is closely allied to the modern French "pret"—a loan or advance money and the circumflex accent suggests that in former times the word was spelled "prest." The word "prest" still appears in English dictionaries as meaning "to put out as a loan" and in old accounts it is found used in this sense as far back as in the days of Queen Elizabeth for in a statement of her expenses in 1552, made by "Thomas Parrye, Esquyer," we find that "The said Mr. Parrye is charged with certen somes of money by him receaved and to him payd," of which the first is "The remayne with the prest of last yere." The word has remained in constant use and always suggests the idea that a sum has been advanced and is to be returned or accounted for.

BONDS

Q. Could you possibly secure for us the solution of this problem or enough aid thereon to enable us to type a statement showing the solution?

This is the problem:

It is desired to make an issue of $2,750,000 of bonds, all to mature before the expiration of 30 years, i. e. between 1923 and the close of 1952. The bonds to bear 6% interest payable semi-annually.

It is desired to pay off the principal and interest in this wise: the sum of principal and interest, payable each year, during the period, to be as near an equal amount as possible.

We wish therefore to type a Statement which will show:
1. The Years 1923 to 1952 listed down.
2. Amount of Bonds Outstanding at the beginning of each year.
3. Interest paid each year.
4. Principal matured and taken up each year.
5. Sum of Interest paid and Principal (matured) paid, each year.

The footing of column 4 should equal $2,750,000.00

A. We duly received your letter in which you ask us what amount would require to be set aside annually to pay off in thirty years an issue of $2,750,000 6% bonds, interest payable semi-annually, "the sum of principal and interest payable each year to be as near an equal amount

4

as possible", and to send you a typewritten statement showing how the calculations work out.

For the purposes of the calculations we have assumed that the bonds are to be dated July 1, 1922, that interest will be payable on January 1st and July 1st, that the bonds are to be issued in denominations of as low as $100.00, that redemptions are to be effected on each interest date, and that the retirement of the bonds is to be completed July 1, 1952.

The following statement shows on the basis of the foregoing assumptions, that by setting aside approximately $99,400.00 each half-year, or approximately $198,800.00 per annum the principal amount of the bonds will be amortized in thirty years and the interest payments met as they fall due.

The amount of $99,400.00 is arrived at as follows:

It is apparent that the amount required to be set aside semi-annually is that amount which, with compound semi-annual interest at 3%, will, at the end of sixty half-yearly periods, equal the amount of the issue (viz., $2,750,000.00) plus interest accumulations thereon under these same conditions.

The amount of a semi-annuity of $1.00 at 3% per half-year for sixty half-years is $163.05344.

The amount of $1.00 at the end of sixty half-years at 3% per half-year is $5.8916.

The amount of $2,750,000.00 at the end of sixty half-years at 3% per half-year is, therefore, $2,750,000.00 x $5.8916, or $16,201,900.00.

RETIREMENT IN THIRTY YEARS OF $2,750,000
6% BONDS, INTEREST PAYABLE SEMI-ANNUALLY

		Amount outstanding at the beginning of each half yearly period	Amount set aside semi-annually (approximately) ($99,400.00)	Interest paid semi-annually	Bonds redeemed at each interest date
1923	Jan. 1	$2,750,000	$99,400	$82,500	$16,900
	July 1	2,733,100	99,393	81,993	17,400
1924	Jan. 1	2,715,700	99,371	81,471	17,900
	July 1	2,697,800	99,434	80,934	18,500
1925	Jan. 1	2,679,300	99,379	80,379	19,000
	July 1	2,660,300	99,409	79,809	19,600
1926	Jan. 1	2,640,700	99,421	79,221	20,200
	July 1	2,620,500	99,415	78,615	20,800
1927	Jan. 1	2,599,700	99,391	77,991	21,400
	July 1	2,578,300	99,349	77,349	22,000
1928	Jan. 1	2,556,300	99,389	76,689	22,700
	July 1	2,533,600	99,408	76,008	23,400
1929	Jan. 1	2,510,200	99,406	75,306	24,100
	July 1	2,486,100	99,383	74,583	24,800
1930	Jan. 1	2,461,300	99,339	73,839	25,500
	July 1	2,435,800	99,374	73,074	26,300
1931	Jan. 1	2,409,500	99,385	72,285	27,100
	July 1	2,382,400	99,372	71,472	27,900

5

			Amount outstanding at the beginning of each half yearly period	Amount set aside semi-annually (approximately) ($99,400.00)	Interest paid semi-annually	Bonds redeemed at each interest date
1932	Jan.	1	2,354,500	99,435	70,635	28,800
	July	1	2,325,700	99,371	69,771	29,600
1933	Jan.	1	2,296,100	99,383	68,883	30,500
	July	1	2,265,600	99,368	67,968	31,400
1934	Jan.	1	2,234,200	99,426	67,026	32,400
	July	1	2,201,800	99,354	66,054	33,300
1935	Jan.	1	2,168,500	99,355	65,055	34,300
	July	1	2,134,200	99,426	64,026	35,400
1936	Jan.	1	2,098,800	99,364	62,964	36,400
	July	1	2,062,400	99,372	61,872	37,500
1937	Jan.	1	2,024,900	99,347	60,747	38,600
	July	1	1,986,300	99,389	59,589	39,800
1938	Jan.	1	1,946,500	99,395	58,395	41,000
	July	1	1,905,500	99,365	57,165	42,200
1939	Jan.	1	1,863,300	99,399	55,899	43,500
	July	1	1,819,800	99,394	54,594	44,800
1940	Jan.	1	1,775,000	99,350	53,250	46,100
	July	1	1,728,900	99,367	51,867	47,500
1941	Jan.	1	1,681,400	99,342	50,442	48,900
	July	1	1,632,500	99,375	48,975	50,400
1942	Jan.	1	1,582,100	99,363	47,463	51,900
	July	1	1,530,200	99,306	45,906	53,400
1943	Jan.	1	1,476,800	99,304	44,304	55,000
	July	1	1,421,800	99,354	42,654	56,700
1944	Jan.	1	1,365,100	99,353	40,953	58,400
	July	1	1,306,700	99,301	39,201	60,100
1945	Jan.	1	1,246,600	99,398	37,398	62,000
	July	1	1,184,600	99,338	35,538	63,800
1946	Jan.	1	1,120,800	99,324	33,624	65,700
	July	1	1,055,100	99,353	31,653	67,700
1947	Jan.	1	987,400	99,322	29,622	69,700
	July	1	917,700	99,331	27,531	71,800
1948	Jan.	1	845,900	99,377	25,377	74,000
	July	1	771,900	99,357	23,157	76,200
1949	Jan.	1	695,700	99,371	20,871	78,500
	July	1	617,200	99,316	18,516	80,800
1950	Jan.	1	536,400	99,392	16,092	83,300
	July	1	453,100	99,393	13,593	85,800
1951	Jan.	1	367,300	99,319	11,019	88,300
	July	1	279,000	99,370	8,370	91,000
1952	Jan.	1	188,000	99,340	5,640	93,700
	July	1	94,300	97,129	2,829	94,300
				$5,960,006	$3,210,006	$2,750,000

6

Q. One of the difficulties which has always attended the preparation of estate accounts has been the proper division of items between corpus and income, and it appears to me that this difficulty is increased by the rules prescribed by the Treasury Department in Regulations 45 and 62. The question has lately arisen in this office in connection with a rather large estate for which we are rewriting the accounts for a number of years.

Reference is made to paragraph 293 of Regulations 62, which states:

"The expenses of the administration of an estate, such as court costs, attorneys' fees and executors' commissions are chargeable against the corpus of the estate and are not allowable deductions."

It has been my practice to charge the initial court costs and attorneys' fees in connection with the probate to the corpus of the estate and I have always charged the annual fees payable to executors or administrators to the income, together with such current expenses as attorneys' fees for current services, rent of safe deposit boxes, telegrams and other similar expenses.

It seems to me that all such expenses should be charged on the estate accounts against the income, although an adjusting statement may be necessary in order to reconcile the estate books with the returns made to the Internal Revenue Department, in which such items as those mentioned above must be deducted.

We shall be glad if you can give us any information bearing on the subject, especially as to whether or not the plan suggested in the concluding paragraph of the memorandum is that which is usually adopted in the best practice.

A. We have your letter regarding the proper division in estate accounting of items of expenses between corpus and income.

In the first place it must be realized that estate accounting differs in many respects from commercial accounting, and that in estate accounting what may or may not be done is covered very minutely by the statutes and by the practices of the probate or surrogate courts in the state where the deceased had legal residence. Many items of expense, which in commercial accounting would be prima facie operating expenses, are in estate accounting properly held as chargeable against the corpus of the estate.

The reference in Paragraph 293, Regulations 62, that "the expenses of the administration of an estate, such as court costs, attorneys' fees and executors' commissions are chargeable against the corpus of the estate and are not allowable deductions" is, in our opinion, entirely correct for estate accounting purposes. While the laws differ in the various states, it may be said that the general rule regarding expenses is that unless expenses are directly connected with the income of the estate they must be charged against corpus. Thus, in the case of one large eastern estate, where a large proportion of the income of the estate consisted of rentals from apartment houses, the probate court permitted charging the cost of janitor service and supplies and of fuel for the apartments against the income rentals, but the salary of an office man retained by the Executors to rent the apartments and in general to look after the properties was charged against corpus.

7

Unless specifically relating to the income of the estate, all current expenses for court costs, attorneys' fees, executors' commissions, rent of safe deposit boxes, and all similar expenses are chargeable against the corpus of the estate. The inquirer should ascertain definitely the statutes and court practices of the state in which he is residing, but the Internal Revenue Department regulations are in accordance with good estate accounting practice, and the estate accounts should be so compiled.

PHOTOSTAT WORK

Photostatic reproductions of most of the articles listed in the Accountants' Index or Journal of Accountancy may be obtained from the library at a rate of 25 cents a page (8½ in.x11 in.), 30 cents a page (11½ in.x14 in.), 50 cents a page (14 in.x18 in.) or 90 cents a page (18 in.x22 in.). Enlargements or reductions can be made within the limits of dimensions of each size print. Members and associates of the American Institute of Accountants are entitled to a discount of 20 per cent. Material not filed in the library, such as reports, letters, etc., should be sent by registered mail or messenger with full instructions. This work will be treated as strictly confidential. Unless the order is large, all copies will be mailed within twenty-four hours.

SPECIAL BINDERS

Binders which were ordered for the convenience of members for filing their library bulletins are ready for sale at the price of $1.25 each.

8

American Institute of Accountants

Library and Bureau of Information

[The Committee on Administration of Endowment authorizes the publication of special Bulletins, of which this is one, on the distinct understanding that members are not to consider answers given to questions as being official pronouncements of the Institute, but merely the individual opinions of accountants to whom the questions were referred. It is earnestly requested that members criticise freely and constructively the answers given in this or any other Bulletin of this series.]

CAPITAL STOCK

Q. The Blank Corporation was organized with an authorized capital stock of 200,000 shares of no par value.

It issued 102,000 shares or 51% of the total authorization to a company for assets which exceeded the liabilities taken over by $550. A value of $9,450.00 was placed on the goodwill and the following entry passed:

Assets other than goodwill	3,450	
Goodwill	9,450	
To liabilities		2,900
To capital stock		10,000

A certain promoter purchased the above 102,000 shares from the parties who owned the previous company and who had sold out to the new company for said 102,000 shares for $10,000 cash. The sale, while not affecting the corporation in any way, was the basis upon which the goodwill valuation was determined.

This promoter then made an agreement to purchase the remaining 98,000 shares at $2.00. In reality he was to sell them for what he could and turn over $2.00 for each share sold.

At the end of two months he had sold 3,000 shares and paid $6,000 to the corporation therefor.

The stockholders then held a meeting, procured authority from the State to change the capital stock to par value stock, a total authorization of 4,000,000 shares at a par value of $1.00 per share. They further decided to call in and retire all the no par value stock and issue to each holder of such 20 $1.00 par value shares for each one share of no par value stock held.

The promoter is, therefore, entitled to receive 2,040,000 for his 102,000 no par value shares and each other stockholder 20 to 1 also. The stockholders have paid the promoter anywhere from $2 to $20 for each no par value share, but the company has received only $2.00 for each share and has no knowledge of what each stockholder has actually paid the promoter for his no par value stock.

In setting up the par value stock given in exchange for the no par value shares, what account is to be charged? In other words, take an example, the promoters own 102,000 no par value shares. In this case capital stock account shows a credit of but $10,000 as the actual value received for these shares. Now the capital stock should show a credit of $2,040,000, or $2,030,000 more than now appears to its credit. What can be done, or, what account can be debited with $2,030,000?

We believe the transaction represents a fraudulent issue of stock. No value will be received for the 2,030,000 shares as well as the additional shares to be received by the other stockholders who have paid the promoter less than $20.00 for the no par value shares purchased.

1

As it is, therefore, in our opinion impossible to make a proper entry to cover the issue of the par value stock in exchange for the no par value shares, what would you advise this corporation to do in order to save itself from future difficulties and to enable it to draw up a proper balance-sheet at this time?

A. It would appear that after the corporation had issued 102,000 shares of stock, no par value, it placed a valuation of $10,000 thereon, that being the equity of the stockholders after taking into account as an asset goodwill, valued at $9,450.00. The disposition of $10,000.00 cash, received for the 102,000 shares, is not disclosed.

If we regard the second transaction with the promoter as not a sale, but a roving commission to attempt to sell 98,000 additional shares, paying the company $2.00 for each share, apparently the corporation at the end of two months would show a capital stock valuation of $16,000.00, representing 105,000 shares of no par value stocks. This assumes that there is neither loss nor profit during the two months' period. Assuming also that, for illustration, we may build up a balance-sheet based on the original statement, the adjusted balance-sheet would be as follows:

Current assets	$9,450.00	Liabilities	$2,900.00
Goodwill	9,450.00	Capital stock — 105,000	
		Shares of no par value	16,000.00

This gives each share of no par value stock a value of 15.2 cents, assuming that the goodwill could be realized at its face value.

We are reluctant to follow the proceedings to the point of valuing 105,000 shares at the exchange of $20.00 per share par value or $2,100,000, and suggesting a form of balance-sheet based thereon. If the question submitted covers all the facts, our advice, as requested in the last paragraph, would be that the company come down to earth, and adjust its capitalization to a reasonable relation to its apparent business.

The issue of 105,000 no par value shares, in itself, seems altogether disproportionate to the net asset value shown by the balance-sheet; the resolution to exchange each no par value share for 20 shares of a par value of $1.00 each results in a capitalization so preposterous as to suggest that some factor in the situation is not disclosed in the question.

PUBLIC STENOGRAPHER

Q. What is the ratio of the expenses of a public stenographer as compared to the income? That is, what part of each dollar received by a public stenographer should be paid for employees, for rent, for advertising, etc., so that a profit could be made?

A. There are two kinds of public stenographers—1st: The reporting stenographer, exemplified in some states by the certified shorthand reporter, who does not take dictation ordinarily, nor do typing work. 2nd: There is the public stenographer who takes dictation, such as letters, memoranda, briefs, etc.

As to the first—the expense for typing is about one-third of the gross amount received by the stenographer for the job. Comparatively few shorthand reporters employ typists by the week. The typing work is usually contracted for and cost varies according to the number of copies. It is safe

2

to say one-third for typing is correct. In addition to this, there are the usual office rent and telephone. There is no expense for paper or carbon, as the typist furnishes these.

As to the second class, the cost depends upon the amount of business in the office. For example, some copying offices have as many as fifteen or twenty stenographers and typists, some doing only typing and others both. An office of this kind, I should say, will earn fully 50%, and this takes into account all overhead charges, such as cost of paper, carbon, repair of machines, rent and telephone.

My own work as a certified shorthand reporter has been somewhat out of the ordinary for the past ten years, being devoted almost wholly to legislative reporting. In many cases I have furnished up to one hundred copies, the highest number, down to about forty copies; in some instances about ten copies. Of course, where I furnish forty to one hundred copies the work is mimeographed and is done in relay form. This requires the highest class of reporting, and stenographers receive seventy-five cents per page net, the typists (who write on a wax stencil) receive twenty-five cents per page, and to this should be added the cost of running on the mimeograph twenty-five cents per page, and in addition the cost of paper, ink, separating, binders and delivering. It is fair to say the total cost is $1.50 per page.

BONUS

Q. A client of our office told us today that he wished to pay a bonus to a certain group of employees. He said the bonus was to be 10% of the audited net profits for 1921 after deducting:
 (1) The bonus.
 (2) Federal income and excess profits tax for 1921.
 (3) New York State franchise tax (4½%).
 (4) A reserve of $500 to take care of Federal capital stock tax.
 (5) A reserve of $6,000 to take care of possible back taxes.
The bonus to be used, of course, in computing taxes. The audited net profits for the year amounted to $205,600.26. Invested capital to be used, $342,420.51.

A. This solution is subject to the following assumptions:
 (1) That the net audited profits are not subject to deduction for New York State taxes paid in 1921. No mention was made as to the amount of these taxes, and as the New York State tax shown in the computation does not become a liability of the corporation until the year 1922, no deduction of that amount has been made before determining the federal income and profits tax. A correct solution of this problem could only be made by taking into account New York State taxes paid in 1921. These taxes are deductible from income for federal income and profits tax purposes.
 (2) That the problem has been correctly stated when it provides that the employees shall receive a bonus of 10% of the net earnings after deducting, among other items, the bonus. As this phase of the problem really means that the employees are to receive 9% of the profits after the other deductions are made it seems absurd to state that they are to receive 10% of such profits.

It is assumed that the reserve of $500.00 for capital stock tax is that which will attach as a liability in June, 1922.

3

Reserves for contingent expense such as is the "Reserve for back taxes" are not deductible for tax purposes.

Net audited profits		$205,600.26
Bonus of 10% accruing to employees		10,660.85
Taxable income		194,939.41
New York State franchise tax		$8,772.27

Federal income and profit taxes
    Excess profits taxes
    Excess profits credit

8% of inv. cap.	$27,393.64		
Specific exemption	3,000.00		
Total E. P. credit	30,393.64		
20% of inv. cap.	68,484.10		
Taxable @ 20%	38,090.46	$ 7,618.09	
Remainder of income } 126,455.31			
Taxable @ 40% }		50,582.12	
Total excess profits tax		58,200.21	

Income tax

Taxable income	194,939.41		
Less E. P. tax	58,200.21		
Taxable @ 10%	136,739.20	13,673.92	
Total federal tax		71,874.13	
Total taxes		80,646.40	
Net audited profits			$205,600.26
Less reserve for capital stock tax		500.00	
Less reserve for back taxes		6,000.00	6,500.00
			199,100.26
			80,646.40
Less federal and state taxes			
			118,453.86
			11,845.39
10% deduction before dividing with employees			
			106,608.47
Net profit subject to bonus			
Bonus 10% of above amount		$10,660.85	

BONUS CONTRACT

Q. A company has a contract with its manager, which stipulates that the manager is to receive a bonus of 20% of the net profits above a certain fixed amount. Assuming that the net profits of the company before deducting the manager's bonus was $60,000 for 1920 and $40,000 for 1921, what would be the amount of bonus to be paid in the two years provided the manager was to receive 20% of the annual net profits in excess of $25,000.

No question of federal taxes is involved, but the point has been raised as to the propriety of deducting the 1920 bonus from the net profits of 1921 in computing the 1921 bonus.

Also, should interest received on bonds owned by the company be included in the net profit upon which the bonus is computed?

A. There does not seem to us to be any justification for treating

4

the bonus paid in respect of the operations of one year as a charge against the profits of the succeeding year. We know of no case in which such a contention has even been advanced.

In regard to the second inquiry, whether interest received on bonds owned by the company should be included in the net profit upon which the bonus is computed, we think the answer depends on the precise terms of the contract. The question states that the manager is to receive a bonus of 20% of the net profits above a certain fixed amount; the term "net profits" clearly requires further definition. If the contract itself is not clear on the point the way in which the fixed amount is determined probably throws some light upon it. If, for instance, the fixed amount were a percentage on the entire capital and surplus invested in the business, it would be natural to bring into account all income of the business from whatever source. If, however, the fixed amount were a definite return on the capital of the company and the bonds represented an investment of the company's share of the profits in previous years which had not been distributed, it would be entirely equitable to exclude the interest on such bonds in arriving at the sum on which the manager's commission would be computed.

NEWSPRINT PAPER MILL

Q. I wish to get an opinion whether or not spoiled material should be included as an element of cost where the circumstances are as follows:

A newsprint paper mill had a contract to sell paper during the six months period ended December 31, 1920, on the cost-plus basis. The contract reads as follows:

"Production costs are to be determined as follows: The actual cost of ground wood, sulphite, alum, color, sizing, and all other materials which become a part of the paper purchased during the six months ending December 31, 1920, shall be added to the inventory value as of June 30, 1920, and from the total amount thus obtained the inventory values of corresponding items at December 31, 1920, shall be deducted. To this amount shall be added the direct conversion or manufacturing costs, including labor, power, lubricants and all other customary expenses of operating and maintaining the paper mill property with $2.00 per ton of paper as depreciation of buildings and equipment, actual cost of all insurance and all other charges for local property taxes and federal capital stock taxes, but exclusive of income taxes and excess profit taxes. The costs shall also include wrapping and finishing and selling, administration and general expenses, as shown on the books of the company. Salaries of officers and managers are to be included at $1.85 per ton for all paper manufactured."

The paper mill does not have a cost system. The cost on this contract was figured on the basis of the percentage of the tonnage shipped to the customer, to the total newsprint produced during the period. For instance, if the total quantity of newsprint manufactured during the period was 10,000,000 pounds, and the total cost was $800,000, the unit cost would be $8.00 per one hundred pounds. If the customer got 7,000,000 pounds of the 10,000,000 produced the cost to the customer would be $560,000, to which cost would be added the profit of $70,000, which is one cent per pound on the paper shipped the customer as provided for in the contract.

During the latter part of the period of the contract 350 tons of ground-wood pulp in the warehouse was damaged in such a way as to make it impossible to use it, by some organic growth, of course through no fault

5

of the paper mill management. Ordinarily this pulp, which had cost $35,000, could have stayed in the warehouse eight or ten months longer without showing any signs of spoilage.

Approximately two-thirds of the newsprint produced during the period was shipped on the contract, and it is the contention of the paper mill that the customer should stand his proportion of the cost of the spoiled pulp, while the customer contends that he should not stand any of the cost of the spoiled pulp.

A. It appears that if the total cost during the period involved was $800,000 and the estimated cost of $8 per 100 pounds was based on an output of 10,000,000 pounds, and that such cost per 100 pounds did not include the element of spoilage, this cost per 100 pounds would be somewhat increased when the discovery was made that 350 tons of ground-wood pulp had become damaged so as to make its use impossible, because of the fact that the total number of pounds produced during the period would be decreased.

It would seem proper to calculate the cost per 100 pounds for the period by dividing the total cost of $800,000 by the actual number of pounds of good paper resulting from the operations. The cost of paper delivered to the customer in question should then be determined by taking the number of pounds delivered at the correct cost per 100 pounds, based on the whole period of operations. The effect obviously would be to include in the cost to the customer the element of spoilage.

Such a procedure would, of course, call for an adjustment in the settlement between the mill and the customer which, however, is not part of the problem submitted by you.

LAND COMPANY

Q. Our firm is now engaged on the audit of a land company, whose main operations consist of the sale of building lots. This concern, some thirty years ago, acquired three large tracts of undeveloped ground. Contrary to the ordinary usage in these cases, when money was expended for improvements and betterments, the amount was not charged—as it should have been—to the respective tracts, but was immediately charged out as an operating expense. When these lots were sold, the gross amount of the sales was credited to the tracts. The results of these entries is that at this time when perhaps three-quarters of the tract have been sold, the remaining quarter stands on the books at a ridiculously low valuation.

As our audit only goes back a period of five years, and as it is to all intents and purposes practically impossible to trace back the entires for 30 years, would it not be the proper thing to do to inventory the unsold portion of these tracts at what would be considered a conservative value?

Of course, it must be well explained that it is difficult to place a market value or price at which similar lands could be purchased today in large amounts, but we can, with a degree of conservatism, arrive at a valuation, which, upon resale, would yield something like 100 per cent. gross profit, and this is the figure that we had thought of using.

The difficulty which confronts us at this time is that this concern has been sending statements to the stock exchange year after year, showing a surplus which is very much underestimated, and, of course, if we on our balance sheet undertake to set up the value of these lands at anything like a fair price, it will automatically increase the surplus from some two hundred and fifty thousand up to a million, and we naturally realize the seriousness of the situation, as no doubt this statement will have a material influence on the value of this stock on the exchange.

Of course, it is understood that we will qualify our balance sheet on

6

the subject of land values, stating that the amount is not the book value but an appraised value, and we can get the president of the company as well as the secretary and perhaps the chairman of the executive committee to certify to the fact that the land is well worth the appraised valuation used. Our report will also suggest that an expert appraisal be made of these lands.

We are, of course, troubled on the one hand by the fact that our balance sheet will greatly enhance the value of the stock on the open market, but on the other hand, we are not forgetting that the stockholders are entitled to know the truth with respect to this land, and it is our humble opinion that this method will more clearly reflect the true condition than if we were to attempt to analyze the tract account with the limited material at our disposal.

A. We think there is certainly no obligation on the auditors to go back over the accounts of the thirty years' operations with a view to restating the unsold land at a correct figure. Apart from the question of taxation we think it would be entirely in order for the auditors to accept the value of the lands at the commencement of the period covered by their audit, applying correct principles to the transactions since that date and stating in their report or certificate that they have accepted the opening balance and are satisfied that it was less than the fair market value of the land. It would appear, however, that for tax purposes a valuation at March 1, 1913, and correct treatment of the accounts since that date are essential. We think the auditors might, in the circumstances, adopt the same basis for general acounting as for tax purposes. We should not be disposed to advise the auditors to place their own valuation on the unsold land, however conservative their valuation might be. If any appraised value is to be used we think the responsibility therefor should be placed on the officers of the company or on qualified experts employed by them.

No doubt the auditors are alive to the possibility of a qualification regarding tax liability being necessary as a result of the unsound accounting methods as well as a qualification as regards the understatement of the remaining land values.

NEWSPAPERS

Q. The following is quoted from "Auditing" by L. R. Dicksee, and edited by R. H. Montgomery, 1908, p. 70, which explains what I mean by establishment account.

"Every periodical is started at a loss, and it is usual to debit this loss to an establishment account; when the concern pays—and so acquires a goodwill—the cost of such goodwill is represented by the amount to the debit of establishment account, which thus virtually becomes a goodwill account. There is no great objection to this system, and it is much in favor on account of the information it affords to the intending purchaser of a recently established paper; but, when a periodical is once fairly started, the auditor should require a very good reason to be furnished him before he sanctions the transfer of an unexpected loss to the establishment account; if such a loss arises from an increase of matter (in quantity or quality) or a reduction in price, it may be in the nature of capital outlay, as tending to increase the permanent value of the concern, but an unexpected loss is likely to have the contrary effect."

If a newspaper during its first year lost $20,000 and during that year secured four thousand subscriptions, would it be proper to capitalize these

7

subscriptions at say, $5.00 each, which would consume the entire amount of loss in establishment account?

What I am anxious to know is how establishment account values are determined, i. e., if there is any fixed practice with reference to handling of said account.

A. We have your inquiry concerning a question referred to the Bureau of Information as to how "establishment values" are determined for newspapers and we also note the quotation from Dicksee's "Auditing."

In reply we may say that this quotation fully covers the principle. It would seem therefore that the entire loss incurred by a newspaper up to the time that it should be on a paying basis may be capitalized. There is no fixed method of determining the length of the establishment period but the capitalization of the first year's loss as the cost of establishment does not seem unreasonable.

BROKERS

Q. A member of the New York Stock Exchange, in addition to conducting his brokerage business, is an active trader on his own account. His own open trades, long and short, at most times embrace as many as 50,000 shares of stock and substantial values in bonds; all of these open trades have been entered into purely for trading purposes, not for investment. We understand that the practice described is quite general and would like very much to know the prevailing opinion as to whether these open trades, both long and short, should be adjusted to market values for the purposes of stating the trader's financial position at a given date and the results of his trading operations for a given period, or whether the long trades should be inventoried at cost and the short trades at sale prices until the transactions are closed by sale or purchase. The position of the bureau of internal revenue seems fairly well settled, and our interest in the matter is more from the independent standpoint of good accounting practice than from that of applying the income tax laws.

A. We have received the following answer to your question:

In our opinion a member of the New York Stock Exchange who, in addition to conducting his brokerage business, is an active trader on his own account and has open trades, both long and short, should adjust to market values both the long and short open items for the purposes of stating his financial position at a given date and the results of his trading operations for a given period. This practice, we believe, is general where the transactions are entered into for the purpose of profit and not for permanent investments.

If the securities do not have a ready market value or are carried as investments, or if it is desired to present a very conservative balance sheet, the securities should be valued at cost or market, whichever is lower. In other words, the losses are taken into account but no profits are included until actually realized by sale.

MOVING EXPENSES

Q. To obtain increased facilities for future operations a corporation leases a new factory site and building. Should the expense of moving from the old location to the new location be treated as a deferred charge to operations and written off over a period of years, or written off entirely in the year in which it was incurred?

A. In our opinion the expense of moving from the old location to the new location may be set up as a deferred charge to operations if considerable, and written off over the period of the new lease not to exceed five years.

8

American Institute of Accountants
Library and Bureau of Information

NOVEMBER, 1922   SPECIAL BULLETIN No. 16

[The Committee on Administration of Endowment authorizes the publication of special Bulletins, of which this is one, on the distinct understanding that members are not to consider answers given to questions as being official pronouncements of the Institute, but merely the individual opinions of accountants to whom the questions were referred. It is earnestly requested that members criticise freely and constructively the answers given in this or any other Bulletin of this series.]

BONUS

I submit hereto attached what, in my opinion, appears to be the correct solution of the bonus problem presented on page three of Special Bulletin No. 15. This solution is subject to the following assumptions:

(1) As in the solution contained in the Special Bulletin, the franchise tax based on 1921 income has not been deducted in the calculation of the 1921 federal tax. The correct franchise tax deduction from taxable income (see A. R. R. 1153, 1-43-558) would be the liability based on the 1920 taxable income, in accordance with the New York State Tax Return, filed on June 30, 1921, for the period from November 1, 1921, to October 31, 1922.

(2) The $500.00 reserve for capital stock tax will not become a liability until June, 1922, the correct 1921 tax having been deducted before arriving at the audited profit. The obvious effect, if this assumption is correct, would be the deduction of two years' capital stock tax. Accordingly the $500.00 reserve has not been deducted from the audited profit before calculation of the Federal Income and Excess Profits Tax.

(3) Reserve for possible back taxes, $6,000.00, represents either a provision for possible additional federal income and excess profits taxes, or a contingent liability for other taxes. In both instances the amount cannot be deducted before calculation of the Federal Income and Excess Profits Taxes.

SOLUTION

Net audited profits		$205,600.26
Let the bonus be represented by	X	
Then taxable income equals	$205,600.26—X	
Calculation of federal tax:		
Excess profits tax credit	$ 30,393.64	
20% of capital	68,484.10	
Taxable at 20%	38,090.46 =	7,618.09
Balance at 40%	137,116.16—X=	54,846.46—.40X
Excess profits tax		$ 62,464.55—.40X
Income tax:		
Income	$205,600.26—X	
Less excess profits tax	62,464.55—.40X	
Balance at 10%	$143,135.71—.60X	14,313.57—.06X
Total federal tax		$ 76,778.12—.46X
Income		205,600.26— X
Federal tax	$ 76,778.12—.46 X	
Franchise tax	9,252.01—.045X	
(4½% of $205,600.26—X)		
Reserve for capital stock tax	500.00	
Reserve for back taxes	6,000.00	
Total deductions		$ 92,530.13—.505X
Income on which to calculate bonus (X)		$113,070.13—.495X

1

Therefore X equals...	113,070.13—.495X

$$\frac{113{,}070.13 - .495X}{10}$$

Or 10X equals...	113,070.13—.495X
Or 10.495 X equals...	113,070.13
Therefore X equals....................................	$ 10,773.71

PROOF

Net audited profits...		$205,600.26
Bonus		10,773.71
Income subject to tax...		194,826.55
Federal tax:		
Income $194,826.55		
Excess profits tax credit................................. 30,393.64		
20% of capital... 68,484.10		
Taxable at 20%... 38,090.46=	7,618.09	
Balance at 40%... 126,342.45	50,536.98	
Excess profits tax...		$ 58,155.07
Income tax:		
Income $194,826.55		
Less excess profits tax.. 58,155.07		
Balance at 10%...$136,671.48	13,667.15	
Total tax..		$ 71,822.22

Income		$205,600.26
Bonus ....$ 10,773.71		
Federal tax 71,822.22		
Franchise tax 8,767.19		
(4½% of $194,826.55)		
Reserve for capital stock tax.............................. 500.00		
Reserve for back taxes.............................. 6,000.00		
Total deductions		97,863.12
Net income for the calculation of the bonus..........		$107,737.14
Bonus at 10%...		$ 10,773.71

The Bureau of Information has received other comments to the same effect.

BANK BALANCES

Q. In the course of securing confirmations from depositors of balances in banks, in connection with audits, I have received confirmations from a certain bank, reading as follows:

......................BANK

The balance to the credit of the...account as shown by our books at the close of business.................................appears to be $...................................

I would appreciate an opinion as to whether an auditor, under those circumstances, should qualify his report to the client in view of the conditional phrase in the above noted form of certificate, wherein it is stated that the balance "appears" to be.

A. We are in receipt of your letter, and do not think that it would be necessary for an accountant to qualify his report because a certificate given by a bank stated that the balance "appeared" to be a certain figure. We think, however, that he might well write to the bank pointing out that as long as they undertook to state the balance as shown by their books there would seem to be no good reason why they should not certify what the balance was, rather than what it appeared to be. He might point out further that banks are vitally interested in the work of accountants, and that therefore the latter might fairly ask for the fullest co-operation from the banks.

2

BALANCE-SHEET

Q. I submit herewith a question with regard to the proper method of submitting a balance-sheet under certain circumstances.

A partnership which had been doing business for a considerable number of years has for the past two years passed through a very critical crisis in their business. They suffered considerable losses and were compelled to make additional contributions of capital in order to maintain their original investment.

While this additional capital helped considerably, it was not sufficient to finance the business, and they were compelled to sell their accounts receivable. These accounts receivable were sold on the basis of 60% advanced against the accounts receivable purchased, the remaining 40% to be remitted by the purchaser when the customer paid the account.

The books of the concern as they stand now show accounts receivable 100 X dollars and due to purchaser of accounts 60 X dollars.

Our client in closing his books has applied the liability to the purchaser against the accounts due from the customers, basing his contention upon the fact that the accounts receivable no longer belong to him, but that 40% equity in the accounts is due him from the discount house, and it is his desire that the balance-sheet reflect only the 40% due therefrom.

While I quite agree with our client as to the facts above stated, I am in a quandary as to the ethics of permitting a balance-sheet to be issued where accounts have been sold and no indication thereof appearing on the balance-sheet.

Our client is absolutely honorable and desires to see the right thing done, but they fear the effect of a balance-sheet which would reflect the sale of their accounts. I, on the other hand, think that a statement which does not show the fact that the accounts are sold would be misleading and would reflect upon my integrity as an accountant.

I wish that you would give me your opinion with regard to the method to be pursued in handling this matter.

A. We feel that inasmuch as when discount houses purchase accounts receivable there is usually a liability on the part of the vendor to reimburse the discount house for any accounts they may not be able to collect, the fact should be disclosed on the balance-sheet that certain of the accounts receivable have been sold, either by way of a footnote or by an explanatory heading under current assets.

CAFETERIA CHAIN RESTAURANTS

Q. What are the percentages of cost to gross revenues in the operation of cafeteria chain restaurants?

A.

Food supplies (including cigars and cigarettes)	38.98%
Wages (general, exclusive of managers' salaries)	19.45%
Rent (less sub-rentals and roof privileges)	3.45%
Food consumed (bakery dining room)	.70%
General expenses	17.22%
Administrative expenses	1.85%
Net profit from operations	18.35%
Total	100.00%

DEPRECIATION OF WOOD WORKING MACHINERY

Q. I am very desirous of finding a flat rate of depreciation which could properly be applied upon the machinery and equipment of a factory manufacturing wooden office chairs.

A. I am afraid that I cannot refer you to any authority on this subject —at least, any publication that covers this subject in detail. There are numerous publications and articles by experienced accountants, covering depreciation of metal working machinery and equipment, but I cannot seem to remember one that covered wood-working equipment in anything but the most general way.

My own experience, which has covered the production of handles, auto-bodies, sewing machine cabinets, phonograph cabinets, school, church and

3

theatre furniture, office furniture, chairs, and filing cabinets, leads me to fix the flat rate of depreciation on the machine tools in a wood-working plant at ten (10%) per cent annually. Auxiliary equipment, such as jigs, forms, templates, wooden patterns, etc., at from 25% to 50%, according to the conditions.

I have found the above figures reasonable. Wood-working machinery does not become obsolete as quickly through change of design as does metal-working machinery—in fact, I know of some machinery in a wood mill which has been running for twenty-seven years, and is still turning out work, while, on the other hand, wood-mill machinery does not get the attention and repairs that steel-working machinery does, owing to the lack of facilities for turning out repair parts that always exist in a metal-working shop. Jigs, forms and patterns are usually of wood, and usage deteriorates them rapidly, so that three years is usually the limit of their existence.

CUSTOMER'S ACCOUNTS

Q. What executive in an organization should, under best and most modern recognized accounting principles, be responsible for keeping the customer's accounts and the reasons for such opinions?

The particular question in mind is "Should customer's accounts be kept under the supervision of the treasurer where the treasurer is not the accounting executive?"

A. We are of the opinion that the responsibility for customer's accounts should rest with the comptroller's department or some department exercising similar functions, if not so named.

We do not regard it as desirable that the treasurer should have supervision of the customer's accounts. The treasurer is essentially a custodian, and handles cash and securities. It is not consistent to combine the handling of cash with the keeping of customer's accounts, and many irregularities have in the past occurred because this combination has been permitted.

UNREALIZED GROSS PROFIT FROM LEASES

Q. C. N. (individual) turns over his assets and liabilities to the C. N. Corporation as follows:

Sundry assets	XXXXXX	
Accounts receivable (leases)	$50,000.00	
Sundry liabilities		XXXXXX
Unrealized gross profit		$20,000.00
(Bal.) net worth		30,000.00

The M. F. Corporation, consisting of two stockholders (1) the aforesaid C. N. and (2) B. K., each owning 50% of the stock of this corporation, also turns over the assets and liabilities as follows:

Sundry assets	XXXXXX	
Accounts receivable (leases)	$ 6,000.00	
Sundry liabilities		XXXXXX
Capital stock and surplus		$4,000.00
Unrealized gross profit		2,000.00
The new corporation issued to		
C. N. 530 shares		$53,000.00
B. K. 30 shares		3,000.00
Total		$56,000.00

How does the new corporation show on its books the unrealized gross profit of $22,000?

A. If before the formation of the corporation there was unrealized gross profit from leases of $22,000 ($20,000 plus $2,000) there is nothing stated that would suggest that this profit has been realized merely by a change in the form of proprietorship. Neither is there anything in the inquiry that would show or even suggest that any "goodwill" exists, but the new corporation, apparently, has issued $56,000 of capital stock for $34,000 of assets and has arbitrarily created an item of "goodwill" amounting to $22,000.

The accounts of the new corporation, on the above assumption, and assuming that it was proper beforehand to include the unrealized gross profit

4

in the books as accounts receivable (which, lacking detail information, may also be questioned), would stand as follows:

Sundry assets	XXXX
Accounts receivable (leases).........................	$56,000.00
Goodwill	22,000.00
Sundry liabilities	XXXX
Capital stock issued......................................	$56,000.00
Unrealized gross profit..................................	22,000.00

EXECUTORSHIP ACCOUNTS

Q. The executor of an estate has engaged me to write up and audit the books for the estate, furnishing decree judicially settling accounts of executors as a basis for starting the current accounts, and a letter interpreting a certain portion of the decree. It seems to me that the interpretation given by the executor is not in accordance with the decree and would be an injustice to one of the beneficiaries.

Being a legal matter, am I governed by interpretation of counsel for the estate? Also, how should I proceed in the matter?

Attached you will please find extracts from the decree and portions of letter interpreting the decree.

EXTRACT FROM DECREE JUDICIALLY SETTLING ACCOUNTS OF EXECUTOR

"In addition to the cash on deposit in the...................Bank amounting to $XXXX; and it appearing that said ABC as one of said executors, having fully accounted for all of the money and property of the estate of said deceased which have come into the hands of said ABC, etc., since February 14, 1916, to and including October 29, 1920, and said accounts having been corrected, adjusted and settled by said surrogate, and a summary statement of the same as corrected having been made as above and herewith recorded; it is

"ADJUDGED AND DECREED that said ABC has received as beneficiary of said estate the sum of $13,000 in excess of the amount received by said XYZ; and it is further

"ORDERED, ADJUDGED AND DECREED that said ABC forthwith pay into said estate in cash said sum of $13,000.

"ORDERED, ADJUDGED AND DECREED that if said ABC does not within ten days after the entry of this decree so deposit said sum of $13,000 and the further sum of $5,800 for costs, disbursements and legal expenses of this proceeding, said entire amount of $13,000, plus said sum of $5,800, shall be charged to said ABC individually as an advance payment on his present and future distributive share in the income of said estate."

EXTRACT OF LETTER INTERPRETING THE DECREE

"The three items, namely, $13,000, $5,800 and $1,100, together, in my opinion, comprise a surcharge against ABC. You will note the decree states that these shall be considered as an advance payment to him and that, in effect, no payments shall be made to him until this amount *from his share* shall have been restored to XYZ. This to me means that ABC can claim no money from the estate until the sum of $39,800 has been paid by the estate to XYZ. Half of this latter sum XYZ would receive any way under the Will, the other half represents a repayment by ABC to him under the decree."

A. Executorship accounts must always be kept in accordance with the statutes or with the rulings of the surrogate or probate court of the state in which the decedent had residence, and, therefore, the decree of the court must be carried out in accordance therewith. The accountant is governed by law in setting up his accounts and if he believes that the interpretation of the counsel for the estate is incorrect or is not in accordance with the decree, he should secure the proper interpretation of the decree from the court itself.

In accordance with the information furnished, it would appear that ABC is ordered to pay into the estate the sum of $13,000.00 plus $5,800.00 in court costs, and plus an additional $1,100.00 (which is not explained). If ABC pays this amount into the estate the sum of $6,900.00 evidently would

5

go to settle court costs and other expenses incurred. **The remaining $13,-000.00**, however, would be divided between ABC and XYZ, each one receiving in cash, if the amount is distributed, the amount of $6,500.00.

The decree further provides that if ABC does not within 10 days after the entering of the decree pay into the estate the sums ordered, these sums, aggregating $19,900,00, will be considered as an advance payment on his future and present distributive share in the estate. This does not mean, as the executor apparently interprets the decree, that XYZ is to receive from the estate $39,800.00 (twice the sum of $19,900.00) before ABC may receive additional funds from the estate.

This may be illustrated as follows:

$13,000.00 has already been realized, and has been retained by ABC. ABC is liable, in addition, for $6,900.00 additional charges which must also be realized from the estate and which must represent a part of ABC's distributable share. This means that ABC has realized $19,900.00 from the estate, and now XYZ must realize a like $19,900.00 before ABC can receive any further distribution. Thus, if $39,800.00 is realized, XYZ will receive one-half of it, or $19,900.00 in cash. Likewise, ABC may also receive $19,900.00 of it, but this amount is represented by the $13,000.00 already retained by ABC, and by the $6,900.00 of court fees and other charges for which ABC is accountable.

The decree does not mean that XYZ is to receive his 50% share, and in addition to receive the 50% share due ABC. It simply means that ABC has already received the full amount of his distributable share, and that he can receive no more until XYZ has likewise received $19,900.00, or its equivalent.

SCHOOLS

Q. Will you kindly advise me as to the most up-to-date method of keeping accounts of payment made to employees, more especially where the number of employees is very large, say, two or three thousand, and particularly in connection with public schools, the payment to teachers?

I might give you my idea as to how they should be carried in order to obtain the best result with a minimum amount of work. I would make a special deposit out of which to pay the salaries and have a special check book upon which to make the withdrawals. In making my entry for the disbursement, instead of enumerating each individual item, I would make one entry, specifying that it included check number so and so to check number so and so, so that one amount might include two or three thousand checks.

In addition to this, I would put in a card system, having a card for each individual receiving salary, and on the card indicate the month, number of check and the amount. While I realize the fact that the keeping of these cards is some job, at the same time it seems to me it would be less work than to post monthly on the cash book two or three thousand items, and the card record is to enable the office to promptly show when a payment was made to an individual, the date, number of check and the amount, so as to avoid the necessity of having to run through thousands of names when looking for one, and in the hurry miss the very one you are looking for.

Any advice that you may offer in this matter will be greatly appreciated.

A. A simple and at the same time a fully adequate system for handling school teachers' monthly or semi-monthly salaries in large cities may be provided through use of a columnar salary record with space at the left for the name of the teacher, the authorized compensation, and such memoranda regarding appointment, etc., as have a bearing on compensation or term of appointment. There should be a column for each payment period. The teachers' names should be arranged by schools and the schools should be arranged in some logical order; a sufficient number of blank lines should be left under each school at the beginning of the year to provide for changes in personnel. The payment columns should be totaled by schools and recapitulated in a grand summary at the end.

6

A special deposit and a special check book are a matter of choice. There are certain obvious conveniences in having such checks kept separate from the general checks; on the other hand, the multiplication of bank deposits has disadvantages. The checks for any periodical payment should in any case be in a consecutive series and their total determined for comparison with the total of the salary list, to which we have referred.

The suggestion that entering each individual payment in the cash book is laborious and unnecessary is perfectly sound. If, however, the expenses of the different schools are kept separate, as should be done, the total for each school should be entered as an item in the cash book. A columnar book of the type described can be made full enough to do away with the necessity of maintaining currently a card system or any other record of the type, as provision can be made in drawing up the form of the record for any peculiar requirements, such as overtime, or other special compensation. A permanent card file should be kept for the personal records of the teachers, but this is an administrative rather than an accounting feature.

FINANCIAL ACCEPTANCE COMPANIES

Q. I am desirous of securing information in regard to the accounting procedure followed by financial acceptance companies, that is, a corporation which purchases from dealers the installment obligation received by such dealers in payment of the personal property (in this case automobiles) sold by them.

The installment obligation consists of a note payable in monthly installments secured by a chattel mortgage, both the note and the chattel mortgage being executed in favor of the dealer and assigned by him, the endorsement on the note being "without recourse." The charges made vary according to the length of time covered by the installments. The difference in the charges between a four-payment obligation and a twelve-payment obligation not being on a ratable basis.

Information is also desired as to the general practice in regard to the apportionment of prepaid charges under the conditions mentioned; also, what would be a relatively fair rate for a reserve for anticipated losses?

A. A financial acceptance company is one which buys notes and acceptances of various kinds, and one of the most common of which covers the purchase of new and second-hand automobiles. These notes, covering the purchase of pleasure cars, trucks, and motor vehicles used for farming, are ordinarily for eighty per cent. of the purchase price, whether the vehicle be new or second-hand.

The notes are usually two-name paper, being made by the purchaser and endorsed by the dealer. Only occasionally are these notes endorsed "without recourse." Sometimes the notes are three-name paper, the manufacturer agreeing to take back the car at a specified figure reducing each succeeding month. The notes are in all cases secured by a chattel mortgage on the property covered by the loan.

These notes are ordinarily payable in ten monthly installments. Sometimes one note and sometimes ten separate notes are given. The interest is included in the face of the notes, as well as a fixed service charge—the latter being a percentage charge on the value of the property purchased. In addition, the property is insured for one year against fire, theft, accident, etc., and this charge is paid by the borrower, ordinarily in cash, though occasionally this charge will be included in the notes.

The service charge is closed into income account in the month in which the charge is made. The prepaid interest is apportioned according to the number of notes outstanding each month—thus, on the basis of ten monthly installments, the first month would receive 10/55 of the prepaid interest income, the next 9/55, 8/55, and so on. For simplicity, the interest is usually computed on all notes, regardless of their exact date, as accruing from the 1st or 15th of the month. Charts, also, are prepared showing each of the ten months' interest income, the charts being based upon various principal amounts loaned. If more or fewer than ten installment notes are given the interest would be apportioned accordingly.

7

Although it is customary practice to close the service charge into income at once, the more correct way would be to apportion this charge monthly over the life of the notes, either proportional to the total number of notes originally outstanding, or perhaps in the same manner as the prepaid interest. To close out the service charge at once means that the company always has taken up more income than has actually been earned. The reason, however, for this procedure is that the notes are rarely defaulted upon, and, in addition, the accounting procedure is thereby simplified.

The insurance premium charged the borrower is credited to a special insurance account, and this account is charged for the cost of the insurance. Usually there is a profit made on the insurance, and this is closed into income either at once or apportioned over the term of the notes.

A fair reserve for anticipated losses is one-tenth of one per cent on all new business, except in the case of loans made on second-hand automobiles, where a rate of one-half of one per cent. may be adopted.

DEPARTMENT STORES

Q. In connection with some department store auditing, I should like to obtain the experience of other stores. What I specifically wish is the rate of turnover for as many departments as possible, together with the ratio of expenses to sales for the corresponding departments.

Departments	Expense Percentage Based on Sales	Times Stock Turned
Silks	27.01	1.94
Dress goods	43.52	2.10
Wash goods	19.94	3.92
Bedwear	20.70	4.13
Linens	25.6	2.15
Drapery	17.25	2.92
Rugs	22.27	2.66
Trunks	21.31	3.57
Pictures	33.06	3.29
Art embroideries	28.50	5.54
Lamps	24.83	1.22
Gloves	16.04	2.64
Hosiery	10.26	5.88
Knit underwear	19.07	2.82
Laces	36.89	1.60
Handkerchiefs	13.73	3.18
Ribbons	20.74	2.51
Small wares	20.29	4.39
Toilets	10.55	3.66
Leather	16.98	5.71
Neckwear	16.08	7.35
Stationery	23.13	4.30
Men's furnishings	22.77	3.03
Little folks	37.13	3.09
Girl's store	37.79	3.38
Undermuslins	24.60	6.97
Patterns	35.57	3.06
Men's clothing	27.24	6.36
Boy's clothing	55.19	4.58
Candy	22.04	13.76
House furnishings	34.30	1.59
China	20.81	1.30
Silverware	25.67	1.35
Furniture	34.17	3.09
Toys	18.59	2.09

NOTE 1.—Interest on investment included in expenses.

NOTE 2.—Stock turned arrived at by dividing the sales by the average weekly stock on hand at retail.

8

American Institute of Accountants

Library and Bureau of Information

FEBRUARY, 1923   SPECIAL BULLETIN No. 17

[The Committee on Administration of Endowment authorizes the publication of special Bulletins, of which this is one, on the distinct understanding that members are not to consider answers given to questions as being official pronouncements of the Institute, but merely the individual opinion of accountants to whom the questions were referred. It is earnestly requested that members criticise freely and constructively the answers given in this or any other Bulletin of this series.]

CAPITAL STOCK

The special bulletins issued by the Institute invite criticism with regard to answers given to questions in the bulletin. I need not, therefore, apologize for taking exception to one of the answers in Special Bulletin, No. 15. I refer to the first question in that bulletin which relates to the statement of capital stock in circumstances which are rather extraordinary.

May I be permitted to say, however, that however repugnant the transaction referred to in the question may be to accountants, the answer is not responsive. The question itself, in my opinion, is incomplete in the sense that it does not give the state under the laws of which the transaction was put through. I am inclined to think, however, that the transaction, as stated in the question, is one which would be legal in certain states, but I do not think it can be answered intelligently without knowing under what guise of legal authority it had been done.

Assuming, however, that I am right in my belief that the transaction was legal, it seems to me that your correspondent, and every other accountant confronted with situations perfectly legal, but somewhat unsound, needs to be informed as to the way in which the transaction should be reflected in a balance-sheet. I have been accused myself of being a heretic, because I insisted it was the duty of an accountant to recognize a legal fact and to reflect it literally in a balance-sheet, but in such a way as not to mislead. If there is a legal method of doing a thing there must be an accounting method of recording the fact and the accountant should adopt that method whether or not in his opinion the law is a sound one.

In the case under discussion my suggestion is that the proper method of stating the capital of the company is as follows:

Capital, $16,000.00.
> represented by capital stock of the par value of $2,100,000.00, consisting of 2,100,000 shares of a par value of $1.00 per share issued in exchange for 105,000 shares of no-par value of a stated or paid-in value according to the financial plans filed under the laws of the State of ———— of $16,000.00.

Your correspondent in answering the question suggests that the company should come down to earth. The promoters will be lucky if it stops there.

NEWSPRINT PAPER MILL

In accordance with the invitation at the head of Special Bulletin No. 15, I beg to offer the following criticism of the answer to the "Newsprint Paper Mill" question:

As I read the question, it is to be definitely assumed that the quantity of newsprint manufactured during the period was 10,000,000 pounds, which would not be affected in any way by the spoiling of wood pulp.

The item that would be affected is the cost of $800,000.00, which would be increased to $835,000.00, due to the closing inventory of materials being that much less in value than was at first reckoned. In other words, the "total cost" of $800,000.00 would not actually be the total cost, by reason of the fact that the spoiled wood pulp had been erroneously included in the closing inventory.

STOCK DIVIDENDS

Q. When a stock dividend is declared in the case of a stock having par value, it is clear that the surplus account will be reduced and the capital stock account increased by an amount equal to the number of shares issued as a stock dividend multiplied by the par value thereof.

In the case of a stock dividend declared in no-par capital stock, what amount, if any, should be transferred from the earned surplus account to the stated value of the no-par capital stock?

A. The following opinions have been received:

A stock dividend declared in no-par capital stock should read to the effect that a dividend of blank dollars per share is payable in stock. At the date of payment a corresponding amount will be transferred from earned surplus to capital, thereby reducing the available earned surplus for cash dividends and accomplishing one of the main objects of a stock dividend. The amount of surplus so transferred would, of course, be optional with the board.

Our opinion must be given with certain reservations, because the state in which the corporation operates is not supplied, but generally speaking, in absence of action by the directors fixing the dollars per share or amount to be transferred, there would be a choice of two ways: one, the number of shares included in the dividend times the stated value per share, or that percentage of the stated or of the actual capital, which the number of shares of the dividend bears to the number of shares previously outstanding.

Where a company is incorporated in a state requiring no stated value to be carried of no-par-value stock, surplus account might be taken as representing the value or equity of such stock and only a memorandum capital stock account, without values, need be carried. In this case, no transfer would be made and notation only of the dividend and the corrected number of shares outstanding would be necessary.

As a general rule, however, companies incorporated with no-par-value stock have on their books a capital stock account for such stock in the amount that the assets acquired were in excess of the total of liabilities and the par value of preferred stock issued or at least a proportion of such excess. In such instances where no stated value is required, no transfer from surplus would be necessary.

Where, however, the certificate of incorporation calls for a stated capital of so much per share outstanding, a transfer of that amount times the number of shares distributed as a dividend should be transferred to the already opened capital stock account. This account would then show the total shares outstanding at the stated value per share.

Again, if the certificate of incorporation calls for a round amount of stated capital and not a per share value of stock outstanding, this round amount would appear on the books as the capital, and would not be altered by a transfer upon the payment of a stock dividend of no-par-value shares, unless with that end in view the charter was altered, in which case a corresponding figure would be transferred from earned surplus.

A stock dividend on no-par-value stock is in itself merely a means of increasing the number of outstanding shares. Such a dividend, if coupled with the capitalization of a part of the earned surplus, appears as reasonable a proceeding as the declaration of a stock dividend on a par-value stock. The transfer to capital account of a portion of the surplus could probably be accomplished by a resolution of the directors, but this is a legal question concerning which state laws may vary, and upon which one should obtain competent legal advice.

The usual method followed in declaration of stock dividends is for the board of directors to pass a resolution containing about the following:

"———— to stockholders of record of ———— date a dividend of —— per cent. payable in the common capital stock of this company to be issued at par." Quite frequently the total amount to be distributed is named in place of or in addition to the per cent.

It would seem that if there were a stated value per share of the no-par capital stock, that if a stock dividend were then declared and that if the resolution provided for distribution of a given number of shares of stock without mention of the amount of money, which those shares represented, then the transfer from surplus to the stated value of the no-par common stock would be the stated value per share multiplied by the number of shares distributed. However, the query arises why a corporation should desire to distribute a stock dividend declared in no-par stock unless it also desired to sell additional shares to obtain new capital and the stock dividend is resorted to in an attempt to equalize equities as between the old shareholders and the new shareholders in the event the latter should buy shares at a lower price than the known or assumed true value of the stock.

The differences in no-par stock laws of different states and the doubtful points involved in their interpretation are so great and the entire subject of no-par stock is so beset with uncertainty and opportunities for transgressing both moral and economic laws, that we are loath to answer this abstract question by any statement of general application. All of the facts involved in and surrounding the proposed action should be known before deciding upon either the propriety of the stock dividend itself or the bookkeeping entries involved thereby.

———————

The question of the values to be set up for no-par capital stock is one that is subject to a great many interpretations. In the first place, no-par capital stock is quite frequently issued without any amount being paid in therefor, either in cash or in other property. The real value behind each share of no-par stock is the total of the capital stock account (if any is set up), plus the total surplus account divided by the number of shares of no-par stock issued. If a stock dividend is issued in no-par stock, the total of these two accounts remains unchanged and the value of each share of no-par stock is reduced corresponding to the increase in the number of shares brought about by such stock dividend declaration.

It would, therefore, appear to be necessary that the directors in declaring a stock dividend on no-par stock should state in their resolution that so much value should be taken from the surplus account, transferred to the stated capital stock account, to be divided in the issuance of no-par stock of a certain number of shares at a fixed amount, thus making capital out of what was formerly surplus.

This would have the effect of taking out of this surplus account an amount that would otherwise be subject in the discretion of the directors for distribution as cash dividend.

In declaring a stock dividend on no-par capital stock, no distribution in money value could certainly be considered unless that amount was stated, and under the new revenue law a serious question might arise as what portion of earned surplus would be accumulated, which might be subject to a 25 per cent. additional tax.

———————

I find on looking through my library that my copy of "Corporation Procedure," by Conyngton, Bennett and Pinkerton, states on pages 1152 and 1153 that "when a stock dividend is payable in stock without par value, the only entry required on the general books is one indicating the number of shares thus disposed of," and that no change is made in the amount of the surplus account or of the capital stock account.

I find, however, on looking at the Journal of Accountancy for December, 1920, on page 459, that Mr. Finney, editor of the Students' Department, furnished as a part of the answer to the question therein contained the following statement:

"The account with stock without par value should be credited with only those amounts actually paid in on the stock, and with any surplus transformed into fixed capital by action of the directors, such action being analogous to the declaration of a stock dividend."

Since receiving your inquiry, we have had quite a discussion in the office on your question, and we have come to the conclusion that we agree with Mr. Finney rather than with Mr. Conyngton, et al.

My reasoning is in this manner:

I have always assumed that the real purpose of a stock dividend was to transfer from the surplus account to the capital account an amount which, so far as possible, would increase the capital account to a sufficient amount to represent approximately the actual capitalization, or an amount which fairly represented the capital which the corporation needed to carry on its business.

If, in the case of declaring a stock dividend of no-par-value stock, it is contended that no change is made in the surplus account, it leaves the corporation where it cannot take out of the surplus account, which is available for dividends, an amount to be added to permanent capital, and this disability prevents withdrawing the amount to a position where it will not be subject to the payment of dividends.

If, however, a cash dividend is declared and the amount of this cash dividend is paid in for new stock, there is no argument against adding the price that the company receives for the new stock to the capital account. This procedure would have exactly the same effect as transferring a similar amount from the surplus account to the capital account and issuing the same number of shares as a stock dividend except that, in the latter case, the stockholders would not be subject to a surtax on the dividend at the time the dividend was declared, but would defer the payment of the tax until the stock received as a dividend was realized upon in cash by them.

Under these circumstances, it would seem entirely obvious that a corporation having no-par-value common stock should not be deprived of its privilege of investing permanently in the capital of the company's accumulated earnings which were actually needed in the conduct of the business and which the directors felt it would be for the interest and safety of the business to have designated as capital instead of as surplus. As I see it, there is no other means of accomplishing this except by declaring a stock dividend, unless a cash dividend is paid to the stockholders and then paid back to the company for new stock.

We have also studied the New York state law regarding no-par-value stock and thus far have been unable to find any requirement of the law which prohibits the payment of a stock dividend.

It is, therefore, our conclusion and opinion that in a case of this kind we should recommend to our client that a stock dividend be declared, that the amount of dividend decided upon be transferred from the surplus account to the capital account, and that the requisite number of shares be added to the outstanding stock. We should expect, of course, to call in the old stock certificates and exchange them for new certificates, which would show the total shares of stock outstanding after the stock dividend.

I presume the question arises, if this is done, as to how many shares should be issued to cover the amount which it was decided to transfer to capital. As you have not asked this question, I will not attempt to answer it except to say that I should judge this might depend very largely upon the circumstances in the case of each corporation and what the directors considered to be the wisest course under those circumstances which might exist.

Any dividend declared, whether in cash or stock, must be capable of translation into dollars and cents. Dividends may be declared as a lump sum; an amount per share; a per cent of the par value of the outstanding capital stock, or a per cent of the credit to the capital stock, no-par-value.

The credit to capital stock account, by a charge to surplus, would be the amount of the dividend declared.

Assume that 10,000 shares have been issued and that a dividend of $10.00 per share payable in stock has been declared, the amount to be transferred from earned surplus to capital stock, no-par-value, would be $100,000.00. The dividend being payable in stock raises a number of points. If the stock has been authorized to sell at $10.00 per share, it would simply be a matter of the issuance of 10,000 shares of stock. Theoretically, there would be no advantage in issuing the additional 10,000 shares, as the original 10,000 shares would have the same book value as 20,000 shares. Practically, there may be quite a decided advantage from the standpoint of selling the shares. It is a well established fact that it is easier to sell 20,000 shares at $10.00 each than to sell 10,000 shares at $20.00 each. This law of psychology is often the reason why stock dividends are declared.

When the stock dividend declared per share is less than, or greater than a multiple of the amount at which additional shares of no-par-value share have been authorized to sell, then it becomes necessary to issue fractional stock certificates to such stockholders whose dividends are less than the authorized selling price of a share or in excess of any multiple thereon.

Naturally, any surplus remaining after all charges and dividends of preference have been taken care of, belongs to the no-par stockholders. Furthermore, the very nature of no-par stock requires that any dividends to its stockholders have to be paid at a given amount per share rather than a percentage per share which obtains in the cases of capital stock having par value.

This being true, it will be necessary that any stock dividend would have to be declared in a definite amount of dollars and in order to cover the outstanding stock in even shares, would have to be in such an amount as represents the per share value then covered on the books or else such value as would represent a fractional value based on the outstanding book value as a capital stock liability.

In this connection I bring to your attention the point made by an extremely able attorney on the question of taxing surplus, that the surplus remaining after all other charges had been covered belong to the no-par stockholders and simply increases the intrinsic value of their holdings. Therefore such surplus would not be taxable by the federal government provided such a tax is eventually instituted.

COMMISSIONS

Q. A manager is to receive 10 per cent. commission after deducting income taxes and $50,000 from $190,000 income. The fiscal year ended August 31, 1922. The invested capital is $500,000.

A. The solution to the problem is as follows:

Commission $10,612.50
Tax 33,375.04

Attached is a copy of a computation in support of these figures.

FISCAL YEAR ENDED AUG. 31, 1922

A Invested capital $500,000.00

Excess profits credit 8 per cent. of invested capital.................... 40,000.00
Specific exemption 3,000.00

B Total excess profits credit...$ 43,000.00

C Gross income before commission...............................$190,000.00
D Less commission (see K below).............................. 10,612.50

E Net income $179,387.50

Computation of taxes, 1921 basis:
Income not over 20% of invested capital (A).........$100,000.00
Less excess profits credit (B)................................... 43,000.00

Remainder taxable at 20%..	$ 57,000.00	$11,400.00
Income over 20% of invested capital at 40%.... _.	79,387.50	31,755.00

F   Total excess profits tax...$ 43,155.00

Income tax:

Net income (E)	$179,387.50	
Less excess profits tax (F)........................$43,115.00		
Specific exemption	43,155.00	
Balance taxable at 10%..	$136,232.50	13,623.25

G   Total taxes (1921 basis)...$ 56,778.25

1922 basis:

H   Income tax, 12½% of (E)................................   179,387.50   22,423.44

4/12 of G	$ 18,926.08
8/12 of H	14,948.96

I   Total taxes ....$ 33,875.04

Proof

Income before deducting taxes or commission (C)..$190,000.00		
Less taxes as above (I)................................$33,875.04		
Plus (arbitrary)	50,000.00	83,875.04

J   Net income subject to 10% commission...................$106,124.96

K Commission at 10% of (J)..$ 10,612.50	
Commission as above (D)..	10,612.50

You may inform your inquirer that we do not use an arithmetical or algebraical formula for working out problems of the kind submitted by him where there are a tax and commission dependent upon each other.

Formulas could, of course, be prepared, and in the early days of the income tax when these problems arose, we used to devise such formulas, but found in practice that we could arrive at the solution more quickly by what we call a trial-and-error method, that is, by assuming a certain commission and working out the resulting tax on that basis, then adjusting the commission on account of any error disclosed in the proof until we arrived at a figure of commission that would exactly balance with the amount to be arrived at after deducting the final and correct amount of tax.

The arbitrary deduction of $50,000 in the proof is the $50,000 referred to in the first telegram submitted by you. In this telegram it states that the manager is to get 10 per cent. commission after deducting income taxes and $50,000.

DIVIDENDS

Q. I should like to obtain information with reference to handling dividends paid by an oil producing corporation from a reserve for depletion account.

In this instance the reserve for depletion is the result of several years' accruals and at the time the dividends were paid from this depletion reserve, there was no surplus.

What accounts are used on the general books to record the handling of the dividends?

In preparing a balance-sheet at the close of a fiscal year, how are the accounts effected by the reserve for depletion and the dividends reflected on this statement?

A. We know of no accounting theory which countenances the declaration of dividends out of a reserve for depletion. This reserve, if it represents what the title of the account indicates, is merely an offset to the value of the property, and is built up through a charge to cost and credit to the reserve, based on the estimated production.

The usual entry for dividends is to charge dividends declared and credit dividends payable. In the closing accounts the charge for dividends payable goes against the surplus, while the liability for the payment of the dividends appears on the balance-sheet. This, of course, is all predicated on the assumption that the dividend is not to be paid until after the date of the balance-sheet.

On the balance-sheet the reserve for depletion appears either as a deduction on the asset side from the property account, or on the liability side, depending on the procedure with regard to the preparation of the balance-sheet. The liability for dividends payable appears on the right-hand side, under the head of current liabilities.

ICE CREAM COSTS

Q. Please advise if you have anything relating to costs in connection with the manufacture of ice cream.

A. The Bureau of Information has received the following statistics:

COST ON GALLON BASIS FOR THE YEAR 1921

On hand Dec. 31, 1920	3,355	gals
Made year 1921	397,074	"
	400,429	"
Less on hand Dec 31, 1921	3,768	"
Made to sell	396,661	"
Actual sales	395,711	"
Short	950	"

Gallons made, 397,074:	Cost	Per gal.
Ingredients	$175,275.43	44.1c
Mfg. wages	$ 10,238.11	2.6
Power house expense	10,938.56	2.7
Packers and papers	6,251.09	1.6
Coal, light and power	11,570.84	2.9
Repairs	9,567.83	2.4
Ice	10,734.29	2.7
Salt	11,299.77	2.9
Repairs, tubs, cans and cabinets	6,246.69	1.6
Porters, oils and general expenses	17,806.32	4.5
	$ 94,653.50	23.9
Drivers' and salesmen's wages	$ 20,058.00	5.0
Auto expense and gas	25,343.08	6.4
Advertising	28,229.42	7.1
Express and sundry delivery	46,098.37	11.7
	$119,728.87	30.2
Office expense	$ 13,527.82	3.4
Superintendents and officers	21,325.00	5.4
Interest, taxes and insurance	8,097.67	2.0
Bad debts	1,881.04	.5
Depreciation	31,981.64	8.0
	$ 76,813.17	19.3
Total expenses	$466,470.97	117.5
Profit	36,934.22	9.3
Selling price	$503,405.19	126.8c

MORTGAGE INVESTMENT COMPANY

Q. 1. A mortgage investment company loans money on a mortgage amounting to $10,000.00, maturing in five years, interest at 7 per cent, payable semi-annually. On this the mortgagor receives only $9,000.00. Thus the mortgage company has an earning in excess of the stated interest of $1,000.00. The security for this mortgage would be real estate of an appraised value in excess of $20,000.00. The mortgage company has been accustomed to taking the discount into their earnings in the month when the mortgage was entered into. Contemplating an audit they wish to have their accounts set up in such a manner that the auditor will be justified in giving them an unqualified certificate as to both balance-sheet and income statement.

(a) Should such discount be amortized over the life of the mortgage or should it be reserved as an earning at time of maturity?

(b) Should this mortgage be set up as an asset at $10,000.00 with an opposing account representing unamortized discount or should it be carried at its cost, $9,000.00, with no offsetting account?

2. A mortgage company deposits its mortgage securities with a bank under a trustee agreement and the trustee certifies the mortgage company's collateral trust bonds, 20-year maturities bearing interest at 6 per cent. against the securities. The mortgage company then through its own sales organization places these collateral trust bonds on the market, paying the salesmen a commission of 10 per cent.

(a) Should the commission paid the salesmen be absorbed as a business expense in the month when the bond is sold, along with the expenses of the sales department, or, (b) should this commission be amortized over the life of the bond in the same manner as would be done if they had sold these bonds to an investment banking house at a discount?

The first question is very similar to the one appearing in Special Bulletin No. 9, page 7, but I believe taken in conjunction with the second question that it might call for different treatment than if it stood entirely alone.

A. 1. (a) The ordinary procedure in the case of discount on bonds or mortgages is to amortize the discount over the life of the investment, and in the case of the $1,000.00 discount referred to in this question it would be proper to apportion the discount, at least with approximate accuracy, over the life of the mortgage.

(b) The mortgage may be set up in the books at $10,000.00, and an unamortized discount account carried as a deferred credit for $1,000.00. Periodically at the time of interest payments the portion of the discount earned should be transferred to interest income. In the balance-sheet the unamortized discount may be deducted from the face value of the mortgage, or may be shown as a deferred credit on the liability side of the statement.

2. The expense of marketing the bonds referred to should not be confused with ordinary selling expense and may be set up as a deferred charge to be apportioned over the life of the bonds, just as if the bonds had been sold at par, less 10 per cent., through an investment house. It would be conservative, however, to write off the expense in the period in which it was incurred.

---

1. (a) If each year is to receive its proportionate share of income, the discount should be apportioned over the life of the mortgage. If the discount is reserved until maturity of the mortgage, the amount thereof will appear in earnings in the last year only, unless, of course, the last year is credited only with its proportion of discount and the remainder credited to surplus. The first-named method appears to us to be preferable.

(b) Either method is correct. It is a more or less uniform practice for mortgage companies to set up their loans at par with an opposing account representing unamortized discount.

2. Commissions to salesmen should be treated as a selling expense in the month in which the sale is made.

American Institute of Accountants

Library and Bureau of Information

MARCH, 1923   SPECIAL BULLETIN No. 18

[The Committee on Administration of Endowment authorizes the publication of special Bulletins, of which this is one, on the distinct understanding that members are not to consider answers given to questions as being official pronouncements of the Institute, but merely the individual opinion of accountants to whom the questions were referred. It is earnestly requested that members criticise freely and constructively the answers given in this or any other Bulletin of this series.]

LUMBER BROKERS

Q. Will you kindly send me as soon as possible cost information based on net sales for concerns that sell hardwood lumber, or in fact any kind of lumber, by the car load. I might have used the term lumber brokers.

	Per Cent
A. Average cost of sales	94.07
Average salaries	2.51
Average all other costs	2.45
Miscellaneous income	.64
Average gross profit	1.61
	100.00

DUAL TELLER SETTLEMENT SYSTEM

Q. Will you kindly obtain for us at the earliest opportunity an outline of the dual teller settlement system for banks.

A. In this system there are two outstanding features to be kept in mind: (1) currency transactions only are considered on the tellers' proof sheets and (2) although the tellers' windows are marked to designate a certain group of customers, it is not vital in the operation of this system that the customers transact their business through the designated window. This designation is made merely for the purpose of dividing the customers and equalizing the work of the various tellers.

The individual teller's proof sheet submitted provides on the reverse side for currency only received and paid out. On the sample deposit ticket submitted there is shown thirty dollars ($30.00) currency in the deposit. When the customer makes this deposit the teller counts the currency and, if correct, marks on the deposit ticket the designation for currency, usually a large "C." He then enters the deposit showing the customer's name and amount on the reverse side of his proof sheet under the caption "Distributing Department Currency." This deposit is then set aside for the proving and sorting departments who take the checks and other items in the deposit and sort and prove as explained hereinafter.

Entries for currency paid out by the teller are entered in the columns "checks on us," "distributing department checks," "coupons," etc., the clearance items being included with the distributing department checks and segregated later by the sorting department. The form provides for morning clearance and can be used if desired, in which event, the clearance items are separated from the distributing department checks.

On the recapitulation side of this sheet there is proof for receipts and disbursements of cash by the teller so arranged as to be self explanatory. The total checks cashed are entered on the debit side and the currency received is entered on the credit side, as noted on the form. Any other cash transactions by the teller are noted in the proper place on the proof sheet. The balance at the beginning of the day is entered on the credit side under the caption, "cash carried over" and the balance at the end of the day is entered on the debit side opposite "cash on hand."

1

PROOF SHEET

PAYING AND RECEIVING TELLER NO. _____

NATIONAL BANK SAVINGS & TRUST CO. OF _____

192_

DEBIT	DEPARTMENTS	CREDIT
	Transit	
	A. H. Chalmers	
	P. H. Chalmers	
Check Cashed	National Banks	
"	(Clerks) Branch Dept. (German)	*Cash Obtained On*
	Note Teller	
	Draft Teller	
	Collection Teller	
	Return Teller	
	Coupon Teller	
	Paying and Receiving Teller	
	Foreign Department	
	Savings Paying	
	Savings Receiving	
	Country Banks	
	General Books	
Bal. End	Cash Carried Over	*Bal. Beginning*
	Cash on Hand	
	PROOF	

2

CASH ON HAND	DEBIT	COUNTRY BANKS	CREDIT
Gold Coin			
Gold Certificates			
Legal Tenders			
Standards			
Silver Certificates			
Fractional Silver			
National Bank Notes			
Federal Reserve Notes			
Nickels and Pennies			
		GENERAL BOOKS	
TOTAL CASH			

I CERTIFY TO THE CORRECTNESS OF THE ABOVE

_____
TELLER

3

RECAPITULATION PROOF SHEET

PAYING AND RECEIVING TELLERS

NATIONAL BANK SAVINGS & TRUST CO., OF _____ _____192___

DEBIT	DEPARTMENTS	CREDIT
	Trust	
	A. M. Clemens	
	F. B. Clemens	
	Individual Banks	
	(Checks) Distrib. Dept. (German)	
	Note Teller	
	Draft Teller	
	Collection Teller	
	Return Teller	
	Comm. Teller	
	Paying and Receiving Teller	
	Foreign Department	
	Savings Paying	
	Savings Receiving	
	Country Banks	
	General Banks	
	Cash Carried Over	
	Cash on Hand	
	PROOF	

4

CASH ON HAND

CASH ON HAND	COUNTRY BANKS	DEBIT	CREDIT
Gold Coin			
Gold Certificate			
Legal Tender			
Standards			
Silver Certificates			
Fractional Silver			
National Bank Notes			
Federal Reserve Notes			
Rebate and Pennies			
	GENERAL BOOKS		
TOTAL CASH			

I CERTIFY TO THE CORRECTNESS OF THE ABOVE

_____ TELLER

5

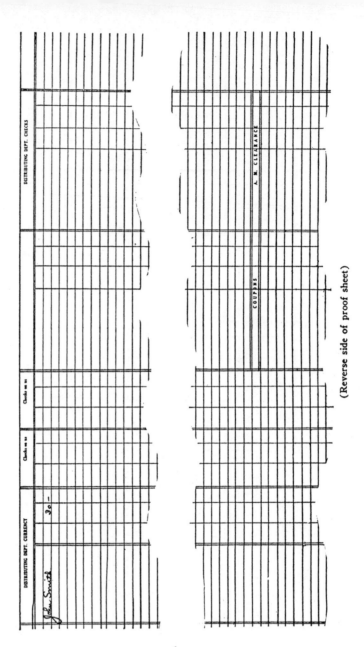

(Reverse side of proof sheet)

6

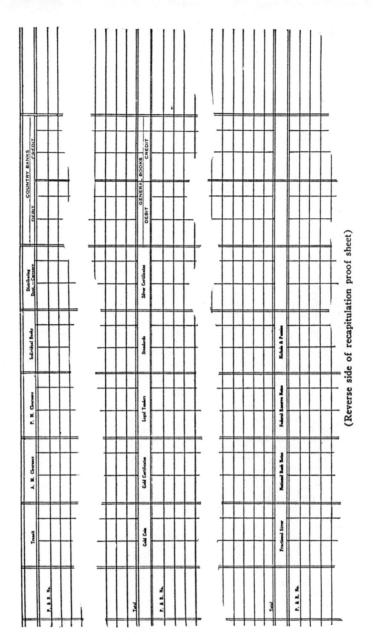

(Reverse side of recapitulation proof sheet)

7

The teller's sheet is balanced in this manner and turned over to the clerk entrusted with the recapitulation who begins on the reverse side of the "recapitulation proof sheet" and enters the totals from the various tellers' sheets. We do not believe it is necessary to go into the details of the recapitulation of the tellers' sheets as this is merely mechanical and can be worked out by following the form submitted. The balance of the total cash is accomplished in the same manner as the individual teller's.

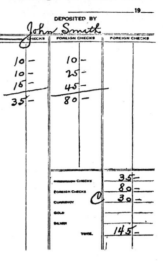

Going back to the depositor's ticket which was laid aside by the teller when he counted the currency and entered same upon his proof sheet. This ticket, together with others taken in by the teller, are turned over to the sorting department and balanced in groups of, say fifteen to twenty tickets. This is accomplished by sorting the checks and items of a group of tickets into stacks of "checks on us," "clearance items," "transit items," etc., totaled on the adding machine, and balanced to the totals shown on the deposit tickets, the currency items, of course, not being taken into consideration. From the totals of the sorting department are prepared the proper entries for the general books.

The "paying and receiving tellers' proof sheet," "paying and receiving tellers' recapitulation proof sheet" and a sample deposit ticket illustrate the operation of this system.

FEDERAL INCOME TAX

Q. A corporation makes its federal income tax returns on the basis of cash receipts and disbursements. That is, all cash received is considered income and all cash disbursements as deductions. During the year 1922 it paid a liquidating dividend. In view of the method of accounting, is the liquidating dividend a deduction for income tax purposes?

A. Dividends, whether from earnings or from capital, are never deductible in determining taxable income.

The federal income tax is levied on net gains or profits. Dividends are a distribution of gains and profits or a return of capital, and hence cannot be considered in any calculation of profits.

Furthermore, it would be quite unusual for all cash received by a corporation (or even an individual) to represent income, and for all cash disbursements to represent expense. For example, reimbursement of a loan would be cash received, but it would not be income, neither would money loaned be expense even though it were a cash disbursement.

NORMAL

Q. We have a case in which it is quite important to define the term "normal" as used in the tax law of 1919. The circumstances are these:

A, an individual, leased to B, a corporation, a piece of property at $12,000.00 a year under the terms of which lease B was to pay A in addition to the $12,000.00 the "normal" income tax on the rent. B leased the property to C, another corporation, and wrote the same provision into the lease

8

covering federal taxes in the following terms—"also normal income tax on all rentals paid in excess of $12,000.00 per annum."

C has consistently refused to pay any income tax to B on the ground that a corporation has no normal tax.

A glance at the 1919 revenue acts bring out the following points. The law consisted of:

Title   I—General definition.
Title   II—Income tax.
Title   III—War profits and excess profits tax.
Title II consisted of four parts as follows:
Part 1—General provisions.
Part 2—Individuals (Normal)
                   (Surtax)
Part 3—Corporations.
Part 4—Administrative provisions.

Structually it would seem that the word "normal" as herein used applied distinctively to individuals, but it is our belief that the surtax stood in the same relation to the "normal" tax in the case of individuals as the war profits and excess profits taxes stood to the tax on corporations and, therefore, the tax on corporations under part 3 of title II could be properly called the "normal" tax.

We believe that corporation C is taking refuge in a pure technicality and we would like your opinion on the subject.

A. As you suggest the "normal" tax is the tax of 4 per cent and 8 per cent of an individual's taxable income and the term is used to distinguish this tax from the surtax of an individual. It would seem to the writer that corporation C is depending upon a mere technicality to avoid payment of an amount it contracted to pay and that if this case were litigated a court would hold that inasmuch as the said corporation agreed to pay a certain tax, which by simply loose construction of the contract was termed a "normal" tax, that the said corporation C had undertaken to pay the same "normal" tax that corporation B had undertaken to pay to the individual.

Very little else can be said with respect to this question, except that it has not been unusual to refer to a corporation's tax of 10 per cent or 12 per cent of its taxable income, as the normal tax, and it is possible that corporation B could show instances where the word "normal" had been so used.

That the word "normal" tax has been used by the department of internal revenue to designate the income tax of a corporation as distinguished from excess and war profits tax, we quote the following:

"Any amounts, however large, received as dividends from a foreign corporation taxable upon income derived from sources within the United States, however small such income may be, is exempt from the normal tax under section 216 (a), or, in case the recipient is a corporation, under section 234 (a) 6."

The above quotation is from Accumulative Bulletin No. 1 and is found on page 265 of said bulletin.

RESERVES FOR CONTINGENCIES

Q. A corporation which makes an annual statement of financial condition as of October 31 has reported annual profits approximately as follows:

Year ended October 31—

1920	$1,500,000.00
1921 (loss)	250,000.00
1922	525,000.00
Total	$1,775,000.00

9

It seems that in 1920 a reserve for contingencies in the amount of $625,000.00 was deducted from profits. In 1921 the entire reserve was absorbed and another reserve of $625,000.00 was set up out of surplus, and in 1922 the reserve was reduced in the amount of $437,500.00 and credited to profits. Accordingly the true profits of the three years were as follows:

1920 ....$2,125,000.00
1921 (loss) 875,000.00
1922 .... 87,500.00

Total $1,337,500.00

From this statement it seems that net profits for the three years have been overstated $432,500.00 and that profits or losses have been equalized over the three years in a way that, to say the least, is certainly misleading.

We are of the opinion that reserves for contingencies are nothing more or less than surplus temporarily appropriated and that losses should be charged against the operations of the year in which they occur. Consequently we believe that reserves for contingencies are chargeable against surplus and should be credited to that account when found to be no longer necessary.

In addition to advice as to the proper method of dealing with the reserve, we should like to be informed as to whether, as a member of the Institute, an accountant could with propriety certify that the profits for the fiscal year ended October 31, 1922, were $525,000.00. If the reply to the latter proposition is in the negative, is the offense of such a nature as to jeopardize the accountant's membership in the Institute?

A. There is no doubt in our minds but that in the case you cite the true profits for 1922 amounted to $87,500.00 and that the transfer of $437,500.00 from reserve for contingencies to which you refer should be credited to surplus, inasmuch as when the reserve was established it was charged against surplus. However, in 1920 the amount of $625,000.00 credited to a reserve for contingencies and charged against the earnings of that year was merely a segregation of net profits, and we do not think that any serious objection can be raised in returning the amount to the income of 1921, provided the facts are disclosed in the published accounts.

SURPLUS

Q. A corporation had outstanding 7,500 shares of stock having a par value of $10.00 each and had accumulated a surplus of $1,500,000.00. In January, 1921, it changed its capitalization from 7,500 shares of $10.00 each to 15,000 shares of no par value, but made no entry on its books. Because of the present agitation for a tax on surplus, the management wishes to make the books reflect the change in the capitalization by transferring the amount of $1,500,000.00 from surplus to capital, on the theory that that portion of the present surplus was capitalized at the time the new stock was issued.

(1) My contention is that no part of the surplus was capitalized; that the present capitalization is exactly what it was originally, except that it is represented by twice as many shares of no par value, which in the aggregate are worth no more than the original ones. Therefore, if a tax on surplus should ever be assessed the mere fact that the surplus was in the capital account would make no difference.

(2) The management of the company contends that the surplus accumulated or the deficit sustained each year should be credited or charged, as the case may be, directly to the capital stock account. While, in theory, this may not be incorrect, yet it seems to me that it is at least advisable to keep the original investment separate from the surplus accretions. My opinion is that the capital investment in this case is $75,000.00 and not $1,575,000.00, as the company contends. It might be stated that no stock dividend was declared.

10

A. It does not appear that any change has taken place in the capitalization. The changes which have taken place are the form of stock and number of shares representing ownership. There is neither more nor less capital than before, nor has the amount of surplus changed. The change in the form and number of shares does not automatically convert the surplus into capital. Action by the directors specifically transferring the surplus to capital is necessary before such combination may be regarded as having taken place. Capitalization is usually interpreted to mean the amount which appears in the capital account. Hence, before it would be proper to make the books reflect a capitalization of $1,575,000.00, it would be necessary to have the directors authorize the transfer of $1,500,000.00 from surplus to capital.

Such procedure might be entirely proper, but apparently ill-advised. To so dispose of surplus might result in embarrassment if future operations fail to provide profits out of which dividends may be paid, and put the corporation in the illegal position of paying dividends out of capital. When all the surplus is transferred to capital the door to future dividends is closed until sufficient additional profits have been made to provide for such dividends. The experience of many concerns in the latter half of the year nineteen twenty should be sufficiently practical to deter any corporation from taking this unnecessary step.

It is evident that in order to solve many of the present-day problems of non-par stock the consideration of a few sensible fundamentals is necessary. Capital is a portion of wealth invested in an enterprise with a view to gain. Surplus is an accumulation of net gains derived primarily from operations. It may also spring from increases, due to economic conditions, in values of possessions. Dividends are declarable only out of surplus. This is not only in accordance with sound economics, but controlled in most states by law.

The proprietary equity represented by capital stock without par value is the excess of assets over liabilities. But this equity needs some classification. It would be about as logical to issue an income statement showing one item for expenses without classification as to set up a balance-sheet with the proprietary equity shown as a lump sum. Part of it is capital on which dividends may not encroach. Part of it is perhaps surplus resulting from operations and available for dividends. Some of the equity may be surplus arising from revaluation of assets, and while available for dividends, legally is not in the form of liquid assets which may be distributed in satisfaction of a dividend declared.

BONDS

Q. The following questions have arisen in connection with a bond issue and with reference to the proper method of presentation on a balance-sheet. The facts are:

The company has executed a closed mortgage against property carried upon the books at $20,000,000.00, which is less than the appraised value given by independent appraisers. This mortgage has been issued to secure an issue of $10,000,000.00 first mortgage 6% bonds, and the trustee (in this case a financial institution) has turned over to the company bonds duly signed by such trustee. The company disposes of $9,000,000.00 of these bonds to the bankers at 95 retaining $1,000,000.00 in the treasury for corporate purposes. Bonds in the treasury have been signed by the corporate officers and are in the same form as those that are outstanding in the hands of the public. Questions at issue are:

1. Are there $10,000,000.00 of bonds issued, or, are there only $9,000,000.00 of bonds issued?

2. Is the company correct in insisting that the $1,000,000.00 of bonds are treasury bonds, and that being treasury bonds they should be shown as an asset at this amount?

3. Is the company obliged to turn over to the trustee the semi-annual interest on $10,000,000.00 of bonds, and clip coupons on treasury bonds and present them for collection in the regular way?

11

4. Are the $1,000,000.00 of bonds entitled to share in the proceeds of a foreclosure of the mortgaged property, if,

    (a) in the company's treasury at the date of foreclosure;
    (b) if pledged to secure bank loans on other indebtedness;
    (c) if sold at bargain price (best price obtainable) immediately before commencement of foreclosure proceedings.

A. 1. As perhaps the best available source of information, the Interstate Commerce Commission, in its Classification of Income, Profit and Loss, and General Balance Sheet Accounts for Steam Roads, effective July 1, 1914, page 52, note B, states that "for the purposes of the balance-sheet statement, funded debt securities are considered to be nominally issued when certified by trustees and placed with the proper officer for sale and delivery, or pledged, or otherwise placed in some special fund of the accounting company. They are considered to be actually issued when they have been sold to a bona fide purchaser for a valuable consideration, and such purchaser holds them free from all control by the accounting company. All funded debt securities actually issued and not reacquired and held by or for the accounting company are considered to be actually outstanding. If reacquired by or for the accounting company under such circumstances as require them to be considered as held alive and not cancelled or retired, they are considered to be nominally outstanding."

The term treasury bond is not used by the commission but includes either nominally issued or nominally outstanding bonds which are held by a corporation in its treasury upon its own behalf. This view has also been adopted by public utility commissions, so in the above case there are $10,000,000 of bonds issued.

2. In accordance with the above quotation, the company is correct in insisting that $1,000,000 of the bonds are treasury bonds. They should be shown in the balance-sheet as a deduction from the $10,000,000 of bonds issued.

3. As long as the bonds have been certified by the trustee and have not been cancelled, it makes no difference to the trustee, for interest purposes, in whose possession they may be. The trustee has no way of determining where the bonds are, and in theory the issuer must pay over to the trustee the full amount of the interest on the issued bonds, and must in turn present the coupons on the treasury bonds.

These matters are ordinarily covered in the indenture of trust or other agreement, and, as a practical matter, the issuing corporation usually turns over to the trustee merely the equivalent of the interest on the issued bonds. That is, the issuer would turn over to the trustee the cash to cover interest on bonds outstanding in the hands of the public and the actual interest coupons for treasury bonds. In the assumed illustration, the borrowing corporation would deliver semi-annually to the trustee $30,000 in coupons and $270,000 in cash.

4. This is a question in law and should be referred to one properly qualified to give such advice. However, it is our understanding that if the bonds were (a) in the company's treasury at the date of foreclosure these bonds would share in the proceeds of the foreclosure to the same extent as any other outstanding bonds. In case the claims of creditors were not fully satisfied from the proceeds of the foreclosure, the creditors could obtain a deficiency judgment and participate in the share of the proceeds of the foreclosure applicable to the treasury bonds. If the bonds (b) were pledged to secure bank loans or other indebtedness the holders of the notes could sell the bonds to protect themselves, and thus the bonds would be outstanding in the hands of the public and would participate in the proceeds of the foreclosure. If the bonds (c) were sold at the best price obtainable immediately before foreclosure took place they would share in the foreclosure proceeds. In the latter case, if the purchaser were a stockholder of the corporation, in some jurisdictions the question of collusion might be raised. Ordinarily, however, treasury bonds would share equally with all other outstanding bonds in the proceeds of a foreclosure.

12

American Institute of Accountants
Library and Bureau of Information

MAY 1923,   SPECIAL BULLETIN NO. 19

[The Committee on Administration of Endowment authorizes the publication of special Bulletins, of which this is one, on the distinct understanding that members are not to consider answers given to questions as being official pronouncements of the Institute, but merely the individual opinions of accountants to whom the questions were referred. It is earnestly requested that members criticise freely and constructively the answers given in this or any other Bulletin of this series.]

LIBRARY BULLETIN

So many requests have been received for copies of the library bulletins that it has been decided to print more than are actually required for Institute members. These copies will be distributed gratis to organizations at the discretion of the Committee on Administration of Endowment. The price of copies to persons not entitled to free distribution is ten cents each.

CIRCULATING LIBRARY

Beginning in June, the library will accumulate a collection of books, pamphlets, etc., for circulation. Duplicates of the books most in demand, excepting of course out-of-print or very expensive volumes. will be acquired and will be available to the membership on the terms laid down in the following regulations. Data from reference books not available for circulation will be abstracted as heretofore. There may be some delay in completing the collection of duplicate copies, but an effort will be made to obtain the most important as soon as possible.

REGULATIONS FOR CIRCULATING LIBRARY

Members and associates of the American Institute of Accountants may borrow books, pamphlets and magazine articles subject to the following regulations:

(1) Application must be made in writing.

(2) Books may be retained for a period of two weeks from the date stamped in the books. Allowance will be made for time lost in delivery.

(3) Renewal may be granted provided no application from another member or associate has been received for the same book.

(4) A charge of ten cents for each week or fraction of week will be made for each book borrowed. Books retained beyond the period of two weeks or renewal thereof, shall involve a fine of five cents a day, plus three cents for each notice of delinquency sent.

(5) When books borrowed are shipped by mail or express, the borrower shall pay the cost of shipment in both directions.

(6) Charges paid by the library, fees and fines must accompany the books when returned.

(7) The borrower must bear the risk of loss, including the risk of transit and must pay the expense of replacing any book lost. If a book is damaged, the borrower must pay the amount of damage.

(8) Works of reference, magazines as a whole, and volumes which cannot be replaced at all, or without great expense, will in no case be included in the circulating library.

1

(9) A non-member shall have the right, subject to the above regulations, to borrow from the circulating library, provided he presents a written order from a member or associate who shall guarantee payments for fees, carriage, loss or damage.

(10) In order to facilitate handling of orders, it is requested that the following information be given in full:

    (a) Subject.

    (b) Detail in regard to books as given in Accountant's Index.

    (c) As full information as possible for references not contained in Accountant's Index.

    (d) If more than one book or pamphlet is desired on any subject, borrowers are requested to be as specific as possible in description of matter wanted.

DIVIDENDS

With reference to the question and answer on "Dividends" appearing in Special Bulletin No. 17, February, 1923, the Bureau of Information has received the following comments:

The reply states:

"We know of no accounting theory which countenances the declaration of dividends out of a reserve for depletion."

Possibly so, but it is a fact that cash distributions are occasionally made and charged against depletion reserves. The distributions are recognized by the Federal Income Tax Department in Article 1546, Regulations 62, 1922 Edition, and are not taxable.

Whether such "distributions" are legal or whether (in the event of a debit balance at surplus account) they would constitute an impairment of paid up capital stock and infringe the laws of the state is a legal question dependent on the particular state laws.

In the state of Washington, for example, it is illegal to declare any dividend except out of net profits, or make any distribution which would impair the legally authorized capital stock (which in the state of Washington must be fully subscribed at the incorporation of the company as a requisite for a license to do business). This provision of course is intended as a safeguard to creditors.

Privately owned timber companies, however, occasionally make cash distributions to their stockholders out of depletion reserves, and while apparently illegal before the formal liquidation of the company, the directors take the position that, there being practically no liabilities, no interests are being prejudiced thereby.

Permit me to offer the following in addition to the answer given. The question presented had to do with the proper method of handling dividends paid from depletion reserve, for balance-sheet purposes.

At the outset, it may be stated that a depletion or depreciation reserve, as the terms generally used, measure a hole in an asset. In other words they provide the means for informing those interested, in terms of money value, just what portion of capital asset has been converted into another form, say cash. In dealing with depletion the fact should not be lost sight of that depletion of cost and depletion of value, which latter operation brings up realized appreciation, although of the same character, require different treatment. Since the question did not indicate the presence of a value factor only depletion on cost will be considered. Assume the following conditions:

Producing property (cost)	$100,000		Capital stock	$100,000
Less: Depletion reserves	10,000			
		$ 90,000		
Cash		10,000		
Total		$100,000	Total	$100,000

2

A dividend is declared payable, in the sum of $10,000 and it is expressly stipulated that this payment is from depletion reserve. We have then:

Producing property (cost)	$100,000	Capital stock		$100,000
Less: Depletion reserve	10,000	Less: Liquidating dividend, b e i n g dividend declared payable from depletion reserve.		10,000
				$90,000
Cash	10,000	Dividend payable		10,000
Total	$100,000	Total		$100,000

Resolving the transaction down to facts we have, simply, that the company has converted certain capital assets into cash, and that the board of directors has, by virtue of its action in declaring a dividend from depletion reserve, ordered to be transferred from capital account to current liabilities the amount of capital converted into cash, as measured by the depletion reserve. It is, of course, understood that the term dividend is used in a general sense; the payment thereof will represent a return of capital, and the fact should be very clearly stated.

STUDENTS' ACCOUNTS

Q. Will you kindly advise me what is the best method of handling the charges to students' accounts in a secondary institution. In other words, from what source do these entries come?

In some institutions they carry a student's charge sheet or book, and in others they make the entry through the journal, which takes a considerable amount of time.

Is there such a thing as a students' register which would carry the names of all students and to a greater or less extent, take care of all charges made during the scholastic year including two semesters.

A. I understand your correspondent wishes information respecting charges to students' accounts and rather objects to the use of the journal because of the time taken up in such use, and suggests a student register, and that this information is required as it applies to secondary institutions.

Our experience is that in any secondary institution where the number of students is limited, the use of the journal is unobjectionable, the time taken in keeping it being inconsiderable, and the opportunity of description in connection with the charge being ample.

Where the number of students is large, however, we have found the use of a charge card very satisfactory. A sample used by ———— University for ten thousand students is given herewith. Classification is made by departments, each of which sends to the bursar a list of students with the proper charges. This supplies a check on the amounts sent in on registration day on the charge card.

The student first registers in the office of the dean or registrar of his particular department, receiving one of these cards with the proper charges indicated. He then takes it to the bursar's office and pays the charge indicated on card No. 1. Card No. 2 also is retained by the bursar from which card is posted the amount of cash paid. It is then filed away for reference.

Card No. 3 also shows the amount paid by the student and is returned to the dean or registrar of his particular department.

CHARGE CARD (sample)

CHARGE CARD (sample) 1. ED
1922

xM *John H. Smith*
 (Given Name)   (Initial)   (Family Name)

PRINT NAME ON
LINES MARKED X

New York City N.Y.   Phone ———
Home Address

Bay State Rd. Boston   Phone ———
Local Address   (Street and No.)   (City)   (State)

Aid $ ———   Source ———

Registration Fee	10 —	10/26			126 —
Tuition	116 —				
Registration Fee					
Tuition	100 —				

2. ED

PAID $ 126.   School

Received from

X *John H. Smith*   OCT 26 1922 $ ———

on account of tuition.   **BURSAR**

TO BE RETAINED BY THE BURSAR

3. ED

PAID $ 126.   School

Received from

X *John H. Smith*   OCT 26 1922 $ ———

on account of tuition.   **BURSAR**

——— UNIVERSITY   4 ED

Bursar's Office, ———

xM *John H. Smith*

TO ——— UNIVERSITY, DR.

Tuition, First Semester

Tuition, Second Semester **PAID $** 126

OCT 26 1922

BURSAR

Make checks payable to " ——→ UNIVERSITY "

CHARGE CARD
(Ledger card)

—B100
1922   1   ED   1923

XM _____

PRINT NAME ON
LINES MARKED X

(Given Name)   (Initial)   (Family Name)

Home Address _____ Phone _____

Local Address _____ Phone _____

(Street and No.)   (City)   (State)

Aid $ _____ Source _____

Registration Fee					
Tuition					
Registration Fee					
Tuition					

2   Post from this card to ledger card   ED

School

Received from

X _____

on account of tuition.

TO BE RETAINED BY THE BURSAR

3   Returned to dean or registrar as case   ED
           may be

School

Received from

X _____

on account of tuition.

4   —————— UNIVERSITY   ED
           Bursar's Office, ——————

Students receipt
for payments

XM _____

TO ——————— UNIVERSITY, DR.

Tuition, First Semester			
Tuition, Second Semester			

Make checks payable to " —————— UNIVERSITY "

5

Card No. 4 supplies the student's receipt for cash paid.

Where scholarships are granted or any additional charges or credits authorized, the system is similar and the ledger cards alphabetically arranged furnish full details relating to each student.

In transactions subsequent to the first registration, the items are posted to the ledger card containing the first entries, and the cards numbered 2, 3, and 4 are used as explained in the first instance.

Probably an adaptation of this card system might be useful in secondary institutions having three or four hundred students.

INTEREST DURING CONSTRUCTION

Q. About two years ago we were asked by a firm of investment bankers to express our opinion as to how interest charged during construction should be treated in the accounts of a public utility company to which they were acting as financial agents. We gave our opinion at that time, but the question has come up for consideration again, and we are now asked if we can obtain also an expression of opinion from some well recognized institute or association on accounting matters.

We understand that the Institute has an established research department, and we shall be obliged if you can put the matter before that department and advise us of its opinion.

The following exhibits show an alternative treatment of this interest.

EXHIBIT "A"

Operating revenue		$600,000
Operating expenses and taxes:		
Operating expenses	$350,000	
Taxes	15,000	365,000
Operating income		235,000
Other income		25,000*
Total income		$260,000
Deductions from income:		
Interest on bonds	90,000	
Interest on notes payable	10,000	100,000
Net income		$160,000

*Includes $22,500 interest charged during construction, capitalized and here credited, this note, however, not being disclosed on the published accounts.

EXHIBIT "B"

Operating revenue		$600,000
Operating expenses and taxes:		
Operating expenses	$350,000	
Taxes	15,000	365,000
Operating income		235,000
Other income		2,500
Total income		$237,500
Deductions from income:		
Interest on bonds	90,000	
Less		
Charged to construction	22,500	
	67,500	
Interest on notes payable	10,000	77,500
Net income		$160,000

A. The Bureau of Information has received the following opinion:

The regulating bodies having jurisdiction over public utilities as a rule specifically authorize the charge to capital of interest on the company's own or borrowed funds during the period of construction; only a few of them direct the treatment to be given to the credit for the interest. The instructions which are probably the most authoritative and at the same time cover the question are those of the Interstate Commerce Commission.

The Interstate Commerce Commission holds for electric railways that when interest during construction is charged, corresponding credit is to be made to the account which was charged as such interest accrued; but that if no interest actually accrued or was paid, the credit should be made to income from unfunded securities and accounts. (Accounting Bulletin No. 14 covering Interpretations of Accounting Classifications for Electric Railways—Case 308).

We are of the opinion that under the conditions regarding the charge of interest during the period of construction, which are approved by the commissions, this ruling of the Interstate Commerce Commission is both authoritative and in accordance with sound accounting principles.

MUNICIPAL DEPARTMENTS OF FINANCE

Q. The ————Chamber of Commerce is making a study of the city budget and a survey of the various municipal functions. Our work, in connection with the department of finance has raised one question and it has been suggested that we refer the matter to you for your advice.

The situation in the department of finance is as follows: the offices of comptroller, treasurer and purchasing agent are combined and one official serves in this triple capacity. This was done with the intention of effecting a saving in the salaries paid. Besides this, the city employs a local accounting firm to make the audit required by state law. The work is continuous throughout the year.

Does the situation described above conform to sound accounting principles? If not, have you any suggestion or comment to make?

A. The combination of the duties of purchasing agent and of treasurer is not usually regarded as sound. It is in many ways desirable that the treasurer's duties should be confined to the collection, custody and disbursement of cash and the care of securities, etc. the comptroller. In some cities, the principal duties of the comptroller have to do with the collection of taxes in arrears and the custody of tax records of prior years; he has little, if any, responsibility in connection with the audit of accounts. If the duties of the comptroller at ————are of such a nature their consolidation with those of the treasurer is not open to objection. If, however, the comptroller's duties include those of audit or of control over the auditor, they should unquestionably be held by an officer separate from the treasurer though quite properly in the same city department.

SUBSIDIARY COMPANIES

Q. A foreign corporation owning over 95% of the stock of two domestic companies has a loss in one of these companies. Would a book transfer of this loss to the foreign parent company affect the tax consolidation situation of the domestic companies and in any way endanger their tax benefit for offset of loss against profits?

A. The book transfer of a loss by a domestic corporation to its foreign subsidiary could, in our opinion, be interpreted as prima facie evidence that the foreign parent corporation had agreed to make good the loss of the domestic subsidiary; the transfer is equivalent to a contribution by the foreign corporation to the domestic subsidiary and such a contribution might be regarded as income to the domestic company. We do not say positively that this interpretation would be given, because we think it is an open question whether the contribution would

7

be regarded as a non-taxable gift or not, but we think the unfavorable interpretation referred to is one that distinctly might, in the terms of your inquiry, "endanger their tax benefit for offset of loss against profits."

If the transaction were the other way around, and a domestic corporation were to take up on its books the amount of the income or loss of a foreign subsidiary, we do not believe the income would be taxable unless actually received as dividends, nor that the loss would be deductible unless actually realized through liquidation of the subsidiary. It is not an uncommon practice to give effect to the profits or losses of foreign subsidiaries on the books of a domestic parent corporation by taking them up in accounts designated as investment appreciation or depreciation accounts, in which guise the transfers are not involved in the domestic company's income in any way.

This procedure suggests to our minds that a similar course might be followed by the foreign parent corporation of a domestic subsidiary if the object of the transfers spoken of in your question is to permit the parent corporation to keep its investment account in the subsidiaries in consonance with the capital and surplus of those subsidiaries. Under this method the subsidiary would not require to make any entries for the transfer of the profit or loss, the only adjustments being made on the books of the parent corporation.

DEPRECIATION—BILL-BOARDS

Q. What is the rate of depreciation on bill-boards?

A. The bill-board is erected on leased space, the lease usually being subject to termination on thirty days' notice in case of sale of the property. The average life of these leaseholds, usually less than the average life of the bill-board itself (one client reports the leasehold averaging five years and the bill-boards six to seven years) determines the rate of depreciation.

The principal element of cost in a bill-board is labor and transportation of the crew and material, the actual cost of the material itself being relatively insignificant. The uprights deteriorate rapidly, and their replacement involves the reconstruction of the whole bill-board.

Depreciation should, therefore, be based on the average term of the leaseholds. A reasonable value should be given to material salvaged from structures reconstructed on long-term leases or torn down on terminated leases, this value to be credited to the undepreciated cost of the structures.

COST OF CONSTRUCTION

Q. Under a contract for installation and realignment of equipment which provides for 15% for overhead and 10% profit, kindly advise concerning the following items?

1. Would (a) board of men
        (b) local railroad fares
        (c) actual cost of auto transportation fo men
        (d) estimated cost of auto transportation of men
        (e) incidental expenses of foreman
come under direct cost of job?

2. What would be the proper cost of materials from contractors' stock?

3. Is it proper to figure the 10% profit on top of the 15% for overhead?

A. In the absence of explicit understanding in the contract or of trade practices all direct costs of the work should be included. These costs comprise materials, payrolls, and any direct burden incurred with reference to the construction. The profit should be computed, in the absence of expressed stipulations to the contrary, on the total direct cost, including burden. The proper cost for materials would be the figure at which similar materials could be purchased for the work concerned.

8

American Institute of Accountants
Library and Bureau of Information

[The Committee on Administration of Endowment authorizes the publication of special Bulletins, of which this is one, on the distinct understanding that members are not to consider answers given to questions as being official pronouncements of the Institute, but merely the individual opinions of accountants to whom the questions were referred. It is earnestly requested that members criticise freely and constructively the answers given in this or any other Bulletin of this series.]

BONDS

In Special Bulletin No. 18, page 11, a series of questions and answers relative to bonds signed by a trustee and not actually sold appears.

While the answers are very clear and pretty fully cover the questions, there is one particular in which something more may be said.

"2. In accordance with the above quotation, the company is correct in insisting that $1,000,000.00 of bonds are treasury bonds. They should be shown in the balance-sheet as a deduction from the $10,000,000 of bonds issued."

This answer is correct but hardly sufficient. "In accordance with the above quotation" puts a limit on it. It will probably not be denied that they are treasury bonds absolutely. They have been signed and registered by the trustee and are outstanding so far as the trustee knows anything to the contrary.

But the trustee's signature cannot change the nature of an obligation such as is involved in these bonds and the obligation cannot be to the issuing corporation by itself. Therefore, in preparing the balance-sheet the liability of the company is only for the bonds held by the public and it necessarily follows that $9,000,000. is the net obligation with respect to these bonds.

"A bond is merely the evidence of an indebtedness and entitles the holder to recover of the maker the amount evidenced by its terms. Independent of establishing the right of such recovery the bond has no value."

As a matter of information and in order to disclose all the facts it is proper to state in the blance-sheet the total amount of the mortgage or $10,000,000. and deduct therefrom that portion of the bonds the company would not be called upon to pay, were the mortgage to be paid off concurrently with the date of the balance-sheet.

EXPENSES

Q. We would thank you to let us have your valued opinions as to whether the following expenses are properly chargeable to capital through organization expense and plant account. Briefly the history of this company is as follows:

1

The ————————Light & Power Co., a concern for whom we are engaged in making an audit as well as installing a system, was chartered some time in March, 1922. They thereupon entered into an agreement with a contractor whereby he was, for a certain stipulated price, to build a power house for the purpose of generating electricity which was to be sold to consumers in the city of... The contractor, however, was not to construct any of the pole lines, according to his contract, but this was to be done by the company itself.

This agreement with the contractor was carried into effect to such a point that on or about the 1st of November the plant was in such a condition that it could generate current; but the company which, as before stated, was to put up the pole lines had at that time only managed to erect sufficient poles to supply current to one customer. As the weeks elapsed however, it extended its lines until on January 31st, which is the closing date of our audit report, it had approximately five miles of lines: but, as these lines traversed a very thinly settled territory, the possibilities were that it could only sell current to about one-fifth of the number of customers that they were capable of carrying.

Our idea is that a company can properly capitalize its initial expenses up to the time that it is ready for doing business; but due to the simple fact that it did sell altogether in the three months operation some $800 worth of current, we do not interpret this as meaning that the plant was a going concern. It was compelled to commence operations at the time it did, due to obligations contained in the franchise which it obtained from the city of ——————. Had it not been for this, it would not have started operations, as it was not profitable to do so, but it was, as explained above, an exigency of the situation.

We have treated the item, tentatively, of income for the three months mentioned as a deduction from the cost of installation, as we felt that it would not be proper to make an operating statement for this period.

For your information we will state that, in the following analysis marked schedule 1, we are in no doubt as to the items 1, 2, 3, 4 and 5, feeling that they are properly organization expense. As to item 6, salary of the secretary, $750.00, it was necessary that the secretary be on the ground even had no current been sold. So, under the circumstances, we believe that this item is properly chargeable to organization expense.

Items 7, 8, 9, 10 and 11 were necessary, for the simple reason that, in order to comply with the terms of the franchise, it was necessary to operate. From a common sense standpoint, no concern would have involved itself in these heavy operating expenses when the largest possible return in the way of sale of current was known to be less than $1,000. So it is evident that this expense was incurred simply as a necessary organization expense.

Item 12, salary and commission paid solicitors, was paid for soliciting rights of way to build their line. It is true that, to a small extent, the amount covered services of the solicitors in soliciting new business; but we may state that ninety per cent of the time of the solicitors was consumed in securing rights of way.

The other items from 13 to 21, both inclusive, are such as are ordinarily incurred by concerns similarly circumstanced.

2

Organization expense   January 31, 1923.

Commission on sale of Capital stock	$37,866.00	(1)
Legal expense	1,835.00	(2)
Advertising	418.99	(3)
City tax on franchise	500.00	(4)
Salary of commercial engineers	1,695.00	(5)
Salary of secretary (paid)	750.00	(6)

Power house:

Salary of engineer, operators and oilers	$3,076.86	(7)	
Fuel and lubricating oil	2,705.36	(8)	
Maintenance	42.05	(9)	
Water for boiler	285.09	(10)	
Supplies and expense	63.30	(11)	$6,172.66

Salary and commission— Solicitors	317.55	(12)
Rent & repairs in lieu of rent (office)	578.42	(13)
Salary of porter	160.00	(14)
Rent—Right of way— Cable crossing	100.00	(15)
Stationery, printing & office supplies	321.12	(16)
Auto expense	44.52	(17)
Taxes	69.78	(18)
Telephone and telegraph	85.35	(19)
Interest and discount	1,788.61	(20)
Other expenses	480.03	(21)

Total	$53,183.03

Less:

Income from current furnished	$814.14	
Profit on sale of appliances	13.70	
Interest earned on notes receivable	9.02	$ 836.86

Total organization expense	**$52,346.17**

A. In our opinion it is permissible to regard the income from sales of current as incidental up to the time when the project as planned is reasonably complete and ready for operation. This principle, however if carried to an extreme, might produce results which would be entirely misleading and interfere with a true reflection of the success or failure of the project as an operating proposition.

While we see nothing in the list of items which might not be capitalized during a reasonable period of construction, it would appear to be more conservative to charge all of these items, with the possible exception of commission on the sale of capital stock, to an organization expense account, and write down the organization expense over a shorter period of time than would be the case if the items were included in cost of plant property and depreciated on the usual basis of depreciating physical property.

There is no objection, of course, to including commission on sale of capital stock in organization expense rather than as a part of the cost of plant property, and, in fact, it would be more conservative to do so, particularly if the organization expense is to be written off over a short period of time.

3

Q. What method of inventorying of granulated sugar produced by a beet sugar company from beets, a portion of which are grown on its own land and a portion purchased from farmers, conforms "as nearly as may be to the best accounting practice in the trade or business and as most clearly reflecting the income"? (See Section 203 of the Revenue Act of 1921.)

The beet sugar company on whose behalf the above question is asked, was incorporated in 1901, and from that year until 1919, inclusive, it consistently inventoried its granulated sugar on hand at realizable market value, on the grounds that that method of inventory was the one that most clearly reflected its income, and also that, at any rate up to the year 1914, that method was the one generally adopted by the industry.

On December 31, 1920, the company changed its basis of valuing inventories from realizable market to cost, the reason being that Article 1582 of the 1920 edition of Regulations 45, promulgated January 28, 1921, provided for the first time that inventories must be valued at (a) cost or (b) cost or market, whichever is the lower; whereas prior to the 1920 edition of the regulations, these two bases of valuations were apparently permissive, the word "should" being used instead of "must" in the first sentence of Article 1582. For this reason the company felt that it had no option but to comply with the direct provisions of the regulation, although it felt at the time that in so doing it was using a basis of valuation in inventorying granulated sugar which was arbitrary and did not as clearly reflect the net income of the company.

As an illustration of the arbitrariness of the use of cost: the company now purchases its beets from farmers on the basis of what is known as a 50-50 arrangement, which is that the farmers shall be paid for their beets 50% of the average price realized for the sugar produced from their beets, the production being the same ratio of the beets purchased from the farmers which the total sugar produced by the company during the season is of the total beets purchased from farmers and grown by the company. The result of this is that the cost of the granulated sugar cannot definitely be ascertained until the season's production of sugar has been entirely disposed of, which, in most years, is not until May or June of the succeeding fiscal year, the company's fiscal year being the calendar year. The company also conducts a general farming business, and the question of apportionment of expenses between the general farming and the beet producing departments is claimed to be more or less arbitrary.

The examination has been made by the treasury department of the returns filed by the company for the year 1917. The inventories of granulated sugar used in determining the net income and in determining invested capital were valued at realizable market, and the treasury department has ruled that this basis is unacceptable to it and that the inventories in question must be valued on the basis of cost or cost or market, whichever is lower.

The company claims that it has consistently used the basis o. market for fifteen years prior to 1917, that that basis clearly reflects its net income, and that the treasury department has no right to require it to change to the basis of cost or cost or market, whichever is the lower.

A. It is noted that the company pays "50% of the average price realized from the sugar produced from the beets" and it is claimed that under this arrangement the cost of the granulated sugar cannot be definitely ascertained until the entire product for the season is sold — which is not until May or June of the following year.

The proper basis for valuing the inventory is undoubtedly "cost or market, whichever is lower" provided of course that the cost can be accurately ascertained.

4

It is also noted that up to 1920 the company has valued its inventory on the basis of the "market" and if it pays for the beets on the basis of 50% of the average price realized for the sugar it must have set up a liability for the cost of the beets on the basis of the market at the close of the year. It is therefore not quite clear why the cost of the beets should not be ascertained on that basis. Any difference between the cost of the beets on the basis of the market at the close of the year and price at which finally settled for with the growers is of course adjusted in the following year just as any difference between the inventory and the sales would be adjusted.

It is further noted that the company conducts a general farming business and the question of apportionment of general expenses between general farming and the beet producing departments is cited as an argument against the method of valuing the inventory at cost. The identical situation exists on many sugar estates and we have experienced no difficulty in arriving at a satisfactory basis for apportioning general expenses between different departments.

The fact that the company has used consistently the basis of market for fifteen years prior to 1917 could not possibly be used as an argument for continuing this practice if it is wrong.

AUTOMOBILE BODY PLANTS

Q. What is the factory burden for overhead rates and commercial burden rates used in automobile body plants.

A. From statistics in our possession, we find that an average factory burden rate to productive labor for automobile body plants for the year 1922 was approximately 100%. The percentage of administrative, general and selling expenses to sales value was approximately 3.5%. The administrative, general and selling expenses were also equivalent to approximately 15% of the productive labor. Of course, the administrative, general and selling expenses are normally measured against the sales value of the product.

ESTATE ACCOUNTING

Q. "A", a bachelor dies in 1917 leaving an estate of approximately $100,000.00, consisting of personalty as well as leases in oil and timber lands, a coal mine, etc. In addition to minor legacies he provides for annuities as follows: X.—$500.00 per month out of principal, Y—$50.00 per month out of income, Z—$75.00 per month out of income. Ten years after the death of the last annuitant the corpus is to be used for the establishment of a foundation for medical research.

The will appoints three executors "to conduct and carry on each of the business interests"————————"each one as long as it proves profitable"————————"and to distribute the income from the various stocks and interests and finally dispose of the principal assets" and apply the proceeds to the foundation mentioned above.

The executors appointed under the will were close friends and business associates of the testator, two of them having been in his employ. Their combined compensation is fixed in the will at 17% of the annual net income of the estate.

In view of the above it is essential that the line between principal and income be very closely drawn. We have construed income to include the revenue derived from the sale of oil and gas, well drilling, and dividends received, but we do not include profit realized on the sale of assets listed in the inventory of the estate, which profit will be added to the corpus.

We have classified the expense in two divisions,—principal expense and operating expense. Principal expense includes all expense incurred in maintaining the assets left by the testator which are non-productive as to income, such as the expense of keeping up the old homestead,—taxes, repairs, etc. Principal expense will also include

5

the lease rentals on timber lands and on oil lands originally leased by the testator, upon which development has not yet begun and are therefore unproductive. As soon as development is begun on these lands the charge for the lease rentals will be made to operating expense.

The operating expense is charged with all expense incurred in maintaining and operating the income producing assets, whether left by the testator or acquired by the executors. Thus the payroll to operate the coal mine and oil wells, repairs, taxes, insurance, etc., are operating expense.

Expense of administration of the corpus as well as of the income operations of the estate are segregated as office expense and include bookkeeper's salaries, stationery, telephone, light, etc. In the early life of the estate this expense was properly applicable to the corpus as principal expense, inasmuch as nearly all of the time spent by the office force was in getting the inventory listed, selling some of the assets, etc., but at present, very little time is spent in this manner, most of their effort being directed toward overseeing the operations of the oil wells and coal mine, which assets being income producing, determine that a large part of the charge for office expense shall now be made against income.

Note that this is not a question of life tenant and remainderman, because there is no life tenant. The purpose of this inquiry into the accounting procedure of the estate is to determine the amount of commissions to be paid to the executors. As this is based on the net income it will be based on the amount obtained by deducting the operating expense from the operating income.

Please criticize the above treatment of principal and income. Should you disagree with the above, will you please state your position, giving reasons?

Will you also advise if it is in the practice in the State of New York to set up estate accounts, especially the large estates, on the double entry basis and make reports to the courts based on double entry procedure. Here it is customary to report cash receipts and disbursements only. This makes no provision for depreciation or depletion and from an accounting standpoint it is incorrect.

A. In New York State trustees are paid a commission on the total amount of money passing through their hands, including expenses paid. In this case the will sets up a standard of compensation not otherwise provided by any law. Under these circumstances it seems wrong to apply to the word "income" the very technical meaning attributed to it in estate law. These laws contemplate income as all the income derived from use of the assets, but none of the income derived from profit on sale of assets; neither do they deduct loss on sale of assets.

Where the assets are of such wasting or increasing character as oil lands and timber lands, there is still more reason to use business sense rather than legal technicality.

As the general practice is to pay commission on all income, on all capital received, on all expenses whether capital expenses or not, and on all capital paid out, we are of the opinion that a reasonable construction of the word "net income" would be the amount of net gain during the year, whether it arises from the use of the assets or their sale, and that any loss on sale of assets should be deducted from the income subject to commission. This would tend to equalize any possible error of judgment in apportioning timber income between capital and income accounts.

In one trust with which we have dealt the court has ruled that income from sale of timber must be apportioned between sale of capital assets, representing sale of timber existent when the trust was established, and income representing sale of timber not included in the valuation of the land when it was acquired.

6

We cannot see that lease rentals on timber and oil lands not yet developed are expense of any kind. They might more properly be treated as payments increasing the value of the capital asset. When development progresses to the point of production these rentals will, of course, be operating expense.

We think that the trustees should make up accounts, exactly parallel to the accounts that would be kept by a business man, taking up depletion and depreciation as expenses; and treating development expense and carrying charges of undeveloped property as additions to capital values, not as expenses for this purpose, and that commission should be paid on the net income so determined. That is to say, the income should be computed as a commercial organization would compute it for purposes of reporting income to the federal government.

This, of course, makes idle the minute division of expenses as between principal and income accounts.

Finally, at the next accounting of the trustees to the court the computation of commission by this method should be submitted for approval; indeed approval might be asked for at any time.

If the court should rule that income is to be interpreted in any other sense, then the court will prescribe rules therefor; the case is not covered by existing rules and I recommend the rule of reason. It is unreasonable to suppose that these trustees will sell capital assets even at a good profit if they get nothing for their work, and especially if they were paid commission on income from the property if they refrained from selling them.

Note that the trustees are to conduct each of the business interests "as long as it proves profitable." Surely the undeveloped property is not profitable unless the increasing asset value is considered; and if that increasing value rendered it possible to sell it now at a large profit is it not reasonable to believe that they would be expected to sell it, realize the profit, and take 17% for themselves?

The rules for executors contemplate the delivery of property to legatees at once, hence capital profits are considered as errors in the original valuations, not as income; trustees are not subject to that assumption.

The memo refers to executors. In New York State such administration is necessarily by trustees and on the appointment of trustees the rules governing executors are much relaxed, the trustees being free to keep accounts and conduct business largely according to the approved methods of general business.

In New York all decently conducted estates keep double entry books. The form of report for the court accounting is readily filled out from them if they have been properly kept. But the prescribed form of report is more primitive. We find, however, that courts do not reject—but rather welcome—reports that loan toward the accountants standard of business reports, including some tabulations instead of an interminable string of items paid or received.

Briefly, the New York State form provides for—

1. Schedule of assets taken over
2. " increases of assets (or decreases)
3. " income received
4. " payments to legatees—capital
5. " payments to legatees—income
6. " expenses —income
7. " expenses —capital

with a summary showing—

1 + 2 less 4 + 7 and
3 less 5 + 6

7

BAKERIES

Cost And Profit On Basis Of Barrels Of Flour Used In Year 1922 In Bakery Plants Below 25,000 Bbls. Consumption

	No. 1	No. 2	No. 3	No. 4	No. 5	No. 6	No. 7	No. 8	No. 9	No. 10	No. 11
Flour used bbls.	5,860	5,765	23,254	12,463	7,920	13,100	12,752	19,599	24,816	16,653	20,721
Flour	$7.30	$7.28	$7.00	$7.28	$7.84	$7.12	$7.32	$6.97	$7.18	$7.87	$7.33
Other materials	1.89	2.11	2.07	1.97	1.09	2.07	2.38	2.13	1.99	2.59	2.39
Bakers wages	1.47	1.80	1.49	1.51	1.42	1.28	1.87	1.15	1.24	1.43	1.29
Operating; repairs, fuel, light and power	1.13	1.13	1.13	.90	.95	1.11	1.37	1.12	1.07	1.55	1.68
Wrapping and packing	.38	.68	.37	1.27	.57	.72	.72	.60	.86	.87	1.17
Horse, wagon and auto exp.	.89	1.82	.86	.74	1.18	1.07	1.07	1.17	.84	1.26	.58
Drivers and route men	1.16	1.85	.81	.72	1.65	1.18	1.55	1.69	.97	1.66	.68
Delivery and shipping	.88	.59	.61	1.34	1.97	1.11	.26	.29	1.41	.46	1.22
Advertising	.02	.29	.45	.32	.19	.16	.43	.69	.19	.21	.75
Manager's	.50	.86	.96	2.06	1.18	.63	.43	.29	.78	.75	.87
Office expense	.72	.50	.61	.16	.30	.17	.25	.21	.94	.87	.32
Interest, taxes and insurance	.31	.27	.25	.33	.65	.60	.32	.17	.28	.47	.11
Bad debts	.12	——	.02	.30	——	——	.06	.01	.04	.02	——
Depreciation	.51	1.10	.48	.46	1.41	.91	1.09	.65	.75	.84	.55
Total cost	17.28	20.28	17.11	19.36	19.38	17.28	19.12	17.14	17.94	20.97	18.96
Profit per bbl.	2.24	.12	1.45	.98	1.30	2.38	1.19	2.24	2.42	1.11	1.36
Selling price per bbl.	$19.52	$20.40	$18.56	$20.34	$20.68	$19.66	$20.31	$19.38	$20.36	$22.08	$20.32

Cost On Percentage Of Sales

	No. 1	No. 2	No. 3	No. 4	No. 5	No. 6	No. 7	No. 8	No. 9	No. 10	No. 11
	%	%	%	%	%	%	%	%	%	%	%
Materials used	47.06	46.03	48.86	47.73	43.18	46.74	49.70	46.90	45.02	47.40	47.84
Manufacturing	15.16	17.69	16.12	17.80	14.23	15.81	19.80	14.85	15.58	17.40	20.37
Selling and delivery	15.08	22.21	14.70	14.26	19.19	13.58	15.51	19.80	16.74	16.28	15.76
Administration and depreciation	11.21	13.49	12.52	15.34	17.18	11.75	11.46	6.86	10.77	13.88	9.35
Total cost	88.51	99.42	92.20	95.13	93.78	87.88	96.47	88.41	88.11	94.96	93.32
Profit	11.49	.58	7.80	4.87	6.22	12.12	3.53	11.59	11.89	5.04	6.68
Sales	100.00	100.00	100.00	100.00	100.00	100.00	100.00	100.00	100.00	100.00	100.00

Compiled by
JOHN C. McALPINE

American Institute of Accountants

Library and Bureau of Information

DECEMBER 1923,   SPECIAL BULLETIN No. 21

[The Committee on Administration of Endowment authorizes the publication of special Bulletins, of which this is one, on the distinct understanding that members are not to consider answers given to questions as being official pronouncements of the Institute, but merely the individual opinions of accountants to whom the questions were referred. It is earnestly requested that members criticise freely and constructively the answers given in this or any other Bulletin of this series.]

PREFERRED STOCK

Q. The "A" corporation purchased from the "B" corporation certain plant assets and good will, agreeing to pay X dollars representing 60% of the purchase price and shares of a specially created preferred stock of the "A" company representing 40% of the purchase price. The payments of the money and shares of stock were spread over a period of about five years.

The "B" corporation upon receiving the shares of stock credit the par value against the total purchase price of the property, but immediately write the value of the stock off the books of account upon the theory that the stock has no known value. The process of reasoning by which the "B" company evolves the above theory is:

(1) There are two issues of preferred stock preceding the issue which it has received in part payment for its property.

(2) There is a bond issue preceding the above mentioned preferred stocks.

(3) The business of the "A" company has fallen off to such an extent since the purchase of the property of the "B" company was made that the "A" company has not operated the plant of the "B" company since its acquisition above 25% of its capacity.

(4) 60% of the purchase price of the plant (which is being received in cash) is greater than the sound value of the property sold by the "B" company.

(5) The preferred stock received by the "B" company has no known market value although the preceding issues of stock are listed on the N. Y. Stock Exchange and are quoted below par.

The question which we wish answered is:

Should a stockholder of the "B" company, upon receiving the shares of preferred stock of the "A" company, as a dividend of the "B" company return, in his individual tax return, any value for the said preferred stock? The said stock bears 7% interest cumulative and is callable at the option of the "A" company at 102 and accrued interest.

It must be remembered that the "B" company carried this stock at no value in its assets, and that therefore the surplus is not affected by a distribution of the stock and that at present no one knows what value. if any, the stock has.

A. According to Article 1547 of Regulations 62, dividends received by a stockholder of the "B" company in the form of preferred stock of the "A" company. are income to the recipient to the amount of the market value of such property at the time of its receipt.

It is stated in the question that the preferred stock has no known market value. but it is noted that this statement is coupled with a reference to the New York Stock Exchange. The fact that stock is

1

not listed or quoted on a stock exchange does not carry the implication that the stock has no value, even though preceding issues of the same company are quoted below par. The various other conditions stated certainly have a bearing on the value of the preferred stock, but taken as a whole do not necessarily indicate that the stock is without value. In this connection that part of Solicitor's Law Opinion 962, which deals with the fair market value of stock received, is of interest.

If all channels have been explored and it is conclusively determined that the stock had no market value at the time of its receipt, no income will accrue to the recipient from this source until it is realized.

INSURANCE PREMIUMS

Q. A corporation takes out a considerable amount of fire, tornado and similar insurance for a period of three years. At the end of its fiscal year, it reduces the amount of the premiums paid to a short rate or cash surrender value.

Is this item a current asset, or must it be considered as a deferred charge?

A. In the case cited, we do not see that any valid objection can be taken to the inclusion of the cash surrender value of insurance premiums amongst current assets.

The practice of reducing unexpired insurance premiums to their cash surrender value and including them in the balance-sheet as current assets while in a sense conservative can hardly be recommended. It results in overcharging one period with insurance to the advantage of the following period, and to that extent destroys the value of comparisons of earnings and operating costs. Unexpired insurance is so generally looked upon as a deferred charge that its inclusion even at its cash surrender value amongst current assets might create an impression that an attempt was being made to inflate current assets.

CUSTOMERS' ACCOUNTS

Q. What is the common practice in connection with the verification of customers' accounts? Is it usual for accountants to send statements of account to all customers carried on the books of a client, asking them to confirm the correctness of their accounts, without obtaining the client's authority, or should they in all cases obtain this authority before so doing?

A. Under no circumstances should confirmations be sent out to customers without the authority of the client. Some clients are averse to making known to outsiders the fact that their accounts are being audited; others object to the practice of sending out confirmations to customers because of the expense involved. The practice, so far as we have observed, is to rather urge the client to have it done, and if not done, to make proper qualification.

EXPENSES

Special Bulletin No. 20 contains an inquiry regarding the treatment of organization expenses and other items in the case of a light and power company. The conclusions arrived at are generally correct in principle but the question cannot be answered completely without a knowledge of the state in which the operations of the public utility referred to are carried on.

The decisions of state commissions having jurisdiction over the public utility should be referred to and also considered in the light of the Galveston Electric Case in the U. S. Supreme Court, the decision having been written by Justice Brandeis.

SALT

Q. Will you kindly send me a chart of accounts relative to the production of salt.

A. The following chart of accounts is relative to the production

2

of salt by a mining company and by a company which produces salt by the evaporation process.

These accounts do not show the classification of the operating expenses in as much detail as might be desired. The labor has not been classified to show the cost of the various operations.

Chart of Accounts for a Salt Mining Company

Sales
Allowances and discounts on sales

Cost:

Labor
Superintendents' salaries
Fuel
Powder
Fuses
Candles and carbide
Electric power
Oil, waste and packing
Plant repairs & maintenance
Car boards
Feed and stable expense
Mine office and general expense
Bags, barrels, packages, etc.
Transportation
Plant depreciation
Depletion of salt deposits
Property taxes
Insurance
Repairs and maintenance of laborers' houses
Rents received from laborers' houses
Farm expense

Selling expense:

Salesmens' salaries
Salesmens' expenses
Commission
General sales expenses
Salaries of officers and clerks, sales dept.
Branch office expenses (detail by branches)
Rent of warehouse, etc.
Salaries and expenses, warehouse and store
Delivery expenses, including depreciation of automobile trucks

Administrative expense:

Salaries, administrative dept.
Salaries, account dept.
General expenses, administrative dept.
General expenses, miscellaneous
Legal expenses
Taxes, other than federal income taxes
Bad debts
Interest earned
Interest paid

Reserve for federal income taxes.

PAPER INDUSTRY

Q. We desire to set up classifications in plant asset records for the various units that should be separately valued in a paper mill. The paper machine itself, of course, consists of many different units that might receive a very detailed classification in such plant asset records.

To what extent would the members experienced in this line, advise us to sub-classify a large paper machine in a modern paper mill?

A. In our opinion, there is seldom a necessity for a more elabo-

3

rate general ledger classification than suggested by the following:

Land
Buildings
Manufacturing Equipment:
    Material preparation
    Conversion
    Finishing
Steam Equipment
Maintenance Equipment
Office Furniture and Equipment.

The division of manufacturing equipment may be dispensed with in most cases.

MINING COMPANIES

Q. I wish to obtain the collective experience of the various members of the Institute on the following points:

1. What is the accounting treatment by large mining companies of compensation paid to employees under the workmen's compensation acts of the state in which they are mining, where they do not pay premiums to an insurance company to take care of losses, but assume all liability themselves? Generally, accidents resulting from mining operations are classified into two divisions by the workmen's compensation acts; non-fatal and fatal. In the former group are accidents which incapacitate a workman temporarily and those where a workman suffers the loss of a member of the body such as an eye, arm, finger, etc., without resulting in death, while the latter includes deaths occurring at the time of the accident or as an immediate result of the accident. Under the state act I have in mind the workmen's compensation must be paid, subject to certain rules and regulations, as follows:

Temporary incapacity: a certain percentage of weekly wages to be paid during the incapacity of the workman, not to exceed a certain amount per week or a certain number of weeks.

Loss of member of the body (called a specified injury): a certain amount is fixed by the state for each member. This amount must be paid in full, in weekly installments, regardless of the liability of the man to work within the time weekly installments are paid.

Death: a fixed amount to be paid in weekly installments to heirs.

Under the law compensation payments take rank immediately after preferred claims for taxes and wages and in the case of the bankruptcy of the company would be paid in full prior to payments to general creditors. The state may require the company to make periodical deposits with it out of which all claims arising under the act may be paid by the state.

2. Payments for taxes on land owned adjacent to mines but not used for mining purposes, which might include land upon which company houses are built and rented to employees.

3. Payments for maintenance expenses of inactive branches of the mine.

4. Various federal revenue acts permitted mining companies to charge against the income reported to the federal government depletion based on the fair value of their mineral deposits at March 1, 1913. In many cases this value was in excess of the original cost of the mine lands. How was the excess value treated on the company's books and was the whole depletion allowed by the government charged as an operating cost on the company's books? Also how was the new value at March 1, 1913, treated on the company's balance sheet?

With regard to the first and last questions I would appreciate it if illustrative entries could be submitted showing the various accounts affected. With regard to the second and third questions, are such payments considered as direct operating costs or charged to a miscel-

4

laneous account which is deducted after net profit from operations is ascertained?

A. It is our practice where mine operators are self-insurers to set up as a liability the compensation due for injuries or fatalities, charging operating expenses with same. "Cost of mining to compensation insurance reserve."

We invariably recommend, and insist as far as we can, that an insurance fund be opened and as awards are made that the amount of liability be taken out the business and paid into this fund. Then that all compensation claims be paid out of it, the same being debited to "compensation insurance reserve."

Taxes on land not used for mining purposes would be charged to taxes and not operating expenses. Taxes on land on which company houses are built should be charged against "house revenue."

Such a condition has not come to our notice. In our opinion, however, such payments should be set up separately on profit & loss account. If you refer to old workings being used to bring out minerals or for ventilation, then such expense should be charged to operating cost.

It is our practice to increase the value of the mineral deposit and set up a special reserve in respect of same, "reserve for re-valuation of mineral deposits," (i. e., substituting ore deposits, coal lands, or whatnot) and so show on the balance-sheet.

It is not our practice to treat depletion as an operating cost; but to set it up monthly as a charge to profit and loss. Profit and loss to depletion reserve."

The "reserve for re-valuation of mineral deposits" will eventually become surplus, supposing that mining will be continuous to exhaustion, and it would be correct accounting to carry from the reserve account to a "surplus from depletion on appreciation," a sum equal to the same proportion of the depletion that the appreciation bears to the total re-valuation.

_____

We have found in our files the following data:

1. **Workmen's Compensation:**

Only one of our clients, so far as we can find, has not recently carried workmen's compensation insurance and this one has, during the past year, taken out such a policy, so that its present practice will not throw any light on the question asked by your correspondent.

Prior to taking out the policy, all payments on account of workmen's claims were charged directly either from cash disbursements or voucher record to a claims and accidents account which was a part of mine expense.

Another client which does not now carry compensation insurance sets up a reserve each month on the basis of premiums formerly paid when such insurance was carried.

2. **Taxes on Land Not Used for Mining Purposes:**

We can find no case which exactly meets the conditions stated by your correspondent. In our opinion, however, the tax should be apportioned between the land which yields an income and that which does not, the former, of course, being a deduction from the income received, while the latter would be included in the carrying charges of non-operative property.

3. **Payments for Maintenance of Inactive Branches:**

In the only case which has come under our observation, these were charged off as expense to be deducted as net profit from operations after ascertained. In this treatment we fully concur.

4. **Depreciation on Appraised Value and Excess of Cost:**

We find no case of this kind, but we have a parallel one of depreciation on appraised value of assets in excess of their cost. The amount of appreciation was carried to a surplus arising from appreciation. The periodical credit to reserve for depreciation is apportioned between cost and appreciation by an entry similar to the

5

following:

Debit surplus arising from appreciation		$1,000.00
Debit depreciation (operating expense)		8,000.00
Credit reserve for depreciation		$9,000.00

SILK HOSIERY COMPANY

Q. A silk hosiery company operates its plant on the basis of three shifts covering in all twenty-four hours.

The officers of the company are desirous of writing off depreciation to cover the unusual wear and tear on the machinery.

Will you kindly furnish me with the standard rates of depreciation on machinery used in the manufacture of silk hosiery and also if possible your recommendations as to what addition to the percentages should be made to cover the unusual circumstances before mentioned?

A. Our observation is that depreciation on silk working machinery is somewhere between 5% and 10% per annum; nearer 5% than 10%, however. We have in mind one case where the company has agreed with the treasury department on the rate of 6⅔%, based on a 15 year life, to cover all kinds of silk working machinery for fabricating and knitting. We are informed, however, that for machinery used in the manufacture of silk hosiery, taken by itself, this rate is fairly liberal and that a twenty year life is a fair basis if used in making fashioned hosiery; though if the machinery is known as "circular" a life of 12 to 15 years would be nearer the mark.

As to the effect of operating the plant on a 24 hour per day basis this obviously increases the wear and tear greatly and the depreciation rates should be increased. But as there is an element of obsolescence in the adoption of depreciation rates we do not think the rates should be increased in full direct proportion with the increase in the working time. The company's management will have to use their own judgment as to the effect of increasing the working shifts but our guess would be that the depreciation rates for a 24 hour day should be raised by from 50 to 100% over those for a normal working day of 8 or 10 hours.

NEWSPAPER COSTS

Q. I am desirous of obtaining information regarding comparative costs in connection with a large city newspaper. What should be the general cost of each department?

A. The only information we have at hand is in connection with a newspaper in a city of a population of approximately 700,000, which has a morning, evening, and Sunday edition.

The following are certain statistics regarding the operation of this paper for two consecutive recent years:

	Later Year		Prior Year	
	Ratio to Total	Ratio to Gross Earnings	Ratio to Total	Ratio to Gross Earnings
Gross Earnings:				
Subscriptions and paper sales		22.17%		22.31%
Advertising		77.83		77.69
		100.00%		100.00%
Operating Expenses:				
Newsgathering and editorial	22.36%	17.70%	18.81%	16.03%
Composition and printing	56.60	44.79	61.81	52.69
Circulation	9.14	7.23	8.51	7.26
Maintenance of property and plant	.76	.61	.60	.51
General expense	11.14	8.81	10.27	8.75
	100.00%	79.14%	100.00%	85.24%
Profit from operations		20.86%		14.76%

6

TREASURY DEPARTMENT'S ADJUSTMENT OF
DEPRECIATION

Q. We are interested in ascertaining the practice of members of the Institute in regard to the placing, upon the books of clients, entries adjusting values due to disallowance of depreciation or in some cases additional allowance for depreciation.

The point is, that settlements are made in the matter of federal income taxes for say, 1917 and 1918, in which adjustments for depreciation have a part. Are entries made on the books at once upon the receipt of such settlement or are members of the Institute withholding the making of such entries until they have received notification of the government's audit of more of the subsequent years?

Our belief is, that if one were to wait until the government "caught up" in the checking of the current year, several years might elapse and in the meantime, adjustments might be forgotten, so that the books would not show the proper results of settlements already made.

A. It does not follow that because the treasury department adjusts depreciation for income tax purposes, the taxpayer is bound to follow them in the rates and calculations adopted for book purposes. There are cases where the taxpayer adheres to his own rates and must, therefore, maintain a running difference between the depreciation calculations for book purposes and those for income tax purposes.

But assuming, as your inquirer seems to assume, that the treasury's rates are acceptable to the taxpayer, we always advise that once the rates and basis have been agreed upon, the taxpayer should make his adjustments at once for the years covered by the settlement and should also adjust subsequent years, though not yet reviewed by the department to the revised basis adopted as that of the taxpayer even though initiated by the treasury department.

CAPITAL GAIN—2 YEAR HOLDING PERIOD

Q. When does the two year period, which is a qualification of "capital gains", begin to run for the beneficiary of an estate or trust in the case of property received as a distribution of corpus or of stock dividends.

A. So far as we know, no regulation or ruling has been issued on that specific question. Our opinion is, however, that in case of distributions, both of corpus and stock dividend shares, the distributee (the beneficiary) should calculate his two year period from the date of the decedent's death. In other words, we regard the beneficiary as acquiring, as of the date of death, a vested right to, and beneficial interest in, any property subsequently distributable to him, and consider that the incidence of an estate or trust, while it may defer the time when such property is reduced to possession by the beneficiary, does not in the meanwhile transfer such right or interest to itself and, therefore, cannot alter the distributee's right to regard himself as the beneficial owner of such property from the date of decease.

Our opinion is based on conclusions we have drawn from several treasury rulings:

I. T. 1759 provides that whether or not the executor or testamentary trustee is the same person, the two year period begins to run from the date of the decedent's death. In other words, the incident of control by an estate before the property passes to a trustee does not thereby destroy the trustee's right to compute the two year period, if he sells the property, from the date of death. By analogy this would also seem to be true if a beneficiary stood in the trustee's shoes, or both an estate and a trust intervened between the date of death and ultimate possession by the beneficiary.

Again, I. T. 1660 provides that if property constitutes the subject matter of a specific legacy, it is acquired as of the date of death.

7

Furthermore, O. D. 667 rules that an estate cannot derive a taxable gain from the transfer of property to a legatee, and that the basis for determining gain or loss on a sale of the property received by the legatee is the value of such property at the date of the testator's death whether the devise or bequest be specific or residuary. We believe that since a capital gain is computed in precisely the same manner as any other taxable gain, obviously it cannot be maintained that the taxable gain for a beneficiary is based on the value of the property at date of death, and, on the other hand, that if such gain is a capital gain it is based on some other value as of a different date.

In the case of the stock dividend, I. T. 1765 provides that the two year period starts from the date of the acquisition of the stock upon which the stock dividend is declared. In other words, if the original shares formed part of the corpus of the estate or trust, the two year period on the dividend shares would also commence upon the date of decease.

VALUATION OF COPYRIGHTS

Q. What is the mathematical basis for valuing copyrights of a going book-publishing concern? This is in connection with the sale of a business.

A. The primary element to be considered in valuing a copyright is its probable future earning power. The mathematical determination of the value of future earnings based on an average of past earnings (commonly used in the case of other intangibles as patents and goodwill) cannot ordinarily be recommended in the case of copyrights. Earnings from copyrights are too erratic and subject to fluctuation. Past results do not ordinarily reflect on accurate measure of future earnings. A "best seller" in fiction may produce large earnings during the first three years of its life; in subsequent years its returns may be negligible. On the other hand, a standard text book may, through proper management and publicity, be made to produce an increasing amount of income each succeeding year of the life of the copyright. It is clear that a true value of the copyrights of a book publishing company may be arrived at only by a careful appraisal of the probable earnings of each individual copyright after taking into consideration the peculiar conditions attaching to each.

Once the estimated future earnings are agreed upon, a mathematical basis may be used to determine the fair value of the copyrights through application of the "present worth" formula to each years earnings:

$$P = A + (1 + i)^n$$

In which P = present worth

A = amount to be received

i = agreed interest rate

n = number of years

8

American Institute of Accountants

Library and Bureau of Information

FEBRUARY, 1924   SPECIAL BULLETIN No. 22

[The Committee on Administration of Endowment authorizes the publication of special Bulletins, of which this is one, on the distinct understanding that members are not to consider answers given to questions as being official pronouncements of the Institute, but merely the individual opinions of accountants to whom the questions were referred. It is earnestly requested that members criticise freely and constructively the answers given in this or any other Bulletin of this series.]

CUSTOMERS' ACCOUNTS

In Special Bulletin No. 21, the answer to the question regarding customers' accounts on page 2 seems to imply that customers' accounts receivable should either be uniformly confirmed by communication with the customers or the balance-sheet in this respect should contain a qualification.

We are afraid this answer may be misleading to some of the younger accountants who are not fully familiar with the procedure followed in practice. Only a little consideration of the immense volume of accounts receivable to be verified and the confusion and delay that would be involved in confirming them by correspondence is sufficient to convince an inquirer that the use of written confirmations cannot be applied by any means universally. The fact is that this method is the rare exception rather than the rule. The bulk of accounts receivable are confirmed by inspection of the accounts alone, with attention given to the composition of the balance (as to its containing new or old charges, etc.), the age of the account, the frequency of payments, the history of the debtor in the past as indicated by the account, the standing of the debtor and the volume of business done with him by the client, coupled with inquiry from the officials or employees in charge of credits and familiar with the status of the customers' balances, etc. It would be a physical impossibility to confirm even a small proportion of customers' accounts receivable by letter within the time allotted to the completion of most audits, besides which such a course is in the majority of cases unnecessary, provided the concern under audit is properly managed in this direction, attends to its own credits and collections properly, and there is no reason to suspect any padding of the accounts. The verification of accounts receivable by letter is commonly resorted to for the purpose of detecting the failure to account for all collections on the part of an officer or employee responsible for cash collections—that is, it is employed in cash audits as much as for any other purpose. It is not commonly a part of a current or routine audit, but is rather a special or extraordinary step.

We have had in mind in the above paragraph industrial or mercantile businesses. In the case of brokerage audits, confirmations of customers' accounts by letter are an essential part and one of the principal objects of the audit.

BAKERIES

Q. I note a very interesting chapter on bakery statistics in Special Bulletin No. 20.

I would appreciate it if you would furnish me with a little more information relative to No. 3 and No. 9 for the reason that a client in a similar business has had a serious problem in reference to costs, selling and delivery expenses, etc., and the chart has brought to light certain conditions which are not applicable to his plant. What are

1

the lb. loaf output and selling price per lb. loaf? Does the item horse and wagon and auto expense contain depreciation on that class of equipment, or does the depreciation item specifically cover all depreciation on plant equipment, delivery equipment and office fixtures? What is the approximate locality of plants?

A. Plant No. 3 is located in the middle south and the price per loaf is 7½c. Plant No. 9 is located in middle Pennsylvania and the price per loaf is 7c for the greater part of the year in question.

Horse and wagon expense does not carry any of the depreciation on the delivery equipment. All of the depreciations in the cost schedule.

DEPRECIATION—HOTELS

A. Corporation "A" owns a vacant lot on which there is a mortgage of $80,000.00.

This corporation has $172,500.00 of full-paid capital stock. It is proposed to borrow $800,000.00 with which to pay off the aforesaid mortgage, and erect a hotel on the site now vacant.

Corporation "B" is to lease this hotel from Corporation "A," and agrees to take a thirty-year lease, paying Corporation "A" the following:

First: A guaranteed 5% to the stockholders of Corporation "A" on the $172,500.00 worth of stock outstanding. This amount to be .... $ 8,625.00

to pay taxes and insurance on the property owned by Corporation "A," same estimated at 18,000.00

to pay interest on the $800,000.00 bonds the first year's interest being 6½, or..................................... 52,000.00

to pay a 4% tax on the above interest, said tax the first year to be 2,080.00

to pay annually, as rental on hotel to be built by Corporation "A," for the amortization of the bonds issued by Corporation "A," an additional sum, the first year to be approximately 20,000.00

Making a total rental of $100,705.00

paid by Corporation "B," the operating company, to Corporation "A," the holding company.

This aforesaid rental will be an income of Corporation "A," against which they will be allowed to deduct for income purposes the tax of $18,000.00

the tax of 2,080.00

the interest on bonds 52,000.00

Totaling ....$ 72,080.00

Net income to Corporation "A" ....$ 28,625.00

The hotel to be erected is a reinforced concrete, fire-proof hotel, on which it is estimated the probable life will be thirty-five years, making the annual depreciation approximately 3%.

The questions that arise are:

First: Is thirty-five years life correct for a hotel of this kind?

Second: Whether Corporation "A" has the right to write off annually the rate of depreciation allowed, on the cost of the building only?

A. It is probable that thirty-five years is a fair estimate of the life of such a building as that referred to in the question, though it must be recognized that the building may last much longer or for a shorter period than this.

With reference to depreciation, the accounting view would be that the depreciation should be charged to the income of Corporation "A"

2

before net income would be déterminée. There being no agreement to the contrary, this would be the correct procedure and the net income of Corporation "A" could be determined only after the depreciation had been computed and charged to income.

RETIREMENT OF PREFERRED STOCK

Q. A preferred stock issue is sold under an agreement calling for the retirement of parts of this stock at regular intervals. Should the debit at this time of retirement be to treasury preferred stock or to preferred stock authorized? The reply might hinge on whether the corporation would, under the law, have the right thereafter to reissue any part of the preferred stock thus repurchased without again going through the formality of securing the authorization of the secretary of state for an increase in the capital stock.

A. The proposition as stated is: "A preferred stock issue is sold under an agreement calling for the retirement of parts of this stock at regular intervals." There seems little doubt that this arrangement as to the periodic retirement of the stock would be embodied in the certificate of incorporation filed with the secretary of state at the time of obtaining authorization of the issue, and that the effect of so doing would be to authorize the corporation to reduce its capital accordingly from time to time. It may be, however, that in strict compliance with the law it would be necessary, in order to carry out the obvious intent at the time of the issue of this stock, to file an amended certificate before proceeding with the actual retirement of the stock from time to time. This feature, however, appears not to be germane to the point at issue.

It being manifest that the intention at the time of the issue of the stock was to actually reduce the capital periodically, it seems that the treatment of the stock redeemed as treasury stock is out of the question. It is difficult to imagine a situation where stock would have been sold under such an arrangement for partial retirement from time to time had it been contemplated that the stock thus "retired" would be subsequently reissued. In issuing preferred stock with a redemption provision the interests of all the preferred stockholders and of the common stockholders are involved. For the protection of the interests of the preferred stockholders whose stock is not redeemed, and of the common stockholders, it seems manifest that a corporation would be acting in contravention of the original agreement if it were to reissue the stock redeemed without specific authority therefor being granted by both the preferred and common stockholders.

In view of the foregoing, it is our opinion that the entry to be made in the accounts at the time of retirement of any part of the preferred stock should be to debit the account representing the preferred stock outstanding however that account may be designated, thus reducing the preferred capitalization.

PARTNER'S LOSS

Q. A & B owned jointly piece of land worth $14,000.00 and decided to build a house on same and they agreed to let in C in the venture he paying into the business $7,000.00. C paid in cash $4,000.00 and gave his note for $3,000.00. It was agreed that all should share equally any profit or loss.

Result of the sale is as follows:

Property sold for $10,000.00 less 5% commission $9,500.00
Rent received $2,500.00
Less commission 127.50 2,422.50

Total amount realized from sale $11,922.50

3

Cost of building, and money used in building:

Cash received from C $4,000.00
Less amount paid for truck 1,250.00
                                                     ————————
                                                     $2,750.00
Note and interest on money borrowed from Bk.....$5,090.36
Cash advanced by A & B 983.39
                                                     ————————
Total cost of building $8,823.75

NOTE: All outstanding obligations paid except the $3,000.00 note given by C which is outstanding and still due. Do not take into consideration the value of truck as it was considered worthless at the time of the settlement.

QUERY: What was each partners' loss and what is the amount that C owes, if any, to A & B his note payment of the $3,000 note? Plus interest of $375.

A. The phraseology of the query is not altogether clear but it is assumed in the answer given below that the reading should be "What was each partners' loss and what is the amount C owes, if any, to A and B on his note of $3,000.00?"

The property account would appear on the books as follows:

Land $14,000.00
Total cost of building 8,823.75
                                             ———————— $22,823.75
Less net amount realized from sale....   9,500.00
Loss $13,323.75

From the figures furnished, the profit and loss account would reflect the following position:

Loss on property $13,323.75
Loss on truck purchased 1,250.00
                                            ———————— $14,573.75
Less:
Interest on assessed note 375.00
Rent received (net) 2,422.50
                                            ————————
                                                      2,797.50
                                                      ————————
Net loss $11,776.25

This loss under the terms of the agreement is to be shared equally by A, B and C. As each of the partners had originally an interest of $7,000.00 in the business, after distributing this loss A's and B's capital account would show a credit each of $3,074.58 and C's $3,074.59. On the debit side of the ledger, cash would show a balance of $5,848.75, notes receivable $3,000.00 and interest accrued on notes receivable $375.00. Of the cash on hand A would be paid $2,924.37 and B $2,924.38, while the difference between these payments and the amounts due A and B respectively, as above, would be made good to them by C out of the interest accrued on his note. This would necessitate his paying A $150.21 and B $150.20. C's credit balance of $3,074.59 would be satisfied as follows:

Cancellation of note $3,000.00
Cancellation of balance of interest due on
note:
     Total interest due $375.00
     Less paid A and B 300.41   74.59
                                                    ————————
                                                    $3,074.59

In checking over the figures submitted to us it is noticed that after the commission has been deducted from the rent, the net amount should

4

be $2,372.50 instead of $2,422.50 as stated. Under the circumstances we have assumed that the commission actually paid was $77.50 instead of $127.50.

CANDY STORE SERVING LIGHT LUNCHEONS

Q. We are desirous of obtaining percentage statistics covering the operation of the popular priced retail store which serves light luncheons in connection with a soda fountain and candy business. The specific percentages desired are:

> Gross profit to sales
> Rent   "   "
> Clerk hire   "   "
> Light   "   "
> All other expenses to sales
> Net profit   "   "

If the business is departmentalized so that these statistics are available by departments, so much the better.

A. Answering your communication asking for information in respect to percentages of costs, etc., in a candy store which also serves light luncheons in connection with a soda fountain, the following is a comparative statement of a profit and loss account with percentages for the years 1921 and 1922.

It should be pointed out that the rental charge is exceedingly heavy and to that extent the percentages may require adjustment. You will note the profits are very small, indeed, but we believe that it is chiefly due to the rental charge. Furthermore, we are of the opinion that this store should do a considerably larger business than they are doing, considering the rent they are paying.

PROFIT AND LOSS ACCOUNT WITH PERCENTAGES OF THE X. Y. Z. CANDY COMPANY

Departmental gross profits:

	1922		1923	
Candy:				
Sales	$59,694.02		$67,925.72	
Cost of sales	37,231.65		40,887.17	
		$22,462.37		$27,038.55
Soda fountain:				
Sales	$58,576.40		$51,702.95	
Cost of sales	12,399.96		11,910.71	
		46,176.44		39,792.24
Restaurant:				
Sales	$68,114.80		$67,281.80	
Cost of sales	39,244.97		37,477.76	
		28,869.83		29,804.04
Total gross profit		$97,508.64		$96,634.83
Less expenses:				
Clerk hire	$32,175.85		$31,670.55	
Rent	36,000.00		36,000.00	
Light	1,695.32		2,025.93	
Other expenses, including depr'n.	23,863.45		26,464.91	
		93,734.62		96,161.39
Balance, net profit		$ 3,774.02		$ 473.44

5

Gross profits to sales:	Percent	Percent
Candy	37.63	39.81
Soda fountain	78.88	76.96
Restaurant	42.39	44.30
Average gross profits		
all departments	52.32	51.70

Expenses to sales:		
Clerk hire	17.26	16.95
Rent	19.31	19.26
Light	.91	1.09
Other expenses,		
including depr'n.	12.81	14.15
	50.29	51.45
Balance, net profit	2.03	0.25

AUTOMOBILE AGENCIES

Q. I shall be very much obliged if you can procure for me from some of the members who have handled accounting work for automobile agencies the information which is listed below.

Percentages of new car sales represented by the following:

Cost of new car sales
Advertising
Insurance—fire and liability
Rent
Taxes
Allowances and replacements
Gasoline, oils, greases
Heat, light, power
Interest
Maintenance of buildings and equipment
Maintenance of shop cars
Miscellaneous office supplies and expenses.
Postage
Telegraph and telephone
Office salaries
Salaries of officials
Salesmen's salaries and commissions
Superintendent and foreman's salaries
Shop expense (including wages not charged to repair
   orders, used cars and new cars)
Unloading and setting up new cars

I should also like to know the average gross profit of the parts department and the net profits after deducting wages; also, the annual turnover in the parts department, that is, the number of times the mean average of opening and closing inventories will divide into the cost of sales for the year. I shall also be interested in knowing the experience of other accountants as regards the gross profit and loss or net profit and loss on handling used cars taken in on new sales.

As these percentages probably vary according to the class of car handled, it is well to mention that the figures would interest me most if they applied to an agency handling two cars, one selling at about $650 and the other at $1400, both prices including freight and taxes.

If percentages cannot be obtained for the particular accounts which I have listed I shall be very interested in having figures covering any classification that is available.

A. In reply to your inquiry we have pleasure in furnishing herewith such information as we have been able to gather relating to accounting statistics of automobile agencies.

6

Percentage (composite, based on six agencies chosen at random) of new car sales represented by items listed below.

New car sales	100.00%	
Cost of new car sales	84.19	
Advertising	1.046	
Insurance	.6788	
Rent	1.532	(3 agencies)
Taxes	.8716	"
Allowances and replacements	.323	"
Gasoline, oils, grease	Information not available	
Heat, light, power	.3841	
Interest	1.5969	
Maintenance, buildings and equipment	.1489	(2 agencies)
Maintenance, shop cars	.4638	"
Miscellaneous office supplies and expenses	.2725	
Postage	.0654	(3 agencies)
Telegraph and telephone	.2032	
Office salaries	2.681	(5 agencies)
Salaries of officials	4.646	(4 agencies)
Sales, salaries and commissions	3.622	(5 agencies)
Superintendent and foremen salaries	Information not available	
Shop expenses (including wages not charged to repair orders, used cars and new cars)		"
Unloading and setting up new cars		"

Percentage of gross profit, parts department to sales, parts department, etc.

Parts department:

Ratio of gross profit to sales	28.64%	(5 agencies)
Ratio of selling profit to sales	5.34	(one report only)
Rate of turnover	1.247	(one agency only)

Ratio of profit on sales of used cars to sales of such cars.

Profit, 2 agencies—average,	10.64%	profit	
Loss, 4 agencies—average,	2.742	loss	
Composite average of these 6	1.721	profit	

FLORISTS' SHOPS

Q. For the information of one of my clients, I should like to be informed concerning the operation of retail florists' shops.

What is the average percentage of gross profit and what are the justifiable ratios of delivery, advertising, salaries and miscellaneous store expenses, also what is the average per cent net profit on sales?

A. We have your letter regarding operations of retail florists' shops, and we are pleased to give you the following figures:

Sales	100.00%	
Cost of sales	61.54%	
Gross profit	38.46%	
Delivery expenses	9.49%	
Advertising	2.81%	
Salaries	10.44%	
Miscellaneous store expenses	18.99%	41.73%
Net loss		3.27%

However, we would point out that the above figures are based solely upon the operations of one florist for the year ended August 31, 1915, as our files contain no other reports of such a nature.

7

Q. I am auditor for a rubber tire and tube manufacturing company in this state. They have initiated a campaign for increasing business and going into new territory. For instance they propose to spend $60,000 or more in advertising and there will be additional salaries besides traveling and other expenses for salesmen, which means in reality a largely increased selling expense.

The directorate does not wish to charge all this expenditure up in the year 1923, contending that it is expenditure for future sales results, that cannot be expected to be offset this year against the expected expenditure and have instanced that the United States Rubber, the B. F. Goodrich Co., the Kelly Springfield Tire Co. and others carry large assets under "deferred charges" or "organization expenses," costs of financing and promoting schemes to increase sales. I have pointed out that if it can be done it is preferable to charge these expenditures as expenses rather than capitalize—yet in so doing we all can see that no surplus can be shown, therefore no dividend can be declared, which of course all corporations are anxious to do. I have also explained that in the case of the income tax all deferred charges must be carried to the profit and loss account of the year as they cannot be deducted in any future year.

Would you concur that capitalizing is sound accounting and if not why do companies carry millions of dollars as an asset under "deferred charges?"

A. The specific question submitted appears to be whether it would be in accordance with sound accounting practise to capitalize expenditures for advertising and selling expenses incurred for the purpose of increasing sales and opening up new territory.

Expenditures of this nature should not of course be capitalized, but there are, however, special cases in which it may be fair and reasonable to carry forward some proportion of selling expenses incurred to a subsequent period in which results therefrom are expected. These expenses should be carried as a deferred charge to operations and not as capital expenditures.

It is not practicable to lay down any specific rule in regard to what proportion of the expenditures in any particular case might be properly carried forward without full detailed knowledge of the facts, as each case must be considered on its own merits. In every case the greatest care is necessary to see that any amount carried forward is not only reasonable but safe, so that the risk of carrying it at a value which cannot be ultimately provided for out of the margin of profits to be realized in the contemplated operations over a reasonable period may as far as possible be eliminated.

It might be pointed out further that your correspondent is in error in assuming that for tax purposes all deferred charges must be carried to the profit and loss account for the year in which incurred. Under the income tax regulations it is permissible to carry forward expenses which have been incurred in advance of accrual and charge them against subsequent periods in which they accrue.

8

American Institute of Accountants

Library and Bureau of Information

APRIL, 1924   SPECIAL BULLETIN No. 23

[The Committee on Administration of Endowment authorizes the publication of special Bulletins, of which this is one, on the distinct understanding that members are not to consider answers given to questions as being official pronouncements of the Institute, but merely the individual opinions of accountants to whom the questions were referred. It is earnestly requested that members criticise freely and constructively the answers given in this or any other Bulletin of this series.]

EQUITY IN PURCHASED PROPERTY

Q. A corporation is purchasing land and buildings for plant purposes, the purchase price of which is $100,000. The purchase is being made on contract which specifies that $10,000 shall be paid down and the balance in ten equal installments annually thereafter, the title to be retained by the vendor until full payment has been made. At the end of the first year the corporation has an equity only in this property of the down payment or $10,000. Is it proper to show it on the balance-sheet among the plant assets as follows:

Land and buildings	$100,000
Less unpaid balance on purchase price......	90,000
Equity	**$10,000**

Or should land and buildings be shown on the assets side of the balance-sheet as $100,000 and land contract payable on the liabilities side as $90,000. Would it make any difference if title passed to the corporation or if it did not until final payment was made?

A. In reply to your letter with reference to showing the equity in purchased property in the balance-sheet, we would state as follows:

Where the title has not passed to the property it is proper to include only the equity among the capital assets, viz.:

Land and buildings purchased on which title has not passed	**$100,000**
Less—Unpaid balance	90,000
Purchaser's equity	**$10,000**

In case the title to the property has passed to the purchaser, the property should be shown as an asset and the land contract payable as a liability.

FIRE LOSS ADJUSTMENT

Q. Will you kindly favor me with an expression of opinion as to whether or not the principle contended for in the following memorandum relating to fire loss adjustment is correct.

In a conversation with a fire insurance adjuster he again expressed to me his objection to the omission by Mr. ——— of depreciation on labor and freight in his computation of the fire loss, and added that it is the invariable custom of insurance adjusters to depreciate the total installed cost of buildings and machinery. I told him I thought they were wrong, and that they would have to arrange a more equitable adjustment for the B——— Co.

From an accounting standpoint, in the ordinary course of events both of these elements must be depreciated along with the factory cost of machinery and other materials, and it is on this theoretical ground no doubt that the adjusters base their contention that depreciation must be figured on the total installed cost for determining the amount of the fire loss.

1

It is important to bear in mind, however, that we are not dealing with an ordinary situation, but are face to face with the practical necessity of replacing the lost property.

The cost to replace the plant with property in a like condition (second-hand) would be less than to replace it new, the difference presumably measuring the depreciation it had suffered, but it would cost no less to install second-hand machinery or material than it would to install new, consequently the logical conclusion would seem to be that from a practical, economic standpoint, the F. O. B. factory cost of machinery and material only should be depreciated to determine the true fire loss, and that it would be wrong to calculate depreciation on labor for the reconstruction of buildings and reinstallation of machinery.

The same principle would apply in regard to freight and haulage.

A. In reply to your letter in which you request an expression of opinion regarding the soundness of the principle contended for, we beg to state that although not in accordance with the practice of insurance brokers we consider the principle fair and sound.

COLLECTIONS

Q. I wish to obtain the opinion of your association regarding the following question:

Under the supervision of which department, namely, the accounting or the treasury, should collections be handled?

(a) Where there is no regular credit department, and
(b) Where there is a credit department.

A. In all well-organized concerns the collections will be handled by others than those who keep the customers' records. This ordinarily will be the function of the treasurer, or of some department under the direction of the treasurer. Oftentimes where a separate credit department exists it is under the general supervision of the treasurer. In any case, the handling of collections should not be left to the bookkeeper.

Q. Thank you for your letter regarding the supervision of collections. It occurs to me that you might be willing to ask the Bureau of Information for a little additional information in connection with this matter.

The answer includes the following sentence: "In any case the handling of collections should not be left to the bookkeeper." Apparently the idea is to insure against theft of money. I do not quite see how this makes any difference if the bookkeeper has nothing to do with receiving the cash or the handling of it but merely sends out the letters and other forms necessary in following up delinquent accounts.

A. With further reference to our letter we feel that inasmuch as a bookkeeper usually has the opportunity to write off accounts as doubtful and may conceivably manipulate the credits for cash receipts, it is not good practice for him to communicate with customers in regard to delinquent accounts as there is always a chance of customers sending remittances with their replies which in some cases may be addressed to the bookkeeper direct. In other words, it is always more conservative practice to have the bookkeeper confine himself to his books and to leave the correspondence with the outside world in the hands of another executive.

ACQUISITION OF REAL ESTATE

Q. The writer cannot find any positive ruling as to whether, in connection with the purchase of land, the following are chargeable to expense, profit and loss, or capitalized:

Abstracting of title
Commission to real estate agents
Recording of deeds
Surveying
Title insurance
Legal expenses regarding purchases, and any other incidental expenses incurred in the purchase.

2

Will you advise where a positive ruling on the above may be found and if not will you kindly advise the usual practice of the Institute.

A. In the majority of transactions covering the acquisition of real estate, the cost of furnishing abstracts of title, title insurance, commission to real estate agents and surveying attaches to and is borne by the seller and not the purchaser. The problem submitted, however, apparently covers a case where the purchaser bears these costs.

Such being the case, all of the above costs constitute cost of acquiring the property and are usually and, in my opinion, properly capitalized. It will be readily seen that the cost enumerated above are not logically current expense of transacting business even if the business be that of buying and selling real estate, but are incidental additions to the purchase price.

A CORPORATION PROBLEM

Q. I am handing you herewith a problem which I would appreciate your submitting to the members of the American Institute of Accountants for an expression of opinion.

During the years 1917 to 1920, inclusive, the "X" Corporation, 95% of whose stock was owned by "A," purchased manufacturing materials from him, giving him credit therefor on its books in an account called the "Y" Company, which was not a corporation, but the style under which "A" conducted the business, he being the sole proprietor thereof. In the same period "A" withdrew monies from the "X" Corporation for his personal use, some of which was charged to his personal account, which was not the "Y" account, and the balance to expense accounts which were subsequently charged against the profits of the various years.

The charges to expenses appear to have been made by the bookkeeper because of the lack of information as to the accounts to which these should have been charged.

Upon examination of the tax return by the revenue bureau the above mentioned withdrawals in the expense accounts were disallowed as deductions and considered to be cash dividends paid. The minutes show that the only dividends declared and paid during the period under consideration were a cash dividend on February 26th, 1917 of 100%, and a stock dividend of 100% on June 30th, 1917.

The original balance-sheet of the corporation at December 31st, 1919, was as follows:

Assets:

Cash		$2,589.73
Notes receivable		1,500.00
Accounts receivable—customers		44,421.93
Inventories		8,366.16
Accounts receivable:		
Stockholder "A"	$30,189.95	
"Y" Company owned by stockholder "A,"		
Cr. balance	22,956.35	
		7,233.60
Equipment		29,157.14
Automobiles		2,221.83
Total		$95,490.39

Liabilities:

Notes payable	$20,000.00
Accounts payable—trade creditors	3,823.47
Accrued expenses	5,559.00
Reserved for depreciation	14,066.45
Capital stock	10,000.00
Surplus	42,041.47
Total	$95,490.39

After an audit of the accounts had been made, the balance-sheets were restated, that for 1919 being submitted for discussion.

3

Assets:

Cash		$2,589.73
Notes receivable		1,500.00
Accounts receivable—customers		44,421.93
Inventories		8,366.16

Accounts receivable:

Stockholder "A"	$30,189.95	
Add: Personal items of Stockholder "A" previously charged against Surplus:		
1917	35,317.67	
1918	33,654.73	
1919	5,420.49	
	$104,582.84	
"Y" Company owned by Stockholder "A," Cr. balance	22,956.35	
		81,626.49
Equipment		29,157.14
Automobiles		2,221.83
Total		$169,883.28

Liabilities:

Notes payable		$20,000.00
Accounts payable—trade creditors		3,823.47
Accrued expenses		5,559.00
Accrued income and excess profits taxes—past due		43,165.14
Reserve for depreciation		14,066.45
Accrued income and excess profit taxes—current		4,076.19
Capital stock		10,000.00
Surplus	$42,041.47	
Add: Personal items of Stockholder "A," previously charged against Surplus through profit and loss account	74,392.89	
	$116,434.36	

Less: Income and excess profit taxes:

Past due	$43,165.14	
Current	4,076.19	
	47,241.33	
		69,193.03
Total		$169,883.28

It is my opinion that the withdrawals being neither expenses nor dividends, should have been charged to the personal account of "A," such account receivable being considered as an offset to the account payable to the "Y" Company as the latter was for all practical purposes the account of "A."

The attorneys in this matter are seeking for confirmation of my opinion, and I therefore request that the question be submitted through the Institute to some members thereof.

A. Assuming that the items of expense, aggregating $74,392.89, were properly chargeable against "A" and not expenses of the "X" Corporation, it appears proper that they should increase the debit account of "A" and serve as an offset to the account payable in favor of the "Y" Company, of which "X" was the sole proprietor. There is apparently no basis for considering these charges to "X" as cash dividends, since a dividend may only arise through a formal setting aside of profits or surplus by the directors. The whole question, as we see it, is whether or not "X" received the money as dividends or payments on account; and we are of the opinion, from the facts stated, that there is no authority for considering such payments as cash dividends.

4

The question is whether these sums disallowed as expenses are to be regarded as dividends or as charges against the personal account of the principal stockholder. The fact that the principal stockholder already had an open account for withdrawals on the books of the company would support the claim that these withdrawals should be treated as charges to this account.

I am regarding the liability account in favor of the stockholders' other company as a part of his open account, the net balance of which is, therefore, to be considered as the account receivable. Whether these charges should be considered as an account receivable would depend somewhat upon the circumstances, that is, whether there was a real intention on the part of the stockholder to repay the money withdrawn to the company, and whether, in case such was his intention, he was able to do so. Assuming the answers to these queries to be in the affirmative, I should advise maintaining the position that the sums drawn were in the nature of accounts receivable.

The objection to this claim would be that the drawings increased cumulatively, a condition which would not indicate any intention or possibility of repaying them. This would rather indicate that the stockholder was draining one company for the benefit of his other interests; and when it is considered how easily a controlling stockholder could thus create a fictitious nominal invested capital by setting up as an asset amounts drawn out by him, it cannot be denied that the treasury department has a very good reason for taking the stand it does. The fact that these withdrawals were not declared as dividends and paid pro rata to all stockholders does not control the interpretation of the transaction because the treasury department is governed not by the restraints of corporation law but by the evident facts in the case.

To sum up, I would make the best case possible for the corporation and could argue in favor of the inquirer's attitude, but fear that unless the circumstances very clearly support that view the treasury department will be able to maintain the position it takes.

The points at issue are whether the withdrawal of monies by "A" from the "X" corporation were in effect constructive dividends, or were merely advances chargeable to his personal account.

The fact that "A" who was a 95% stockholder, withdrew monies aggregating more than $100,000 for the years to December 31, 1919, would indicate that "A" was obtaining the same advantages in effect as if dividends had been actually distributed even though no dividends had been declared. Probably it was on this basis that the department considered the withdrawals, which it was later claimed had been charged to surplus in error by the corporation, to constitute distributions of surplus profits.

The withdrawals by "A" exclusive of the $74,000 charged to expense accounts, aggregated some $30,000 and this was about $7,000 more than the liability of the corporation to the "Y" company, or "A" in this case. Had the liability to "Y" aggregated more than the advances to "A," it would seem reasonable to assume that the withdrawals were in effect payments to "A" for materials purchased through the "Y" Company, and could be applied as such at least to the extent of the indebtedness.

There may be other facts pertaining to the matter which would alter the case and make it more favorable to the corporation, but in view of the evidence presented in the inquiry it would appear that the department was justified in assuming that the withdrawals of "A" constituted constructive dividends.

It should be noted that even if the corporation could satisfy the department that the withdrawals of "A" were not dividends, the stockholders might be subject to tax imposed under Section 220.

DEPRECIATION—MARBLE COMPANY

Q. What depreciation rates should a marble company use?

A. The rates should be governed, as in all other industries, to a

5

great extent by the policy adopted as to maintenance of the equipment. In one company a scientific method has never been adopted, although it is our opinion that the rates used are approximately correct since the company is very liberal in charging to operations items of equipment, which conceivably might be capitalized by a less conservative management. Facts such as these, therefore, should be taken into consideration in arriving at proper rates. The company we have in mind has never attempted to apply varying rates of depreciation to the various items of plant equipment, but has adopted a rate of 8% on all mill machinery and fixtures and 4% on mill buildings. In instances where an analysis is not available for the buildings and machinery showing, respectively, the value of buildings, machinery and equipment, a composite rate of 6% has been used.

It is the practice of two marble companies that have come under our observation to charge to operations such items as gang saws, edge polishers, carborundum cleaners, rubbers, cutoff saws and water pipes in the mill building, after the initial investment therein has been capitalized. On the initial investment the water pipes are depreciated at the rate of 2½% per annum and the remaining items on the basis of a ten-year life. It is our opinion that such bases are conservative. All water pipes used in the quarry are charged to operations.

Such items as electric motors, compressors, marble lathes, tanks and pumps do not necessarily call for special treatment by reason of the fact that they are used by marble companies. In the case referred to, a rate of 8% is used for electrical equipment and shafting. All shafting after the initial equipment has been capitalized is charged to operations.

DEPRECIATION—FLOUR MILLING INDUSTRY

A. It has been the practice of flour mills to operate twenty-four hours a day. The annual rates of depreciation on buildings and equipment have been based on such full time operation. At the present time, however, due to overexpansion, the general experience in the milling industry is that only from ten to twelve hours daily will produce sufficient flour to meet demand.

We are endeavoring to adjust straight line depreciation rates to conform with the situation outlined, and we shall be much pleased to obtain your opinion upon the following points:

(1) Should flour mill depreciation be based upon number of barrels of flour produced rather than upon number of months or years elapsed?

(2) If (1) is answered in the affirmative, should buildings be treated in the same manner as machinery and equipment, or should they be depreciated on a time basis only?

(3) Assuming that depreciation (wear and tear) be computed on a unit of production rather than a time basis, would it not be necessary to charge "obsolescence" on a time basis in addition to the unit basis for wear and tear only?

(4) What rate would you suggest for
(a) annual straight line depreciation, including obsolescence, for flour mill machinery and equipment?
(b) same, for steel and concrete buildings, mill, and elevator?
(c) rates per barrel, wear and tear only, for machinery?
(d) annual rates for obsolescence for machinery and equipment?

A. Replying to your questionnaire relative to depreciation in the flour milling industry, we submit the following:

1. Flour mills, especially the larger ones, usually operate on a 24-hour basis and base depreciation on that schedule. It is generally recognized that some depreciation occurs even when machinery is idle. If such deterioration can be determined it would be appropriate to provide for it. Depreciation is usually based on the normal working schedule rather than on barrels produced, and such schedule should not be varied for temporary fluctuations.

6

2. Building depreciation is usually based on the useful life. Except where the vibration from the operation of heavy machinery is a factor, the depreciation sustained would not vary materially, whether the plant is operating to capacity or not, if anything an idle building depreciates more rapidly.

3. The factor of obsolescence on flour mill machinery has been found to be practically nil. If obsolescence were a factor, it should be treated separately from that of depreciation.

4. (a)

	24 hr. basis	12 hr. basis reduced
Rolls	4%	2½%
Reels	6	3½
Purifiers	6- 8	3½-5
Sifters	10-12	6-7
Packing machinery..........	10-12	6-7

  (b)   1½%-2%
  (c)   3 cents
  (d)   See Number 3

Note: To obtain an average rate for the entire machinery and equipment, apply the above rates to units and reduce to total to one average rate.

Reduce the 24-hour basis to 12-hour basis as follows:

          12 hour normal time
          12 " overtime
           6 " factor for overtime 1½
          ─────
          30 hours

Considering one and one-half rate for overtime (any hours above an established normal time), and using five percent as an average depreciation rate for 24-hour basis:

       24 hours—reduce 5%
       18 "   6/30 — 1/5   4%
       12 "   12/30 — 2/5   3%

CONSOLIDATION OF ACCCOUNTS

Q. A corporation which owns and operates several large hotels, but which has no mortgage or other funded debt, acquires for a cash outlay of $500,000, 100% of the capital stock of another corporation which owns one hotel and has a bonded indebtedness of $1,500,000. The parent corporation then leases the building and equipment from the subsidiary for a rental consideration sufficient to enable the latter to redeem its bonds as they mature serially and pay the interest on the obligation. The parent corporation does not assume nor guarantee the bonds of the subsidiary.

Current liabilities are negligible.

Interested persons argue that the consolidation of the balance-sheets results in imposing a liability upon the parent corporation which has not been assumed, and that the subsidiary could be abandoned by the parent corporation without impairing the business of the latter.

Is it proper to publish a balance-sheet of the parent corporation showing "investment in subsidiary company, $500,000?"

If a consolidated balance-sheet is considered necessary, is it permissible to take up the equity in the consolidation property account, or must the gross value be taken up and the bonds set out specifically as a liability?

The bonds existed at the time the property was acquired by the subsidiary company. Would the amount thereof be considered a purchase money obligation?

A. While there is, of course, no legal obligation on a company to publish a consolidated balance-sheet so long as that of the parent company shows its true financial position, yet the proper and best practice in the circumstances mentioned in your letter would be to consolidate the accounts. The liability of the subsidiary company for outstanding bonds would then be shown in the consolidated balance-sheet in such a manner as would clearly indicate it was not a liability of the parent

7

company but applied against the properties of the subsidiary company which would be shown separately in the balance-sheet from those of the parent. We would not favor showing the parent company's equity in the property of the subsidiary company as an asset nor would we describe the bonds of the subsidiary as purchase money obligations.

In the case you mention the parent corporation leases the property of the subsidiary for a rental sufficient to enable the latter to redeem its bonds serially as they mature, and to pay the interest on its obligations. This, in our opinion, is a material factor in the financial position of the parent company inasmuch as while technically the parent does not guarantee the bonds of the subsidiary, yet in effect it has, as a going concern, a liability for their repayment. Such being the case if a balance-sheet of the parent company only is prepared a note should be attached stating the terms of the lease under which the parent company operates the properties of the subsidiary.

CHOCOLATE AND CHOCOLATE PRODUCTS

Q. What is considered an usual turnover of average inventory in the candy manufacturing business?

What is the usual proportion or about what would be a correct proportion of fixed assets to total assets in a well balanced candy manufacturing business?

A. The turnover is 6.75 for a manufacturer of chocolate and chocolate products.

This manufacturer rents his building, but the machinery and equipment at its depreciated value is 44% of the total assets. Equipment is about 1/3 depreciated. If effect were given to the original cost, the percentage to total assets adjusted would be only 35%.

EXPORT ACCOUNTS RECEIVABLE

Q. Will you kindly advise the form of verification used by accountants on export accounts receivable, particularly with Cuba, Porto Rico and South America.

A. We have no special form for verifying export accounts receivable with customers in such foreign lands as Cuba, Porto Rico, or South America, but we see no reason to depart from more or less standard forms of confirmation letters for accounts receivable or open accounts of any kind. In the cases with which we have been familiar, the clients have been very chary about permitting us to send independent confirmation letters to their customers or correspondents. Our clients have their own form for calling for a confirmation of the balances with their foreign correspondents. These letters are written in Spanish, but they contain a statement somewhat to the following effect:

"We take pleasure in enclosing herewith extract of your account current as of December 31, 19 , showing a balance of in favor of   U. S. gold, which statement we should thank you to examine and if found correct to kindly forward under advice to us."

SALT—COST

Q. What is the actual cost per ton of salt by evaporation?
A. The cost per ton of salt by evaporation is as follows:

Undried "at works"............ $4.3575
Dried "at works"............... 5.5075

These costs include a depreciation charge of $1.14½ per ton, but do not include depletion.

HARDWARE—EXPENSE

Q. What should the administrative, office and selling expense be in a concern manufacturing counters, brass and steel hinges and metal stampings? These counters are sold to quite an extent to the retail trade and the hinges and stampings is a jobbing business.

A. The percentages of such expenses to the sales of two representative hardware concerns during two recent years averaged 18%.

8

American Institute of Accountants

Library and Bureau of Information

SPECIAL BULLETIN No. 24

JANUARY, 1925

[The Committee on Administration of Endowment authorizes the publication of special Bulletins, of which this is one, on the distinct understanding that members are not to consider answers given to questions as being official pronouncements of the Institute, but merely the individual opinions of accountants to whom the questions were referred. It is earnestly requested that members criticise freely and constructively the answers given in this or any other Bulletin of this series.]

CONSOLIDATION OF STATEMENTS

Q. A corporation owns real estate which it transfers to a building corporation it has organized, taking in payment all the capital stock of said building corporation. The building corporation then borrows money on long-term or serial-mortgage bonds for the improvement of the property. The parent corporation does not go on the bond of this mortgage nor guarantee it, but takes a lease on the property from the building corporation sufficient to pay the interest and sinking fund (or serial maturities) of the mortgage bonds.

The question at issue is whether it is or is not good business practice and good accounting practice for the parent corporation not to consolidate the statement of the building corporation with its own, when it makes its annual report to the stockholders.

Of course, if the statements are consolidated, the mortgage debt will show on the consolidated balance-sheet of the parent company, and if they are not consolidated, the parent corporation's investment will be represented merely by "capital stock in building corporation" at the original cost of the property.

A. The facts in the question presented seem to be that the property of the parent corporation has been improved with borrowed money for which certain assets have been mortgaged and the problem is how to disclose these facts. The interposition of another corporate entity does not really alter the situation although it does influence the method of presenting it.

A statement of assets and liabilities would be as follows:

Parent company
Investment in capital stock of building co. $100,000
Cash 200,000

Capital stock $300,000

Building company
Land $100,000
Building 300,000

1

Capital stock	$100,000
Mortgage	300,000

Combined
Land	$100,000
Building	300,000
Cash	200,000

Capital stock	$300,000
Mortgage	300,000

If the accounts are not consolidated the parent company's balance-sheet shows an asset on which no opinion of value can be formed. It may have much, little or no value.

If the accounts are consolidated the consolidated balance-sheet shows a liability which does not lie against all the assets but which nevertheless may ultimately extinguish assets of more than its face value, i. e. if the mortgage covered both the land and building and was foreclosed leaving no equity.

Of course the combined balance-sheet is the usual thing but if there be objection to publishing that the situation might be met in one of two ways: (1) publish a separate balance-sheet of each company; (2) publish the balance-sheet of the parent company with a note at the bottom reading somewhat as follows:

"Building company (of which this company owns the entire capital stock) has tangible assets of a value of $400,000.00 which are mortgaged for $300,000.00."

Undoubtedly the best practice would be to consolidate the accounts of the building corporation with those of the parent company as the mortgage could then be clearly shown in the consolidated balance-sheet as a debt of the subsidiary company and the operating results of the building corporation would also be properly recorded. There would then be no question but that the auditors could give a clean certificate to such a statement stating that the consolidated accounts clearly set forth the financial position of the combined companies and the results of the operations.

Should the parent company, however, decline to consolidate the accounts of the building corporation with those of the parent company then care should be taken in the balance-sheet to show the investment in the stock of the building corporation as a separate item, and to indicate clearly that it is subservient to the mortgage. At the same time the losses, if any, of the building corporation should be reflected in the accounts of the parents company.

There are a good many accounting questions about which a definite statement may be made as to whether a certain treatment is or is not good business practice and good accounting practice. We think though that this is not one of them. In our opinion the two balance-sheets may be consolidated, or need not be consolidated, without a question arising that the treatment is not good practice.

It is not uncommon for mercantile houses to form a distinct corporation to hold the buildings in which they do business, and perhaps others. The usual procedure is for the active company to lease the

2

property under terms which will permit the real estate company to meet all its charges, and thus conduct its affairs without incurring a deficit. If the forecast of charges upon which the rental named in the lease is based proves incorrect an adjustment is usually made, which still permits the real estate company to avoid a deficit in its operating account.

If the proprietors choose to consolidate the two balance-sheets, there is no objection to their doing so. If they prefer to show the financial position of each corporation separately, we think that the interest of the active company in the real estate company may be properly, and adequately, expressed as an investment on the balance-sheet of the active company.

We are not wholly in agreement with the position expressed in the last paragraph of the question. If the real estate company receives enough income to cover its charges and runs along with a small surplus, the active company's investment may be carried in the balance-sheet at original cost. If the rental agreed upon proves too small to meet charges against it and no adjustment of it is made, with the result that a deficit occurs, the valuation of the active company's investment should be adjusted accordingly at suitable intervals.

EQUITY IN PURCHASED PROPERTY

The following is a partial quotation from a letter referring to the first problem in Special Bulletin No. 23.

In this question, the opinion is given that where land and buildings are purchased on contract, the purchase price to be paid over a period and the title to remain in the vendor until full payment has been made, the proper manner of showing the item and the liability thereon in the balance-sheet is to show the full cost, less the unpaid balance and to bring out the net equity, presumably all on the asset side of the balance-sheet.

I do not agree with this procedure for the following reasons:

(1) The liability side of the balance-sheet should reveal all of the liabilities, whereas by the answer given it would not do so. The liability on the land contract is secured by title remaining in the vendor to the property. However, in the event of default the creditor would be a general creditor to the extent that the property did not satisfy the unpaid balance. This is especially true in the case of plants acquired during the recent period of extremely high prices, and which might not in normal times, come anywhere near realizing the purchase price. In addition, in the event of bankruptcy of the industry, it might be very possible that the plant at a forced sale would bring a very low figure. Surely, a banker for instance, scrutinizing the balance-sheet has the right to expect all of the liabilities to appear upon the liability side. Of course, the liability is shown but would it not be more properly shown as a liability among other liabilities. In addition, those payments due on such a land contract within a very short time from the date of the balance-sheet, assuming the contract is payable in annual installments, represent a very current liability to be satisfied out of the current assets.

(2) The liability on the land contract, is almost identical with the liability upon a mortgage, the only real difference being the matter of the passing of title. I do not believe anyone would favor deducting a mortgage from the asset on the asset side of the balance-sheet and yet the equity of the purchaser is, as in the case of the land contract pur-

3

chase the purchase price less the balance due on the mortgage, assuming for instance that the mortgage was given in connection with the purchase and not as the basis for a loan.

The member who furnished the original answer makes the following comment on the letter above quoted:

On further consideration we think your correspondent is right, assuming that the vendor has a right against the corporation as a creditor quite apart from the lien on the land. Where the liability is solely against the property a statement in the form suggested in our previous letter would be appropriate. In considering the whole question it is, we think, important to bear in mind first, that disclosure of facts is the first and most vital requisite of a balance-sheet; and secondly, that while it is very important to bring in all liabilities there is sometimes a danger that the introduction of assets entailed in the introduction of liabilities into a balance-sheet may result in the statement being more misleading than if both were omitted.

However, in the case forming the subject of the question, it is clear that a plant was being built on the land purchased, so that presumably the vendors would have a security on the plant when constructed as well as on the original land, so that the better practice would be to show the unpaid purchase as a secured liability.

BONDS

Q. In your Special Bulletin No. 20 issued in September, 1923, an explanation is made of the answer to question two relative to bonds signed by a trustee and not actually sold, covered in Special Bulletin No. 18 page 11. Having submitted the original question to your bureau, I am taking the liberty of again addressing you with reference to the additional comments made.

The original answer to question two was satisfactory and I am not aware of the reasons for the additional information, but this was no doubt brought up by some member of the Institute. There is, however, a statement in Bulletin No. 20 which seems to me to be in conflict with certain statements made in answer to question four. In Bulletin No. 20 it is stated that the trustee's signature cannot change the nature of an obligation such as is involved in these bonds and the obligation cannot be to the issuing corporation by itself. Therefore in preparing a balance-sheet the liability of the company is only for the bonds held by the public and it necessarily follows that $9,000,000.00 is the net obligation with respect to these bonds. It is also quoted as follows: "A bond is merely the evidence of an indebtedness and entitles the holder to recover of the maker the amount evidenced by its terms. Independent of establishing the right of such recovery the bond has no value." From the above quotations I am of the opinion that it is the intention to state that these bonds in the treasury at the date of foreclosure would not be considered outstanding bonds and that in the distribution of the proceeds received from the sale of pledged property under the mortgage, that such proceeds would be distributed only to the $9,000,000 of bonds outstanding in the hands of the public. This is directly contrary to the statement made in Bulletin No. 18 as to question four in which it is stated as follows: "However, it is our understanding that if the bonds were (a) in the company's treasury at the date of foreclosure, these bonds would share in the proceeds of the foreclosure to the same extent as any other outstanding bonds.

4

In case the claims of creditors were not fully satisfied from the proceeds of the foreclosure, the creditors could obtain a deficiency judgment and participate in the share of the proceeds of the foreclosure applicable to the treasury bonds." The question as to whether or not the treasury bonds would share in the proceeds of the foreclosure is a very important one and in order that the possible point at issue may be clearly stated it will be assumed that the following is a statement of fact:

Bonds authorized	$10,000,000
Outstanding in the hands of the public	9,000,000
In the company's treasury	1,000,000

As a result of a foreclosure under the mortgage, the property pledged realized $8,000,000. As far as the trustee is concerned there are outstanding bonds of a total amount of $10,000,000 and he is therefore in position to pay off from the proceeds from the foreclosure 80% of this indebtedness.

In accordance with the answer to question four the bonds outstanding in the hands of the public would be paid to the extent of $7,200,000 and there would revert to the company's treasury $800,000 which would be available for distribution amongst the general creditors. The public bond holder would secure a deficiency judgment amounting to $1,800,000 which would share proportionately with the unsecured creditors provided that the other assets of the concern together with the $800,000 available from the treasury bonds would not be sufficient to take care of all liabilities.

I would have you advise if the conclusion drawn above is in accordance with the answer submitted by your bureau.

A. The bureau has received the following comments:

There is a legal aspect to this question and not being a lawyer I submitted your letter to two attorneys of high professional standing and attainments and my reply is based on their statements to me. Restating the problem in its last form:—

"A"

Property valued @	$20,000,000
Mortgage	10,000,000
Mortgage bonds sold	9,000,000
Mortgage bonds not sold and retained by trustee	1,000,000
"B" Mortgage forclosed and properly sold for	8,000,000

Mr. X says that the trustee is now in position to pay to purchasers of $9,000,000 of the mortgage bonds 80%, or $7,200,000 and they lose 20% of their investment or $800,000.

My advisers say that the trustee is legally bound to pay the holders of the $9,000,000 bonds sold, 8/9ths or 88 8/9%; that property valued at $20,000,000 was mortgaged to secure a loan of only $9,000,000 net and that every cent of the $8,000,000 obtained by the sale under foreclosure of the property mortgaged goes to the purchasers of the mortgage bonds. That the mere issue of $1,000,000 of so called treasury bonds creates no obligation or equity by which common creditors can participate in the proceeds of the sale of the mortgaged property.

I must say that this is in accord with my views based on fairness and justice, else what would be the position of the ordinary bond buyer?

5

If he bought a $1,000 bond at par he might be in the position of sharing the security supporting that bond to the extent of 10%, 20% or even 50% with common creditors in case of bankruptcy. Why do people buy bonds anyway if it is not to secure themselves against loss as far as possible by buying an interest in the real property of the issuing company which cannot be endangered by possible bankruptcy?

It seems to me that if, as in Mr. X's illustration, common creditors can participate to the extent of 20% in the mortgaged property by the mere fiction of having certain papers signed and sealed by the trustee and delivered to the treasurer of the company, a feeling of uncertainty would be introduced into the bond market, which would have a very bad effect on that business and on business in general.

Let me quote a decision by a special master in the case of a political subdivision in which the debt was to be stated and it was urged by one litigant that the bonds held by the commissioners of the sinking fund were a part of the debt.

> "I am satisfied that the great weight of reason and authority is against the contention of the plaintiff and I, therefore, find that the sinking fund (bonds) *** were not a part of the debt. *** The (town of W) can hardly be debtor and creditor at the same time."

As a parallel to the case under discussion the political subdivisions' property and credit were the security, the bonds outstanding in the hands of the public were the actual debt and the sinking funds bonds the "treasury bonds." I am prepared to furnish references to this decision, if they are desired.

A hypothetical case is stated and you are asked as to whether the facts of this hypothetical case are interpreted in accordance with the printed answer to part four in Bulletin No. 18.

In my opinion they are interpreted in accordance with the answer in Bulletin No. 18, but it is my further opinion that the answer to this part of the problem in Bulletin No. 18 is incorrect.

If $10,000,000 of bonds are certified, $9,000,000 sold, and $1,000,000 held in the treasury, the company issuing the bonds owes only $9,000,000 unless it can be said that the company owes itself $1,000,000, which is a patent absurdity. The mortgage is, of course, security for the debt and only for the debt. Since the debt is only $9,000,000 the mortgage can be security for only $9,000,000. This would mean that the bondholders would receive the entire $8,000,000 assumed proceeds of the disposal of the mortgaged property and no portion of the proceeds would be returned to the issuing company.

MINING COMPANIES

In looking over Special Bulletin No. 21, I notice some questions on mining companies. Question two inquires about taxes on land owned adjacent to mines but not used for mining purposes, which might include land upon which company houses are built and rented to employees.

The bituminous mines for which we are auditors charge taxes against the department to which they apply, and taxes on land used for dwellings, company stores, club houses, hospitals, theatres, pool rooms, farm, dairy, bath houses, gasoline stations, schools, churches, etc., are charged to the tax account in the "rents" group of accounts. (Each

6

activity is the.. charged rent). If the land is not used for the ancillary operations mentioned, its possession is generally necessitated by the operation of the mines and the future extraction of the minerals underneath and is consequently a proper charge against the mining or extraction of the coal or whatever mineral it might be.

Relative to question four about depletion of the fair value of mineral deposits March 1, 1913, when such value was in excess of the original cost, it is the practice of bituminous mines that have come under our observation to charge depletion (operating expenses) with the full amount of depletion allowed by the government and to credit reserve for depletion. At the same time an entry is made charging surplus arising from appreciation (of leaseholds, or mineral deposits if owned) and crediting surplus with that portion of the depletion on the value written up. This is done to show the actual cost of mining based upon March 1, 1913 valuation. This method is also followed in the case of values placed upon discovery.

SERIALLY-MATURING FUNDED DEBT

Q. Will you please advise us as to the general practice in treating serially-maturing funded debt for balance-sheet purposes.

A. There is little uniformity of treatment in American balance-sheets of funded debts represented by serial notes maturing monthly or at other frequent intervals. Instead there seem to be three methods as follows:

(1) It is quite generally the practice with regard to public utilities to consider all funded liabilities as being classifiable under the long-time liabilities heading. This practice is followed even though some of the notes may mature very soon after the date of the balance-sheet. The reasoning back of this treatment is that such a debt is usually refundable, that the debt did not create any of the current assets, and that the working capital should not be reduced because of such indebtedness. The disadvantage in such treatment lies in the fact that it does not serve warning to the inspector of such a balance-sheet that a liability in addition to those in the current liability group must be met at an early date. Unless arrangements have been made for the early renewal or refunding of such debt, the balance-sheet does not properly display the immediate financial problems of the business.

(2) A method frequently followed is to split such a funded debt into two amounts, bringing into the current liabilities group the total of such notes maturing in the current financing period, allowing the remainder of the group to appear among the long-time liabilities. This treatment is not wholly satisfactory as it is more desirable for a particular debt with its necessary comments to appear but once on a balance-sheet. Further, the question immediately arises as to how much of the debt should be put into the current group. In other, words, how long is the "current financing period." There seems to be a growing tendency to consider twelve months as a proper basis for the majority of commercial concerns, though this is far from being a generally accepted period.

(3) While it is true that balance-sheets should follow certain definitely prescribed and generally accepted forms, this must not prevent initiative in the treatment of special problems. While generally the liabilities are grouped under two broad classes—namely current and long-time—the problem of the serial funded debt above referred to is

7

probably best met by the creating of a third group to be placed between the long-time and the current. This group may appear on the balance-sheet as follows:

Serial equipment notes payable
(Maturing $20,000 on the first day of each month)....$1,2000,000

Such a treatment shows the current liabilities in total, uninfluenced by these funded notes, and at the same time allows the observer of the balance-sheet to exercise his own judgment as to the amount of serial notes which he desires to consider as current for his own interpretation. In such usage the heading for the long-time group of liabilities would probably be other funded debt or other long-time liabilities.

VALUATION OF RAW SILK INVENTORIES

Q. I understand that raw silk is quoted and traded in on a basis that includes ninety days credit terms and that it is a general practice of silk manufacturers to value the raw silk inventories on this ninety day term basis, regardless of the fact that a part of the raw silk inventories may have been purchased for cash or paid for in yen, thus taking advantage of exchange and interest fluctuations between the local and foreign markets.

The difference between the ninety-day basis and cash basis is carried direct to income upon the theory that it is a cash discount or a profit on foreign exchange.

This practice raises an interesting question relative to the valuation of raw silk inventories and I will be grateful if you will advise me relative to the accepted practice of accountants on this subject.

A. We know of no instance in which silk on hand at the close of a fiscal period, bought on a cash basis, is valued on the ninety-day basis, taking up as a profit the difference between the ninety-day basis and the cash basis.

Those companies with which we are acquainted, and who are importers of silk as well as manufacturers, purchase silk say in China and against these purchases drafts are drawn under letters of credit. Although the purchase is made in yen, the drafts are drawn in dollars or sterling, converted at the current market rate, and in general the amount of the draft is taken up at cost. At the close of a fiscal period, the raw silk on hand is taken at cost, or if the market has declined, at market.

In the case of one large company in particular where drafts are drawn in sterling, the cost of the raw silk purchased is definitely known at the time of purchase owing to the fact that under the company's arrangements with the banks, the sterling rate is fixed at the time a sterling draft is drawn.

In the case of two large importing and manufacturing companies, with whose accounts we are familiar, discount or interest for the period covered by a draft is included in the amount of the draft. One of these companies takes up as cost of raw silk the full amount of the draft. The other charges the portion of interest and discount included in the amount of the draft to the interest and discount account—the balance being charged to the cost of raw silk.

We fail to see how the taking up of a profit arising through the difference between the ninety-day basis and the cash basis can be justified. In our opinion, the accounting relative to the purchase of raw silk is similar to that relative to the purchase of any imported commodity on which current quotations are made.

8

American Institute of Accountants
Library and Bureau of Information

SPECIAL BULLETIN No. 25

February, 1925

[The Committee on Administration of Endowment authorizes the publication of special Bulletins, of which this is one, on the distinct understanding that members are not to consider answers given to questions as being official pronouncements of the Institute, but merely the individual opinions of accountants to whom the questions were referred. It is earnestly requested that members criticise freely and constructively the answers given in this or any other Bulletin of this series.]

DEPRECIATION—BALL PARKS

Q. I would appreciate it if you would give me some information in regard to what depreciation accountants are taking on ball parks. This ball park is a concrete building and while much smaller is on similar lines to the Yankee stadium.

A. Ball parks are not so numerous that there is any general practice or consensus of opinion regarding rate of depreciation. From our experience with the treasury department concerning rates of depreciation for concrete buildings, we imagine the treasury would not allow for income tax purposes a rate higher than 1½ per cent. per annum or, at the outside, 2 per cent., with the possible exception of any items of equipment which can be distinguished from the structure proper, which can be shown to have a shorter life.

The factor of obsolescence should receive consideration when so long an expected life is used as a basis for the depreciation rate as in the above case. The treasury department, however, would not under its present rulings make any allowance for obsolescence until it was more definitely in sight than is probably the case today with ball parks.

CHARGES OF PUBLIC ACCOUNTANTS

Q. I am anxious to ascertain the general custom among public accountants with respect to charges for consultations. We make no charge for consultation where we are regularly employed as auditors. In other words, where we are employed on an annual basis as auditors our clients have the privilege of consulting us without charge on our part. I will appreciate it if you will endeavor to ascertain, if possible and consistent, what the general practice is in this regard and advise me.

A. We encourage our clients to consult us on any matters of an accounting nature in connection with which they feel we may be of assistance. If we have an annual retainer we rarely charge for such consultations. However, if the consultation occupied any considerable portion of the time of the principals and if, in our opinion, our advice was of considerable value to the client, we would not hesitate to make an additional charge.

1

Our experience, is generally speaking along the lines indicated by your correspondent, that is to say, that where we have clients for whom we act as auditors on the basis of a regular contract of employment, we are quite prepared to give them the benefit of consultation services during the year without additional charge. Cases have arisen, however, where the nature of these services manifestly have been such, as to clearly come outside the scope of the regular contract arrangement, and in these cases we have arranged with the client for a special charge either on the basis of agreed per diem rates or a lump sum for such special services. Of course, in cases where a new client desires advice or consultation services this is always made the basis of a special charge by arrangement with him at the initial interview.

BUILDING MATERIAL TRADE

Q. We should like to secure some figures relative to the cost of the operation of building materials companies dealing in plaster, cement, miscellaneous materials and structural steel combined. The sales average between one million and one million and a half dollars.

A. We submit a statement giving operating statistics relative to two companies in the building material trade.

OPERATING STATISTICS OF
COMPANIES SELLING BUILDING MATERIALS

	Cost of sales	Gross profit	Operating expenses	Net profit
Company located in the Middle West (average sales $450,000 per year)				
1923	85.47	14.53	12.78	1.75
1922	86.09	13.91	10.81	3.10
1921	86.79	13.21	11.18	2.03
Company located in New York State (average sales $900,000 per year)				
1920	77.30	22.70	20.95	1.75
1919	83.27	16.73	16.39	.34
1918	77.78	22.22	21.51	.71

Percentage to net sales

DISTRIBUTION OF COST ON THE BASIS OF SALES IN A PATENT LITIGATION CASE

Q. In a patent litigation case, the plaintiff has reported profits arising from infringement sales. These profits have been determined by percentages based on total sales.

For your information, the following figures were taken from the plaintiff's report.

Total sales	$426,744.80
Infringement sales	77,792.86
Percent of infringement sales to total sales	$ 18.23
Costs:	
Materials, labor and burden	$221,972.15
Selling and administrative	149,742.29
Total	$371,714.44

2

```
Infringement sales .........................  $ 77,792.86
Deduct:
    Cost of sales—
        18.23% of $221,972.15........$40,462.81
    Selling and administrative—
        18.23% of $149,742.29........ 27,298.02
            Total deductions ........———————  $ 67,760.83

    Net profit from infringement sales .......  $ 10,032.03
```

You will note from the foregoing that costs have been distributed on the basis of sales. Will you please give an opinion on' this method of distribution? It is possible to determine the cost of material and labor from the records and to arrive at a burden rate based upon direct labor.

A. It is our opinion that the distribution of costs on the basis of sales in such cases is incorrect and inequitable. From our experience in manufacturing establishments we would say that it is very unlikely that the percentage of gross profit on each of the articles manufactured would be the same, because an article upon which the manufacturing costs were twenty cents and sold for thirty cents, that therefore another article upon which the manufacturing cost was fifty cents would sell for seventy-five cents. It has been our experience that the selling price of an article is not necessarily based only on the cost of the article but also upon the supply and demand for that article. In the case in question one of the articles manufactured was an infringement upon a patent right, and in view of the fact that probably only one other manufacturer had the right to manufacture and sell the article so infringed upon, the demand for the article allowed a greater percentage of profit on the selling price of that article than on the balance of the articles manufactured upon which in all probability no patents were existing, and were therefore being sold in a competitive market at lower percentage of profit.

For example, suppose the true cost of the infringement sales was $5 of a total cost of manufactured articles of $40 and that the total sales were $120, of which $30 were for infringement sales. On the basis set forth in the case in question, the cost of the infringement articles would be $10 which on its face is incorrect.

We understand from the statement in the third from last paragraph in your letter that it is possible to determine the cost of materials and labor entering into the manufacture of the infringement sales from the records and to arrive at a burden rate based upon direct labor. If this is the case it is our opinion that the only correct, fair and equitable cost in this case would be the aggregate costs of such labor and materials entering into the manufacture of the infringed article plus the burden based upon direct labor entering into the cost of all articles manufactured, both infringed and others.

If no analysis of the sales and administration expenses can be had in respect of the amounts chargeable to infringement sales, and other sales it is our opinion that the best and most equitable method for the distribution of such expense is the one used, as set forth in the question.

The question involves the determination of profits on certain sales. The sales in question were infringement sales and it is proposed to ascertain the percentage relationship that infringement sales bear to

3

total sales and to apply this percentage to the total profit on all sales for the purpose of determining profit on infringement sales.

It seems to me that it would be more nearly accurate to determine the material, labor and burden applicable to the infringement sales, especially if the material, labor and burden cost for the infringement sales were likely to be in a different percentage of the selling price of such articles than the general average of 18.23%.

The apportionment of selling and administrative expenses might possibly be made the subject of study. If the cost to sell the articles which constitute the infringement sales, is high or low in proportion when compared with the selling cost of the other sales, the use of the average percentage would not produce the most nearly correct results. If, on the other hand, no determination can be made of the relative cost of making the infringement sales, then the use of the average percentage is probably the only method which could be employed for the purpose of determining the selling and administrative cost in connection with the infringement sales.

There is some question as to whether selling and administrative expenses should be deducted before arriving at the net profit from the infringement sales, but if such selling and administrative expenses are incurred in connection with the infringement sales, I believe a deduction for a proper amount of such expenses is permissible.

LUMBER INVENTORY

Q. Will you kindly procure for us from the best authority available an expression of opinion on the following points relative to the method of valuing a lumber inventory at cost or market whichever is lower.

(1) What constitutes an item in the lumber inventory? Our experience indicates that lumber inventories are usually recorded in terms of board feet of certain specifications as to kind, grade, size, etc.; and a unit of the inventory or an "item," if you please, usually consists of a pile or a fraction of a pile.

(2) If a lumber company divides its inventory into sections, each section consisting of all lumber manufactured from the same species of timber, can such a section of inventory be construed as an "item" within the meaning of the regulations?

(3) Is it not a violation of the principle to value an inventory by groups such as white pine, yellow pine, cedar, fir and larch by applying the principle of valuation to the aggregate market value and the aggregate cost of each of the groups, rather than to the items within the group?

(4) Would not an auditor, making an examination of the accounts of a lumber company for credit purposes, be remiss in his duty were he to pass an inventory purporting to be priced upon the principle of cost or market whichever is lower and were he to accept the test applied to the aggregate of each group, rather than to the items within the groups and more especially so if the latter application indicated a much lower aggregate value?

A. It is assumed that the question relates to the inventory of a dealer and not that of a manufacturer. The cost of each "item" can usually be determined by a dealer, but not usually by a manufacturer.

4

(1) An "item" is usually the total feet of a given kind and size (or group of sizes within the same price bracket) of a given species in the dealer's yard or sheds, regardless of its location in different piles. However, if a quantity can be identified as a particular purchase, it can probably be inventoried separately from the total quantity.

Sometimes an "item" is an unsorted or mill-run lot of lumber and it might even be a lot which includes various species.

(2) Yes, if the section is composed of a group of items within the same cost-price-bracket; or if it is a mill-run purchase; or if high-price and low-price lumber in the section exist in the same proportions as in the stock purchased.

(3) a. No, if the proportions of high-price and low-price lumber in the groups are practically the same as in the purchases.

b. Probably not, if the lumber is purchased unsorted; that is, at a price for mill-run lumber which is sorted for sale by the dealer. In the case of a mill-run purchase, however, the dealer would probably be permitted to determine the cost of the unsold lumber, if it could be identified, by allocating to each grade obtained from the mill-run purchase that portion of the total cost which the market value of the grade bears to the market value of all grades in the mill-run purchase.

(4) Yes, if he found that the proportions of upper—and lower-priced lumber in the group differed materially from the proportions in the purchases.

A MERGER

Q. Corporation A is organized as a merger of several concerns manufacturing the same product. The net assets of the merged corporations (without including goodwill) total $10,000,000. The new corporation issues securities as follows in payment of same:

First preferred stock, 100,000 shares, par value $100—$10,000,000.
Second preferred stock, 50,000 shares, par value $100—$ 5,000,000.
Common stock, 50,000 shares, no par value.

The issue of first preferred stock is underwritten at 90 and the proceeds paid to the vendors in lieu of the stock.

What would be the entries on the books of Corporation A for recording the above transactions? In preparing the balance-sheet of Corporation A, could any of the following items be merged with plant account?

(1) Second preferred stock issued.
(2) Common stock, assuming that it had a declared value of $5 per share.
(3) Discount on first preferred stock.
(4) Discount on a bond issue in the event that bonds were issued and sold at a discount in order to obtain working capital.

A. We append a list of the journal entries which, in our opinion, correctly record the transactions stated. In preparing the entries we have assumed that the directors decide to dispose of the discount on capital stock by charging it to goodwill.

Discount on bonds is usually treated as a deferred charge to be written off during the life of the bonds, and the other three items mentioned in your letter should, in our opinion, be merged with the plant account.

JOURNAL ENTRIES

The several asset and liability accounts aggregating net $10,000,000

5

Vendors		$10,000,000

To record the purchase of the assets and liabilities of the merged corporation as per agreements dated

Cash	$ 9,000,000	
Goodwill	1,000,000	
First preferred stock		$10,000,000

To record the sale for cash at $90.00 per share of 100,000 shares of first preferred stock par value $100 sold to A. B. & Co. in accordance with underwriting agreement dated ....

Note: The difference between the par value of the stock and the consideration received therefor, viz. $1,000,000 has been charged to goodwill in conformity with a resolution by the board of directors dated ....

Vendors	$ 9,000,000	
Cash		$ 9,000,000

To record the payment to vendors of the proceeds of the sale of the first preferred stock.

Vendors	$ 1,000,000	
Goodwill	4,000,000	
Second preferred stock		$ 5,000,000
Common stock 50,000 shares of no par value		

To record the issuance to the vendors of the following securities being the balance of consideration payable to them under agreements dated ....

50,000 shares of $100 each of second preferred stock

50,000 shares of common stock of no par value

Note: The difference between the tangible liability to be discharged to the vendors and the par value of the second preferred stock, viz. $4,000,000 has been charged to goodwill in accordance with a resolution of the board of directors dated ....

Q. It is possible that the proposition stated in my letter was not clearly outlined, inasmuch as the reply does not give me all of the information I desire.

If I am not imposing too greatly on the privileges accorded by your department, I would appreciate a reply to the following:

Is is permissible for a corporation to charge any of the following items to plant account:

    (A) Stock discount.

    (B) Bond discount.

    (C) An issue of no par value common stock with a stated value of $5 per share?

6

If the appraised value of the properties, for which the stock and bonds were issued, equalled the par value of such securities, would the reply be any different than if such appraised value were less than the par value?

A. Inasmuch as neither stock discount, bond discount nor no-par-value stock issued for intangible property has any tangible value, it would appear axiomatic that neither of these three items should be included in plant account.

The appraised value of physical properties would have no bearing whatsoever on the treatment of stock discount, bond discount and no-par-value stock.

SALT — COST

Q. Referring to the Institute's Special Bulletin No. 23 (April 1924) and particularly to the matter of Salt-Cost appearing on page 8, the question seems to be a very general one and is perhaps for that reason answered in the same manner.

At what point does the questioner expect his salt (by evaporation) to be costed? And where were ascertained the values of $4.35 3/4 for undried and $5.50 3/4 for dried salt "at works"?

Deducting depreciation charge of $1.14 1/2 per ton as stated, the figures above mentioned would appear to be $3.21 1/4 and $4.36 1/4 respectively. Are these tonnages long (2,240 lbs) or short?

At one place, where large quantities of salt are shipped to this country, the price for coarse dried salt is F. O. B. vessel 8 cents per bushel (30 bushels to the ton) or $2.40 per long ton. If we assume that the freight thence to New York, say, $3.00 to $3.50 per ton is no more than that from the works, quoted in your bulletin, there would seem to be considerable difference between the rate of $2.40 and that of $4.36 1/4 for dried salt.

Can the answerer to the query in bulletin be more specific as to his prices?

A. Replying to your letter requesting further information regarding cost of evaporated salt, we would advise that the costs, previously given you were before loading charges.

The approximate cost for labor in loading salt into cars and vessels was about 45 cents per long ton. The evaporated salt costs as previously given should not be confused with the coarse salt as shipped to this country from foreign ports. The nearest comparison of such salt would be the very poor grade of rock salt mined in some parts of the United States.

DEPRECIATION—SHEDS

Q. We are making earnest efforts to ascertain the proper rate of depreciation on buildings, which are known as sheds, which are used in retail lumber yards. The lumber is stacked upon the shelves and taken out as deliveries are made.

The sheds used by retail lumber yards in cities usually have concrete foundations and are constructed of reasonably substantial lumber. The rate on this type seems very well established.

The corporation, whose income tax interest are receiving our attention, had twenty-two yards, all in small towns, with the exception of one which is in a city of some twenty thousand inhabitants. All of

7

these sheds were built of light timber (2x4), have no foundations and are subject to very rough handling of lumber.

We can find no authority on this particular subject.

A. In a well established community the depreciation on a lumber shed of good construction, with concrete foundations, should be from 3% to 5%. In a new town, or a shed of ordinary construction, the rate should range up to 10%. In a "boom" town—oil or other basis—more than 10% could probably be justified.

ACCOUNTANT'S LIABILITY

Q. I would appreciate it if you would submit the following question regarding an accountant's liability to certain of your members for their consideration and advice.

The president of a corporation to whom the auditors report directly has the books of his company audited monthly. He desires only the monthly transactions audited and the financial statements prepared as per books.

To correctly reflect the company's financial condition, certain adjustments are necessary in the form of increased reserves for bad debts, depreciation, etc. However, no entries of this nature are desired, or permitted to go through the books.

Under the circumstances do you consider the auditor sufficiently protected if the monthly balance-sheet and profit-and-loss account are stated to be prepared as per books and are not certified to? It would, of course, be desirable to qualify the statements by foot-notes.

You will understand that the president of the company in question objects to any other qualifications.

A. In my judgment, if an accountant is not permitted to make all verifications and adjustments that he considers necessary for an unqualified certification, he should make perfectly clear in the body of his certificate the respects in which the audit is not complete. From my viewpoint, it would not be sufficient, in the absence of complete verification and adjustment, to state that the monthly balance-sheet and profit-and-loss account are stated to be prepared as per books. We should always keep in mind the fact that the statements may be considered by persons who would not understand that the words as per books, mean that essential verifications and adjustments have not been made.

CONVERTERS OF COTTON GOODS

Q. Will you endeavor to procure for me bad debt statistics of converters of cotton goods who sell to the retail and wholesale trade?

A. We have searched our files for information of this kind and were able to find only one case. For the year 1923 this case shows a ratio of .34% of uncollectible accounts written off to net sales and for nine months of the year 1924 a similar ration of .12%.

We regret that we are unable to give you more extended experience and trust that the above information will be of some value to you.

8

American Institute of Accountants

Library and Bureau of Information

SPECIAL BULLETIN NO. 26

March, 1926

DISTRIBUTION OF OVERHEAD

Q. We are desirous of obtaining information regarding the distribution of overhead in the following case:

A company is engaged in manufacturing goods for sale primarily in domestic markets, although it sells a considerable portion of its product abroad. We should like to know what percentage of the total overhead of the company should be allocated to the product manufactured for domestic markets, and what percentage to that manufactured for foreign markets. We should like to ascertain the policy of the larger industrial companies in this respect.

A. The approved practice is to distribute manufacturing department overhead over the whole product evenly, no matter whether for domestic or foreign destination; to distribute general (administrative) overhead in the same manner; and to keep separate any overhead that can be allocated specifically to (a) domestic sales or (b) foreign sales. If there is any other overhead that can not be properly allocated either to foreign or to domestic sales it should be apportioned in proportion to the amount sold.

The general principle is that overhead should not be shifted from domestic to foreign trade or vice versa merely to produce an appearance of consistent profit. It is better to realize fully just what profit is made on each and to be able to estimate the amount that may be sacrificed to keep a foreign trade that is not the primary object of the business but is maintained either to dispose of surplus merchandise or to bring production up to an amount suitable for the size of the plant.

BOND DISCOUNT

Q. A question has arisen regarding the definition or meaning of good accounting practice in dealing with the term "bond discount." The question arises in connection with the computation of invested capital under the federal revenue acts of 1917 and 1918. The facts are as follows:

1. A corporation offers to exchange its interest bearing bonds for the stock of another corporation.

2. At various dates, which extended over a considerable period of time, stockholders of the second corporation exchanged their stock for interest bearing bonds of the first corporation. The offer of exchange dealt only in par values of the stocks and bonds.

3. On or about the dates these exchanges were made, the stock of the second corporation was selling on the New York stock exchange at prices below the face value of the bonds. As stated above, the exchanges

1

were made over a period of time. The prices on the New York exchange varied from day to day.

4. The bonds were redeemed at par several years before 1917.

5. The second corporation was dissolved and its assets merged with those of the first corporation before 1917.

The treasury department contends that the difference between the market price of the stock of the second corporation and the face value of the bonds of the first corporation should be set up on the books as discount on bonds, and that such amount should be amortized over the life of the bonds. The effect of this ruling is that actual earnings are eliminated from invested capital.

The taxpayer contends that the bonds should be treated as the equivalent of cash; that it obligated itself to pay the face value of the bonds for the stock of the second corporation; that the treasury department can not under the law or the regulations indirectly amortize any part of the purchase price of the stock. Even though it might be admitted that an unwise purchase had been made, the cost of the stock was mostly transferred to goodwill when the second corporation was dissolved so that an attempt is being made to write down the book value of goodwill. As a matter of fact the goodwill is worth several times the par of the bonds issued to acquire it.

Queries:

1. What is bond discount?

2. If the treasury department's position is correct, under what theory of accounting can it be justified?

3. As a matter of accounting procedure how could the accounts be accurately written up, especially as stockholders made exchanges at various times over a period of two years when the market price of the stock and bonds fluctuated from day to day?

Note. The only purpose of the query is to secure a trustworthy definition of the term "bond discount." The tax situation is explained at length in order to show the position of the treasury department.

A. Good accounting practice requires that bond discount should be set up as an asset and amortized over the life of the bonds.

There is a most logical reason for this, which I will endeavor to elucidate as follows:

Bond discount is an expense incurred for the benefit of a corporation and per se for its stockholders. As bonds are issued with the view of deferring the repayment of the capital so obtained to a future date, and during their tenure the shares of stock may change hands, and as the benefit to the corporation of issuing the bonds extends over their life, it would not be correct treatment to charge to the stockholders the total cost of issuance of the obligation at date of issue because the then stockholders would bear a greater portion of the cost than was actually theirs and future stockholders would obtain an unjustifiable advantage.

From Montgomery's "*Auditing Theory and Practice*" is quoted an opinion by the Superior Court of Pennsylvania in the Ben Avon-Ohio Valley Water Company case, in which the court held, among other things, that:

"While corporations should not be permitted to capitalize their lack of credit, still, where bonds are sold at a reasonable discount and bear a fair rate of interest, such discount should be allowed."

In the case cited, the government's position, the difference between the fair market value of the stock given exchange for the bonds and the par value of the bonds is held to be equivalent to bond discount.

In all the revenue acts the commissioner is authorized to prescribe a system of accounting that will correctly reflect income. True income under good

2

accounting practice would not be reflected by entering the exchange on the basis of par for par because the stock the first corporation received in exchange for its bonds was not fairly worth par, and to show the new stock as an investment at par in the corporation's books would inure to the benefit of the stockholders at date of transaction and the possible detriment of the shareholders of later years.

Good accounting practice provides that books be kept to show cost of assets and expenses. Good accounting practice, however, permits deviations from this practice to account for fluctuations in value over or under cost, as affected by appreciation and depreciation of fixed assets, and in fluctuations in value of stock in trade, investments, etc.

The stock of the second corporation seemed to cost par value to the first corporation, but the financial status of the first corporation would not be accurately reflected by valuing this stock at date of its acquisition at par value.

This loss in the transaction is exactly equivalent to a case where a corporation sells its bonds for cash at less than par value. In the latter case good accounting practice would require the setting up the difference between cash received and the par value of the bonds as a deferred asset to be amortized over the life of the bonds.

The fact that the exchange was effected over a period of time at different prices for the stock does not alter the situation for it follows that the obligation on the bonds did not take effect until they had been sold.

Conclusion:

(1) Bond discount is the price or bonus paid for borrowed money or value.

(2) The treasury's position can be justified by the sections of the several acts that require taxpayers to keep their books in such a manner as will correctly reflect income in accordance with the best accounting practice.

(3) As to accounting procedure in the instant case the accounts could be accurately written up by making entries at dates the actual exchanges were made of bonds for stock, somewhat as follows:

Bond discount   ———
Stock of B Corporation at
 market value at date of   ———
 exchange to bonded debt   ———
     ————————

An expression of opinion is desired as to what is a proper definition of the term "bond discount". The inquirer has expressed the opinion that if stock of one corporation is acquired by another corporation in exchange for the latter's interest bearing bonds, the cost of the stock acquired should be entered on the books of the purchaser at the par value of the bonds and that no bond discount exists in such a transaction.

The inquirer points out, on the other hand, that the treasury department holds that the bonds were issued for the market value of the stock exchanged for them and consequently, the difference between the market value of the stock on the date it was exchanged and the par value of the bonds should be set up as bond discount on the books of the purchaser and amortized over the life of the bonds.

The term bond discount, in the ordinary case, represents the difference between the par value of issued bonds and the actual cash proceeds received by the issuing corporation at the time the bonds were issued. Bond discount represents the additional amount which has to be paid at the time of maturity of bonds issued, over and above the cash or its equivalent received at the time of issue.

The question, therefore, is whether the consideration received upon the issue

3

of the bonds is the market value of the stock exchanged therefor, or whether the stock should be considered as being of a value equal to the par value of the bonds issued in exchange.

We think there can be no doubt that the corporation issuing the bonds received property of a cash value equal to the market value of the stock and, therefore, it would be proper accounting practice to charge the difference between the market value of the stock and the face value of the bonds to bond discount and prorate the same over the life of the bonds.

The real question at issue, as no actual cash passed, is "what are the respective market values of the bonds and stock"? We have assumed that the bonds have no quoted market and that their value would be at the time of issue the same as the stock acquired. If, however, the bonds were actually sold at par or better immediately after their issue, then, in our opinion, it would be proper to charge the par value of the bonds as the cost of the stock and there will be no "bond discount". This would no doubt mean, however, that the individuals exchanging the stock would have made a profit which would be taxable in the year in which it was exchanged; the amount of the profit being the difference between the face value of the bonds and the original cost of the stock or March 1, 1913, value if acquired prior to that date.

We see no insuperable difficulty because the bonds were issued at different times over a period of years and that the stock had different values on different dates of acquiral. The facts as to each transaction are determined at the time and the proper amount could be charged to bond discount. There should be no difficulty in determining the annual write-off of bond discount over the life of the bonds.

————————

We have given consideration to your inquiry and submit the following opinion thereon:

1. Bond discount is the difference between the value received when bonds are issued and the nominal amount that is to be paid to liquidate that liability. Wildman in his *Principles of Accounting* describes it as interest collected in advance for the difference between the amount of the principal and its present worth. If the value received is in a form other than cash there may be difficulty in measuring the resultant bond discount. This seems to be the difficulty that prompted the question that you have submitted to us.

2. Discount being interest, collected in advance as stated above, it is an expense chargeable ultimately to surplus. It should be amortized over the period between the date the liability is incurred and the date when it is liquidated. In the interim, the unamortized portion of the discount is a deferred charge. The treasury department therefore rightly holds that bond interest as it is amortized is a deductible expense which reduces invested capital.

3. The inquirer undoubtedly has a record of the dates at which the bonds were issued to acquire the stock and the amounts respectively issued and acquired. There should be no difficulty then in ascertaining the market value of the stock acquired by referring to the stock exchange transactions nearest the dates of exchange. The difference between the market value of the stock acquired and the par value of the bonds issued therefore is the amount of discount.

The inquirer does not state how the transactions were recorded in the books. We assume from the information given and from the fact that the treasury department contends that the discount should now be set up that both the stock acquired and the bonds issued were set up at par. We can readily understand the difficulty which your inquirer has in seeing the import of the treasury department's contention.

This difficulty may possibly be lessened by consideration of the following illustration, for which purpose it is assumed that the stock had a par value of $100, a market value of $75, that bonds of a denomination of $100,000 were

4

offered which the holders of the stock declined to accept, and that the bonds were then sold through a banking house which took them at 75. From the sale of $100,000 par value of the bonds the corporation received in cash $75,000. To retire the bonds the corporation has covenanted to pay $100,000; therefore, the bonds have been sold at a discount of $25,000, which sum must ultimately be charged to surplus, thereby reducing the corporation's invested capital. With the $75,000 in cash received from the sale of the bonds the corporation went into the market and acquired $100,000 par value of the stock at its market value of 75.

The effect of these transactions upon the surplus and invested capital of the corporation is exactly the same as it would be had the $100,000 of bonds been issued directly to the holders of the $100,000 par value of stock.

The inquirer is in error when he contends that the amount paid to retire the bonds determines the value of the stock acquired. Such is not the case as will be seen if it were considered that the corporation had covenanted to retire the bonds at 110. In such a case there would be a futrher deductible expense in the premium paid upon retirement of the bonds, being the amount of cash paid over the nominal value of the bonds.

The cash payments only liquidate the liability. The factor that determines whether or not bond discount enters into the original transaction and the amount of the discount is the value of the consideration received upon the issue of the bonds. Therein appears to be the inquirer's only possible opportunity to avoid the effect of discount upon its invested capital and that is to marshall an array of facts which will show that the price at which the stock was traded on the exchange did not represent the true market value. This will be a difficult proceeding but not necessarily an impossible one. Factors other than the actual condition of the company often influence the trading prices. If such factors existed they should be cited. For example the corporation may have had a good earning power but for reasons satisfactory to itself reinvested its income rather than distribute it in the form of dividends, which would have the effect of lowering the trading price. Another factor which might be cited is the actual value of the assets back of the stock which again is not necessarily a determining factor in fixing the trading price.

The difficulty in dealing with the treasury department on this matter will be that the trading exchange value is generally recognized as a fair and reasonable one and that the burden of proof is upon one who would assert another value.

The transfer of the cost of the stock to the goodwill account does not necessarily render the latter proof against assault by the income tax unit; on the contrary it may support the treasury department's contention that upon the dissolution of the second corporation there remained no asset of a reasonable value that could be set up on the books in place of the value previously carried for the stock. In other words the books of account appear to support the treasury department's contention that the stock when acquired was not worth its par value and that consequently the bonds were issued at a discount and the invested capital has been reduced by the amortized amount of such discount.

Your definite query as to a trustworthy definition of the term bond discount can only be answered, it seems to me, by stating that bond discount represents the difference between the amount realized from the sale of bonds and the face amount of such bonds when they are sold for less than the face amount.

I appreciate the fact that the practical meaning of bond discount as applied to the problem in question is now a matter between the treasury department and your inquirer. No outside opinion is of any value. However, I can not forego saying that I believe the treasury department to be in error in its position for the reason that the quoted market price of any stock does not neces-

5

sarily represent its real value to a buyer for control. In the case cited it is quite within reason to assume the stock acquired in exchange for bonds was actually worth the face amount of the bonds. If this were true then the fact that bonds were given in exchange for stock would not make the fact measurably different than if cash had been paid therefore.

In order to accept the treasury's position as correct it must be assumed first that the company's credit conditions were such that its bonds could not have been sold at par for cash and stock acquired in exchange for the bonds was not worth the face amount of the bonds issued in payment for same.

Your query as to accounting procedure may be answered by saying that I believe if a bond discount is recognized as proper that no attention should be given to the fluctuations in the market price of the stock during the period in which the exchanges were made. It seems to me that the basis taken should be the market value at the date when the offer to holders of the stock was made.

We submit the following:

1. Bond discount, as the term is generally understood in accounting practice, represents the excess of the face value of the bonds over the cash, or cash equivalent, received by the issuing corporation at the time of their original issuance.

Ordinarily bond discount should be amortized over the life of the bonds, but if any of the bonds are retired before maturity, the unamortized portion of such bond discount as is applicable to the bonds so retired should be charged off to Profit and Loss during the year of their retirement.

2. Referring to the case cited, it appears that the issuing (first) corporation acquired stock of another (second) corporation in payment for its bonds, and that the cash value of said stock, based on representative sales of such stock on the stock exchange, was less than the par value of the bonds. If this be an established fact it seems to us that the difference between the cash value of the stock and the face value of the bonds represents bond discount. However, if any of the bonds were sold for cash about the time of these transactions at a higher value, such transactions may be considered as better evidence of their true cash value at the date of issue than the cash value of the stock, on the assumption that the issuing corporation could have obtained cash for its bonds in this amount had it not exchanged such bonds for the stock of the second corporation.

3. As to the accounting procedure required to accurately record the numerous transactions which occurred at various times, we think that the discount involved in each transaction should be separately determined. Of course, if the cash value of the stock remained constant for a period of time, the discount in all transactions within that period could be determined in one computation. In our practice we have had several engagements in which a series of such transactions was involved, and in each case we found it necessary to actually determine the premium or discount in each day's transactions.

REAL ESTATE IMPROVEMENTS

Q. A real estate company was incorporated to acquire land and thereon to erect and afterwards operate an office building.

The total cost of the land and building was $3,500,000 which included the cost of the tangible property and interest on capital, insurance and taxes during construction, and the sum of about $90,000 being the cost of advertising and a special corps of men who were employed to secure leases for the building so that immediately on its completion the lessees took possession and revenues commenced without any loss or delay.

6

Queries:

  (1) Was it proper to capitalize this $90,000 and leave it as part of the capital cost subject to regular depreciation charges?

  (2) Should the $90,000 be included in "deferred charges"—not a part of the capital cost of the building. If so, on what basis should the charge be extinguished?

Saliers in his "*Accountant's Handbook*," page 448, says:

"Construction costs sometimes properly involve capitalization of repairs, because all costs necessary to bring a plant to operating condition represent capital expenditure. Among these are—interest on borrowed money, engineering, supervision, legal expenses, taxes and overhead."

and on page 808:

"Initial capitalization legitimately covers not only cost of tangible assets but also certain intangible elements in form of promotion, engineering and developmental expenses. Frequently these are capitalized in a single account such as organization expenses or deferred expenses. Ultimately, depending on the nature of the items and the policy of the management, these are either written off or are permanently capitalized. Interest during construction is usually permanently capitalized."

A. There is no doubt that such items as interest and taxes accruing during construction of a building are chargeable to the cost of construction. The outstanding example in these cases is the Interstate Commerce Commission which has always approved of this method.

The item mentioned in your letter, namely $90,000 being the cost of advertising and preliminary selling expenses, is, in my opinion, of an entirely different nature. It should not be charged to the cost of building but should be set up as a deferred charge which may be distributed over a period to be determined by the proprietor; I should think, usually three to five years. In the instance you mention, the term would probably be determined by the length of the leases secured through these disbursements.

The matter is open for discussion and I dare say you will find some excellent accountants who may differ from me in the above view but rather wide experience in such matters leads me to think that the plan I have suggested is the one safe course to follow.

A distinction should be drawn between cost of construction and cost of operation and I incline to the opinion that the cost of advertising and soliciting of prospective tenants is an operating and not constructing cost.

In our opinion it is not proper to capitalize the $90,000 as a part of capital cost but that the sum may be included in deferred charges for a short time.

Under the circumstances, we believe that this deferred charge should be extinguished against the earnings of the first year because it seems to represent a proper off-set to income which may have been secured through the early leasing of the premises.

CERTIFIED BALANCE-SHEETS

Q. In making an annual audit for one of my clients who has a small issue of preferred stock which has a retirement provision, this provision being that 10% of the profits, after preferred stock dividends and taxes, is to be set aside in a sinking fund for the retirement of this stock. I placed a qualification on the bottom of the balance-sheet before certifying the same as follows: "Subject to the creation of a sinking fund of 'X' dollars for the retirement of preferred stock," which according to my idea is correct.

My client contends that inasmuch as the balance-sheet which is being certified is as at December 31st, that it is physically impossible to set up this sinking

7

fund before the end of the year. He, therefore, objects to this qualifying statement.

A. There seems to be no particular reason why the qualification referred to should not be omitted. Except for the amount of premium that might be paid for the preferred stock retired the operation would not affect the surplus at all. It is not stated that the provision is to take the form of setting aside actual cash for the purpose of retiring the stock, and even if it did the cash could not be set aside before the profit and amount of retirement fund dependent thereon were determined.

Perhaps the matter could be adjusted by a note, not a qualification, saying that a retirement provision existed; or the preferred stock could be described in the balance-sheet as having a retirement provision.

The objection of the company to a qualification in the certificate after it had done all that it could do at December 31 is not without some force and unless the auditor believed that the omission of the qualification would give such a presentation as to mislead some one to his disadvantage, we think it might well be left out and a note such as suggested above substituted therefore.

INSTALMENT FURNITURE BUSINESS

Q. Some instalment furniture companies are desirous of adopting a reserve system for providing for losses on accounts. We should like to obtain from you data regarding the percentage of sales set aside by companies of this nature, to take care of losses on bad accounts.

We should also like to ascertain the manner in which a reserve of this character should be established, and the character of the items chargeable.

A. This question must be answered in two ways, according to the method of accounting for profits, namely:

(1) where all the profit is taken into income in the period during which the sale is made, and

(2) when the profit is taken into income only as collected, in accordance with the practice which is permitted by the United States treasury department for income tax purposes.

Under the first condition it seems to us that provision for uncollectible accounts should be made periodically (according to the fiscal period), by a charge against income and a credit to reserve of an amount representing a certain percentage of the net sales during the period. Your information to the effect that losses in this kind of business run from seven to ten per cent seems to be about right, but if the particular concern has been in business long enough to determine what its losses may be expected to be, the experienced rate should be used. The charges against the reserve would consist of the amounts of accounts definitely determined to be uncollectible, less any recoveries through repossessions of furniture. The balance of the reserve should be adjusted periodically (say once a year) to accord with conditions as they appear at the time.

Under the second condition mentioned above, only such profit would be taken into income as was realized in cash. If this practice is adopted, it seems to be unnecessary to create any reserve for uncollectible accounts. It will, of course, be necessary to make adjustments of the accounts receivable from time to time to give effect to failure of realization, but such adjustments would not affect the income. It should not be necessary for us to outline the bookkeeping procedure incident to the keeping of accounts upon this basis.

The only figures which we have are of one large furniture instalment house whose losses in the year 1924 averaged about $3\frac{1}{2}\%$ of their sales and during the year 1923 about 5%.

8

American Institute of Accountants

Library and Bureau of Information

SPECIAL BULLETIN NO. 27

MAY, 1926

[The Committee on Administration of Endowment authorizes the publication of special Bulletins, of which this is one, on the distinct understanding that members are not to consider answers given to questions as being official pronouncements of the Institute, but merely the individual opinions of accountants to whom the questions were referred. It is earnestly requested that members criticise freely and constructively the answers given in this or any other Bulletin of this series.]

AN IRRIGATION PROJECT

Q. Company A is engaged in the business of irrigation. In other words it furnishes water to rice planters for the irrigation of land. For this service it receives one-fifth of the rice crop.

Water is pumped from different streams known as bayous or estuaries. In recent years, during seasons of drought, the rice crop was damaged through salt water backing up and entering into these bayous or estuaries.

In order to eliminate this risk and consequent damage, Company A and other irrigation companies in the same territory conceived the idea of bringing fresh water from a dependable fresh water stream into their irrigating canals. To consummate this plan, it was necessary to excavate a canal. Plans were worked out along practical lines; all irrigating companies in the territory contributing towards the cost of the canal.

An independent agency was necessary to finance and carry out the work. Therefore a corporation (call it the Company B) was formed simply and solely for the purpose of limiting the liability of the companies contributing towards the construction of the canal.

The irrigating companies (not the rice farmers) pay to Company B for the water they use, the money collected from this source by Company B being applied to construction and maintenance.

It is therefore apparent that, while the irrigating companies are benefited indirectly by the enterprise, it is the rice planter who receives the real benefit.

Under an agreement with the government under which the canal was constructed, Company B is not permitted to earn any profit from its operation, and the plant, when completed, is to be turned over to the government.

The irrigating companies contributing towards the construction of the canal received stock covering the amount of their respective contributions. This stock was issued merely as an evidence of their contribution and not as evidence of any financial interest in the canal constructed by Company B.

Company A contributed $15,532.35 for which it received stock which was charged to profit and loss.

From the above it will be noted that Company A has no financial interest in the enterprise and receives no return from Company B for the money contributed towards the construction of the canal.

It will further be noted that the contribution was made for the benefit of the rice planters by which, of course, Company A was the beneficiary indirectly.

Should the amount ($15,532.35) be treated as a capital expenditure, or as a contribution made for the good of the business?

A. It would not be possible to give a final opinion as to the treatment of the expenditure referred to without further information as to the terms of the

1

agreement with the government. Assuming, however, that Company B is entitled to the perpetual use of the canal, the amount expended may, in our opinion, be properly carried as a capital expenditure and would be subject to the same treatment in the accounts as other expenditures on canals, etc. Any facilities abandoned as a result of the change in the source of water supply should be written off against surplus or against any reserves previously established for such contingencies. ―――――――

Q. In further explanation of the proposition I wish to state that under an agreement with the government, the canal in question, which is being built for the purpose of bringing fresh water into the rice canals, is to be turned over to the government as soon as completed. Those who contributed to the cost of constructing the canal have no financial interest in it.

From your letter it would appear that those who answered the question are under the impression that Company B is the only one entitled to use the canal. This is erroneous. The canal was built for the benefit of the rice industry as a whole and all irrigating concerns and others have the right to use the water at a nominal charge.

A. After giving due consideration to the additional information furnished, we see no reason to change our opinion. Even although the construction of the canal results in a direct benefit to the industry as a whole and the canal is available for use by other parties, we do not think, in view of the substantial direct interest of Company A in the rice crop, that the expenditure should be considered as a voluntary contribution made primarily for the benefit of the rice growers without regard for the company's own interests.

We take it that Company A is in business for the purpose of earning profits and the expenditure referred to was made for the protection of its income. Under these circumstances we consider the amount expended may properly be treated as in the nature of a capital expenditure. At the same time we see no serious objection to writing off the amount against surplus on the ground of conservatism should the company desire to do so.

SICK LEAVES

Q. What is the practice of large public accounting firms in handling sick leaves of members of their staffs? What is their practice as to salary payment or sick benefits when a member of the permanent staff is absent because of illness? If regular salary is continued, for how long are the payments made?

A. The members of the permanent staff of this firm are paid upon the basis of monthly or annual salaries, no deductions are made for absence either on account of sickness or other causes nor are there any payments made for over time. There have been instances where employees have been absent from the office for several months at a time due to sickness and the salary check was regularly sent to them.

We have no program for sick benefits, but there have been at least one or two occasions when the firm made advances in time of need which later were absorbed by an increase in salary over a period of several years. For how long a time salaries would continue to be paid, I am unable to say; this would depend somewhat upon the person who was away on sick leave, as well as upon the surrounding circumstances. If the person was a valuable staff member or an old employee, and there was a reasonable assurance that he would return to the office and continue to be a part of the organization the disposition would be to continue salaries for a reasonable length of time.

RATE BASE

Q. In 1922, John Doe obtained from the city of A a franchise to build and operate an electric light and power plant; the only consideration for the

2

franchise is a nominal annual franchise tax assessed by the city against all franchises.

John Doe sold the franchise to the B company of which he was one of the organizers for X shares of its capital stock of a par value of XXX dollars. B company constructed the plant and is operating it. The stock of B company was sold at par less a certain commission paid to the brokers. The operation of B company for the period ending December 31st, 1923 resulted in a loss of XXX dollars and in a loss of XXX for the entire period ending February 28th, 1925.

In a statement of assets on which the company should be allowed to earn a fair return, the cost of the franchise, (XXX dollars) is not included for the reason that it was issued by the city without cash consideration. The operating loss for the period ending December 31st, 1923 (XXX dollars) was allowed as going value.

Will you kindly obtain opinions on the following questions:

1. B company having purchased the franchise from John Doe for XXX dollars of its capital stock, should not this amount be included in a rate base? State reasons.

2. B company's operations having been continued to show a loss after December 31st, 1923, should not the loss for a longer period be considered as going value instead of the loss for the period ending Dec. 31st, 1923 and if so, for what period?

A. The decisions of public service commissions and of the courts generally would indicate that

(1) B company purchased the rights of John Doe; it obtained the rights he had, for he could sell them no more. If John drove a hard bargain it makes no difference, the company could acquire nothing that John did not have to sell them. If the franchise had been exercised by John he could have based a rate on what the franchise cost him. One of the parties to the franchise is the city granting it; its rights were not diminished by the sale of the franchise by John Doe to a company; one of those rights was the operation of the utility on a rate based on the amount received by the city for the franchise. The opinions of the courts on inflations of apparent cost by transfers between successive owners of properties and franchises are exhaustively set forth in Maires vs. Flatbush Gas Company, New York Public Service Commission, First District, case No. 1541.

(2) Losses in the early period of operation are to be taken as such. The absence of need for renewals makes the cost of operation of a new plant less than in later years and if a profit can not be made in the first few years when the cost of repairs and renewals is small the prospect for the future is not bright enough to justify adding losses to book investment. Capitalization of losses is, in general, bad accounting. See U. S. Supreme Court, Galveston Electric Co. vs. City of Galveston, Public Utilities Reports 1922D page 159:

"A public utility can not erect out of past deficits a legal basis for holding confiscatory for the future rates which would on the basis of present reproduction value otherwise become compensatory". Page 165 "It does not make past losses an element to be considered in deciding what the base value is". Page 166 "Past losses obviously do not tend to prove present values".

REPORT NOTES

Q. At various times in the past, we have had our attention called to notes printed by other accountants on their reports and official statements intended to provide some restriction as to the use which shall be made of this material by clients, or possibly by others. For example, "Our reports and certificates are issued with the understanding that, if published, either they must be repro-

3

duced in their entirety, or, should it be desired to publish any reference to or abstracts from them, that such shall be submitted for our approval."

At a recent partners' conference, we gave consideration to the desirability of using some similar phraseology on our reports, and we are therefore writing to inquire what data is available in the office of the Institute as to phraseology of that character, or similar character, used by other accountants. Would you be willing to make a systematic canvass of a few leading firms to find out whether they have used anything of this kind, and if so, to get the exact wording which they have used?

A. This firm uses the following:

"The publication of any condensation or modification of statements herein contained, or the use of our certificate detached from its context, or the use of our name in connection with the sale of securities or other publicity, will not be sanctioned unless first submitted for our approval."

We never have used any extended restricted footnote on any of our reports, but have endeavored to cover this situation by putting on either a footnote or a parenthetical clause under the heading of the statement reading somewhat in this form:

"This report is subject to the comments, qualifications, etc., contained on pages — to — of this report."

We have always tried to be very careful to put this note in such a place that it could not be removed without showing that the sheet had been mutilated. On one or two different occasions, we have had matters come up in connection with note brokers where footnotes, etc., were omitted, but have never felt that the insertion of such a paragraph as you quote would prevent a third party from omitting the footnotes if he was determined to do so.

In one case of rather recent date, a banking house used our name in a manner which we did not think they were justified in doing as a basis for their report, and we were finally forced to have our attorney take it up with them in order to get the matter placed in the proper light before the public.

To the best of my present recollection, we have had only three cases in twenty-eight years where it has come to our knowledge that our statements were used in a manner which did not meet with our approval.

One of these was never rectified, and we declined any further work from the concern.

The second case we were reasonably satisfied was an error on the part of a clerk in the note broker's office and it was corrected as soon as the matter was called to his attention.

The third case needed the services of our attorney, as above referred to.

We have never used any language similar to that contained in your letter and which we understand a few other firms of accountants have adopted, because we have felt that it was unnecessary. No one has any legal right to misquote another on a material point and anyone deliberately so doing is subject to legal action if damage results to the misquoted party. On the other hand, if no damage results, no penalty could be enforced at law whatever restrictions the party issuing the report may have sought to impose.

We have, however, always taken the precaution when issuing balance-sheets or profit and loss accounts, which were not themselves certified but which were accompanied by reports to have the following words typed at the top of such statements, "Subject to report herewith". This notation in our opinion puts anyone on notice who may see the statements, that they are properly qualified in the text of the accompanying report.

4

It has not been our practice to have any note printed on our reports stating that our authority is needed for the publication of any excerpts. Of course, in accordance with the practice of most accountants, we have always insisted upon our clients submitting for our approval any extracts made for publication of any of our reports.

We would advise that no restriction has ever been printed on our official reports or statements which would require the client to refer any extracts to this office before making publication of same.

This matter was very thoroughly considered some years ago and our conclusion was that such printed restrictions were no deterrent to any client who wished to use the report with outside parties or for some ulterior purposes.

We may say that we have never considered it necessary to preface our reports with any warning that they must be reproduced in full, if at all, or that extracts quoted must first be approved by us. In our experience we cannot recall a case where our reports have been abused by any serious misrepresentations. The responsibility for misuse of the reports is entirely upon the user and this responsibility seems to be pretty uniformly recognized among our clientele. This legal and moral responsibility is our real safeguard and, in the absence of any adverse experience, we do not now believe it is necessary to convey in advance the kind of warning referred to by your inquirer, which is almost a reflection upon the intelligence of the business community.

Besides this, there is nothing improper in making quotations or extracts from reports so long as these extracts are complete and clear in themselves and do not give a false impression. The keynote is whether the quotation from, or reference to, our report, is intended to misrepresent the facts as we have reported them or has the effect of so doing.

We have considered it to be neither necessary nor desirable to print such note on reports or certified statements.

We have never used any restrictive phraseology in our reports. We feel that the point is well taken, however, and can understand how in some cases it might be advisable from a precautionary point of view.

Frankly speaking, however, we have never felt the necessity of adopting any such precautionary measure as we have been sufficiently fortunate in our relations with our clients to know in advance as to any desires they might have in the matter of publishing any reports, or portions thereof, issued by us and to feel assured that they would never take such a step without our previous knowledge and approval.

Our firm has not used a statement of the kind submitted. We presume that the "understanding" mentioned in the clause, in order to have legal effect, would have to be made a part of the original contract covering the employment of the accountant; and it would be difficult, in the ordinary course of affairs, to arrange for such a specific understanding. It is conceivable that the clause might be valuable, even if without legal effect, as a deterrent; and, without having any specific knowledge of the facts, we presume that this is the reason for the use of the clause.

When a balance-sheet is submitted as part of a report, it is our custom to note on the balance-sheet that it is subject to the comments contained in the report. When we attach a certificate to a balance-sheet or a profit and loss account, we assume that it will not be changed, and so far we have not had trouble on this score.

5

Q. Will you kindly advise me how I had best act under the following circumstances:

I am employed as the accountant for a close corporation. One of the principal stockholders, who employed me, has instructed me to make entries on the books increasing his salary for the year 1924. There has been no authorization of this increase. On the other hand the chances of this being passed by the board at the next meeting are reasonably certain. This stockholder is indispensable to the company. Therefore, can I rightfully make this entry on the books and prepare a qualifying report?

A. It would, of course, be irregular to make an entry on the books increasing the salary of this officer for the year 1924 before the amount had been authorized by the board of directors, assuming, of course, that his salary had previously been fixed by the board of directors. I think, however, that circumstances in the case have some bearing, that is to say, if the officer in question is a majority stockholder and it is reasonably certain that the increase will be approved by the board the bookkeeper might be justified in placing the entry on the books and calling attention in his report that this increase had not been formally approved by the board of directors.

It is, of course, always better to handle these matters in a regular manner and the bookkeeper would do well to try and impress this fact on his employer. If the increase in salary is voted upon at a meeting held subsequent to the first of the year the internal revenue department will undoubtedly reject this additional salary as a deductible expense in 1924.

Strictly speaking, no important change in the salary of an officer of a corporation of this character ought to be made without evidence that it has been passed upon by the directors or stockholders of the company. In the circumstances, and in the event, however, of the matter being made the subject of a qualification in the report, it would appear that no harm would result, and if it is impossible to get the proper authority before the report is issued I would, under similar circumstances, be prepared to pass the item.

I think the accountant referred to, under the conditions outlined, would be entirely justified in making entries on the books covering the increase in salary of the official referred to for the year 1924. It would be in order for him to see that this increase was authorized at the next meeting of the board of directors, and, if the increase was not authorized, to then bring the matter to the attention of the proper officers of the company, either by qualifying his report or by making a special report on the subject.

INTEREST CHARGED TO CONSTRUCTION

Q. An electric utility corporation prior to 1924 financed its improvement program out of borrowed money obtained through the sale of bonds and included as a construction cost the interest on money so used. In 1924, however, the company obtained its funds for construction purposes from the sale of preferred capital stock.

The company claimed that it had a right to include interest as part of its construction costs for 1924 even though the improvements were financed out of other than borrowed money and advanced in support of its position the ruling of the Interstate Commerce Commission under Case 308 in Bulletin no. 14, which reads as follows:

"Query: To what account should a carrier credit the amount of interest which has been charged to construction? This company has no funded debt.

6

Are we permitted to charge to construction the interest on the company's working funds used for construction purposes?"

"Answer: Interest charged to construction shall be included in account no. 547, "Interest during construction" and corresponding credit shall be made to the account which was charged as such interest accrued. If no interest actually accrued or was paid, account no. 547 may include a reasonable charge for interest during the construction period on the carrier's own funds used temporarily, the corresponding credit being made to account no. 208, "Income from unfunded securities and accounts."

Admitting the justification of including interest as a construction cost in order that the plant accounts of all utilites should be stated on the same basis, the following claims have been made with respect to the credit arising from the charge to construction for interest:

"A" claims the credit should apply as an offset to interest expense
"B" claims the credit should be made to Other Income
"C" claims the credit should be made to Capital Surplus

It is recognized that there is a difference between theoretical accounting and its practical application in view of current practices and usage and it is a practical solution in connection with an actual case which is now desired.

We would be glad of any information which would disclose the current practice of utilities with respect to the above and in the event that this practice favors the claim of "A" or "B" what justification has been advanced for including the credit in surplus available for dividends.

A. Cost of construction should be charged with interest on funds devoted to construction. The counter credit should be made to the interest deduction account previously charged with such interest if the moneys used had been borrowed. There is no general or substantial agreement, however, with respect to the account to be credited when the construction moneys were derived from earnings or from payments by stockholders.

My personal view is that the credit in the last mentioned case should be to a capital surplus account, probably the premium on capital stock account.

STEEL PLANTS

Q. We would appreciate it if you could obtain the opinions of other accountants in respect to the questions asked, which are as follows:

(1) In an average steel plant in the United States what percentage of the plant valuation is represented by spares? By this is meant, mechanical, electrical and all others taken as a whole.

(2) What is the valuation of electrical and general stores separately or collectively in relation to the valuation of the plant, finished output, or any other available basis?

(3) What is the common practice in handling the item of spares in the accounting? It is desired to determine whether spares are charged direct to costs or whether they are put in a spares account and charged to costs and credited to the spares account as used.

(4) How is general works expense allocated to each department? Our practice has been to proportion the general works expense according to the operating expenses in each department. In other words, a department which has a high operating expense, such as the sheet mill, has to stand a much larger proportion of the general works expense than the sheet bar and billet mill.

7

A. I take up the questions in the order in which they were submitted:

(1) If by spares is meant, mill rolls, annealing boxes and repair parts generally, the average for the plants which we examine shows a percentage of these items to the plant and equipment valuation of 3% to 3⅓%.

(2) We are unable to give any data with reference to the ratio of electrical and general stores separately, but we find that the ratio of the total of spare parts, repair parts and manufacturing supplies to the total plant valuation varies from 4½% to 8%.

(3) In the plants under our observation the spare parts are charged to an inventory account and when put into use, credited out and charged as a deferred expense and prorated monthly on a tonnage basis. Past experience determines the rate to be used. Necessarily each plant will have to base the extinguishment charge on its own experience.

(4) In the plants coming under our observation, it is the practice to charge the departments direct with supplies as used and such items of expense as are a direct charge. Overhead is apportioned on the tonnage basis.

MUSICAL RECORDS

Q. We are interested in securing some authoritative opinion on possible depreciation rates on matrices used in the manufacturing of musical records. These matrices, of course, last a considerable length of time but we find nothing in the tax regulations which might assist us in determining upon specific rates.

A. The depreciation of records, by which we imagine the questioner means the depreciation of the matrices from which phonograph records are molded, is not at all governed by physical deterioration but by the number that can be sold and the price that can be obtained for them. There is no uniformity in the rate at which demand falls off and some of the largest manufacturers write off the entire cost against the first profit made from the sale of the records, and also write off all records that have not made a profit within a very short term. This seems to be the best plan; specific rates are inapplicable.

Gold matrices, of course, are written down only to the amount represented by the gold value.

FERTILIZER INDUSTRY

Q. In the fertilizer industry what is the percentage of repairs to net sales?
A. In one plant, whose annual sales fluctuate from $800,000 to over $1,000,-000, the percentage relation of repairs to net sales was as follows:

1925	.0042
1924	.0058
1923	.0044
1922	.0107
1921	.0218

This plant renders and digests animal refuse almost entirely and sells animal greases and by-products, such as hides, bone, etc. and finished fertilizer. Its chart of accounts thus far will not lend itself to any comparative cost statistics, but the cost for repairs was as above.

8

American Institute of Accountants

Library and Bureau of Information

DECEMBER, 1926   SPECIAL BULLETIN No. 28

CHEQUE DATED BACK

Q. Will you kindly endeavor to ascertain, as quickly as possible, the authoritative solution of the problems raised by the following situation:

A joint-stock association, engaged in a business which is subject to regulation and supervision by a department of the state in which it is licensed to do business, had, on December 31, its fiscal closing, an account receivable on its books owed by an agent company. When the books of the association were actually closed on January 13 (as of December 31) and the net indebtedness of the agent company accurately ascertained, a bank cheque, dated back to December 31, was drawn by the agent company in favor of the association, covering the portion of its balance which was more than 90 days old on December 31. This cheque was entered on the books of the association as a cash receipt of December 31, and credited to the agent company's account. Transactions similar in every detail to this one have been made at several prior fiscal closings, with the knowledge and approval of the supervising state department, which has accepted these cheques as having been "cash on hand" on December 31.

In dealing with this situation, may a member of the Institute, in rendering an independent report, present a balance-sheet showing the two resultant items of cash and balance of accounts receivable as thus finally shown by the books of the association, state on the face of the balance-sheet that it is "subject to the comments of this report of which it is a part" and in such comments state that the cheque was drawn when the books were actually closed and dated and recorded as of December 31?

This situation described above has arisen because of the desire of the association that the audit report be in agreement with the report submitted by the association itself to the state. The association's attitude, in turn, is based on the fact that the agent company's balance, represented by the cheque referred to, if not treated as cash, becomes an account over 90 days old and therefore an asset not admitted.

A. The first thought that comes to me is, why was it necessary to wait until January 13th to ascertain what should have been paid 90 days prior to December 31st; and the second, was the cheque duly paid in January out of the funds in bank on December 31st? In other words, was everything bona fide and the only reason the cheque was not issued on December 31st, that the balance due by the agent company could not be ascertained until some two weeks later? If that were so then there would be some justification for the procedure, although somewhat irregular.

On the other hand, if the funds wherewith to pay the cheque were not in the bank on December 31st, then it would be clear that the intent of the transaction was to mislead.

1

I would say, under the circumstances as submitted, the accountant should accept the accounts as he finds them, but state in his certificate that the item "cash on hand" included a cheque of the agent company dated December 31, 1925 for $••• which was not received until January 13, 1926, and not content himself with a reference "Subject to the comments in this report of which it is a part."

INTEREST CHARGED TO CONSTRUCTION

The bureau of information has received the following letter referring to the query in Special Bulletin No. 27 (May, 1926), in re *Interest Charged to Construction*.

Unless a ruling of the interstate commerce commission requires that all expenditures on construction account carry interest, it would seem utterly ridiculous that the cost of construction should bear a charge for interest on one's own money.

Where such charge is made and allowed by the commission there can still be no justification for crediting same to surplus available for dividends. It is in no sense an earning, being of the nature of paid in surplus and it is the writer's opinion it should go to a capital surplus account.

RATE BASE

My attention was attracted to the comments under the subject *Rate Base* on pages 2 and 3 of Special Bulletin No. 27. The Brandeis decision in the Galveston Electric case should not be used in too broad an application without very careful consideration. It should be remembered that the court was trying the case which was before it and on the record which was submitted to it.

In past years there was a marked tendency to use the term "early losses" in an embracing sense and because historical records were not adequate to supply information sufficient to make a distinction between actual early costs and true early losses.

Unfortunately the literature on the subject of valuation is limited. Generally speaking it is not up to date and unfortunately the leading authorities on valuation are not given to writing for publication. The most valuable data on valuation in its more difficult phases is hidden away in court records in the form of testimony and is not readily available. The accounting literature on the subject is even more limited than the engineering literature. Furthermore, the very valuable data collected by the committee on valuation of the public utilities group is, I believe, rather confidential and perhaps limited to members.

With all deference, I respectfully suggest that the member of the Institute whose problem is referred to in Special Bulletin No. 27 should not commit himself to a policy which may unjustly injure his client without a quite thorough examination of the precedents afforded by courts and public service commissions.

CORPORATION ACCOUNTS

Q. I would like, if possible, to obtain an answer to the following questions:

(1) Corporation A starts business with a capital of $10,000 and a paid in surplus of $5,000. From time to time the stockholders have paid in additional surplus of $25,000 which shows on the books of the company at present as $30,000 paid in surplus.

Corporation A owns a building valued at $15,000 and a mortgage of $15,000 which it wants to transfer to its stockholders who have organized Corporation B to take title to the building and to the mortgage.

Is it permissible to charge the $20,000 of assets, taken off the books, to paid in surplus?

2

Is such a transfer properly called a "partial liquidation" or "reduction of capital"?

Corporation A also has an earned surplus of $10,000.

(2) Corporation X is preparing a statement to the bank.

It owes $20,000 which is covered by several chattel mortgages which in turn are represented by several series of notes which are payable monthly.

What part of these chattel mortgages and the notes which are due within two months, six months or a year shall be considered current liabilities?

A. Replying to your enquiry, the rights of a corporation to repay to stockholders moneys paid in in excess of the amount of capital stock depend on the intention of the original payments, the manner in which they have since been treated, and the laws of the state in which the company has been incorporated.

If the moneys were originally paid in as temporary advances by stockholders, the company has the right to repay them either in cash or in assets, without conflict with the laws, especially where, as in this case, the capital stock is not impaired and there is an operating surplus. The accounts, in this case, should show the advances as "loans by stockholders," not as surplus belonging to the company.

If, however, the amounts paid in have partaken of the nature of capital, the rights of the company to redistribute them should be decided by counsel, taking into consideration the recorded terms, if any, on which the payments were originally made, whether interest has been allowed on them, whether they were paid in by all stockholders in proportion to their stock holdings, and whether they have been held out to creditors as part of the capital of the company.

In no case would the repayment constitute income to the stockholders.

In reply to the question as to the classification of serial notes as between current and other liabilities, there is no fixed rule, although often those maturing within one year are classed as current. It should give the bank sufficient information if they were set forth separately on the balance sheet as "secured serial notes, maturing $*** each month."

ATHLETIC CLUBS

Q. (1) What is the common practice among the larger clubs in regard to the charge for depreciation on buildings in the statement of operations, especially where the value of the property has a tendency to increase in value and the building is of a steel, concrete and brick construction? Depreciation is not to be considered for tax purposes in a first-class corporation of this kind, and the board of governors of the club are interested in showing as good a statement as possible.

(2) Is there any definite period of time over which to amortize the organization expenses? These expenses include the upkeep of the offices of the club together with costs of securing members for a period of three years prior to the opening of the building and they total about $200,000. This is another question which directly affects the apparent result of operations inasmuch as the quicker we charge off these expenses, the net profit will accordingly be reduced.

Before discussing this matter with the finance committee of the club, we would like to know what is the general practice of large corporations which have been recently organized and have had considerable expense of administration for several years prior to beginning of their operation.

We might add that this organization expense does not include any interest on indebtedness due to construction costs inasmuch as we have decided to capitalize this interest, at the same time crediting to construction costs the interest on deposits received as the result of money borrowed and held in the hands of the trustees during the course of construction.

3

A. In answer to the first question I would say that the common practice among clubs is not to include any charge for depreciation on buildings in the statement of operations. I have reviewed the accounts of a good many clubs and do not now recall any that follow the practice of making a charge for depreciation on buildings.

In answer to the second question I would say that there is no definite period of time over which to amortize organization expenses. In commercial undertakings it is the practice to write off organization expenses in a comparatively short period of time if the result of operations will permit—three to five years being common periods. In clubs, however, I believe from my observation that there is a tendency to capitalize these expenses permanently, the total cost being considered as a part of the permanent investment. It would seem better practice, however, to break up the permanent investment so that members could see clearly the cost of land, buildings, equipment, financing, etc. and then be in a position to write off the intangible portion of the investment whenever result of operations would permit.

There is a general tendency among clubs, whose affairs are guided by committees of members, to arrange the charges producing revenues on a basis which only permits the recovery of actual out-of-pocket expenses. Each committee aims to conduct its own department on such an economical basis that there is no surplus of revenue against which to write off the investment either in intangible form or in the depreciation form of buildings. The losses in such investments are sometimes offset by an appreciation in land values so that when the old building becomes obsolete and it is necessary to erect a new one, the old site may be disposed of at such an advance over cost as to offset any loss arising from the capital invested in buildings and equipment and intangibles. It seems a poor business policy to rely on this accomplishment because it does not always come true. Many clubs do provide for the depreciation of equipment such as furniture, carpets, rugs, linens, silver, crockery, etc.

VALUATION OF SUGAR PROPERTY

Q. A sugar factory in its return of annual net income has been valuing the inventory of sugar on hand at cost or market, whichever was lower.

For the calendar year 1920, cost being lower than market, the inventory was valued at cost, and the following items were included in cost:

> Raw material (sugar cane).
> Factory labor.
> Factory supplies.
> Miscellaneous factory expenses.

The department contends that insurance and depreciation should be included in cost while we contend that insurance is not necessary to the production of sugar, as the taxpayer may select to assume the fire risk. Some factories carry their own insurance. Depreciation is an arbitrary charge against income which occurs whether the factory is operating or not and it can in no wise be considered a manufacturing cost.

Will you kindly submit the question whether these two items should be included in cost and let me know the result.

A. Replying to your letter regarding the inclusion of insurance and depreciation in the price to be used for costing an inventory of sugar, the following is our opinion.

The object of a sugar factory is the production of sugar. In order to safeguard against the risks of fire, insurance is necessary and whether it be carried by the sugar producer or by an insurance company, it is an expense of sugar production.

4

We do not agree that depreciation is an arbitrary charge against income. Depreciation may be said to represent the shrinkage in value of any particular property arising from—

       1—Wear, tear and breakage as a consequence of its employment.

       2—Mere effluxion of time.

       3—Obsolescence.

If it arises from causes in item No. 1 above, it is certainly a charge to the cost of production. For convenience in accounts, an arbitrary reserve may be set aside out of profits. At least to the above mentioned extent it is an expense of producing sugar, the amount of which may be arrived at in various ways.

Our experience in connection with raw sugar producing companies' accounts is that sugar on hand is invariably priced, not at cost or market, but at the estimated realizable value which the tax regulations provide for under the farm method. This method is necessary in order to show the true profit of the year, arising as it does from a crop period of about six months.

Our answer would be that while there are arguments for treating insurance as a financial charge, not part of the cost of production, this theory is not very generally accepted and the common practice—and probably the best practice—is to treat insurance as part of cost of production if it is insurance on the facilities used in production. There is very little argument for not including depreciation as part of the cost of production if it is depreciation of the capital used in the manufacturing operations as represented by the manufacturing plant. The charges for depreciation may be to some extent arbitrary, but the fact of depreciation is not arbitrary, for the consumption of fixed capital, which is depreciation, is just as much a part of the cost of production as the consumption of working capital. It is true that some depreciation takes place when the plant is not operating, and there are other fixed charges as well which go on whether goods are being produced or not. For this reason, in systems of standard cost the normal rates for insurance, depreciation and all other elements of cost are treated as cost, and the excesses as cost variations, or cost of idleness, or whatever else may cause the fluctuations. But even under such circumstances the cost of idleness must in the end be borne by the commodity which is produced, the segregation of the fluctuations from standard cost being made for purposes of analysis and control and for general enlightenment.

We give our opinion in the following paragraph:

It is assumed that the depreciation and insurance referred to are in respect of properties used in the manufacture of sugar and that the mill operated for a normal portion of the period under review. In that case we are of the opinion that both items should be taken up as a part of the cost of manufacture and should be included proportionately in ascertaining the cost of the inventory on hand at the end of the period.

CAPITAL STOCK WITHOUT PAR VALUE

Q. A reorganization of X Corporation provides for the issue of the following classes of stock:

       1,000 shares preferred stock, par value $50.

       1,000 shares Class A common stock, par value $100.

       1,000 shares Class B common stock without par value.

       1,500 shares Class C common stock, par value $1.

The preferred stock is entitled to annual cumulative dividends at 6% and has preference over the common stock both as to dividends and assets.

5

The three classes of common stock are on a parity and equal in all respects.
The stock is issued in lieu of 1,000 shares of common stock of the old corporation, as follows:

One share of preferred stock and one share each of Class A and B common stock for every share of old stock outstanding.

Stockholders have the right to purchase at par one share of Class C common stock for every share of the old stock, the remaining 500 shares are to be sold as the board of directors may decide but not for less than $1 per share.

1,200 shares of the Class C common stock have been sold for $5,200, 1,000 shares to the old stockholders and 200 shares to others.

At date of reorganization the net assets of the corporation were..	$110,000
Add Proceeds from sale of Class C common stock...............	5,200
Total	$115,200

How should the capital stock and surplus be shown on the balance-sheet?

A.   We note that it is stated that "the three classes of common stock are on a parity and equal in all respects," whereas the figures give the parity for A stock as $100, for B stock as indeterminate and for C stock as $1.

Accepting the figures, and not the written statement referred to, the balance-sheet should show:

Capital stock:

1,000 shares pfd., par $50.................................		$ 50,000
1,000 " com., Class A—par $100......................		100,000
1,200 " " " C—par $1.......................		1,200
1,000 " " " B—without par value............		
		$151,200

and per contra:

Assets—Acquired for stock (net)..........................	$110,000
Proceeds sale capital stock.........................	5,200
	$115,200
Goodwill.......................................	36,000
	$151,200

The par value stock must be set up as a liability at its par value.

On sale of the remaining 300 shares of the Class C common stock any proceeds in excess of $1 per share should be credited against goodwill.

MERCHANDISE SHIPMENTS

Q.   I would like to present a question to the members.

In May 1918 a client contracted for 30,000 pounds of merchandise at $3 per pound, to be delivered in more or less equal quantities during the months of September, October, November, and December, 1918.   A large percentage of the goods was to be used in connection with the manufacture of war supplies. The seller did not ship as promised, giving the influenza epidemic as the excuse. During the latter part of November and early in December, he endeavored to make up the shortages in the shipments promised for September, October and November.   The client then refused to accept the delayed shipments, aggregating about 10,000 pounds and the goods went to storage pending an adjustment.

On December 31, 1918 there were 10,000 pounds still unshipped which the seller was ready and anxious to ship in January, 1919.   The purchaser was evidently bound to accept the goods which in the meantime had dropped from $3.00 per pound to about $1.50 per pound.

6

At the end of 1918, the adjustment was as follows:

(1) The purchaser should accept the 10,000 pounds which had been shipped prior to December 31st and which had gone into storage because of his refusal.

(2) The purchaser should accept the 10,000 pounds which had not been shipped prior to December 31, 1918. Instead of having the seller ship them in January, the shipments should be spread over several months, in some instances as called for by the buyer.

There seems to be no question but that the buyer had to consider $30,000 as a liability on December 31, 1918 and could set up only $15,000 as an asset with regard to the merchandise which went to storage.

I maintain that on December 31, 1918 the buyer was also liable for $30,000 on account of 10,000 pounds which the seller insisted on shipping in January, for which it was known that he could realize only $15,000. In my opinion, this condition should have been stated on his balance-sheet on December 31, 1918. In other words, the statement issued by him as of December 31, 1918 should show the facts with regard to both items:

(a) The shipments prior to December 31, 1918 which went to storage.

(b) The merchandise which the seller was prepared to ship in January.

A. It will be assumed for the purpose of this reply that the liability of the purchaser was exactly as stated in the question, although the facts given lead to doubt as to the actual liability.

As to the merchandise shipped prior to December 31st, and to be accepted by the purchaser, it will appear in the inventory at a price in conformity with the stated practice of the purchaser, at either "cost" or "the lower of cost or market." "Market" is said to be $1.50 per pound.

As to the merchandise to be taken in later months, the facts should be shown on the balance-sheet, preferably in a note saying that the company was obligated to accept merchandise to the extent of $30,000 at a price which would amount to $15,000 over present market.

Also, if the inventory be taken at "cost," this being materially greater than market prices, a note indicating the amount of difference should be appended.

Generally speaking, the contention of your correspondent that the statement should "show the facts" is not only correct, but is the key to almost every troublesome matter in connection with statements of account.

RATE OF INTEREST

Q. On January 1, 1926 A borrows $1,000 from a loan association on the following terms:

5% service charge $50.00 payable at once.
$20.00 payable on principal monthly, running for 50 months.

Interest computed semi-annually and payable monthly in the following manner:

1st six months:

8% of $1,000. = 80.00 \div 2 = 40.00$
$\frac{1}{6}$ of 40.00 or $6.66\frac{2}{3}$ payable each month for first six months.

2nd six months:

8% of $(1,000. - 120.) = 70.40 \div 2 = 35.20$
$\frac{1}{6}$ of $35.20 = 5.86\frac{2}{3}$ payable each month for second six months.

And so on.

Borrower's payments each month to cover service charge, principal and interest are then made as follows:

7

1926	Jan.	1	$50.00	1927	May 31	25.06	1928	Oct. 31	22.67
	Jan.	31	26.67		June 30	25.06		Nov. 30	22.66
	Feb.	28	26.67		July 31	24.27		Dec. 31	22.66
	Mar.	31	26.67		Aug. 31	24.27	1929	Jan. 31	21.87
	Apr.	30	26.67		Sep. 30	24.27		Feb. 28	21.87
	May	31	26.66		Oct. 31	24.27		Mar. 31	21.87
	June	30	26.66		Nov. 30	24.26		Apr. 30	21.87
	July	31	25.87		Dec. 31	24.26		May 31	21.86
	Aug.	31	25.87	1928	Jan. 31	23.47		June 30	21.86
	Sep.	30	25.87		Feb. 29	23.47		July 31	21.07
	Oct.	31	25.87		Mar. 31	23.47		Aug. 31	21.07
	Nov.	30	25.86		Apr. 30	23.47		Sep. 30	21.07
	Dec.	31	25.86		May 31	23.46		Oct. 31	21.07
1927	Jan.	31	25.07		June 30	23.46		Nov. 30	21.06
	Feb.	28	25.07		July 31	22.67		Dec. 31	21.06
	Mar.	31	25.07		Aug. 31	22.67	1930	Jan. 31	20.27
	Apr.	30	25.07		Sep. 30	22.67		Feb. 28	20.27

Total
payments $1,286.14

Required:
Effective rate of interest paid by borrower.
Effective rate of interest received by loan association.

A. The problem set forth that a sum of $1,000 was borrowed for which a service charge of $50 was immediately paid and payments of $20 per month, at the end of each month, were made on the principal sum concurrently with interest payments of varying amounts. It was requested that we determine the effective rate of interest paid by the borrower and the effective rate paid by the loan association.

The answer to the problem is as follows:

The effective rate of interest to the borrower is approximately .955% per month or 11.46% per year, compounded monthly.

Owing to the necessity for dropping decimals, a three cents adjustment has been necessary in respect to the final interest payment. It will be noted that in the solution furnished, it has been recognized that the amount of money borrowed was $950. Inasmuch as the service charge was immediately paid on the nominal loan of $1,000, the amount received by the borrower was only $950 and all subsequent payments represented either interest on that sum or repayment of the principal amount. We believe that the answer furnished is both academic and practical, though, of course, if the actual problem only involved an amount of $1,000, it would hardly be worth making the elaborate calculation required in this case in order to record the payments with theoretical correctness on the books of the borrower. Where such a small sum is involved, we would recommend recognizing the nominal amount of the loan and charging the payments supposed to represent interest, together with a monthly amortization of the service charge, to interest. Such treatment, however, would not alter the fact that the actual interest, from a practical viewpoint, was the same as in the answer previously given.

The request for the effective rate of interest received by the loan association should be accompanied by a statement as to how the service charge affects the lender. If the service charge was not offset by expenses, the rate of return to the loan association would be the same as the interest expense to the borrower. On the other hand, if the service charge was offset by expenses, the return to the loan association would be reduced proportionately.

8

American Institute of Accountants

Library and Bureau of Information

JANUARY, 1928   SPECIAL BULLETIN NO. 29

[The Committee on Administration of Endowment authorizes the publication of special Bulletins, of which this is one, on the distinct understanding that members are not to consider answers given to questions as being official pronouncements of the Institute, but merely the individual opinions of accountants to whom the questions were referred. It is earnestly requested that members criticize freely and constructively the answers given in this or any other Bulletin of this series.]

APPRAISAL OF FIXED ASSETS

Q. A manufacturing corporation has acquired, January 1, 1924, machinery to the amount of actual cost, new, $300,000.00.

Their balance-sheet as of June 30, 1927, as follows:

Machinery..........................	$300,000.00
Less, 2½ years depreciation at rate 10 per cent..........................	75,000.00
Net worth as of June 30, 1927.........	$225,000.00

For the purpose of issuing bonds they were compelled to call in a reputable firm of appraisers, and they placed the market value or net worth as of June 30, 1927, at $317,000.00 on this machinery.

Can this corporation in their calendar year statement, i. e., December 31, 1927, take the amount of the appraised value as submitted by these appraisers, i. e., $317,000.00, as the value of this machinery and set up as a surplus the difference of $317,000.00, less $225,000.00, $92,000.00?

A. The difference between the sound value as appraised and the depreciated residual cost of the plant represents an appreciation of value in the nature of an unrealized profit. Conservative practice demands that such an unearned profit should not be buried in earned surplus if brought upon the books, or, at any rate, the fact that appreciation has been given effect to in the accounts should be disclosed in some form or another in the balance-sheet. The exact manner in which such a transaction should be treated depends upon the individual case, depending to a great extent upon whether the appraisal is incident to the acquisition of fixed assets by a new corporation, incident to a change in the capital structure of a corporation, or purely an appraisal of fixed assets involving no other changes of the nature described. It is stated in the instant case that bonds are about to be issued, and in order that the public buying bonds may be well informed as to the true value of the property, it would be highly desirable to give effect in the balance-sheet to the appraised value. However, the appraisal in this case has no relation to a change in capital stock or the transfer of title to the property. The description of the fixed assets, therefore, should make reference to the fact that the machinery has been appraised and that the values stated are the appraised values. Per contra, the appreciation should properly appear in a separate division of surplus account entitled "surplus arising from appraisal of fixed assets," or some similar title.

1

Such unrealized profit or appreciation is specifically exempt from federal income tax under the revenue act of 1926, and, per contra, the allowable deduction for depreciation with respect to such assets is restricted to an amount which will amortize out of profit the cost of acquisition of such assets. The amortization of the appreciation should be provided over the remaining life of the assets by charge against the surplus arising from appraisal.

May we say in closing that in our opinion, under present accepted principles of finance and accounting, the operating accounts of a business are responsible only for the amortization of the cost of acquisition of fixed assets. To charge operations, and ultimately penalize earned surplus, with the amortization of appreciation is incorrect. Many political economists, appraisers and a few accountants hold opinion to the contrary. The problem is one of the moot questions of the present time, and every one admits much of the practical logic which supports the contentions of those advocating the amortization of appraised values out of earnings. In the instance of the appraisal of fixed assets to be acquired the situation is quite different. In such a case, the appraised value becomes the cost of acquisition. Surely, in connection with a change of capital structure, being in the nature of a reorganization, as a result of which capital stock is issued against such appreciation, there remains but one course out of which to provide for the amortization, namely, out of earnings. As a general rule, the term surplus, unless otherwise qualified, should represent surplus arising from earnings, and, per contra, such surplus should be charged with amortization sufficient to extinguish the cost of acquisition of fixed assets.

CANNING COSTS

Q. In connection with the cost accounting of a canning factory which packs corn principally, is it the common procedure to departmentalize or treat the entire operations as a whole? If departments are set up, what is the correct basis for apportionment of overhead expenses, or if entire operations are treated as a whole, what is the correct apportionment for various overhead items?

A. Final costs cannot be prepared more often than once a year, owing to the fact that the packing season is of short duration, whereas the overhead expenditure is constant.

Costs are departmentalized in so far as they apply to factories, which in turn are broken down in various products, those in turn being broken down into various sizes of containers.

Factory overhead is allocated to factories according to actual figures per accounting records, or if actual figures cannot be determined, then it is pro-rated on the basis of pack. General overhead is also pro-rated according to pack.

Labels, labeling, warehouse and shipping costs are allocated on basis of actual figures for factories or, if not known, according to cases shipped. Selling expenses embracing commission, brokerage, salesmen's salaries and expenses, swells and allowances, cash discounts, are allocated on a dollar value on the shipments from the individual factories.

Costs are broken down by factories to various products on the following basis:

Raw material, labor, boxes, cans and jars—Actual.
Coal and power—On a basis calculated on the time necessary to cook the product, in relation to a base time.
Factory and general overhead—Arbitrary figures may be used but the basis should be "pack" quantity.
Labels, etc.—On shipments.
Freight out—On tonnage shipped.
Selling expenses—On sales value of sales.

2

The costs are broken down into sizes on the ratio of the capacity of the container to a No. 2 can. All items with the exception of the following are pro-rated on that basis.

> Boxes, cases and jars—Actual being used.
> Labels, etc.—Actual being used.
> Selling expenses—Sales values being used.

All costs are worked out on a base figure which is taken as a No. 2 can, and then broken down into sizes according to the previous paragraphs.

A. In 1920 the National Canners Association put out Special Bulletin No. 3, which provides for departmentalizing of commodities so far as prime costs are concerned, and so far as direct factory expense is concerned. Prime costs, of course, can be charged without hesitation to cost of the single commodity packed. Certain factory expenses can be charged direct to the product, such as

> (a) Royalties, rentals and other expenses in connection with the machines used exclusively for corn.
> (b) Miscellaneous factory expense and repairs chargeable directly to corn.
> (c) Setting up or taking down machinery used only in packing corn.
> (d) Small tools and appliances used exclusively on corn.

Quoting further from this classification, which by the way is out of print:

> "Some accountants may ask, 'Why have "Corn Factory Expense" for instance?' 'Why not charge all factory expense to general factory expense account No. 75 and at the end of the year distribute the total to the commodities on the basis of the pack?' If this view is persisted in it will, no doubt, save a little bookkeeping; but the results under such conditions will be grossly inaccurate. Charge all items that clearly belong to specific commodity expense accounts to those accounts at once, and charge to general factory expense account only items that cannot be said to belong to one particular commodity."

Factory expense of the sort that benefits all products is distributed at the end of the year to the commodities on the basis of quantities packed. Some items perhaps may be divided on a more equitable basis where a division on the basis of relative quantities packed would be manifestly unfair. In most instances, however, the per dozen or per case basis of distributing general factory expense is usually employed. General expenses paid are distributed on the quantity basis rather than on the basis of relative aggregate sales values, or prime cost, or productive labor costs.

As to cost of distribution, brokerage and sales allowances can be charged direct against the specific commodity. Selling expenses applicable to all commodities are apportioned in proportion to quantities sold.

CONTINGENT RESERVES

Q. Company X on December 31, 1925, prepared and published a profit-and-loss account showing a net profit of $X, which was transferred to surplus account. At the same time there was charged to surplus account a sum of $Y, designated as "reserve for contingencies," which officers of the company then stated as intended to cover general and at that time unforeseen contingencies. Inventories of materials used in manufacturing were valued at cost. During 1925 certain contracts had been made for materials for future delivery, part of which were received by the company in 1926.

Since January 1, 1926, a very substantial drop has taken place in the market prices of such raw materials and the company feels that its earnings have been

3

seriously affected by the relatively high value of raw materials carried over in inventory and by commitments entered into in 1925.

With a view to determining the proper set-up of its accounts for 1926, some discussion has arisen and the company has obtained a number of published statements of accounts of companies engaged in the same line of business certified by various leading accountants. As a result the following questions have arisen relative to the summarized annual statements which it intends to publish:

(1) Can the manufacturing costs with propriety be reduced by the above mentioned sum of $Y and the actual net profit from operations for the year be increased accordingly?

(2) Can the above mentioned sum of $Y with propriety be included as a credit in profit-and-loss account under a designation of reserve brought forward for fluctuation in prices in determining net profit carried to surplus account?

(3) Should the above mentioned sum of $Y merely be credited to surplus account whence it was originally transferred in 1925?

A. In the following we are assuming that both inventories and commitments were at the lower of cost or market as of the close of 1925 and that no part of the reserve for contingencies now under discussion was to cover an excess of cost over market on either of these items.

(1) In our opinion manufacturing costs for the year cannot with propriety be reduced by the reserve for contingencies set up as at the close of the preceding year without incorporating in the body of the published profit-and-loss account or as a footnote thereon a brief explanation of what has been done; and, even in this case, the caption opposite the final amount on the profit-and-loss account for the year which ordinarily would read "Net profit for the year" should undoubtedly have a few words inserted therein—for example, "On the above basis" or "See footnote," directing the attention of the reader to the more detailed explanation of what has been done, appearing elsewhere in the account.

(2) We see no objection to applying the reserve for contingencies, set up at the close of 1925, as a special credit in the 1926 profit-and-loss account below the "Net profit for the year" if a brief wording is inserted explaining that this reserve has been applied to offset the extraordinary losses due to fluctuations in prices. We think this method preferable to that referred to under (1) above.

(3) We think it a better plan than either of these referred to in (1) and (2) to transfer the reserve for contingencies directly back into surplus, and one much less likely to be misunderstood or misconstrued by outsiders reading the published accounts.

CORPORATION ACCOUNTING

Q. A holding corporation has an operating deficit of $54,000. A consolidated balance-sheet of the holding corporation and all subsidiaries shows a surplus of $10,000, after elimination of all inter-company profits. The holding corporation owns all the capital stock of the subsidiaries.

Subsidiary corporation "A" has a surplus of $67,000, all resulting from increase of fixed-asset value, as reported by competent appraisers. The holding corporation's deficit is the remainder of a former larger deficit, after being cut down by a profit of $15,000 during the year recently closed.

The holding corporation carries its capital stock in subsidiary corporation "A" at its cost, which is par.

The holding corporation desires to pay a dividend. It proposes to write up the value of the stock in subsidiary corporation "A" to equal the book value of the stock, which they consider a sound and actual value. The holding corporation would then show a surplus of $13,000.

4

The writing up of this stock would cover the deficit, and in addition release $13,000 of the $15,000 profits of the last year as available for dividends. It is my understanding that the procedure is proper, although perhaps not to be considered as a conservative manner of doing business.

A. The most feasible way, in our opinion, of handling the above situation would be to have the subsidiary corporation "A" declare a dividend to the holding corporation, in the amount of its surplus, either in cash, if sufficient cash is on hand, or if this is not the case, then to increase its authorized capital stock in the amount of the existing surplus, and then declare this as a stock dividend to the holding corporation. Thus a surplus would be created on the holding corporation's books in the amount of $13,000, which could then be declared as a dividend. We think that this method is preferable to the method proposed in the question.

We agree with the writer that the procedure as set out could hardly be considered conservative. The question as framed does not state the causes for the increase in value of fixed assets in subsidiary corporation "A," nor does it state whether or not similar appraisals were made of the fixed assets of the other subsidiary corporations. If so, and these latter showed their assets to be worth approximately the values carried on the books and if the increase resulting from the appraisal of "A" corporation's fixed assets was due to excessive depreciation rates having been charged over the expired life of these assets, in this event the procedure proposed by us would seem to be technically in order, and the dividends could be defended under New York practice. If, on the other hand, "A" corporation had its fixed assets appraised, and wrote them up as a result of the appraisal and the other subsidiaries had no appraisals made of their fixed assets, it is quite possible that there would be offsetting adjustments in the plant accounts of the other subsidiaries due to overvaluations existing on their books. Under this condition the procedure would not appear to be either conservative or defensible.

From a legal standpoint the question arises as to the right of the directors to declare dividends out of a surplus created as the result of a revaluation of capital assets. We understand from New York attorneys that under the laws of that state dividends can be declared out of surplus arising from such sources. We are not sufficiently familiar, however, with the laws of other states to say whether or not this would apply throughout the country.

CORPORATION FINANCE

Q. We have two or three clients who make it a practice to increase the book value of their affiliated companies to cover their proportion of their earnings, crediting the same to their income account and paying dividends out of it.

In the case of a company that owns all of the preferred stock of a company and 50 per cent. of the common stock, all of the voting power being in said common stock, is it proper for the parent corporation to increase the book value at which they are carrying said common stock with their pro-rata of the earnings for any particular period and credit same to an income account, using said income with which to pay dividends? Some of our clients make a practice of doing this, although the partly owned affiliated company is not in position to pay out any cash dividend; in fact, said affiliated company in one of two instances is more or less heavily indebted to banks.

A. There are two principal methods of handling profits and losses of subsidiaries on the books of a holding company, both of which are considered good accounting: (1) the investment is carried at book value, and profits and losses of subsidiaries are taken up on the holding company's books from time to time; (2) the holding company's investment in subsidiaries is carried at cost.

Under method (1) the investment account would be debited with the book value at date of acquisition and subsequently debited for subsidiary profits

5

and an income account credited, the latter account being closed into surplus. The investment account would be credited also for losses suffered by subsidiaries or for dividends disbursed by subsidiaries to the holding company. The investment would approximate at all times the current book value of the holding company's interest in subsidiaries.

Although profits of subsidiaries increase the holding company's net worth, such profits are not available for distribution as holding company dividends as long as the subsidiary elects to reinvest its profits in the business rather than to distribute them as dividends. It is not sound finance for a holding company to declare a dividend on an increase in net worth which is retained by subsidiaries and invested in the business of those companies.

The holding company, therefore, should limit its dividends to the amount of dividends actually received from subsidiaries. But there is still another limitation. For example, in one instance the parent company A owned the entire capital stock of subsidiaries B and C. B made a substantial profit and declared a dividend thereon. C suffered a loss so that the condition of the organization in its entirety as represented by consolidated statements did not warrant the payment of a dividend. Nevertheless A ignored the loss of C, took up the dividend from B as income and declared a dividend out of the resulting profit. The principle that a holding company may distribute dividends to its stockholders to the extent that dividends are received is appropriate, therefore, only when the amount distributed does not exceed the net aggregate profits of the subsidiaries.

Under method (2) the subsidiary investment account on the books of the holding company is carried at cost. Profits and losses of subsidiaries are not recognized on the holding company's books. Dividends received from subsidiaries are credited as income on the books of the holding company. The holding company may properly declare dividends on the basis of such income subject to the limitations discussed in the third paragraph under method (1).

DEPRECIATION OF GREENHOUSES

Q. What are the rates of depreciation customarily taken on greenhouses constructed with concrete foundations and steel frames?

Seven and one half per cent. yearly was taken by a client for the period 1919 to 1922, and without question by the income-tax unit. However, for 1923 the rate has been questioned and after conference a rate of 5 per cent. was allowed. I am not altogether satisfied that this 5 per cent. rate is fair to the client.

A. We had never been able to find any official information regarding rates of depreciation which would apply with reasonable accuracy to greenhouses. We have, however, discussed the probable life of greenhouses of different types of construction with greenhouse men and we have reached the opinion that greenhouses built upon a concrete foundation with steel frames, kept in good repair, could reasonably be expected to have a life of twenty years as a minimum.

Accordingly, it has been our practice to use a depreciation rate of 5 per cent. on the greenhouses and on the heating plant. To offset this moderate depreciation rate, in sections which are occasionally visited by hail storms, the repair charges may prove to be heavy, and it may even be advisable to raise the depreciation rate so as to equalize this charge to some extent. Such damage, however, is restricted to relatively small areas.

LAUNDRIES COST ACCOUNTING

Q. We have several prospective clients in the state who are operating small laundries and feel unable to install a complete cost system such as is prepared by the National Laundrymen's Association.

6

One of them has suggested the possibility of providing for tests of the costs whenever they feel disposed to make them.

A. Test costs must always be accepted with reservations and more especially so when no attempt is made to reconcile them approximately with actual expenditures. On account of fluctuations of business in laundries the value of test costs would depend to a large extent on the judicious selection of the time chosen for making the tests and even then extreme care would require to be exercised to see that due allowance had been made for all indirect as well as direct expenditures.

PARTICIPATION MORTGAGE BONDS

Q. The X Mortgage Company is practically ready to place some participation mortgage bonds on the market. In fact, they have some customers on the waiting list for some at this time.

If it can be done without hurting the sale of these bonds, they would like to have a provision in their trust agreement, or in their prospectus, or in the bonds themselves, that the ratio of bonds issued to the capital stock and surplus of the corporation shall not exceed a certain figure which should be, perhaps, not in excess of five to one, possibly three to one.

The question that is perplexing us and on which we would like to have your counsel is: Will such a provision be, in your opinion, detrimental in the selling of these bonds? Probably in most cases this question would not enter the mind of a purchaser, and on the other hand, if introduced by the X Mortgage Company, it might appear to be an effort to bolster up their collateral and therefore we are rather at a loss to know just exactly what is the proper thing to do under the circumstances.

It is our opinion that these bonds are absolutely good so long as they are held within a reasonable limit. However, we do not wish to leave open an avenue whereby it would be possible for an excessive issue to be sold which would, of course, weaken the guarantee which stands behind these securities by increasing the ratio of bonds to capital.

We will very greatly appreciate your counsel in this matter, and to avoid any possible misunderstanding, will state that the X Mortgage Company does not expect to issue many bonds at this time and will be rather surprised if they have as much as $100,000.00 worth of them to offer within the next twelve months.

Will you also advise whether or not "Participation Mortgage Bonds" is a correct name for this particular kind of a bond. The word "Participation," we think, seems to convey that the bonds would participate in profits and we want to be sure that there can be no legal tangle about this.

A. It appears from the question submitted that, in placing some "participation mortgage bonds" on the market, the X Mortgage Company is considering the desirability of restricting the total of the bonds to an amount such as shall not exceed a given ratio to the company's capital stock and surplus, the restriction to be embodied in the trust agreement, or the prospectus, or the bonds themselves. The ratio in mind is "not in excess of five to one, possibly three to one."

The question perplexing the inquirer is: Will such a provision as is contemplated be detrimental to the sale of the bonds?

It is our opinion that the stated provision would make for a sounder capital structure than would be the case otherwise and, therefore, instead of being a hindrance it should promote the sale of the bonds. We are, of course, confining ourselves to this particular feature of the issue. Further, we believe that a ratio of 5 : 1 is high; the lower ratio of 3 : 1 is more acceptable.

The second question is too vague in its terms to permit an explicit answer. If, as appears to be the case, the bonds are the direct obligation of the company,

7

issued under an agreement between the company and the trustee and secured by the deposit and assignment of mortgages acquired, we do not think the word "Participation" should form part of the description. "Participation" might be construed as meaning a sharing in something—profits; at any rate there is that possible hazard, to avoid which we suggest a more suitable designation. If the bonds are of the nature outlined above, we suggest "Collateral Trust Mortgage Bonds" as an appropriate description.

NEW YORK FRANCHISE TAX BILL

Q. New York franchise-tax bill for the year ending October 31, 1927, is received in December dated December 20, 1926. Should this invoice be entered in the accounts in 1926 and a prepayment shown for the ten months of 1927, or should the bill be excluded from the accounts and an accrual for two months of 1926 shown on the December 31, 1926, balance-sheet? The latter based on the assumption that a prepayment must result from an actual expenditure of cash.

A. The New York franchise tax is a liability on November 1st of each year. If the bill is received in December, it should therefore be entered up as a liability, and a deferred charge for 5/6 of it may be carried forward. Deferred charges do not necessarily mean cash prepayments and since the tax bill is received before the close of the year and will have the effect of reducing the cash and increasing the liabilities, it should be shown in the balance-sheet.

8

American Institute of Accountants

Library and Bureau of Information

MARCH, 1928   SPECIAL BULLETIN NO. 30

[The Committee on Administration of Endowment authorizes the publication of special Bulletins, of which this is one, on the distinct understanding that members are not to consider answers given to questions as being official pronouncements of the Institute, but merely the individual opinions of accountants to whom the questions were referred. It is earnestly requested that members criticize freely and constructively the answers given in this or any other Bulletin of this series.]

GAS AND WATER WORKS COMPANIES—AUDITING

Q. We are engaged upon an audit of a city of a population of 150,000 people with a gas consumption of 34,000 customers. We would appreciate any information which you may be able to furnish us in regard to the audit of the accounts receivable and the accrued income of this size and kind of company. In other words, what we are asking here is for information as to what detail other accountants would undertake to check the income and accounts receivable for gas and water works companies.

A. In so far as revenue and accounts receivable of a small company of this type are concerned, it will usually be found that consumers' accounts are maintained in " Boston " ledger form. The basis of entry in the " Boston " ledger will be in the form of a consumer's contract, agreeing upon either a monthly flat rate or referring to a metered rate. The " Boston " ledger is simply a monthly columnar record listing the names of consumers at the left hand margin alphabetically, and sometimes separately controlled by districts. For each month there are provided columns for the balance unpaid at the beginning of each month, charges during month, payments during month, and balance at end of month. Occasionally two or more of these columns may be combined by the use of red and black ink. The totals of the balance columns serve as balancing media for control accounts of accounts receivable. The column provided for monthly charges serves as the posting medium for revenue accounts, and the payment column provides a check against the cash receipts.

Depending upon the degree of internal control existing in the organization (which ordinarily will not be very great in an organization of the size referred to) the following matters should be subjected to test verification:

    (1) The propriety of charges against consumers' accounts should be tested by a comparison of contracts with ledger charges. Ordinarily this test may be restricted to accounts in which substantial changes in charges occur. Flat rates which have continued for some time past and which indicate regular and recurring cash payments ordinarily need not be checked.

    (2) The mathematical accuracy of metered charges should be tested.

    (3) Tests by means of adding-machine tapes should be made of detailed monthly charges to confirm controlling-account credits for revenue.

    (4) Tests by means of adding-machine tapes should similarly be made of cash payments verifying the cash-controlling-account entries.

    (5) Outstanding balances may be tested against consumers' returned bill cards.

1

(6) Balances of accounts receivable will ordinarily be found to be substantially correct. The companies ordinarily exercise the right of discontinuing service upon delinquency.

(7) Agreement of detailed accounts receivable with control may similarly be established by adding-machine tapes.

In the majority of the tests suggested a verification of from 5 per cent. to 10 per cent., in number of accounts, serves to satisfy the auditor that the accounts are accurately and properly maintained and that both revenue and accounts receivable are substantially correct. It goes without saying, that the best test of revenue is to be found in cash receipts. If charges to customers' accounts are being regularly paid, the legitimacy of the consumers' accounts is confirmed.

Statistics of gas manufactured are usually maintained, based upon main-meter records, compared with quantities sold, and accounting for leakage and other shrinkage loss. These records may well be used in a cursory substantiation of revenue.

The enquirer should also be referred to Brown's Annual Directory of American Gas Companies containing reliable statistics of great interest to auditors in the examination of gas companies.

JOINT FEES

Q. Can you advise me as to any form of agreement in use between members of the American Institute of Accountants, having to do with the apportionment of joint fees in connection with joint engagements?

A. In so far as we are aware, no such general form of agreement is in use nor, indeed, do we believe that it would be practicable to go very far in the way of using a standard form of agreement. Each case is different in some respects from every other case and what would be a fair arrangement under one set of conditions might be quite unfair under different conditions. Further, it seems to us that it ought not to be necessary to reduce to a formal agreement an understanding regarding such a matter. A letter stating the intent of the parties ought to be entirely sufficient and the informality of such a procedure would, we think, tend to put the whole arrangement upon a higher and more satisfactory plane.

VALUATION OF LICENSED ABSTRACTOR'S BUSINESS

Q. Can you supply any information relative to the basis of valuation to be placed on the purchase of a licensed abstractor's business by a title guaranty company?

Aside from tangible assets of fixtures, equipment and accounts, there is the accumulation of work performed in obtaining base titles to property subdivisions and the accumulation of other abstract information, which in the future will be constantly available and a very material time saver in preparing future documents in respect of passing on title.

From your experience, have any methods or rules been determined upon arriving at the valuation of such intangible items as the above, in addition to goodwill value as arrived at on a basis of past earnings?

A. The permanence of the accumulated data relating to titles, etc., suggests a computation similar to one which would be applicable if a valuation of goodwill were involved. It seems to us that the average earnings over a period of years should be a fair basis. After deducting from the average earnings of the period agreed upon, a return of, say, 8 to 10 per cent. on the tangible net assets, the balance of the earnings would be capitalized. In businesses that are more or less stable, the treasury department suggests 8 or 9 per cent. return on tangibles and capitalizes the remainder of the earnings at 15 per cent. To the extent that the "plant" may be subject to obsolescence, depreciation or

2

any other influences which may impair the value, the average earnings should, we think, be reduced by an estimated charge to cover this element. Likewise, any abnormally high or low years should, in our opinion, be excluded from the years selected as the basis for computation.

PARTICIPATION MORTGAGE BONDS

By chance, I read your Special Bulletin No. 29, and was somewhat interested in the question as to the ratio of participation mortgage bonds to capital and surplus and as to the propriety of the term "participation mortgage bonds." The answer was of greater interest, and if non-members are permitted to join in the discussion, I should appreciate the opportunity of adding a thought or two.

The first is that the inquirer refer to the statutes of the state in which the company is organized, as there are usually some statutory restrictions governing the sale of participation certificates, particularly if they are to be legal investments for trust funds. Quite frequently, corporations selling mortgages with a guaranty as to payment of principal and interest must organize under the banking or insurance statute and not the general corporation law.

Where a company lends money on mortgage, it eventually gains possession of "frozen assets" and to continue doing business, it must either increase its capitalization and its "frozen assets" or dispose of its mortgages. The latter is accomplished either by selling the entire mortgage, frequently with a guaranty of payment of principal and interest, or by depositing one or more mortgages under a trust agreement and selling certificates representing a part of the loan. The profit to the company is in the difference between the interest it receives from the mortgager and the interest it pays to the one who invests either in an entire mortgage sold with a guaranty or in a participation. As this is a process of turning over its investment, it is obvious that since the company's profits can increase only through increased loans and sales of them, restrictions on the amount of participation certificates sold must curtail profits.

Presumably when a company lends money on mortgage loans there is a sufficient margin between the market value of the property pledged and the amount of the loan. Conservative practice is not so much in the ratio referred to, but in the ratio of loan to the appraised value and, of course, conservatism in appraising the property is the crux of the matter.

Companies of this type will have by-laws referring to a ratio of mortgages guaranteed with greater frequency than to a ratio of participation certificates. Some companies in New Jersey have voluntarily adopted by-laws whereby there is a limitation on the bonds or other indebtedness. One (Lincoln Mortgage and Title Guaranty Company of Newark) that sells its bonds through a New York investment house (Harris Forbes and Company), published an advertisement containing the following:

> "The company is limited in the issuance of bonds and other indebtedness to an amount not to exceed fifteen times its fully paid capital stock, or a more conservative ratio than governs either the federal land banks or the joint-stock land banks."

The term "participation certificates" is used in chapter 305 of the laws of 1926 of New Jersey and in practice it has been found that where one mortgage is deposited under a trust agreement and part of that one mortgage is sold, the term is used, but where a group of mortgages is deposited, the term "mortgage bonds" is more frequently adopted. Realty Associates Securities Corporation, a New York company, recently issued a prospectus in which reference is made to "Participating interests in bonds and mortgages." It would seem that in this particular field, "participation" is not construed as meaning a sharing in something—profits.

3

The fact that "participation" has another meaning in another line, should not necessitate another descriptive title. As you know, foundry men use certain words as "flasks" and "pigs" with a meaning somewhat different to their ordinary use.

PARTNERSHIP WITHDRAWALS

Q. A client of mine, a copartnership, started business with an original capital of $50,000, as follows: "A" contributed $25,000, "B" contributed $25,000. There were no articles of copartnership, but the understanding between the partners was that no additional moneys were to be invested, no interest calculated on withdrawals, that both were to devote their entire time to the business, and that each partner should draw a salary of $5,200 a year.

At the end of nine months of business, the partners had drawn equal salaries, but one partner had withdrawn, at various times, moneys aggregating $16,000, which of course, was in addition to his salary. It was acknowledged by both partners that the partner who had exceeded his salary account by $16,000 was indebted to the business to that extent, and that he was obliged to return the said overdrawal as soon as possible. As a matter of fact, the overdrawal originally stood in the amount of $17,000, $1,000 of which had been repaid, bringing the amount down to $16,000, which appeared under the heading "'A' personal account" in the general ledger.

At the end of nine months of business, a dispute arose between the partners and a balance-sheet was prepared by an accountant, whereby the item of $16,000 "'A' personal account" was shown in the balance sheet as an asset, while the respective capital accounts had been reduced, through losses to $14,000, $7,000 to the credit of "A" and $7,000 to the credit of "B." The capital account, of course, showed a credit balance collectively of $14,000, only because there was included in the assets, the item of "'A' personal account," $16,000. Two months later, the creditors demanded their moneys and as a result a receiver was appointed.

The question arises, as to whether the item of $16,000 appearing in the balance sheet assets, under the caption "'A' personal account," should have been deducted from the capital account of the partners, or whether the balance sheet as prepared by the accountant containing "'A' personal account $16,000" was correct. As a guide, please remember that the personal net worth of "A" was not known at the time of the overdrawal.

A. Partners' withdrawals are in fact always a reduction of capital employed in the business. There are "border-line" exceptions in cases in which temporarily superfluous capital is lent to a partner, at interest, instead of being lent elsewhere; but fundamentally the principal remains fixed. It follows, therefore, that such withdrawals should be expressed specifically in the partnership balance-sheet as deductions from the partners' capital account. As a matter of fact, the true condition is satisfactorily disclosed when such withdrawals are shown specifically as such, as an asset in the balance-sheet. Per-contra, when the partnership agreement, whether written or oral, provides for the contribution of stated capital sums. it would be incorrect to bury such withdrawals by merely stating a net capital-account balance, thereby lending the impression that the balance stated is the agreed capital of the particular partner.

As a matter of legal principle, the relation of partners to one another is one of mutual trust, and the law demands the exercise of the highest integrity and good faith toward each other. One partner can not, without the consent of the other, apply partnership property to his own debts. The right of one partner to make such an application, with the previous consent or subsequent sanction of the other partner, is clear when the claims of partnership creditors are not thereby impaired. It appears that such sanction existed in the case

4

submitted, and that the firm was solvent at the time. In such circumstances the receiver, or partnership creditors, can not follow such assets into the hands of the partners' personal creditors for the benefit of partnership creditors. It is a general rule of partnership law that it is the right of each partner to have partnership property applied to the payment of partnership debts, and this right is often spoken of as partners' liens upon partnership property. Upon dissolution, under order of court, this rule will be enforced and accordingly partnership creditors will be given a preference in the partnership assets over individual creditors of partners. Each partner is, of course, personally and individually liable for the entire amount of partnership obligations, but each has the remedy of requiring the other partners to contribute their pro rata share. "His liability is said to be as a principal debtor for his own share, and as surety for the other partners for the remainder."

A. It has been our practice to show such drawings on a balance-sheet as a deduction from capital account. This treatment would show the "true" investment of partners in the business at the date of the balance-sheet. Partners, (and this applies as well to sole proprietors), should not be shown as owing money to themselves.

An exception to this rule might be made if the partner repays the withdrawal immediately after the date of the balance-sheet, and prior to its issuance.

PROMOTION EXPENSES

Q. A small ice-cream, milk and cheese corporation decided to expand and increase its sales, and the directors instructed the manager to expend not to exceed $7,000 in an aggressive campaign to get new business and customers.

Starting July 1, 1927, and closing October 31, 1927, $5,500 was spent for this purpose, and this item was charged off as operating expense for the year 1927.

In this way all extraordinary expense is charged off as expense during the year 1927, while the subsequent years would be equally benefited by additional profits. Under these conditions would it not be permissible and good accounting to capitalize this amount of $5,500 and deduct for the subsequent five years their pro rata share of this expense?

Do you believe that the government would permit this handling of this account for taxable purposes?

A. We are of the opinion that the most desirable course, from every point of view, is to write off the entire amount when it is expended.

It can not be denied that the cost of getting new business may, in some cases, be carried forward, as in the case of the expenses of travelers in the fall obtaining orders for spring deliveries. These are cases where the expenses are specifically applicable to certain orders obtained. Where the expenses are, as in this case, general promotion expenses, the profit from which is no more than a hope, it is bad practice to carry them forward. Suppose the campaign fails, what then?

We do not wish to offer any opinion as to what the government might do in assessing taxes.

A. I believe that this could be capitalized in the year spent, and apportioned to the next three or five years, and that the government would have no kick when the internal revenue statement is granted. In fact, I have done this in a number of my plants, and there has never been any serious objection made by the federal authorities.

RESTAURANTS—COST OF SALES

Q. I find some members of the accounting profession are of the opinion that in the case of restaurants, cost of sales, for the purpose of stating gross

5

profit, should include cost of foods only, while others are of the opinion that cost of sales should also include such items as:

China and glassware	Ice
Utensils, pots, pans, etc.	Insurance
Silverware and linens	Laundry
Salaries—Kitchen	Miscellaneous supplies and expenses
Salaries—Dining room	Rent
Advertising	Repairs
Decorations	Mercantile tax
Depreciation	

It seems that those who have expressed an opinion agree that sales include revenue from meals and from sales of fat, garbage, etc.

I would like to know the opinions of several of the foremost members of our profession with regard to this matter and I would appreciate it if you will obtain the opinions for me.

I shall also appreciate it if you will obtain for me the following information:

Average percentage of cost of sales—Chain restaurants—Single restaurants.

Average percentage of gross profit—Chain restaurants—Single restaurants.

Average percentage of general and administrative expenses—Chain restaurants—Single restaurants.

Average percentage of net profit from operation—Chain restaurants—Single restaurants.

A. Sales:

I do not agree with the inquirer in his statement that "sales include revenue from meals and from sales of fat, garbage, etc." It is better practice, in my opinion, to credit the sales of fat, garbage, etc., to the cost of food sold. I am quite certain that all firms engaged in installing food-cost accounting systems follow this practice, in which there has been substantial uniformity in restaurants for a number of years. The same practice is followed in the manual adopted by the American Hotel Association as a basis of preparing uniform financial statements for hotels. The manual, prepared by a committee of hotel accountants on which the Institute and the New York State Society of Certified Public Accountants were represented, states on page 22:

"Cost of food sold should also be credited with the revenue derived from the sale of grease, bones, bread, etc."

I may add that "bread" in this quotation means stale bread sold as such in bulk.

Cost of sales, gross profit and expenses:

The term "gross profit" means to a restaurant man only one thing: the excess of sales over the cost of food sold. The term is used in this sense in all the trade publications and, as far as I know, at all meetings of restaurant proprietors. It is also used in this sense only by food-cost accountants. The list of expenses given in the inquiry includes practically all the usual expenses of a restaurant, so that if they would be all included in the "cost of sales" the result would be the net profit and not the gross profit, except perhaps for such expenses as the salary of the manager and of the bookkeeping office, or the general administrative expenses of chain restaurants.

It is not even practical in restaurants, to determine the production cost by separating what may be called manufacturing expenses from selling expenses.

If a line of demarcation were drawn between the two, many of the expense items which at present have definite meanings for restaurant men would have to be divided between the two classes. The cost of the ice used for preserving the raw material is clearly part of the cost of production, while the cost of the ice used for ice water in the dining room would be rather a selling expense. The laundry cost includes the cost of laundering cooks' uniforms and towels, a

6

manufacturing expense, as well as the cost of laundering the dining-room linen, a selling expense. Even the generally accepted classification of payroll into kitchen and dining-room payroll would have to be disturbed, for the dishwashers and silver cleaners in the kitchen have no more to do with the production than the waiters in the dining room. Other expense items, such as depreciation, repairs, rent, light and heat would have to be similarly divided. Of course, it is not impossible to make the division, even though it would have to be rather arbitrary in the case of such expenses as rent. It is hard to see, however, what practical advantages such a grouping of expenses would have. On the other hand, the fact that there is a rather generally accepted method of expense classification which restaurant proprietors are used to, the fact that the expenses of a restaurant consist of comparatively few items, and the fact that restaurants are usually small business units employing one or two bookkeepers often not with an over-supply of bookkeeping and accounting knowledge—all these facts speak in favor of the classification of the financial results of restaurant operations into sales, cost of food sold, gross profit, expenses and net profit. Furthermore, the percentage of gross profit determined on this basis is information of vital importance to the restaurant proprietor.

It is my opinion, therefore, that the most practical form of the profit-and-loss statement for a restaurant is the one that includes only the cost of food in the "cost of sales" and follows the gross profit so determined with a simple list of expenses without classification into what would be logical groups in a truly manufacturing enterprise.

Food cost and expense ratios:

As far as the percentage of food cost is concerned, the fact that a restaurant is operated as a single unit or as one of a chain does not make so much difference as to stamp either class with a characteristic cost ratio different from the other.

STATE FRANCHISE TAX ON BUSINESS CORPORATIONS

Q. A certain New York corporation whose fiscal year ends on October 31st received a bill from the state tax department at Albany for their New York state franchise tax. This bill is dated November 17, 1927, and is due on or before January 1, 1928, and reads as follows:

"State franchise tax on business corporations for the year beginning November 1, 1927 and ending October 31, 1928."

The contention is made by the corporation's officers that the amount of the bill should be included in expenses for their fiscal year ended October 31, 1927. In every other previous year this corporation has included this tax in the month and year in which paid and if this particular one is entered in the fiscal year ended October 31, 1927, there will be two such charges for that year.

The officers of the corporation contend that the basis on which this tax was computed when filed during the summer of 1927 was on the net income for the fiscal year ended October 31, 1926, and, therefore, that not only this bill should be included, but also 4½ per cent. on the net profit for the year ended October 31, 1927. This would result in three charges for the year ended October 31, 1927, and would without doubt, be disallowed by the federal state-tax authorities.

Inasmuch as the company's practice since the inception of this tax has been to enter it as an expense at the date paid, I contend that the company should continue to do so with the present bill not only for the sake of consistency and simplicity, but also by reason of the quotation in paragraph three above, which clearly states the period for which the tax becomes a liability.

Do you not think that any other method would be contrary to internal-revenue regulations? The corporation is very anxious to include all liabilities at the time of closing each October 31st, but I regard the particular bill referred to as not being a liability as of that date.

7

A.   Under the various federal revenue acts, state taxes are deductible on the accrual basis in the taxable year during which the liability accrued.   This has been decided by the supreme court in the case of United States v. Anderson, et al, and United States v. Towne Manufacturing Company, decided on January 4, 1926.   (See Solicitor's Memorandum 4499A, reported in Cumulative Internal Revenue Bulletin V-1, page 56.)

With particular reference to the accrual of the liability for New York state franchise taxes, the treasury department has held that it accrues on November 1st of the year during which the annual return is due; that is, although the Franchise Tax based on a return filed during July of a particular year is actually based on earnings of a prior period, nevertheless, the tax applies to the fiscal year beginning November 1st, following the date upon which the franchise-tax returns must be filed.   Therefore, the New York state franchise tax for the year beginning November 1, 1927, accrues as a liability on November 1, 1927, and is deductible from the income of the taxable year within which November 1, 1927, falls.   If the taxpayer's fiscal year begins on November 1, 1927, the franchise tax covering the fiscal year beginning November 1, 1927, would be deductible from the income of the taxpayer for the taxable year ending October 31, 1928.   If the taxpayer's taxable year coincides with the calendar year, then the franchise tax for the fiscal year beginning November 1, 1927, is deductible in full from the income of the calendar year 1927.   (See A. R. R. 1153, reported in Cumulative Internal Revenue Bulletin 1–2, page 92; also appeal of Jamestown Worsted Mills, 1 B. T. A. 659.)

In view of the references already cited, it seems unnecessary to state that the treasury department will not allow a deduction in one taxable year of a state franchise tax which applied to a different taxable year, only one year's tax being allowable as a deduction in any one taxable year.

From a technical accounting point of view, it is our opinion that the New York state franchise tax payable on January 1, 1928, which covers the fiscal year beginning November 1, 1927, and ending October 31, 1928, should be prorated over such a fiscal year, that is, one twelfth of the tax payable on January 1, 1928, should be accrued during each of the months of November and December, 1927, and the balance should be treated as a prepaid tax from the date of payment and charged off in equal instalments during the ten months beginning with January and ending with October, 1928.

REPURCHASE AGREEMENTS

Q.   A large chain of retail stores does most of its business on the instalment-sales plan.   The merchandise sold is secured by chattel mortgages or by other legal devices, and the down payment varies from nothing to 15 per cent., while the balance is payable over a period of months, varying from one to three years. The annual volume of sales is several times the concern's invested capital. Hitherto, losses from uncollectable items have been kept within reserve limits. During the past few years, the practice of selling accounts receivable subject to a "repurchase plan" has been gaining headway, so that during the year 1927 approximately 90 per cent. of all newly created accounts receivable have been converted into cash on the basis of repurchase agreements.

The repurchase agreements referred to, provide essentially, that upon the failure of a customer to live up to his instalment payment obligations for a period of . . . days, that the banking organization may, at its option, and without notice, return the said customer's paper to the instalment-merchandise house, which must immediately pay therefor in cash the balance due on such paper, together with accrued interest and certain fixed charges.

The contention of our new client, supported by several banks, is that "leading firms of reputable public accountants" unhesitatingly certify to balance-sheets without reference to the contingent liability represented by the above-

8

referred to repurchase agreements. While our client truly represents to us, on the basis of its own experience, that during the past few years the extent to which it has been called upon to make good on the aforementioned repurchase agreements is negligible, we do not believe that this approach to the subject goes to the crux of it. We can not believe that the existence of a contingent liability, especially of so large an amount, is overlooked by reputable accountants in their balance-sheet certifications and should greatly appreciate word from you as to the attitude and practice of as many of our fellow members as may be willing to make early response.

A. We have on more than one occasion insisted upon mentioning in balance-sheets the fact that the concern had disposed of instalment paper, subject to a repurchase agreement. We believe that in most cases these so-called repurchase agreements call for the finance company's repossessing the merchandise and selling the merchandise to the business concern for the amount outstanding on the paper. Accordingly, it is maintained by some finance companies—and perhaps some accountants and bankers—that the position of the business concern with respect to its obligation to repurchase the merchandise is precisely the same as it is with respect to any other commitments for the purchase of merchandise, which, admittedly, do not have to be recognized in the balance-sheet. Notwithstanding this argument, we believe that any person who is considering the financial condition of the concern is entitled to know that the concern has disposed of its receivables and may have to take some of them back. There is some doubt as to whether this commitment can properly be characterized as a contingent liability, but the fact remains, we think, that it is an important factor in the consideration of financial condition.

If the repurchase agreement does not call for the repossessing of the merchandise by the finance company and the purchase of the repossessed merchandise by the business concern from the finance company, but merely calls for a reversal of the transaction whereby the paper was purchased by the finance company, it seems to us that the situation is not essentially different from an assignment with recourse; and, that being the case, there seems to be a definite contingent liability.

We are very much interested in the statement in the letter that the attitude of the client is supported by several banks. We took the trouble to canvass a number of large banks on this subject, and found that without exception they insisted that information regarding such transactions should be shown in the balance-sheet.

A. It seems that your interrogator might well have directed his client's attention to the provisions in this connection contained in the pamphlet, "Approved Methods for the Preparation of Balance-sheet Statements," published in the Federal Reserve Bulletin for April, 1917. They are as follows:

> *Contingent liabilities*—"It is not enough that a balance-sheet shows what must be paid; it should set forth with as much particularity as possible what may have to be paid. It is the duty of an auditor who makes a balance-sheet audit to discover and report upon liabilities of every description, not only liquidated debts but possible debts. The following are the usual forms under which contingent liabilities will be found:
>> Indorsements......................................
>> Guaranties...
>> Unfilled contracts.................................."
>
> *Notes receivable*—"When notes receivable are discounted by banks the company has a liability therefor which should appear on the balance-sheet. Lists of discounted notes not matured at the date of the audit should be obtained from the banks as verification and their totals entered under 20a if the cash therefor is shown as an asset."

9

Accounts receivable—"Inquiry must be made às to whether any of the accounts receivable have been hypothecated or assigned and the sum total of accounts so listed entered under 20b."

The above references to "20a" and "20b" refer to subclassifications shown under the main classifications of secured liabilities which appears on the liability side of the form of balance-sheet contained in the Federal Reserve Bulletin. These subclassifications are as follows:

"20a—Notes receivable discounted or sold with indorsement or guaranty (contra)."
"20b—Customers' accounts discounted or assigned (contra)."
"20c—Obligations secured by liens or inventories."
"20d—Obligations secured by securities deposited as collateral."

Whether obligations for the repurchase of instalment notes and accounts receivable are shown as direct liabilities in the manner required by the above quotations from the Federal Reserve Bulletin, or are shown as contingent liabilities in foot-notes to the balance-sheet, is a matter to be governed largely by the client's preference; the important matter being, of course, that the balance-sheet discloses the existence of the obligations.

The fact that losses experienced by the company in repurchasing instalment accounts during the past few years have been negligible is quite irrelevant to the question of the necessity of disclosing the existence of the obligation to repurchase the unpaid accounts.

A. It is our opinion that a balance-sheet should show all liabilities, both actual and contingent. The exact liability which the concern who sold the accounts receivable may be called upon to meet, is difficult of determination. Therefore, we feel that reference thereto, in the form of explanatory memoranda on the face of the balance-sheet, should be sufficient. The important thing is that their existence be disclosed and that such data as will give an idea of the nature, status and amount be clearly set forth. In other words, show the total amount of outstanding accounts sold and the nature of the repurchase agreement. If there has been any experience as to the amount which the concern has been called upon to repurchase in the past, this data might be shown for the information of bankers and others who make use of the balance-sheet.

A. In our opinion, reference should be made on the balance-sheet to the contingent liability that exists in respect of instalment notes sold under the conditions set forth in the question above recited.

There are, however, conflicting opinions which might be here considered.

It is contended, in the first place, that the sale of instalment notes, secured by chattel mortgage or similar instrument, is an ordinary and usual practice in many lines of business (e.g., pianos, furniture, automobiles, washing machines); and as interested parties, bankers certainly are fully aware of this well understood method of financing, specific mention thereof is superfluous.

Again, while it may be conceded that a contingent liability does exist in respect of sold paper, this contingency, it is claimed, is so remote that for practical purposes it may be disregarded provided adequate provision is made for such losses on repossession, however, described as experience shows to be necessary or particular circumstances determine. A variant of this latter view is that there is no contingent liability; that repossession losses, including repossessions in respect of notes reacquired, can be computed within reasonable limits and, such a provision being made, the element of contingency is discounted by the direct reserve.

The first of the above contentions is not acceptable because it depends on an unverifiable assumption which, we consider, carries no such sanction as is claimed, while the alternative views mentioned break down under the very

10

test applied, namely, by what practicable measure is it possible to determine the remoteness of the contingency?

Clearly we can not with the required degree of assurance restrict the limits of probability and assign a value to that which, in the nature of the case, is modifiable by varying circumstances. In a word, we can not evaluate the unknown.

It is our opinion, therefore, that, as already stated, cognizance should be taken of the contingent liability that undoubtedly exists, but in order to give full recognition to the contra views herein expressed we believe that reference thereto might properly be made in some such terms as set down hereunder. The notation suggested is indicative of the proposed treatment; it is not offered as a set formula.

> Contingent liability:
>> In the ordinary course of business, the Company has sold customers' paper, secured by . . . The contingent liability thereunder is considered remote.

It will be understood, of course, that adequate reserves should be provided against losses on repossession and that in each individual case the circumstances should be such as to justify the statement that "The contingent liability thereunder is considered remote."

A. One fact in connection with the business under consideration which appears to be essential to a true understanding of its financial position is that its bankers hold large amounts of accounts receivable which it may be required to repurchase for cash in case debtors default. Another fact of importance to one seeking to know the financial status of the business is that experience in the past has been that losses in connection with such "repurchases" have been negligible.

The client apparently urges that the second fact be offset against the first and that both be eliminated from the accountant's report. From the information given it does not appear that such an offset can properly be made.

On the other hand, we feel that it is important that *both* of the facts mentioned be definitely presented, because both of them would be of practical informative value to anyone who may study the statement.

Going a little beyond the scope of the question, it seems to us that the client should logically be entirely satisfied to have the statement presented with both of these facts included, because it would seem that any unfavorable impression which might be made by admitting the amount of contingent liabilities would be more than overcome by the fact that losses in connection with such liabilities had been negligible in the past, and by the effect of the desire to present the "whole picture," a desire which would be evidenced by including these facts in the certificate or in the statement.

TAXATION OF CORPORATION SHARES

Q. A partnership unable to meet its obligations is taken in hand by a committee of bankers to whom it is heavily indebted. The bankers arrange with another corporation, successful in the same line of endeavor, to take over the business. A corporation is formed to take over the affairs of the partnership, and the entire capital stock (one thousand shares of no par value—stated value $1.00 per share) is given to the corporation which has agreed to assume the management. In the takeover the bankers have agreed to cancel one half of the obligations due them, feeling that in this way they will fare better than if they forced the partnership into bankruptcy. At the time the new corporation begins business, due to the cancellation of indebtedness, the one thousand shares have a book value of $300,000 an equity which would appear from the

11

balance-sheet to rest in a third mortgage of $100,000 and about $200,000, in plant and equipment. On the books of the issuing corporation the capital stock appears at the stated value of $1,000, and surplus is credited with the balance of $299,000.

The corporation receiving the shares wishes to treat the book value of the stock, $300,000, as current income. The auditor's first thought was to credit the amount on the recipient corporation's books to surplus, but he is confronted with the fact that the transaction was initiated and consummated during the year under review and feels there may be some justification for its inclusion in the income statement as "Other income" with a full explanation of the facts.

Again, will its inclusion in the income statement subject the recipient corporation to income tax on the $300,000? It may be classed as a gift, hence non-taxable, or at any rate it is an unrealized, and, for some time to come, an unrealizable item and therefore should not be taxed.

The questions for which answers will be greatly appreciated are:

(1) How to treat the receipt of the shares on the books of the corporation acquiring them.

(2) Should the transaction appear in the income statement of the recipient corporation?

(3) Is the transaction taxable to the recipient corporation for federal income-tax purposes?

A. 1. The shares received by the managing corporation seem to be the consideration for its entering into a contract to manage the business of the issuing corporation. We do not think this creates income at that time. The income is to be derived in the future from the earnings of the issuing corporation. We should not treat the receipt of the shares as income unless and until they were sold; then they would be income for the full proceeds. It is not necessary to set them up on the books at all, although it is advisable to do so, at least to give them a nominal valuation for the purpose of recording their existence and ownership on the books of the managing corporation. On this theory, it does not matter whether the stock is valued at $1.00, $1,000 or $300,000. Whatever value is placed upon the shares, however, should be credited to surplus and not to income.

2. We have already explained why the receipt of the stock should not be treated as income, in answering No. 1.

3. We do not believe the receipt of the shares is taxable income. It is from the carrying out of the contract that the managing corporation may expect to receive an income and not from the mere initial consideration received for entering into such a contract. We do think, however, that crediting the valuation of the stock to income account would create a presumption that it was taxable income which would be seized upon by the income-tax authorities in a way to embarrass the managing corporation with a contest, the outcome of which might be doubtful. It would not be good advice, in the light of knowledge that an unnecessary contest is probable, to advise the managing corporation to treat the receipt of the stock as income.

A. We are of opinion that the stock of the reorganized company should be carried on the books of the recipient corporation at a nominal figure of, say, $1.00 and that only dividends on this stock should be credited to income. Our reason for suggesting this procedure is that as the recipient company received the stock of the unsuccessful corporation for services to be rendered the measure of the services will be future dividends to be received, and it would be poor policy to attempt to estimate at this time the liquidation value of the stock merely for the purpose of carrying it at such a valuation on the books of the successful corporation.

12

American Institute of Accountants
Library and Bureau of Information

JUNE, 1928   SPECIAL BULLETIN No. 31

[The Committee on Administration of Endowment authorizes the publication of special Bulletins, of which this is one, on the distinct understanding that members are not to consider answers given to questions as being official pronouncements of the Institute, but merely the individual opinions of accountants to whom the questions were referred. It is earnestly requested that members criticize freely and constructively the answers given in this or any other Bulletin of this series.]

ACCRUAL OF CONTRACTOR'S PROFITS

Q. Corporation A, a contracting company, has a contract with a city for the construction of four public school buildings. Corporation A turns over to corporation B the right to construct one of the buildings. The transfer of contract by Corporation A (a general contractor) to B must be and is approved by the city, but does not relieve Corporation A from responsibility for faithful performance of the contract. The moneys due under this contract are payable to Corporation A, who in turn pays them over to Corporation B. As work progresses the city engineers usually once a month estimate the work and approve payments. The contract states that the approval of payments does not mean an acceptance by the city of the work completed, but that the acceptance by the city is made only when work is completed and the last payment approved. Corporation B agrees to pay Corporation A $100,000 for the transfer of the contract, $25,000 of which is paid on the signing of the contract, and the balance $75,000 payable in monthly instalments extending over a period of ten months, or $7,500 per month. Corporation A claims that the transaction is an actual sale of a contract, hence a profit of $100,000 should be immediately entered as such upon its books. Corporation A has the right to seize the plant, tools, etc., of Corporation B in the event of a default in the terms of the contract and has a claim upon any work performed by Corporation B, and these rights fully secure Corporation A as regards the $100,000 profit.

Is the $100,000 a profit on the signing of the contract, by Corporation B, and should it be immediately entered on the books of Corporation A as such?

If not, does the profit accrue pro rata as payments are made, or does it accrue only on completion of contract?

A. No, the $100,000 is not a profit on the signing of the contract. This contract obligates Corporation "A" to fulfil the terms regardless of the performance of Corporation "B," and it is not an assured profit to Corporation "A" until the work has been approved by the city. The inquiry states Corporation "A" has the right to seize the plant, tools, etc., of Corporation "B" in the event of a default in the terms of the contract . . . and that these rights fully secure Corporation "A" as regards the $100,000 profit.

This should secure Corporation "A"'s profit, but does it? Let us suppose that toward the completion of the work Corporation "B" had expended more than the total contract price (plus extras) and did not have funds to complete the work. It would then be necessary for Corporation "A" to step in and complete the contract, an action which might entail a net loss to Corporation "A."

We have recently had an experience of just this nature in which Corporation "A" sustained an actual loss amounting to 200 per cent. of this "guaranteed

1

profit" in addition to the loss of the "guaranteed profit." In this instance Corporation "A" had, in addition to the securities named in the inquiry, a further security in the form of real estate valued at about 50 per cent. more than the "guaranteed profit."

Article 36 of *Regulations 69* (the Revenue Act of 1926) permits a contractor on "long-term contracts" to report income on this basis of work completed, or upon the completion of the contract, and, in my opinion, the later course is the more conservative.

The profit may be accrued as the payments are made, as in many cases contractors accumulate and take into earnings the proportionate profits on completed work, but I believe that the more conservative method is to accrue earnings only on the basis of completed work.

A. As I understand the important features of the problem presented, they are as follows:

Corporation A has received $25,000 and is to receive $7,500 per month for ten months as the consideration for turning over to Corporation B the execution of a contract entered into by A, but A still stands responsible to the city for the proper performance of the contract and the city pays to A the moneys due for performance of the contract, which A in turn pays to B. Although the inquiry states that "the transfer of contract from A to B is approved by the city," it would seem (since the money is to be paid to A and A is responsible for the performance of the contract) that so far as the city was concerned, A is a contractor and B is a subcontractor to A. If this is correct then it seems to me that we should have to look on the $100,000 as being the compensation which A receives for performance of its contract, rather than an amount paid A "for the transfer of the contract," because A apparently has not made a real transfer of the contract.

We should then be faced with the question as to whether profit on a contract is to be taken up by instalments as the work progresses or should only be taken up on the completion of the work. The principle that a contracting corporation may properly compute earnings during the progress of the work seems sufficiently recognized so that I think the generally accepted basis for such a computation might be applied to the present case. If the services and responsibilities which rest on A seem fairly measured by the initial payment of $25,000 (say for its services in the preliminary work of plans and specifications, drafting and obtaining contracts, etc.) and its further responsibilities seem further measured by the payments of $7,500 per month, this might be a fair measure for instalment computation of earnings. Decision on this question would, however, have to depend on a knowledge of all conditions, which is not given by the brief inquiry.

You will note that this answer is based on a belief that there has not been an actual sale and transfer of the contract, but that A still stands in the position of being the contractor, since otherwise there seems no basis for it to receive from the city the amounts payable under this contract. Under such conditions I can not see the warrant for taking up the profits in advance. The most, I think, which could be done is to take up the profits pro rata as the contract is performed.

MANUFACTURING CONFECTIONERS' COSTS

Q. What information can some of your members supply concerning costs of manufacturing confectioners?

Information of the following sort accepting the dollar of sales as the standard will be most welcome.

Material and supplies used......................	.000
Direct labor.................................	.000

2

```
Factory expense..............................  .000
Selling and administrative expense..............  .000
                                              ──────
Total cost and expense........................  .000
                                              ══════
Sales.......................................  1.000
                                              ══════
```

A general line of hard candies and soft-center candies selling at moderate prices is the product.

    A. Following are costs of manufacture of candy:

```
    Cost of production:
      Raw material...........................  $23.85
      Packages...............................   16.90
      Salaries and wages.....................   13.26
      Supplies...............................     .57
      Fuel, light and power..................    1.23
                                               ───────
                                                        $55.81
    Maintenance and repairs...................              .40
    Shipping and delivering...................             1.18
    General expenses (exclusive of depreciation and
      taxes).................................            19.40
                                                        ───────
    Total....................................            76.79
    Profit...................................            23.21
    Sales....................................           100.00
```

NEWSPAPER PUBLISHING ACCOUNTING

    Q. Will you kindly obtain the following information for me on the subject of newspaper publishing accounting:

    No. 1. Determine the labor cost of the composing room per page.

    No. 2. The number of hours worked per day and the rate per hour.

    No. 3. This information to cover plants publishing both morning and evening papers.

    A. The labor cost per page of the composing room of one client, publishing both morning and evening papers, was $10.10 for the year 1926. This item may appear low compared with a company publishing only a morning or an evening paper. This is due to the fact that advertisements which are to appear both morning and evening may be set up originally for the morning edition and then used for the evening edition with very little additional cost. This reduces the cost per page nearly 50 percent. In view of the fact that this query requests information only as to plants publishing both morning and evening papers, this reduced cost of composing is probably an essential part of the comparison.

    Linotype operators work 36 hours a week or 6 hours a day at a rate of $47.00 a week for day work and $50.00 a week for night work. Other journeymen, proof readers, etc., work 48 hours a week or 8 hours a day at the same rate per week as linotype operators.

PRICING INVENTORIES OF SCRAP METALS

    Q. Have you the data available, or would it be possible for you to ascertain for me, what the accepted practice is in pricing inventories of scrap iron, steel and other metals?

    The case in point is one in which it would not be practicable, even if possible, to ascertain the cost of scraps on hand, and in this business apparently the same market prices govern both for buying and selling, the profit often being dependent upon favorable shipping points and freight differentials.

3

Also in the matter of verifying quantities when it is not practicable to weigh the scrap, can approximate weights of irregular piles be ascertained by measurement?

A. We have the following comments to offer on the several queries set forth in your letter:

1. Inventories of scrap iron, steel and other metals are usually valued at the lower of cost or market.

2. It is assumed from the nature of the question that the company concerned is engaged in the purchase and sale of scrap. In which case, if costs are unascertainable, market should be used less an amount sufficient to provide for the expense of selling the scrap.

3. Most companies seem able to compute weights from measurements.

UNDERWRITING EXPENSES FOR MORTGAGE-BOND ISSUES

Q. One of my clients, a corporation, erected a building and as usual made a building loan. Before the building was finished, a bond issue for $1,000,000 was arranged. The underwriting expenses, legal fees and other items in the underwriting amounted to $90,000. The building loan was paid for out of the proceeds of the bonds. The proceeds of the bonds also supplied the funds necessary to complete the building.

The bonds were known as a 20-year sinking-fund loan and we charged off annually that portion of the $90,000 which we felt was practicable to the year in question. The amount charged off was governed to some extent by the amount paid into the sinking fund, but the total $90,000 was to be wiped out more or less equally over the 20 years.

The building was sold, subject to this bond issue, the purchaser assuming the obligation and relieving the seller as is customary with first mortgages when property is sold. Of course, since my client was the original mortgagee and is the corporation mentioned in the agreement when the bonds were issued, it no doubt still has somewhat of a contingent liability in connection with this bond issue. I should consider the chances rather remote of its becoming liable.

At the time of sale the underwriting expenses appeared in our books as an asset item of $80,000 a deferred charge against future operations. In calculating our profit on the sale, we considered this as one of the cost items. A revenue officer insists that this underwriting balance of $80,000 can not be considered so. His arguments are

(1) The contingent liability and
(2) The fact that my client will have other income against which it could apply this $80,000 over the balance of the 20 years.

This is the first time in my experience that a question of this sort has been raised. It always has been generally understood that the cost of obtaining a mortgage went with the sale of the property mortgaged, and was applied against the profit.

A. We are in receipt of your letter which deals with a case in which a taxpayer claimed a deduction for unamortized expenses incident to the issuance of bonds to finance the cost of a building.

It appears that the revenue agent has disallowed the deduction claimed for such expense when the building was sold and the bonded debt was assumed by the purchaser.

In our opinion the revenue agent is in error in disallowing the deduction and in doing so is acting contrary to article 545 of treasury regulation 69. Neither of the arguments advanced by the revenue agent appears to us to be valid reason for disallowing the deduction.

You will understand, of course, that in expressing the foregoing opinion we

4

are simply passing on the principle involved, in the light of the facts presented in the letter. Naturally if there were any special circumstances which might be material to the question and are not brought out in the letter of your enquirer, it might be necessary to give further consideration to the question raised.

VALUATION OF GOODWILL

Q. We have a question of placing a valuation on the stock of a very prosperous city-directory publishing company, the stockholders of which are considering a proposition of selling their stock to a printing house which prints and binds their books, because the printing house figures that it is an ideal combination.

The only point that is of any special importance is the valuation of copyrights, trade-marks, and goodwill, and I am writing to ask you what rates, in your opinion, should be used.

It has been suggested that the average net tangible assets over a period of five years are entitled to earn about 8 per cent. and that the balance of the average net earnings should be capitalized at one of three rates, namely, 10, 12½, and 15 per cent. We are naturally anxious to place as good a valuation on the stock as can be done consistently, but we want to have your opinion so as to have some authority for the figures that are used and it would be very much appreciated if you would give us an opinion on this.

A. The valuation of goodwill, under the conditions described, is primarily a matter of judgment as to the stability of the profits. Although no definite and positive rule can be laid down by anyone, there are some precedents that carry great weight, especially those set up in computing taxes, where the government often has an interest in setting the value as low as possible and the taxpayer in setting it as high as possible. Some examples of decisions reached upon these valuations are to be found in Income-tax Procedure, Montgomery, pages 509 et seq. The treasury has held that in businesses that are "more or less stable" the goodwill should be capitalized at 15 per cent. after allowing 8 or 9 per cent. on tangible assets; that is to say, the value would be 6⅔ times that part of the profit for one year in excess of an 8 or 9 per cent. return on the net tangible assets. Other treasury methods of computing goodwill may be found on pages 512 et seq. of the book referred to above.

VALUATION OF LICENSED ABSTRACTORS' BUSINESS

Referring to the question and answer in Bulletin No. 30, we have received the following from a correspondent:

The questions relative to valuation of licensed abstractors' business, appearing in the special volume No. 30 are not, in my opinion, fully answered in the answers listed.

The question purely outlines how often at times, the public accountant's work touches that of an appraiser and how a theoretical answer must be qualified or adjusted to give effect to business conditions not clearly reflected by percentages or mathematical computation.

In the valuation of an abstract office, much weight must be given to the increase or decrease in property transfers, as set forth in the past, and what may reasonably be expected in the future. If the abstract office is covering a district that is undergoing a development that may be expected to increase rather than decrease, the matter of cost of establishing the basic books of the abstractor is of importance and should be taken in consideration, in my opinion, in addition to any goodwill earning power that the business has shown.

On the other hand, if the locality has been subject to a retarding movement and real estate transfers have shown little or no increase in volume with the

5

possibility of a small decrease, the previous earning power may, when capitalized, over-state the value.

This is a particular type of business where, in my opinion, it is incumbent upon the accountant to examine the business itself and its future prospects and until this has been done, the capitalizing of earning power is liable to be very misleading even when abnormally high or low years are excluded.

VERIFICATION OF CUSTOMERS' SECURITIES

Q. In the preparation of answers to the New York stock exchange questionnaire for brokers, we should appreciate it if you would advise us as to the detail of verification of customers' securities held by the broker.

We are particularly anxious to obtain information as to whether it is possible to obtain this information without listing in detail each customer and the security held by him.

A. The subject is governed by the printed regulations prescribed by the committee on business conduct of the New York stock exchange for audit under authority of chapter XV, section 2 of the rules adopted by the governing committee, pursuant to the constitution. These rules relate specifically to the questionnaire, and prescribe, in part, as follows:

"Ledger balances and securities shall be verified. Written confirmation of the following should be obtained."

Among the items listed thereunder are:

Customers' accounts:
    Ledger balance
    Securities long and short
    When issued contracts
    Open commodity contracts

The answers to the questions, therefore, are: (1) that customers' securities held by the broker require to be verified in detail, and (2) that listing in detail each customer and his securities is essential for that purpose.

The verification of customers' securities divides itself into two parts, namely, ownership and location.

Ownership is verified by sending to each customer a statement of his account as it stands on the broker's books and requesting confirmation of the money and security balances as at the date of the examination.

Location is verified by tracing the securities through the security-position records to their location as being either on hand, in loans, in transfer, or with other brokers, all of which are verified either by count or by confirmation.

The listing is usually made, for customers in the form of a trial balance, for securities on the confirmation forms.

In relation to customers' securities held in safekeeping, the regulations prescribe as follows:

"Securities in safekeeping shall be inspected and checked with the office record and a written confirmation obtained from the owner."

Here again the answers would, therefore, be the same.

6

American Institute of Accountants
Library and Bureau of Information

MARCH, 1929   SPECIAL BULLETIN No. 32

[The Committee on Administration of Endowment authorizes the publication of special Bulletins, of which this is one, on the distinct understanding that members are not to consider answers given to questions as being official pronouncements of the Institute, but merely the individual opinions of accountants to whom the questions were referred. It is earnestly requested that members criticize freely and constructively the answers given in this or any other Bulletin of this series.]

AMUSEMENT PARK ACCOUNTING

Q. I would be glad to receive any information regarding accounting for amusement parks, particularly whether or not such expenses as advertising, general management and general office expenses are pro-rated among the various devices. If this pro-ration is made, I would also like to know on what basis these expenses are divided among concessionaires—that is, where the park receives only a percentage of the gross receipts is the expense pro-rated to these concessions on the basis of gross receipts taken in by the concessions or on the percentage received by the park?

A. It has been my experience that the concessionaires pay to the park a percentage of their gross receipts and that they are not charged with any of the park's advertising, general management or office expenses.

If, however, in the case in question they are to be charged with a portion of these expenses, the lease or agreement covering the space which they occupy should fully cover the method of pro-ration or other basis of charge.

However, if it is the inquirer's intention to pro-rate in a statement to be prepared, a portion of the expenses against the percentage received from each concessionaire, to do so on the basis of the amount of the percentage received by the park from each concessionaire in relation to the total thus received is, perhaps, as good a way as any. However, it is quite arbitrary and it would seem to me more desirable to state the park's gross income from percentage received from concessionaires and deduct as general expenses all items of advertising, management, office expenses, etc., properly classified.

If, in peculiar circumstances it is desirable to pro-rate expenses against each concessionaire in a statement to be prepared even though the concessionaires are not actually charged therewith it might be advisable to consider pro-ration of the total cost of the upkeep of grounds, etc., on the basis of the space occupied by each concession as compared with the total space so occupied.

A. All amusement parks to a greater or less extent rent or lease out sub-concessions. In some cases the concessionaire pays the head office a percentage of his gross receipts in lieu of rent, or / and other overhead items, and in some cases the head office collects all of the money and returns to the concessionaire weekly or at other periods the amount originally collected by the head office less percentages, overheads, etc. In either case, and providing also for advertising, it is customary to compute the percentage for which each concessionaire is charged on a basis of the gross receipts.

Where concessions are leased to sub-concessionaires the percentage (or in some cases a flat rate) covers the general management and general office expenses. Where the company operates all of its concessions or "rides" the

1

general overhead consisting of advertising, general management, general office expenses, etc., are pro-rated to the various activities in proportion to the amount of gross receipts.

CALCULATION OF INTEREST

Q. A client of ours sends one foreign customer semi-annual statements of account, and a problem arises because of the present method of charging interest.

The customer is charged with merchandise shipped as of the shipment date.

He is also charged with interest from the due date of each bill to June 30th or December 31st, according to which statement is being prepared.

If the due date falls after June 30th on the mid-year statement, then he is credited with interest or anticipation from June 30th to due date.

He is credited with payments and, should they be anticipated, with interest thereon. He is credited with returns as of shipment date, and an attempt is made to adjust the interest charge correctly.

Here is the inconsistency which develops and I would like to be able to explain the fallacy or correct the form of statement. I will reduce my illustration to simplest possible terms as follows:

Statement June 30, 1928

Debit:
Invoice 1, shipped June 15, 1928, due November 1, 1928 $1,000.00
Credit:
Interest from June 30, 1928 to due date November 1, 1928
(4 months at 6%)...................................   20.00

Balance, July 1, 1928................................ $980.00

Statement December 31, 1928

Debit:
Balance of July 1, 1928............................. $980.00
No new charges....................................
Interest for 6 months at 6%........................   29.40

Total debit.. $1,009.40

Credit:
Invoice No. 1 returned............................. $1,000.00
Interest from November 1 (due date to December 31st, 2
months at 6%) 10.00

Total credit....................................... $1,010.00

By returning the goods, customer has gained 60 cents. Conceivably customer by buying tremendous quantities and returning all, would earn quite a sum.

Obviously our client's system of interest calculation is erroneous. Why? What change would you recommend?

A. As is apparent, the customer would gain 60 cents even though he returned the goods and was credited with precisely the same amount therefor as he was originally charged. An analysis of the statements, however, readily discloses the incorrect accounting on which the erroneous credit is based.

The credit for interest in the June statement, namely, 6% on the invoice price from June 30th to the due date, November 1st, is the full amount of interest which would be allowed the customer, provided he anticipated the payment for the whole period of 4 months. If he did not so anticipate the payment but settled on the due date, then the full amount of the invoice would

2

be payable. In brief, the interest shown on the June statement is a contingent credit only.

Now let us suppose that the customer settled on December 31st—two months after the due date. According to the agreed terms he should be charged with two months' interest; and since the customer has been credited, in anticipation, with four months' interest, he should now be charged with interest on the full amount of the shipment for six months, of which the proportion for four months is, in effect, the adjusting offset to the earlier anticipated credit, and the balance the interest actually chargeable.

In preparing the December statement, as shown in the question submitted, interest has been computed, in effect, thus:

Debit:
Interest on \$1,000.00 for 6 months at 6% $30.00
Credit:
Interest on \$20.00 for 6 months at 6% 60

Net debit $29.40

When, therefore, the customer is credited with the full amount of the returned shipment, his account incorrectly shows a credit of 60 cents by reason of the erroneous credit based on the amount of the interest anticipated at June 30th.

Answering the question, "What change would you recommend?" it would seem that the correct position could be readily determined at any time if the provisional interest items were recorded in separate columns of the customer's ledger account, making such adjustments as are necessary according as the customer wholly or partially actually does anticipate payments and extending only such interest as has actually accrued.

A. Manifestly, the method in use is fallacious, as demonstrated by our correspondent. It seems to us that the fallacy is easy to explain, since the customer is credited with interest on \$1,000 and charged with interest only on \$980; in other words, the customer gets the advantage of one-half year's interest on the amount of \$20 which is credited as interest. This whole thing appears to us to be unnecessarily cumbersome and futile. It would seem that interest should be charged only on past-due balances and credited only on anticipation.

CONSOLIDATED BALANCE-SHEET

Q. I would like to ask advice regarding the following:

Company "B" is incorporated with the following outstanding stock:
Class "A"—40,000 shares.
Class "B"—60,000 shares.
40,000 shares of class "B" are owned by company "A."

The class "A" has no voting power unless two years' dividends are in arrears, all voting power up until then being in class "B" stock. The class "A" is preferred as to dividends up to one dollar. Class "B" then receives a set amount and the class "A" then shares equally with the class "B" until the class "A" receives an additional dollar; thereafter all earnings go to class "B." Class "A" is convertible into class "B," three shares of class "A" into one of "B." The class "A" stock is redeemable at \$10.00 per share but in case of a voluntary or involuntary liquidation, both "A" and "B" stocks share alike.

The question is, can companies "A" and "B" be consolidated in preparing a balance-sheet where company "A" owns two thirds of the class "B" stock

3

and none of the "A" stock, giving it a total of two thirds of the voting or class "B" stock, or two fifths of the entire outstanding stock?

A. The consolidated balance-sheet is authorized by accounting and financial practice. It has no legal basis other than for tax purposes.

If the question refers to tax purposes the answer is No. Under the present law 95% ownership is required.

If the question refers to accounting and financial statement the only guide seems to be accounting and financial practice and custom, which makes a categorical answer scarcely possible.

The accounting theory of consolidation is that the facts of operation and management control. Where none but consolidated accounts would present a true picture of the enterprise as a whole the tendency is to consolidate. In our experience we have seldom found consolidation necessary to that purpose in cases of less than 75% ownership.

Indentures securing bonds often state the minimum ownership percentage which determines consolidation—varying from 75% to 90% or 95% or even 100%.

However, it is not solely the percentage which governs—elements of control, management and business and operating relation to the parent company modify the percentage figure. It is conceivable that a 51% ownership might warrant consolidation in one case whereas an 80% ownership in another case might not.

The question is further complicated by the fact that answer would depend upon whether company B's class A stock, with its possibilities of change, might properly be left out of consideration. If it could a 66⅔% ownership of the common would seem to warrant consolidation if the businesses are closely related.

If such case arose in our own practice we are inclined to think we would be guided by the simple rule that where consolidation is possible it should be made if demanded by the true situation of the enterprise as a whole.

A. In the circumstances stated we would recommend that the subsidiary companies' accounts should not be consolidated and in that connection it might be well to quote from the revenue act of 1928 as follows:

"Under the revenue act of 1928, 95% of ownership is required for consolidation."

The question discussed by your correspondent is covered in Dickinson's *Accounting Practice and Procedure* on page 182 under the heading of "What is a constituent company?" and in Montgomery's *Auditing Theory and Practice* on page 388 under the heading of "Definition of subsidiary."

COST OF ENGRAVINGS TO LITHOGRAPHERS

Q. A controversy has arisen between one of my clients and the revenue agents as to the proper procedure in charging off the cost of engravings on stones used by a lithographing company.

The revenue agents say frankly that all their files show that there has been no uniform practice in this matter either as to whether all the cost is charged off to expense or whether some of it is capitalized with depreciation figured. The client is more concerned about handling this matter in the approved method than he is about the effect on income taxes and the revenue agents seem equally willing to abide by the usual practice.

A. We have as a client a firm of lithographers doing a very large business. We have been handling the accounts for a period of ten years.

It is the firm's practice to include in its estimate when bidding on work the cost of engravings on stones, and therefore this cost is billed to the customer and paid for by him.

All of these years the bureau of internal revenue has ruled that this is the

4

proper procedure. It has been our client's custom for a period of forty or fifty years.

We have been informed by our client that some lithographers capitalize the engravings on stones as goodwill. Our client has at the present time some $2,000,000 worth of stones in the basement of the plant, which could be capitalized as goodwill in case the business was sold.

A. We do not know the uniform practice of lithographing companies with respect to the manner in which they handle their engraving-stone account but one of our clients who has quite a large business here, has two separate accounts, one covering the cost of the stones which are imported from Belgium and which are depreciated at the rate of 10% per annum and the other account covering the cost of engraving the stones.

In cases where the engraving on the stone is of such a nature that the company will not receive a repeat order, the entire cost of the engraving is immediately charged to the job. In cases where stones are engraved for cards, letterheads, etc., for which the company will receive further orders in the future, 25% of the engraving cost is immediately charged to the job and the balance is deferred over a period of years based upon the quantity ordered by each customer. This may be a spread of anywhere from four to ten years.

In case the customer wishes to change the design or the engraving, then the amount which is in the deferred-charge account relating to the old stone, is taken out and the cost of the new engraving stated in its place.

DEPRECIATION OF OFFICE BUILDING AND EQUIPMENT

Q. A client of mine is having some difficulty with the internal revenue bureau on the question of proper depreciation of office buildings, accessories and equipment.

It is requested that if possible you secure information regarding what is considered reasonable depreciation on such office buildings. The accounts of the client are well kept and are segregated into the following items:

> Building, ten story, light steel and concrete, first-floor stores, balance offices, erected 1925–1926.
> Plumbing in building.
> Electric wiring and fixtures (not including elevators).
> Elevators, five, all passenger, 3000 pounds capacity, including motors and cables.
> Refrigerating system (for circulating ice water, not including water piping and outlets).
> Water system, for circulating ice water only.
> Linoleum floor covering. Practically all halls and all offices have floors covered with high grade heavy linoleum. (Due to climatic conditions the item of dry rot must be considered. This linoleum laid direct on concrete floor.
> Venetian blinds.
> Signs and directories. (All of most modern type.)
> Office partitions. (Frame and glass, removable.)

In considering this item of depreciation the following local conditions must be considered: First the fact that Miami is within three miles of the ocean and that the Biscayne Bay is within one half mile of the building. Therefore the effect of salt air must be taken into consideration. All window frames are of steel and the action of rust on those and on cables and all other metals in the building must be considered. The local water used in the city is highly chlorinated and in its original state contains a percentage of salt which affects all plumbing, etc.

If you can furnish me with any help in this matter it will be appreciated. Our position down here is peculiar—we have no background on which to esti-

5

mate such depreciation. All of the office buildings here were built during 1924–1926 and we have no experience.

A. I would preface my remarks by the observation which seems to be supported by the experts, by whom I mean practical construction engineers, that it is almost impossible to apply any general rule as to depreciation on all the buildings of a particular type in Miami, and this observation would be particularly applicable to the class of building described in the inquiry as "ten story light steel and concrete." This description, by the way, would be considered by practical engineers as extremely vague and would give rise to such questions as "Are the joints completely covered or only partly so?" "Are the concrete floors laid on plaster or are they laid on metal lathes?" Again it would be asked, "What do you mean by light steel and concrete?" as this definition might apply to a reinforced concrete building.

For the purpose of an answer we will assume that what is meant is a ten-story building with a light steel framework, and let us say poured concrete walls. It is noted further that the building was erected in 1925–1926, during which years not only was the cost of construction about 50% higher than the replacement cost today, but also many buildings (among which may be numbered the office building from which this is written) were hastily and indifferently built, and the specifications certainly did not provide either architecturally or from an engineer's viewpoint for perfect buildings of their respective class.

Considering depreciation, not so much in its relation to the amount which a taxpayer may possibly be allowed to deduct from gross income in respect thereof, but as the gradual reduction in the value of property due to physical deterioration, exhaustion, wear and tear through use in trade or business, I do not believe that outside of the Court House, the Ingraham Building, and possibly the Congress Building, that there is any office building in Miami with a prospective lifetime of over 25 years from the time of construction. By this I mean that any conservative owner (quite apart from its effect on deductions from gross income for income tax) in setting up a replacement fund would consider that there should be added to reserve for depreciation each year 4% of the cost of the building.

In the case of most buildings of this class in Miami, however, the greatest difficulty would be encountered in obtaining from the bureau of internal revenue an allowance in respect of depreciation exceeding 2% to 2½% of the cost of the building. My experience, however, as stated, is that no general rule can be applied and that the depreciation on each building should be considered on its merits irrespective of and without relation to the fact that the building is of a type of construction similar to other buildings in Miami.

Assuming, however, that the building is of perfect construction of the type indicated, viz.: 10 story light steel frame concrete with proper provision for windbracing and of the best material obtainable with proper regard for the action of the weather, there is little doubt that such a structure would have a lifetime of at least 50 years. This statement, of course, presupposes that the peculiar local conditions such as high winds and the erosive action of the salt water can be provided for.

I do not believe, however, that with the exception of the two office buildings mentioned and the Court House (which is a public building) there is any office building in Miami that would qualify under the specifications outlined in the preceding paragraph.

For the other office buildings in Miami, while I am reluctant to express an opinion which would indicate the possibility of a rule applicable to any particular type of construction, I do not believe there is one with a prospective lifetime exceeding 25 to 30 years.

Plumbing: With reference to plumbing, if the most modern equipment is used, there seems to be no reason why this should not endure as long as the structure.

6

Electric Wiring and Fixtures: The fixtures should last as long as the structure. With reference to connections, however, the action of the air of Miami on all rubber insulations and coverings is very corrosive. With proper protection, however, the wiring should be good for 20 years.

Elevators: Elevators deteriorate very rapidly in this climate. It is believed, however, that it is customary for manufacturers to keep these in repair for an annual service charge, so that assuming that this periodic overhaul is adopted, the lifetime of an elevator of the class indicated should be at least 15 years.

Refrigerating System: Probable lifetime 10 years. Action of acid and weather abnormal.

Water System: For circulating ice water only. Excessive lime in the water. Probable lifetime ten years.

Linoleum: Probable lifetime not in excess of 5 years under most favorable conditions.

Venetian Blinds The action of the air on tape very erosive. Blinds should be rebuilt every five years.

Signs and Directories: 20 years' life.

Office Partitions: 10 years.

Speculation as to the probable lifetime of a depreciable asset is more a subject for a professional engineer than for an accountant, and in setting up a reserve for depreciation I have never hesitated to avail myself of the opinion of the former rather than to rely on my own judgment.

It is a matter for comment that the depreciation rates allowable by the bureau are not more flexible, and that there is too much tendency to classify. In other words, assuming that the bureau rate for machinery is 10%, and I have a machine, therefore the lifetime of my machine is ten years.

A. Building, ten story, light steel and concrete, first floor stores, balance offices, erected 1925–26—estimated useful life—40 years.

Plumbing in building—20 years.

Electric wiring and fixtures (not including elevators)—10 years.

Elevators, five, all passenger, 3000 pounds capacity, including motors and cables—cars, tracks, 15 years; motors, pulleys—7 years.

Refrigerating system (for circulating ice water, not including water piping and outlets)—7 years.

Water system, for circulating ice water only—20 years.

Linoleum floor covering. Practically all halls and all offices have floors covered with high grade heavy linoleum. (Due to climatic conditions the item of dry rot must be considered. This linoleum laid direct on concrete floor.) If cemented and shellacked—8 years; if not both—5 years.

Venetian blinds—4 years.

Signs and directories all of most modern type—10 years.

Office partitions (frame and glass, removable)—10 years.

PAYROLL BOOK AS EVIDENCE

Q. In a case now being argued before a referee, we are claiming that a payroll book is a book of account and we need support in this statement. To put this matter before you clearly I quote below a paragraph I have prepared for my brief:

"The payroll book was the book of original entry kept by the company for the particular purpose of recording the amount of wages paid to each employee. It was a time book, kept in tabular form and it showed in an intelligible manner the number of days of labor of each employee and the amount earned for the week. Same was written up in the customary and regular way by the company's employee having this duty to perform. It was written up at the time—namely July 2 to 6, 1927."

7

Counsel opposing me on this matter are claiming that the payroll book is not a book of account as commonly understood, but they are unable to define exactly what particular books the term "book of account" includes. They picture a ledger, cashbook and a journal, and being lawyers their vision goes no further. As you know modern bookkeeping includes, under the description of "book of account," such books as sales book, purchase book, voucher register and many others, each one of which contributes its respective part in a modern bookkeeping system.

The question I am asking help on is this. Has there been any official determination on this point by our profession?

Am having some search made for possible legal determination on this point, but the nearest I have found was one that states that the "book of account," to be accepted as evidence, must be a book of original entry. The payroll book in question was certainly the book of original entry.

A. While I have no doubt in my own mind that a payroll book is a book of account, I had difficulty in finding confirmation. I have now ascertained that *"The Accountant Law Reports"* of July 31, 1909 (page 22), reported a case tried before the court of criminal appeal, in London, on July 16 and 17, 1909. In this case it was held that a taximeter record and the machine itself were accounts, just as much as a ledger and day book. This decision would apply with at least equal force to a payroll book. The report in question is as follows:

COURT OF CRIMINAL APPEAL

July 16 and 17, 1909
(Before Lord Alverstone, C. J., Darling and Jelf, JJ.)
Rex v. *Solomons*

Falsification of accounts—Taximeter—Account—Master and servant—Falsification of accounts act, 1875 (38 and 39 Vict. c. 24) S. I.
Larceny act 1901 (I Edw. VII, c. 10).

The appellant was a taximeter cab driver, and had been in the habit of taking out one of the cabs belonging to the General Motor Cab Company. He had been convicted of falsifying the taximeter, by driving fares, from whom he had taken money, without putting down the flag which set the taximeter at work. There were also charges under the larceny act, 1901. It appeared that on a consecutive number of days the appellant had driven two music-hall artists from one music hall to another and back, without putting the flag of the taximeter down. For each journey he was paid 9s., which was less than the amount that the taximeter would have registered had it been working. At the end of the day, it was customary for the drivers of cabs belonging to the company to sign a paper, which was an account of the day's takings, recorded by the taximeter clerk, from the figures registered by the taximeter itself. Of the amount so registered and checked, the driver was entitled to one-quarter and the company three-quarters. It was contended for the appellant upon appeal against conviction that there was no contract of service between him and the company. It was true that there were various notices and regulations concerning the drivers, one of which was to the effect that a driver who absented himself, without special need, for more than twenty-four hours was liable to instant dismissal, which might suggest a contract of service. On the other hand, there were other matters to show that there was no such contract, such as the lack of any control by the company over the drivers, once the cabs had left the company's premises. Drivers could go where they pleased and were subject to no orders. The common sergeant had told the jury that he had grave doubt as to whether the appellant was a servant within the act dealing with falsification. For the crown, in respect only of the question as to whether a taximeter was an account, it was contended that a taximeter machine was an account within the act of 1875. There was nothing in the statute to show that

8

an account must be on paper. The machine on one side had a record of the number of miles run, which record, in this case, was untrue. The number of miles traversed would show how much the driver ought to have received. The paper, drawn up by the clerk, was copied from the machine, and both paper and machine were accounts, just as much as a ledger and day book.

JUDGMENT

Held that an offense was committed when the taximeter, which was an account within the meaning of the act, was falsified; that the appellant, being a servant of the company, was rightly convicted of falsification under the act of 1875; and that, therefore, the appeal must be dismissed. (127 L.T. 291.)

A. We do not know of any official determination by an authoritative body of accountants on this point. However, we feel sure that all accountants would agree that the payroll book was a book of account. This must be true because in most instances it is the only book in which the individual account with the employee is kept. It is a book of original entry and supports the wages paid which are shown only in total in other books of account including the general ledger. It, therefore, affords the supporting detail for the wages account in the general ledger.

We note that counsel opposing the questioner apparently agrees that a journal is a book of account. It should be remembered that such books as the cashbook, voucher register and payroll book are nothing more or less than journals. These books have been developed as a matter of expediency and economy in operation to record items of like nature. The payroll book, besides containing the account with each employee in terms of hours or days of service, also contains the amount to be paid to each employee. Obviously, the amount due each employee could be made the subject of a journal entry in the general journal whereby wages would be charged and the employee credited. This would be a wasteful process and for this reason the payroll book is adopted, but nevertheless the theory is the same and the payroll book is merely a journal in which a record is made of the amount to be charged to wages and to be credited to the individual employee.

We are quite sure that the court would put an interpretation in defining books of account which would include the payroll book.

A. From my experience of thirty years in practice I should say that the payroll—sometimes prepared on a loose sheet and subsequently bound in book form, or entered originally in a bound book—has always been regarded as the original record or compilation of a firm's or corporation's purchase of services, and, as such, stands on an equal footing with the purchase book or register containing the record of the purchases of material and supplies.

Many works on accounting support this view; and, just to mention a few, I refer to *Modern Accounting Systems*, by Gordon and Lockwood, of the Wharton School of Accounting and Finance, published by John Wiley and Son. See paragraph on "Labor," page 355 of that work; also see "Summary of accounting records" on pages 322 and 323.

I also refer to the book on *Street Railway Accounting*, published by the Ronald Press in 1917 and written by I. A. May, C. P. A., and vice-president of the American Electric Railway Accountants Association. His book contains several references to payroll accounting; one which should prove useful to you is the paragraph entitled "Approving payrolls" on page 159 of that work.

To turn to English writers, I refer to the work *Factory Accounting*, which has long been a standard. The authors are Emile Garcke, managing director of the British Electric Traction Co., Ltd., and J. M. Fels, an incorporated accountant of England. This work was published by the McGraw-Hill Publishing Company of New York in 1912. The pages in this book, 35 to 45, show conclusively

9

that the payroll record, or wages book, as it is called, is an essential original record of any labor-employing organization.

See also the book entitled *Contractors Accounting Practice* by William M. Affelder, Comptroller of Thompson-Starrett Company, New York, published by the Ronald Press in 1924. This book contains many references to, and shows the reliance placed upon, the original record of wages paid as recorded in the payroll. I refer particularly to page 38 and pages 92 to 96.

SUGAR REFINERY PROBLEM

Q. Could you advise me the usual or scientific method of charging off what is known in sugar refineries as "bone-black" or "char."

I understand that char is used for filtration and purification purposes in the refining of raw sugar and that it is used over and over again with the aid of regeneration materials for from three to five years when its life or value would have been exhausted. The cost to revivify is known as char regeneration expense.

A. The handling of bone-black on the books of a refinery with which we are familiar is as follows:

Two accounts are maintained: (a) "bone-black," and (b) "bone-black in filters." Assuming that a new filter is installed, the original charge of bone-black would be transferred from (a) to (b) account above, at the cost of the new bone-black.

After a filter has been in use for a time, it is necessary to revivify the char or bone-black. This is done by burning the bone-black in a kiln, and the cost of this burning is charged to the expense account, "Kiln-men and char handlers."

After the burning, the residue is replaced in the filter, and a certain amount of new bone-black is added to the filter to take the place of that which has disintegrated in the burning. The cost of this new bone-black is again transferred from the (a) account above to (b). During the year the account "Bone-black in filters" is credited, and cost of operations debited with an amount equal to one cent per every hundred pounds of raw sugars melted and passed through the filters.

Thus at the end of the year the balance standing in "Bone-black in filters" account has been reduced by the difference between this one cent per pound of sugar melted, and the charges for additional bone-black added during the year.

After a certain time, the bone-black in the filter reaches a state where it can no longer be used. This bone-black has a certain value as fertilizer, and is so sold under chemical analysis.

TAXES ON COAL MINES

Q. I would be interested to have an expression of opinion from some of the members of the Institute as to (1) the propriety of a coal mining company's charging to property account, rather than to operating expenses, taxes on those lands of the company which are undeveloped and therefore not yet being operated, and (a) whether they know of any actual cases, either in the anthracite or bituminous fields, of companies' treating as capital expenditures taxes on undeveloped coal lands.

A. (1) I am fully on record as believing that it is a proper procedure for a company to charge directly to property account or indirectly through a development account, all expenses connected with the opening up and development of mining property prior to its reaching what might be termed an operating basis. This principle, I believe, can properly be applied regardless of whether the expenditures thus made are such as should be considered applicable to the entire property (as taxes on such lands would be) or whether they were expenditures applicable to a certain part only of the property as certain phases of underground development might be. The distinction would be that those which applied to the entire property would be written off over the entire production tonnage of the property, whereas those which benefited only a certain limited

10

-328-

tonnage would be written off as applicable to that limited tonnage. The question of proper basis in any case is a rather long question which I am not trying here to discuss.

Unfortunately, however, the revenue department and the board of tax appeals have held that, regardless of what may be proper commercial accounting, the revenue act provides that taxes and interest are to be deducted in the year in which the expenses accrue, and therefore a deduction of taxes cannot be carried forward to be written off against the operations of a subsequent year. These decisions might perhaps be modified under section 200 (d) of the revenue act of 1926, with its provision that "The deductions and credits provided for in this title shall be taken for the taxable year in which paid or accrued' or 'paid or incurred' . . . unless in order to clearly reflect the income the deductions or credits should be taken as of a different period." Just what this means and who is to decide whether or not "the deductions or credits should be taken as of a different period" is an interesting question which I suppose will one of these days be finally decided.

On the face of it, it would seem to be decided as to non-producing mines by article 222 of *Regulations 69*, which reads in part:

"All expenditures in excess of net receipts from minerals sold shall be charged to capital account recoverable through depletion while the mine is in the development stage."

This would seem clearly to put the department's sanction on capitalizing "all expenditures," but knowing how prone the department is offhand to change its regulations at any time, and also knowing how ready congress is to change the law itself from time to time, it might prove that even though the commissioner might on the basis of this regulation deny a deduction for taxes in the year in which paid or accrued, this would not give any assurance that such taxes would later be considered as part of the capitalized costs to be written off after the property reached a producing stage.

Accordingly, the taxpayer seems to be in the position that if he does not claim these deductions at the present time he will be told some years from now that he has lost his right to deduct them when paid or accrued and has no right to deduct them in a subsequent year.

Of course, if a company owns only a single non-producing property and has no income from which it could make deductions currently, it will probably lose nothing by capitalizing the items and including taxes as part of the capital cost to be written off pro rata to mineral extraction.

The question directs itself solely to "the propriety" of the procedure and I have expressed quite clearly that I believe it is proper to capitalize such expenditures and have pointed out that the regulations recognize it as proper. I mention the tax situation, however, because I think it is proper for an accountant, in recommending accounting procedure, to take into account the question of whether or not this procedure will involve his company in tax payments which might, by a somewhat different procedure, be avoided.

(2) I think I have said enough above to indicate that it is quite a recognized procedure for mining companies, both as to coal and other minerals, to treat taxes as capital expenditures, as authorized by article 222 of *Regulations 69*, as well as in prior regulations. I think, however, that at the present time probably a majority of the companies are currently deducting as an expense all taxes which they pay because they are afraid that unless they do this they may never receive the benefit of any such deduction.

I think it is understood that I am not trying to advise the procedure to be followed in any particular instance, because I believe it is fully understood that in attempting to answer questions of this kind no accountant can possibly try to give such advice without a much more complete statement of the facts than is contained in the questions submitted.

11

A. It is proper for a coal mining company to charge to a subsidiary account of the property account taxes on lands of the company which are undeveloped and not operated or used, to be charged off from the tonnage extracted when the mines are opened.

We do not know of any instance, however, where coal companies do this. It is not considered practical because there is always a certain amount of the coal lands undeveloped and a division of the taxes between the two classes of land has never been made by any of the coal companies we have examined.

USE OF TERM "WORKING CAPITAL"

Q. I wish to find authority for the proper use of the term "working capital" as used in a prospective balance-sheet prepared for the purpose of reorganization. A specific example would be in the case of a going company which decides additional capital is necessary. The company's balance-sheet is reconstructed indicating how it will appear after the financing is completed. A portion of the new capital is used to pay off present indebtedness, the remaining part of the new capital secured is set up in the current asset position on the balance-sheet and labeled "Working capital."

A. We have to advise you that we do not know of any authoritative source in which the term is defined in the sense you require.

Our own view is that working capital is that part of the proceeds of a capital issue which is not immediately applied in the reduction of capital, or other liabilities, but is permitted to remain in the form of funds for such current uses as may be required in the operation of the business. In other words, a corporation might sell an issue of preferred shares for $1,000,000; use $800,000 to pay off a bond and mortgage on its land and buildings, and keep the remainder in current funds for the purpose of buying additional raw materials, or meeting the payrolls, or settling other current liabilities, as the current transaction of business might require.

The textbooks usually define working capital as net current assets, although the courts have from time to time placed different interpretations upon the term. In such cases the application of the term usually has been restricted to cash.

A. The term "working capital" as ordinarily used is synonymous with the term "net current assets"; that is to say, it is the excess of the current assets over the current liabilities. In the illustration given in your letter it might be perfectly proper to set up the remaining part of the new capital secured in the current-assets section of the balance-sheet, but instead of the term "working capital" there might have been used some such term as "cash provided for additional working capital."

The custom, however, is to state in the head of a balance-sheet giving effect to new financing a summary of the changes which have been given effect to in the balance-sheet, and to cover the question in some such language as the following:

"Balance-sheet
As at . . . .
(Giving effect as at that date to the provisions of the agreement dated . . . . for the sale of $. . . . .% first-mortgage bonds and the application of the proceeds thereof to the retirement of current indebtedness and as additional working capital)"

It is then customary in the balance-sheet itself to add the amount provided as additional working capital into the cash balance and to show the item just as "Cash, $. . . . ."

If the method adopted by your correspondent, however, is followed, the application is just as clear if the alternative terms suggested above are used in place of the bare words "working capital."

12

American Institute of Accountants

Library and Bureau of Information

DECEMBER, 1929   SPECIAL BULLETIN No. 33

[The Committee on Administration of Endowment authorizes the publication of special Bulletins, of which this is one, on the distinct understanding that members are not to consider answers given to questions as being official pronouncements of the Institute, but merely the individual opinions of accountants to whom the questions were referred. It is earnestly requested that members criticise freely and constructively the answers given in this or any other Bulletin of this series.]

STOCK DIVIDENDS

Question. I should be glad to have the opinion of some leading members of the Institute on the proper treatment of stock dividends received from companies which make a practice of declaring such dividends regularly in lieu of cash dividends, such, for instance, as Goldman Sachs Trading Company, North American Company, and South Eastern Power and Light Company.

Answer. I am in receipt of your letter transmitting an inquiry from a member of the Institute regarding the proper accounting treatment of stock dividends received from corporations which declare such dividends regularly in lieu of cash dividends. This is a question of growing importance upon which some difference of opinion exists.

The first view is that such dividends should be treated in the same way as other stock dividends and should not be regarded as in any part a proper credit to income. As is well known, the question in regard to stock dividends in general was before the supreme court and that court felt that the dividends were so clearly not income that it must hold the taxation of them as income to be unconstitutional.

The second view is that such dividends are income to the extent that they represent a capitalization of earnings. It is pointed out that a stock dividend produces substantially the same effects as the payment of a cash dividend and a contemporaneous subscription to capital stock. In the stock dividend cases, however, the court held that the two forms of transactions were not identical and in any case the difference in form might quite properly justify a difference in the taxable status.

A third point of view has been advanced that periodical stock dividends are income to the extent of the market value of the stock distributed. Where, however, the market value exceeds the amount capitalized by the payor corporation in respect of the dividend this course seems clearly to involve the treatment of unrealized appreciation as a credit to income contrary to all established accounting principles.

In my judgment the soundest policy is to take no credit to income for stock dividends received, whether the dividends are irregular or periodical. I believe, however, that a substantial argument can be advanced in favor of treating periodical stock dividends as income when received to the extent of the earnings represented thereby; that is to say, the amount of earnings per share capitalized by the paying corporation in respect of the dividend.

In order to answer your correspondent's question completely it is perhaps necessary to consider the treatment of a sale of stock received as a stock divi-

1

dend. If no credit is taken to income account when a stock dividend is received the cost per share of the total stock held is reduced by reason of the increase in the number of shares held. On a subsequent sale of any of the stock the profit or loss is determined by the reduced cost and enters into the account under the heading of "Profits and losses on sales of securities." If a dividend is treated as income when received to the extent of the earnings capitalized in respect thereof, this credit goes to income account under the heading of "Dividends received," and the asset account on the books is increased correspondingly. A new book value per share is thus determined and forms the basis of a computation of profit or loss on the subsequent sale of the stock. In cases where the distinction between interest and dividend account in profits on sales of securities is of importance, this latter treatment probably results in a fairer apportionment between the two classes of income. I am altogether opposed to crediting income with the market value of dividend stock as and when received, since, as stated above, this involves the inclusion of unrealized appreciation in the income account.

Answer. It is assumed that the question relates to corporate accounting and not to the accounts of individuals.

The proper treatment of stock dividends received in cases in which the distribution of such dividends in effect represents the capitalization of the current income, in the opinion of the writer, is, first, to value the shares of dividend stock received under a specific authorization by the board of directors upon a basis bearing some definite relation to the market value of such stock after the date of record for the stock dividend, and to credit the amount of such valuation to income account as stock dividends received.

The relation, which the price used in such valuation should bear to market must depend upon the judgment of the directors. The market price used as the basis should not be the price for any one day but should represent a fair average of several days. Sufficient margin should be provided by means of a reserve or otherwise between market price and the valuation at which the shares are set up to cover the amount of income tax payable upon the additional profit which would result from a sale of the entire investment due to the receipt of the shares in question. Such a reserve may be unnecessary if the original holding is carried at a value very much below the market for such shares over an extended period. The directors must also decide whether the market price following the record date for the dividend is unduly affected by abnormal conditions.

Second, in stating the income account, the item of stock dividends should be shown specifically with a general indication as to the basis of valuation; as for example, "Stock dividends received taken at average market prices following the dates of record for such dividends." If the amount of stock dividends received is comparatively small, they may be included with other income from investments, which in that case, however, should be described as "(Including stock dividends valued at $—— taken at market prices following the dates of record for such dividends.)"

Answer. This question should be viewed from two angles: first, that of taxes and, second, that of sound accounting principles. From neither viewpoint do I see any reason for departure from the usual method of treating stock dividends. The fact that they are considered in lieu of cash dividends does not seem to me to be pertinent. Actually, the investment of the owner in stocks of each of these companies has not changed and is merely represented by a greater number of certificates. Realization of any income or profit on the investment is postponed until some of the stock is sold or until the payment of cash dividends is begun. The only entries necessary, to my mind, in connection with these divi-

2

dends is an historical entry increasing the number of shares representing the investment but not in any way altering the dollar value at which such investment appears. Of course, if any part of the stock received as dividends is sold, then it is necessary to determine the proper proportion of cost applicable to the shares sold and in that connection, for tax purposes, the stock dividends must be apportioned ratably among the various purchases of the stock on which it is declared in the event that the investment represented a succession of separate purchases.

Answer. When stock is received as a dividend representing a distribution of current earnings, and such stock is sold, it seems to be the consensus of opinion at this time that the proceeds can properly be treated as income, but of course it is more conservative to take into income only the excess of the proceeds of sale over the average cost of all the shares held, including the dividend stock at no value. In any event, the relation of the book value of the unsold stock to its market value must not be overlooked.

When the stock is not sold, there are three alternatives as to the amount at which it may be taken up on the books as an asset and credited to income: (1) at no value; (2) at the amount charged by the issuing company against its surplus; (3) at market value. Obviously, in many cases the first of these alternatives would constitute an unnecessary hardship on the recipient. At the other extreme is the third method. This practice is, of course, in conflict with the traditional accounting theory that profits should not be taken up until realized, but in some cases it appears to be justified. It would seem that the second alternative is the most logical. The theory is that stock dividends from earnings should be valued by the recipient the same as by the issuing company (as in the case of cash dividends), for the reason that the same amount is received by the recipient as is parted with by the issuing company; namely, the amount charged against the surplus of the issuing company, however arbitrary that may be in the case of dividends paid in stock.

It should be borne in mind that all the foregoing applies only to stock dividends representing distributions of earnings, and not to so-called "split-ups". While it is rather indefinite, it is all that we are prepared to say on the subject at present, in view of its controversial nature.

Answer. A short outline of the procedure in the case of the North American Company will serve as an illustration in our consideration of such stock dividends as are referred to in the question.

For a number of years that company, instead of paying cash dividends on its common stock, has paid regular quarterly dividends in common stock at the rate of 2½% per quarter.

The common stock, which is listed on the New York stock exchange, has no par value. During the year 1928 the quoted market price ranged from 58 to 97. During 1929 the price has ranged from 66½ to 186.

The company's earnings for 1928 equaled $4.68 per share on the average number of shares outstanding, but by selling his dividend stock at, say, the middle price, 77½, a stockholder would realize $7.75 per share.

The effect of the dividend policy is, then, that the company retains the whole of its earnings for the further development of its business and properties, while the stockholder who sells his dividend stock receives in cash considerably more per share than he could receive from a distribution in cash of the entire earnings for the year. On selling his dividend stock the equity of the stockholder is reduced since his proportionate share diminishes as the outstanding stock is increased. There should be no reduction in the earnings per share so long as the rate of earnings on the additional capital provided out of profits is not less than that on the original capital. The dividend policy

3

has been effective since October 1923; the following figures are therefore **of** interest:

Earnings per share on common stock outstanding at the end of the year	1928	1927	1926	1925	1924
	$4.51	3.86	3.85	3.12	3.16

Finally, the dividends are charged against surplus at the former par value of the stock, namely, $10.00 per share—the common stock having been changed from par to no par in April, 1927.

Having thus reviewed the dividend policy, it may be at once remarked that the proceeds of the dividend stock do not represent dividends on investment. The policy has been described as being in effect a combination of cash dividends and subscription rights. The latter, it seems clear, is an important factor. In brief, a stockholder selling his dividend stock is realizing a part of his equity and capitalizing a portion of his possible future cash dividends. Any accounting to be correct must take cognizance of this feature.

Answering the question specifically: the dividends referred to, I consider, should be treated by a recipient in the same way as any other stock dividend, that is, to increase the number of shares held without any change in the aggregate value of the investment, the average cost per share being thus reduced.

No income accrues to the stockholder merely by receipt of the dividend stock; income—or it may be a loss—results only as the stock is realized. Even where there is an immediate cash realization of dividend stock, only that portion of the proceeds is attributable to income which is in excess or defect of the average cost of the stock including the dividend stock then sold.

Answer. Stock dividends from the companies mentioned are supposed to be paid from current income. If not sold, they are not taxable. If sold, they are taxable according to a formula which may be found in Montgomery's *Income Tax Procedure.* As far as current income accounts are concerned, I see no objection to entering the market value of the stock dividends as income on the date of receipt, assuming, of course, that the current earnings of the companies paying the dividends are sufficient to justify the distributions and assuming further that the market prices of the stocks are no more affected by the distribution of the stock dividends than is usually the case in the distribution of cash dividends.

I would suggest to your correspondent that a year or so ago an editorial and several letters appeared in *The Journal of Accountancy* discussing the stock-dividend methods of the North American Company.

4

THE DEVELOPMENT OF
CONTEMPORARY ACCOUNTING THOUGHT

An Arno Press Collection

Baldwin, H[arry] G[len]. **Accounting for Value As Well as Original Cost** *and* Castenholz, William B. **A Solution to the Appreciation Problem.** 2 Vols. in 1. 1927/1931

Baxter, William. **Collected Papers on Accounting.** 1978

Brief, Richard P., Ed. **Selections from Encyclopaedia of Accounting, 1903.** 1978

Broaker, Frank and Richard M. Chapman. **The American Accountants' Manual.** 1897

Canning, John B. **The Economics of Accountancy.** 1929

Chatfield, Michael, Ed. **The English View of Accountant's Duties and Responsibilities.** 1978

Cole, William Morse. **The Fundamentals of Accounting.** 1921

Congress of Accountants. **Official Record of the Proceedings of the Congress of Accountants.** 1904

Cronhelm, F[rederick] W[illiam]. **Double Entry by Single.** 1818

Davidson, Sidney. **The Plant Accounting Regulations of the Federal Power Commission.** 1952

De Paula, F[rederic] R[udolf] M[ackley]. **Developments in Accounting.** 1948

Epstein, Marc Jay. **The Effect of Scientific Management on the Development of the Standard Cost System** (Doctoral Dissertation, University of Oregon, 1973). 1978

Esquerré, Paul-Joseph. **The Applied Theory of Accounts.** 1914

Fitzgerald, A[dolf] A[lexander]. **Current Accounting Trends.** 1952

Garner, S. Paul and Marilynn Hughes, Eds. **Readings on Accounting Development.** 1978

Haskins, Charles Waldo. **Business Education and Accountancy.** 1904

Hein, Leonard William. **The British Companies Acts and the Practice of Accountancy 1844-1962** (Doctoral Dissertation, University of California, Los Angeles, 1962). 1978

Hendriksen, Eldon S. **Capital Expenditures in the Steel Industry, 1900 to 1953** (Doctoral Dissertation, University of California, Berkeley, 1956). 1978

Holmes, William, Linda H. Kistler and Louis S. Corsini. **Three Centuries of Accounting in Massachusetts.** 1978

Horngren, Charles T. **Implications for Accountants of the Uses of Financial Statements by Security Analysts** (Doctoral Dissertation, University of Chicago, 1955). 1978

Horrigan, James O., Ed. **Financial Ratio Analysis—An Historical Perspective.** 1978

Jones, [Edward Thomas]. **Jones's English System of Book-keeping.** 1796

Lamden, Charles William. **The Securities and Exchange Commission** (Doctoral Dissertation, University of California, Berkeley, 1949). 1978

Langer, Russell Davis. **Accounting As A Variable in Mergers** (Doctoral Dissertation, University of California, Berkeley, 1976). 1978

Lewis, J. Slater. **The Commercial Organisation of Factories.** 1896

Littleton, A[nanias] C[harles] and B[asil] S. Yamey, Eds. **Studies in the History of Accounting.** 1956

Mair, John. **Book-keeping Moderniz'd.** 1793

Mann, Helen Scott. **Charles Ezra Sprague.** 1931

Marsh, C[hristopher] C[olumbus]. **The Theory and Practice of Bank Book-keeping.** 1856

Mitchell, William. **A New and Complete System of Book-keeping by an Improved Method of Double Entry.** 1796

Montgomery, Robert H. **Fifty Years of Accountancy.** 1939

Moonitz, Maurice. **The Entity Theory of Consolidated Statements.** 1951

Moonitz, Maurice, Ed. **Three Contributions to the Development of Accounting Thought.** 1978

Murray, David. **Chapters in the History of Bookkeeping, Accountancy & Commercial Arithmetic.** 1930

Nicholson, J[erome] Lee. **Cost Accounting.** 1913

Paton, William Andrew and Russell Alger Stevenson. **Principles of Accounting.** 1918

Pixley, Francis W[illiam]. **The Profession of a Chartered Accountant and Other Lectures.** 1897

Preinreich, Gabriel A. D. **The Nature of Dividends.** 1935

Previts, Gary John, Ed. **Early 20th Century Developments in American Accounting Thought.** 1978

Ronen, Joshua and George H. Sorter. **Relevant Financial Statements.** 1978

Shenkir, William G., Ed. **Carman G. Blough: His Professional Career and Accounting Thought.** 1978

Simpson, Kemper. **Economics for the Accountant.** 1921

Sneed, Florence R. **Parallelism in Two Disciplines.** (M.A. Thesis, University of Texas, Arlington, 1974). 1978

Sorter, George H. **The Boundaries of the Accounting Universe** (Doctoral Dissertation, University of Chicago, 1963). 1978

Storey, Reed K[arl]. **Matching Revenues with Costs** (Doctoral Dissertation, University of California, Berkeley, 1958). 1978

Sweeney, Henry W[hitcomb]. **Stabilized Accounting.** 1936

Van de Linde, Gérard. **Reminiscences.** 1917

Vatter, William J[oseph]. **The Fund Theory of Accounting and Its Implications for Financial Reports.** 1947

Walker, R. G. **Consolidated Statements.** 1978

Webster, Norman E., Comp. **The American Association of Public Accountants.** 1954

Wells, M. C., Ed. **American Engineers' Contributions to Cost Accounting.** 1978

Worthington, Beresford. **Professional Accountants.** 1895

Yamey, Basil S. **Essays on the History of Accounting.** 1978

Yamey, Basil S., Ed. **The Historical Development of Accounting.** 1978

Yang, J[u] M[ei]. **Goodwill and Other Intangibles.** 1927

Zeff, Stephen Addam. **A Critical Examination of the Orientation Postulate in Accounting, with Particular Attention to its Historical Development** (Doctoral Dissertation, University of Michigan, 1961). 1978

Zeff, Stephen A., Ed. **Selected Dickinson Lectures in Accounting.** 1978